ACTIVATE YOUR
SUPERPOWER!
CREATING COMPELLING COMMUNICATION

Kendall Hunt
publishing company

EDITED BY

BETH RIBARSKY · JESSICA J. ECKSTEIN

All chapter opener images were created by the editors using Superherotar.framiq.com
with permission to use its output in this text granted from that tool's creator, Ivan Renyé.

Cover image © Shutterstock, Inc.

www.kendallhunt.com
Send all inquiries to:
4050 Westmark Drive
Dubuque, IA 52004-1840

Contents

Introduction

Contributed by Dr. Beth Ribarsky & Dr. Jessica J. Eckstein

So, here's the deal, folks. Intros to books are typically a lot of filler. Because a competent communicator's goal should be effectiveness and appropriateness, we'll keep it concise and useful by sticking to four main things you need to know: why this book is unique, how you should use it, our hopes for you in reading it, and a few acknowledgments.

Why It's Unique

For one thing, we've designed it to be organized in the way most instructors actually teach their courses. Yes, we cover the basic areas of the communication discipline, but we make sure to cover the speech stuff first. We know you'll probably be giving speeches all semester—not just at the end—so it makes sense to cover that *first*. But, we don't just cover public speaking and then forget about it. Instead, Public Speaking Power boxes are in EVERY chapter, providing tips on how that chapter's focus can inform your speech construction and delivery.

Second, we (your editors) are interpersonal communication scholars with A LOT of public speaking experience. And, although we bring a lot to the table (or rather, textbook) through interesting examples and personal experiences, it doesn't mean we're qualified to write about EVERYTHING related to communication. So, we recruited experts on each topic to write chapters pertaining to their area of study. This means you're getting thorough and current coverage!

Third, it's lavender scented to make studying less stressful. Ok, maybe not, but that's a pretty spectacular idea! Between earning our PhDs and all the sample textbooks we receive for classes we teach, we've literally looked at hundreds (if not thousands) of textbooks . . . and many are mind-numbingly dull (and not scented)! Boring textbooks mean students are less likely to read them, missing out on the whole point of assigning them. So, we tried to flip the script by writing in a conversational manner and including plenty of pop culture references and jokes (most made at our own expense). No, you may not think all of it is funny or entertaining, but we think we're pretty hilarious.

How to Use It

Read it.

Our Hopes

As you read this textbook, we hope you'll find our examples enlightening, perhaps even occasionally funny. But, more so, we hope you'll find easy ways to apply the concepts to become more informed and conscientious communicators in your personal and professional lives. We know most of you reading this aren't communication majors (yet), so we emphasize how important these skills and concepts are no matter what your degree. But, personal application is just the first step, so we hope you'll move beyond that.

That brings us to what real heroes do. The world we live in is far from perfect, but that doesn't mean you can't do something to make it a better place. Each of our Activism Hero boxes are focused on things—big and small—you can actually DO to make a difference in the world around you. Whatever your passion is, we hope to help you be heard, be kind, and/or be a superhero. And yes, that's where the (sometimes over-the-top and cheesy) superhero theme comes in. We don't expect you to suddenly be able to leap large communication barriers in a single bound (or message), but these boxes (and the whole book, really) will give you the applied, *practical* knowledge to rise above those around you—putting you on your way to creating change (for yourself and others) in our current world. And, as our good friend GI Joe says, "Knowing is half the battle."

Acknowledgments

Although we're incredibly proud of the finished product, it wasn't easy. So, we owe a few thanks. Together, we'd like to first thank our contributors who were willing to help us see this vision through. We were sometimes heavy-handed with our editing and perhaps forced our (silly) sense of humor on some, but our contributors were flexible and brought great insight to make this book what it is. Second, we'd like to thank Kendall Hunt for their patience, guidance, and making things so easy to get done; shout-outs to Bev and Melissa!

Dr. Beth would like to first thank Jessi for having the chutzpah to take on this beast of a project with her. Without her careful eye, wittiness, and organization, Dr. Beth would still be running behind and freaking out. Next, she'd like to thank her colleagues, Dr. Amie Kincaid and Mr. Ric Perez, who helped brainstorm this textbook proposal and have continued to be wonderful friends and a great support system. Dr. Beth also would like to acknowledge her family's support—she's not sure they quite get what she does for a living (or why she gets paid for it) but support her nonetheless. And, she'd be remiss if she didn't thank her pets who sometimes provided just the right distraction/break. Finally, thanks to Buzz Bomb Brewing for allowing her to camp out and write and Orangetheory Fitness Springfield for helping her burn off those beers . . . and a little stress too.

Dr. Eckstein (Jessi) appreciates her Davit for "need anything?," "your feelings are stupid," and "they're fine"; you're the only reason she dreads death. Next, Jessi begrudgingly adores her furry kids' (Freyja, Penelope, Lola, Henry) constant progress-interruptions to prevent blood-clots. Jessi also owes her original family big-time—Mom/Dad for the work ethic and wit, and Aaron/Jake for the humor (regret we couldn't use your art and comics) and tolerance (goes both ways). Finally, Beth for having me on board and her shared pathetic humor, expectation clarity, compliment- and credit-generosity, and sounding-board-sanity amid frustrations.

We fear this may be the start of something enduring and prolific—professionally and personally. Now, we need a well-deserved break!

Communication Is More Complex and Important than You Think

Whenever you tell someone you're taking a communication class, they most likely think you're just learning about giving speeches (which admittedly is something we cover in this text). But, communication is so much more! Communication is something we oftentimes take for granted. Unfortunately, we usually don't recognize how important and complex it can be until we mess it up. And, miscommunication happens all the time. Think about your everyday life and various situations you've been in; chances are that even in this last week you've had some form of miscommunication, or at the very least, ineffective communication. Did your roommate misunderstand your text message? Were you not able to convince your parents to loan you $20? Don't worry . . . you're not alone. Because there are so many complexities to communication, there are many places for things to go wrong. And, in this era of ever- and so rapidly-changing technology, our communication is even more challenged. So, learning more about the complexities of communication will help you unlock a superpower you never knew you had!

Although superpowers are cool, if you're reading this text, most likely it is NOT because you want to take an Intro to Communication course but rather because it's required. The reason many universities, and even some U.S. states, require you to take a communication course is because of the always-present nature of communication in our lives. This dramatic impact communication has on us and the importance of taking a communication course can be explained by six key factors: practice, development of self, well-being, relational development, career enhancement, and community engagement.

Practice

The first reason an Intro to Communication course is important has to do with the idea of practice. Believe it or not, public speaking is considered one of the greatest fears of Americans' lives. In fact, some people report public speaking as a fear even more frequently than they report fearing death (Dwyer & Davidson, 2012)! Colleges and your professors hope taking a communication course will give you opportunities to engage in public speaking and practice such a scary skill in a safe and comfortable environment. Undoubtedly, you'll still feel nervous, but take comfort knowing your classmates probably feel

It's not really this bad. . .

© vchal/Shutterstock.com

the same way (and likely are more concerned about their own nerves than paying attention to you). And remember, your instructor *wants* to see you succeed.

We also hope as you communicate in your course and with your instructors and classmates, you get to practice interpersonal and small group communication skills. A good communication classroom should be a safe place of practice and experimentation because there's no safer place to practice your skills than around others learning at the same time—all before you get to situations with greater consequences, such as your workplace. Most of us would rather mess up in front of our classmates, where the worst thing that might happen is a poor grade versus your boss firing you. We want good communication skills to become second-nature to you. A communication course is a great place to start to help you overcome some of those fears you might have, whether it be public speaking or even overcoming a bit of shyness in your daily life. When you practice a skill to the point where you do it without even thinking, it's called **overlearning**. In time, you become so proficient at a particular skill, it can reach the level where you seem communicatively omnipotent, omniscient, and exceptional—all features of a real-life superpower!

Understanding Our Sense of Self

Beyond being a safe place for you to practice your communication skills, a communication course is also a great place to understand how and why we see ourselves the way we do—our superhero "origin" story, so to speak—and how this influences how we communicate with others. When we're born, we have no singular identity. Instead, our identity is constructed through our communication with others (Stryker, 1994). From birth, a baby hears messages like "Oh, you're such a good girl!" or "You're such a strong boy!" and is often dressed in certain colors according to their presumed sex/gender to reinforce parents' gender expectations for their babies (Pearson & VanHorn, 2004). These very words and communication toward us help us develop our sense of who we are. Are we a boy? Are we a girl? Are we smart? Are we funny? All this communication with our family, friends, and even strangers is the main thing that affects how we see ourselves. While this has the most dramatic impact on us during our formative years, the way others communicate with and about us continues to shape our view of ourselves throughout our lives (see Chapter 6 for more).

Physical and Mental Well-Being

One often-overlooked benefit of becoming a better communicator is how it helps us become mentally and physically healthier individuals (Tardy, 2000). Have you ever really wanted to tell a friend about something that happened to you or a secret that someone shared with you, but you couldn't? This desire to share that information is a natural human response, but by keeping it private, we often experience a feeling of stress. You might find yourself only being able to focus on that one thing. Your muscles and chest might even feel a bit tight as you sense anxiety building. But, once you're able to share that information, you often feel a mental and physical release—what we call *catharsis* (Pennebaker, 1989). Good communication can make you feel better in many ways.

Catharsis can be amazing!

© Annashou/Shutterstock.com

Researchers have found those individuals who are better at communication tend to have better health overall—both mentally and physically (Floyd & Deiss, 2012). Good communicators, like mutants or superheroes, are above average in several aspects; they often have greater levels of connection with family and friends and lower rates of depression. Because our mental health is interwoven with our physical health, competent communicators also tend to have better overall physical health, including lower rates of diabetes, heart disease, and other chronic health conditions (Pennebaker, 1993; Schwartz & Russek, 1998). If you're still trying to justify taking a communication course, simply remember that you're doing it for your health.

Relationship Development

Communication is obviously instrumental to our inherent need for relationships with family, friends, romantic partners, co-workers, and even your classmates and instructors (Baumeister & Leary, 1995). Our relationships are built, maintained, and destroyed by communication or lack thereof. Relationships can't exist without communication. Period. Many students end up enjoying their communication course because it provides them with a better understanding of how and why they and others behave and communicate the way that they do. It's great to come away from a class or reading a chapter being able to immediately apply the material to your own life. It's our hope that by the end of the course, you'll have developed your communication skills in ways that help you build stronger relationships throughout your own life.

Be a superstar in your relationships!

© Rawpixel.com/Shutterstock.com

Career Enhancement

Perhaps the main reason many places require an Intro to Communication course is because it plays an instrumental role in your career. No matter what your job is, you'll use communication. For example, think of a career as a mortician, where the primary individuals you deal with are not even alive. Even there, being able to listen with empathy and communicate appropriately with family members who may be experiencing the worst moments of their lives can make a significant difference not only for those grieving but also the success of the mortician in their career. Even the mortician's interaction with the deceased body relies on the communication skill of listening because they have to learn where and when to use particular tools or chemicals in the right ways. We're sure you've heard about the many career opportunities open to those with great communication skills. In the box on the next page, we've provided a modern-day list of some unique, fun, and currently in-demand careers you may not have yet considered.

Research has shown the number one reason people get hired to and promoted within a job is because they have effective communication skills (Association of American Colleges & Universities, 2018). Have you ever met someone who is incredibly brilliant (maybe even a college professor) who you simply cannot understand? If so, they've failed in getting their idea across to you; they have failed in communicating. You can have all the knowledge in the world, but if you can't communicate it effectively and appropriately, it's basically worthless

How will you use communication superpowers to change YOUR world?

© Yuganov Konstantin/Shutterstock.com

(Hayakawa, 1972). Thousands of dollars on an education, down the drain! We hope this book and course will help you develop both the *effectiveness* and *appropriateness* of your communication skills in ways that help you achieve success in and out of the college classroom.

Community Engagement and Activism

Finally, one of our goals in creating this textbook was to promote the key role communication can play in helping you become an informed and involved citizen. In other words, communication skills shouldn't just help you—you should be able to use them to make a difference in the world around you. We'll keep referring to the fact that communication skills are like superpowers—they allow you to rise above typical life-challenges, struggle against oppression, and ultimately, help yourself *while* helping those around you. We'll get dorky with this analogy at times, but we will never exaggerate the immense power of communication. If understood and actually practiced (i.e., *overlearning*), these skills *will* set you above most people. Then, it's your own burden of responsibility to use the powers for good and not evil.

HAVE YOU EVER THOUGHT ABOUT BEING A/N:

Animal Trainer
Auctioneer
Bereavement Coordinator
Brand/ing Consultant/Ambassador
Cancer Registrar
CIA/FBI Analyst/Agent
Community Organizer
Concert Promoter/Booker
Copywriter/editor
Cruise Director
Culture Director/Officer
Divorce Mediator
Doula
Environmental Activist
Entertainment Reporter
Event/Party Planner
Fantasy Broker
Fashion Writer/Blogger
Food Critic/Blogger
Funeral Service Manager
Gender Equality Consultant
Headhunter/Recruiter
Hospitality Manager
Imagineer
Motivational Speaker
Art/Museum/Music Curator
Negotiator
Park Ranger
Police Officer
Politician, Local or National
Publicist/Image Consultant
Purchasing Agent
Retirement Home Director
Social Media Specialist/Content Strategist
Sustainability Coordinator
Travel Writer/Blogger
User Experience Designer
Voice-Over Worker/Actor

Professional:
- Apologizer
- Baby-Proofer
- Bridesmaid
- Coach, Life or Weight-Loss
- Conservationist
- Cuddler/Comforter
- Dating Profile Ghostwriter
- Decoy Corporate Executive
- Design Consultant
- Facebooker, Real or Fake
- Fundraiser
- Greeting Card Writer
- Interviewer
- Matchmaker
- Mourner
- Mystery Shopper
- Nail-Polish Namer
- Nanny
- Online Reviewer
- Party Guest
- Personal Historian
- Personal Shopper
- Podcaster
- Product Tester
- Storyteller
- Taster, Food or Beverage
- Tour Guide
- TV Watcher (scanner)
- Vacation Tester
- Video Gamer or Tester
- Wardrobe Stylist

Yes, ALL of these are REAL, current, full-time jobs in-demand as freelance, corporate, *and* nonprofit options for those skilled in the Communication Studies basics covered in this text. Search each title online to learn more!

Source: Jessica Eckstein

Some of the more *interesting* careers communication skills allow you to pursue.

If there's something in the world you care deeply about, becoming a competent communicator will give you the abilities to express your ideas, have others listen to you, and perhaps even persuade others to become involved with your cause/interest. For example, we (Drs. Ribarsky and Eckstein) both have a passion for animals and volunteer with our local humane societies. Because of her persuasive communication skills, Dr. Ribarsky plays a key role in helping construe the importance of animal welfare to others and in getting businesses to help financially support the organization. Dr. Eckstein also uses her ability to listen and adapt her style of communication to interact with diverse (e.g., personalities, moods, backgrounds, opinions) people and animals who've experienced abusive relationships from their partners/owners. Neither of us would be so successful at these things were it not for our communication skills. Thus, even in "little" or local ways, communication skills can help you make a difference in the world around you.

© Cienpies Design/Shutterstock.com

Activism Hero: Make Your Speech Work for You

In your course, you'll most likely be asked to give a persuasive speech. As much as you might dread giving speeches, this is an invaluable opportunity to share your knowledge and experience with others. How many other times in your life will you have a captive audience? When selecting your speech topic, we encourage you to pick a topic you're truly passionate about—not just what you think will make a "good" speech topic. Do you love animals like us? Does nothing infuriate you more than when you see someone littering? Are you fanatical about a political candidate or a law? When you talk about something that *matters* to you, your passion shows in your delivery and *that* is what starts the process of creating change and inspiration in others. In the chapters to follow, you'll learn more about how to adapt *your* passions to your audience. For example, research shows that getting someone to see what they have in common with you in at least one social or cultural group makes them more likely to be persuaded on moral or ethical issues (Teng, Poon, & Yang, 2016). So use that skill: ***What group commonality can you emphasize when talking to your audience?*** Use this connection pro-tip to effectively share your passion with others!

Contributed by B. Ribarsky & J. Eckstein

© barbaliss/Shutterstock.com

Defining Communication

Hopefully, you can now see some practical reasons for and benefits to taking this course—other than you're just required to. Better yet, maybe you're now even a bit excited about digging into the actual ways to become a better communicator. So, let's get a bit more into the meat of what you're actually studying. *Communication* is a symbolic process in which we construct meaning together. Although this definition seems quite simple at first glance, it involves numerous important aspects, the individual parts of which can be traced all the way back to Aristotle (1853)! First, we need to recognize communication uses symbols and/or is symbolic. A *symbol* is anything that represents something else. Symbols can be both verbal and nonverbal. Words themselves don't mean anything; they're just a bunch of shapes we happen to call letters (Salsbury, 2013). For example, if you see or hear the word "cat," chances are you'll think of a furry feline that might say meow. By having a word (or even just a letter) be a symbol for an *artifact*, or the thing it represents to both you (called the *reference*) and to other people (called the *referent*), we can talk about a cat without actually having to physically drag in a poor, screaming, clawing kitty to a classroom.

Nonverbal communication also involves symbols (see Chapter 8). When you see someone smile, you might interpret this as them being happy. When asked how many slices of pizza you want, you can hold up two fingers without saying anything else, and the receiver is able to understand you'd like two glorious pieces of gastronomical delight presented to you. In these cases, the smile and the two fingers are the symbols, and the happiness and the pizza are the artifacts, respectively. And, like any college student . . . or frankly, sane human, you should be smiling because you're getting two pieces of pizza.

A second important part of our definition of communication is process. *Process* acknowledges communication involves varying steps that senders and receivers must undergo when exchanging messages. However, as clear as we like to think a process might be, it's not. Oftentimes, communication doesn't have a distinct beginning or ending. Think about a class you've taken. Just because you're no longer in that class, is the communication process truly over? If you ever still think about that class or use any of the material you learned, we'd argue that the communication process hasn't really ended. Every interaction we engage in somehow influences how we see and interact in the world.

The last part of the definition focuses on constructing meaning together. We are, in fact, studying humans in this textbook. This is not to say bees, dogs, giraffes, and wookies don't communicate with each other and with us—they do! And, if you're anything like Drs. Eckstein and Ribarsky, you're also guilty of talking (OK, fine, having long, in-depth, extended conversations) with your pets. But, for the purposes of this textbook and course, we'll largely study how humans interact with one another. So, that brings us to the *constructing meaning together* part, where we try to generate shared understandings through our exchange of messages. Think back to when we mentioned the word "cat." Depending upon your experiences, you might picture a beautiful Siamese cat. Maybe you envision a classic cartoon-like Garfield cat. Dr. Ribarsky probably thinks of this cantankerous Russian Blue stray she feeds and lets live on her deck, who is affectionately known as A-Hole the Cat. What we do through the process of communication is construct these meanings together in ways that hopefully bring us to some sort of shared understanding—helping move our definitions and visions of "cat" closer to one another.

A-Hole the Cat: Cute but cranky!

Source: Elizabeth Ribarsky

There Is No "S" in Communication

Now that we've defined communication, it's also important for us to define what communication is NOT. You may hear students or even faculty from other disciplines refer to what we study as "communications." You will never hear any of our authors refer to communication as communications. Simply put, there is NO "S" in communication. Communications involve the technical aspects of communication transmissions like telephones, running cable wires, setting up electronics, generating computer programs, designing webpages, and many IT-related jobs. Undoubtedly, all of these skills require and facilitate communication, but they focus only on the use of channels (we'll touch on this in a bit). In contrast, *communication* is the study of what happens between and among individuals and the world around them. What YOU do with others on a daily basis—building/forming/maintaining relationships; coordinating identities; managing cultural interactions; navigating power exchanges, attractions, disparities, conflicts—all involve communication. Give yourself a bit of credit for the immense task you undertake on a daily basis. So again, for future reference, we're just going to leave the "s" off of communication—and if you want to look like you know what you're talking about in front of your instructor, you will too.

The Communication Process

As mentioned in our definition of communication, we recognize communication is a process. When researchers began trying to study and understand the communication process, they began to dissect the various components and, over time, the discipline progressed through three increasingly complex models of communication.

Simple Linear Model

Back in the day (as in, 2000s BC), when communication was first studied as an art form (rather than as a science), the emphasis was largely on public speeches (Hallo, 2004). People got their entertainment and news from public forums where orators would deliver speeches to make people laugh and cry, be informed and persuaded. As a result of that history, the first model we used in our field was also based on direct speech-making and is known as the *Simple Linear Model of Communication*. Despite its name, there are numerous components that make up the model. But, all subsequent models use these components too, so learning the basics of this preliminary model is essential for understanding our current model of communication.

The first three parts we're going to focus on are the sender, message, and encoding. First, the *sender* is the individual who wants to convey (i.e., send) or relay some form of a message. The *message* is whatever idea or thought the sender relays. Sometimes our messages are intentional, but sometimes they're unintentional. For example, as we're writing this text, we are intentionally sending you messages. Or, if you tell your friend, "I'm mad," it's clear you're intentionally sending them a message that you are mad. However, have you ever had a case of "the yawns" where you may not even be tired, but you can't stop yawning? Even though you're not intentionally yawning, you're still sending a message for others to receive. Or, do you or someone you know suffer from RBF ("resting bitch face")? An RBF sufferer might be a perfectly wonderful, sweet, and caring individual, but his or her face might be unintentionally sending a different message. The third part of this beginning sequence is *encoding*, which is the process of the sender choosing which verbal and nonverbal cues to use to relay their message (Schramm, 1954). So, for example, if you want to let someone know that you love them, you may choose verbal symbols (i.e., words) such as "I love you." But, there's also a nonverbal element that goes along with that. If you say "I love you," but you simultaneously roll your eyes, it's a different message than if you say "I love you" while gazing into the person's eyes and smiling.

The next important part of the Simple Linear Model is the transmission channel. The *channel* is the medium through which a message is relayed (Schramm, 1954). Channels nowadays come in so many different forms beyond just face-to-face. You can Tweet. You can text. Maybe you make a phone call, or you send an old-fashioned letter. As simple as the channel sounds,

© seanbear/Shutterstock.com

it's important to acknowledge the impact a channel choice can have. For example, if you're going to break up with someone, what channel are you going to use? Are you going to do it face-to-face or are you going to send a text? Or, will you simply leave a Post-It note like in the infamous *Sex and the City* episode? Channel choice can have a dramatic impact on the thought/meaning behind the message, and in turn, affects how the message is received.

In addition, the channel itself can also affect if the recipient even gets the message in the first place—like when you're in a place with bad cell phone service and try unsuccessfully sending a text message.

Once you've chosen your channel, you then move to the final part of the Simple Linear Model. The first item on this end of the model is the *receiver*—anyone who notices your message. We assume we have *intentional* receivers. As we write this textbook, you are, in fact, our intentional receivers. But, just because you intend for someone to receive your message, that doesn't guarantee they'll get it. Have you ever sent an email, and it somehow gets lost in a SPAM folder? Ever waved at someone and felt a bit like a fool because they didn't see you? Things like this happen all the time. Even though we have intentional receivers, we also have the possibility of *unintentional* receivers. Again, a receiver is ANYONE who notices your message. Dr. Eckstein's most common embarrassment is when someone says hello and she enthusiastically smiles and says "Hi!" back to them before realizing (from their slightly scared look) they were talking to someone else—either behind her or on a tiny phone. So whereas Dr. Eckstein's *intended* receiver of her "Hi" was the stranger talking to someone else, Dr. Eckstein was *their unintended* receiver.

With different types of channels, we run the risk of even more types of unintended communication. For instance, you probably often overhear one side of a cell phone conversation because somehow people forget others can hear them when on the phone. Even though you're not their intended receiver, you nonetheless get to hear about all their gross medical procedures (candling, anyone?), awkward dates (it was your cousin!), or what they plan on having for dinner (canned cheese on cereal?!). You may even want to un-hear the messages you heard, but nonetheless, you are still a receiver. Once somebody receives your message, the final component of the Simple Linear Model falls into place: *decoding*—the process of dissecting the verbal and nonverbal elements of a message to decipher what they mean (Schramm, 1954). Going back to somebody saying "I love you" but rolling their eyes at the same time, a receiver might decode the combination of these elements to mean the sender was being sarcastic. But, even if a sender perfectly encoded and constructed their message, it does not guarantee the receiver will accurately decode the message. If you've ever been in a bad mood, you may have decoded something incorrectly or taken more offense to it simply because you had a negative framework from which you were viewing/receiving a message. All your friend said was, "Oh, you cut your hair!". But because you were already in a bad mood as a receiver, you might infer that your friend hates your new haircut.

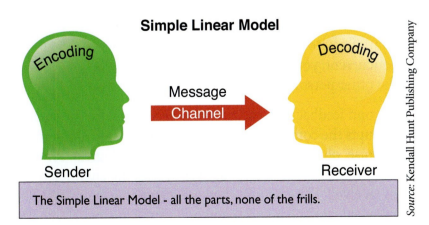

The Simple Linear Model - all the parts, none of the frills.

Source: Kendall Hunt Publishing Company

Bad mood? Bad haircut?
Or, just bad smell?

© Syda Productions/Shutterstock.com

Now, despite all the components of this model, we still call it the Simple Linear Model because it is . . . simple. You have a message. You send the message. Someone receives the message. The end. But remember, it was originally created to explain speeches that focused on the orator, and even in interpersonal settings, the focus was on one person at a time (think of early telephones or walkie-talkies; Hartley, 1928; Wynter, 1854). Nowadays, however, we know that even a silent audience gives something in return.

Interactional Model

As researchers looked at the Simple Linear Model, they decided it was just too simple. Scholars recognized that when we communicate, we're not *just* sending a message and waiting for a receiver to get it. But rather, communication is going on constantly—by all parties involved. Researchers thus noted our communication is *concurrent*, or seems to happen all at once, and there are often many factors that disrupt our communication from being successful. Therefore, two additional factors (feedback and noise) were added in the 1950s to 1960s to create what we call the ***Interactional Model of Communication***.

Feedback is both verbal and nonverbal exchanges between both the sender and receiver (Schramm, 1954). You don't just send a message and call that communication. Rather, feedback is ongoing, so the sender and receiver inherently play BOTH roles in the same encounter. For example, as your friend is telling you a story, you might find yourself nodding your head. You are receiving her message, but you're also sending a message back to her that you're listening and/or you want her to continue with her story. Your communication is concurrent; you're sending *and* receiving while the other person is also sending *and* receiving.

Interactional Model

Encoding
Noise
Message
Channel
Noise
Decoding
Noise
Sender
Feedback
Receiver

The Interactional Model considers a bit more - how all the stuff going on in our heads influences our communication, and that we communicate simultaneously.

Source: Kendall Hunt Publishing Company

Beyond feedback, researchers also accounted for the presence of noise. ***Noise*** is anything that disrupts the communication process at any step along the way. There are three specific types of noise: physical, physiological, and psychological. ***Physical noise*** is anything happening in the physical environment, or even within the channel, that affects how/if a message is sent or received. For example, if you're trying to have a delicate conversation with your friend in a packed sports bar and there's a playoff game on TV, chances are the environment is going to be too physically loud to effectively engage in a personal conversation. Similarly, if you've ever been on a cell phone and you randomly hit a dead spot with no signal, the person on the other end might think you're angry with them (believing you hung up on them) or think you aren't listening because you haven't responded. In this case, because the channel stopped the effective flow of messages, it, too, can become a form of physical noise.

We've all been there!

© standret/Shutterstock.com

Physiological noise deals with the body and might include something like a hearing deficit. This could be a congenital deficit, something that develops over time, or even a temporary situation, such as when your ears get plugged when you get a bad head cold. Nonetheless, because you have difficulty hearing a message, it makes it more difficult for you to receive a message exactly as it was encoded and sent. Another physiological noise is being really tired. Research has shown that driving while tired may be actually as dangerous, if not more so, than driving while intoxicated (Tefft, 2018). A similar thing can happen in the communication process. When you're really tired, it's unlikely you'll receive, or even send, messages as effectively as usual. Perhaps you're exhausted during your 8 a.m. class because you had a bit too much fun the night before; this then prevents you from catching everything the instructor says.

Finally, *psychological noise* is everything within the senders' and receivers' minds that disrupts the sending or receiving of messages. Whereas physiological noise would affect the direct functioning of your *brain* (i.e., physical organ), psychological noise affects your *mind* (i.e., cognitive, emotional thoughts your brain produces). For example, as you read this text, you might be simultaneously thinking about a quiz you have tomorrow in another class. It's similar to trying to convey a complex emotion to someone in-person while they're thinking about the super-hot girl/guy who just walked by. Mental distractions mean we may not be sending or receiving messages as effectively as we could, or should.

© Irina Levitskaya/Shutterstock.com

It is also not unusual for noises to be interrelated. For example, Dr. Ribarsky, as a self-proclaimed foodie, gets unusually excited about food—which can become her Kryptonite. If Dr. Ribarsky missed breakfast, her hunger pangs might create physiological noise. But then, she's likely to begin thinking about all of her lunch options, thus, creating psychological noise. The acknowledgement that both ongoing feedback and noise are always occurring in every communication encounter was a significant contribution of the Interactional Model.

Transactional Model

The Interactional Model added some important components to the communication process, but it failed to account for the fact that our communication is unique and always changing. This third, most complex, and most current (as of this writing) model is referred to as the *Transactional Model of Communication*. What makes this model most comprehensive is that it accounts for the incredible complexity of communication by recognizing that every single interaction we ever have is unique and depends upon every interaction we've had before. This complexity can be described as context. *Context* includes everything that surrounds, embeds, and comes out of the communication process (Berlo, 1960). One way to consider the different types of context we might encounter is by breaking them into four categories: physical, social, chronological, and cultural.

Like physical noise, *physical context* refers to the environment and how the environment might influence the type of messages sent or how a message is received. For example, if you've ever watched a football game, the physical context changes the way in which players interact with one another. You might see them pat each other's butt as a way of saying "good job" or "way to go." However, outside of that playing arena, it's much less likely to happen between players. Over the years, we've taught thousands of students, including many athletes, and have never seen any of them leave our class patting one of their teammates' or classmates' rear ends, saying, "Way to go! Good class!" Just the thought might make you giggle because of how *weird* and inappropriate it would be. The physical context changes the very type of messages being sent or what is considered appropriate within a particular physical context. The physical context can also influence how a message is received. Hearing your first "I love you" from your romantic partner in a quiet, romantic restaurant will probably have a different impact on you than hearing it at a busy, loud, and boisterous football game.

The *social context* focuses on the relationship between individuals and the ways that relationship affects their communication with each other. For example, the way you talk with your professor might be really different than how you communicate with your best friend. Around your friends, you might "swear like a sailor," but in front of your grandmother, not a foul word will cross your lips. The social context will determine whether your swearing really serves an effective *and* appropriate function (Jay & Janschewitz, 2008). Because of the social context, based on the roles you each play in *that* relationship in that particular moment, hearing "I want to see you" from your boss has a very different meaning than hearing the same thing from the attractive classmate you sit next to.

The third form of context is the *chronological*, or timing, context. There are numerous types of time that might influence the type of message you send or how your message is interpreted, such as the time of day, time of year, or even the timing within a relationship. If you get an "I want to see you" text from your boss

We might have needed a swear jar while writing this book!

© Suzanne Tucker/Shutterstock.com

at 2 p.m., you'll probably interpret it completely differently than if received at 2 a.m. Or, if you happened to get your friend a gift close to Valentine's Day, they might construe your innocent gift as an expression of romantic interest, even if that's not at all what you intended. What if you're on a first date and at the end of the date, they told you, "I love you"? Chances are you might find this much too fast and way too soon (and yes, you should see this as a red flag—run away quickly)! These are just a few of the types of chronological contexts that can impact your communication.

© Luis Molinero/Shutterstock.com

Dating red flags?!?! Run for your life!

Finally, the *cultural context* involves the culture that is surrounding the individuals, as well as the relationship. Culture (see Chapter 14) is any group of individuals who share beliefs, values, rights, rituals, and norms and can include aspects like age, race, religion, sexual orientation, or even sex/gender. Cultures are something so complex that they often influence all the other contexts as well. For example, in some churches, it's considered rude to clap, sing, or do anything other than sit there somberly and quietly; if you grew up in a very loud church where people shouted, laughed, clapped, and even danced, you'd still be expected to adapt to the quiet church's rules when you attended there—or risk getting hauled out of there pretty quickly! In this example, the particular culture of a religious type also interacts with physical (e.g., type of church building and service), social (e.g., ministers have different "rules" than congregants/parishioners), and chronological (e.g., traditional Sunday morning services might differ in expectations from holiday pageants or weekday services) contexts.

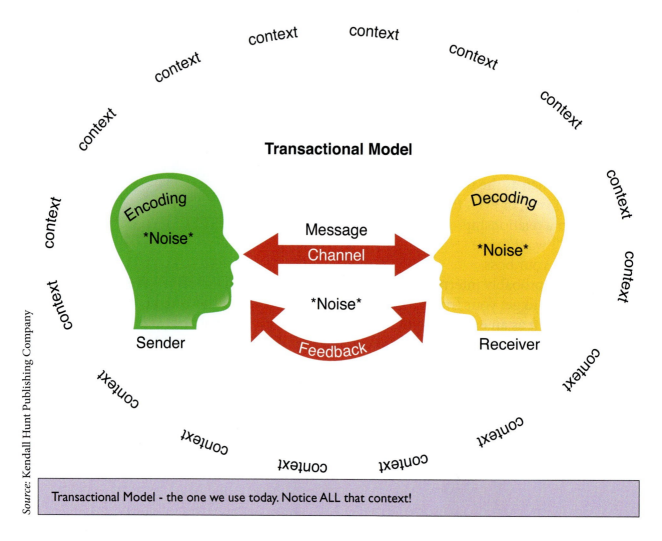

Source: Kendall Hunt Publishing Company

Transactional Model - the one we use today. Notice ALL that context!

The complexity of the Transactional Model (which also incorporates all components of the previous models) further illustrates numerous places where miscommunication can and does happen. When we recognize all these intricacies in the communication process, it's no wonder we ALL make so many mistakes. Try not to be so hard on yourself. Even your authors and instructors who've been studying communication for years still make plenty of mistakes because we're simply humans trying to navigate an incredibly complex process.

Principles of Communication

Beyond these models of communication, it's important to recognize there are numerous principles that help describe and explain the complexities of communication.

Communication Is Unavoidable

Watzlawick, Beavin, and Jackson (1967) famously noted, "You cannot not communicate." These scholars argued we're unable to stop the communication process. Even if someone stops verbally communicating with you, they're *still* communicating. Think about how much you can tell about a person simply from what they're wearing (Expensive brand logos? Dirty overalls?), how they're standing (Superhero-like posture? Slumping into the ground?), their hair (Springfield Illinois is home to the famous Chili Bowl Mullet Man . . . stay classy, Springfield), what their face is doing (Smiling? Creepily winking?), or any number of other aspects that nonverbally communicate to us. Even the timing of the messages or lack thereof communicates. Have you ever sent someone a text, saw a read receipt but *still* haven't received a reply? Even their silence is communicating something to you (Are they plotting their revenge or the perfect witty comeback?). Even in the absence of words, we're still engaging in communication whenever the receiver *perceives* it.

Business in the front; Party in the back!

© Annette Shaff/Shutterstock.com

Communication Is an Unrepeatable Process

This principle is linked to the transactional nature of communication. Because of the various contexts (relationships, environment, time, culture) we discussed, it's impossible to *ever exactly* repeat communication. Every interaction we have is ultimately unique (Berlo, 1960). And, every single encounter influences our worldview and perspectives, and thus, all our current and future interactions. In other words, every interaction—the messages we send, how we receive them, and all the other parts of the model—depend on what happened before. This doesn't mean you'll come away from every single experience with an earth-shattering, grand epiphany. Sure, you could (but holy cow, would that be tiring!). Even our small and seemingly mundane interactions have an impact over time on how we see and interact in the world. Therefore, you could sit in the same room tomorrow and have the same conversation with the same person, but your communication would inherently be different because of all of the interactions you've had within the last 24 hours.

This concept is, admittedly, a bit obscure and requires some grand-scheme thinking of how it influences us day to day. So let's use an experience you've probably had. Perhaps you know a couple (or maybe you're part of one) whose partners have broken up and gotten back together numerous times. You might hear things from them such as: "Okay, let's start fresh. Let's forget about the past and move forward." Pretty simple, right? Does it ever work? Nope! As nice as it might be to wipe the slate clean in so many of our relationships and interactions, it's just not that simple. Everything that has happened in the past will continue—at least to some extent—to influence how each individual sees themselves, each other, and the relationship itself. And once it's out there, we can't take it back, which leads us to the next principle of communication.

Communication Is Irreversible

Perhaps you grew up with the parent who was always telling you to "think before you speak." That's because mom or dad knew that once something is said or done, it can't be taken back. Communication is irreversible. If you're a fan of any TV courtroom dramas, chances are during a cross-examination, you've heard the judge say, "Strike that from the record." What the judge is telling the jury is that they cannot include any of that information that they just heard into their decision-making process. However, we (and so do the lawyers) know that communication is irreversible. So once it's out there, there's no taking it back. Can this information legally change the outcome of a trial? No. Does this information still remain in jurors' heads and have the potential to influence their decisions? Yes.

Any other *SVU* addicts out there?

© sirtravelalot/Shutterstock.com

Communication Has Two Levels of Meaning

Another overarching principle of the communication process is that there are two different levels of meaning in any message that we send: content level and relational level. The **content level** is the actual, usually intended *message* we send to another individual. The **relational level** reveals the type of relationship or connection we have with someone and influences how our message is perceived. If your friend told you, "I really like your shirt," the content level is expressing a feeling about your shirt, and because you are friends, the relational levels tells you this is a compliment, and your friend is being kind. Conversely, if your worst enemy told you, "I really like your shirt," the content level of the message remains the same. However, because of the relationship with your enemy, you're much less likely to take their comment as a compliment; you might view their comment as sarcasm or an insult. Even though message content might remain the same, the relational level can have a dramatic impact on how the message is interpreted.

Communication Does Not Solve All Problems

Of course, all the authors in this textbook are a bit biased in loving communication and recognizing just how powerful it is. We like to think of ourselves as superhero mentors or grizzled "old" sages. But, we also acknowledge communication isn't some magical cure-all. We, of course, encourage you to have open and civilized conversations, but just because you're engaging in clear and competent communication doesn't mean you're going to fix the problem. You've probably been in an argument where you keep rehashing the same thing over and over again but get nowhere. In fact, you might find the more you talk about the issue, the more frustrated you become. Sometimes the old saying of "agree to disagree" rings incredibly true. In fact, one of Drs. Eckstein and Ribarsky's pet peeves is when pop-culture counselors (yes, we're looking at you Dr. Phil!) tell couples they simply need to "communicate more"; many times, part of effective communication is knowing when to just shut up and/or listen.

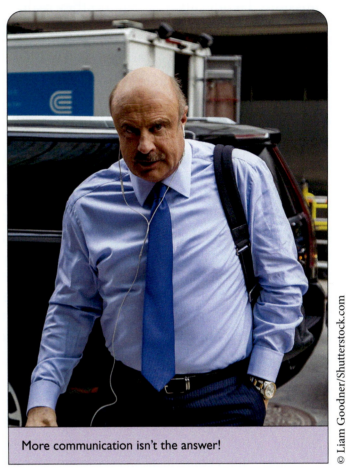

More communication isn't the answer!

© Liam Goodner/Shutterstock.com

Communication Involves Ethical Issues

Like many things in life, communication involves ethics and good and bad practices to consider. Although the ethical issues surrounding communication can span a vast frontier, two factors we encounter frequently include lying and privacy. But what is "right" isn't always as clear cut as you might think.

Because of our particular cultural values, you might be quick to think lying is automatically *un*ethical, but chances are you've already told several lies this week . . . perhaps even today. Undoubtedly, there's a spectrum to the severity of lying (Bok, 1999). There's a significant difference between lying about cheating on your romantic partner and lying that the meal they spent all day cooking tastes great (and not actually like a used shoe with hairy gum stuck to the bottom). Whether big or small, they are still lies. But, what makes one lie ethical and one not? Or, is all lying unethical? As much as we'd like to have an easy answer for you, unfortunately, like most ethical issues, there are many factors to consider and rarely simple answers (Dunbar et al., 2016). For example, does not telling your partner *everything* about your day mean you're lying through omission? Technically, yes. But, do they really need/want to hear about every time you've used the restroom during the day? Probably not . . .

The other significant ethical issue you're likely to experience frequently involves privacy. Privacy encompasses so many areas of our lives. Have you ever been told to keep a secret private but still ended up sharing it with your best friend or romantic partner (e.g., Dr. Eckstein considers even "don't tell anyone" secrets fair game to share with her partner Dave)? Or, if you've been to a doctor's office, you've had to sign an HIPAA (Health Information Portability and Accountability Act) form to protect your privacy by releasing your medical information only to individuals you approve. Do you ever feel like your cell phone or computer is spying on you? You were just chatting about having burgers for dinner, and now you're seeing ads for Red Robin on your social media. Again, like lying, there's not necessarily always a clear right or wrong answer when it comes to issues of privacy (Bok, 1984). Even if you think you're an open book, there're still probably some things you wouldn't share with everyone . . . or perhaps anyone (insert your personal embarrassing childhood memory here). It remains important for all of us to be aware of how privacy impacts how we communicate. Remember, a great communicator considers not only effectiveness but also appropriateness of their communication.

Public Speaking Power: Ethics of Changing Minds & Behaviors

Because ethics come in all shapes, forms, and shades of gray, it shouldn't be surprising that giving speeches also requires significant ethical considerations, including how to change someone's mind or behavior through your speech. How do you feel when someone forces you to do something? Are you angry? Do you dig your heels in a little deeper? You're not alone. Humans inherently don't like change, and being forced to change is even worse. There's a big difference between *coercing* someone by threatening or manipulating them to make them do something and *persuading* or motivating someone to make a change or do something on their own. Research has shown if an individual makes a change on their own or personally commits to it rather than complying through pressure, not only will they be more satisfied with the change but also more likely to stick with change (Helmreich & Collins, 1968). To be effective *and* appropriate public speakers, we must consider how our own and our audience's ethics influence our content and delivery.

Contributed by J. Eckstein & B. Ribarsky

Good Communication Takes Works

The final principle recognizes that effective *and* appropriate communication takes work. We mentioned at the beginning of this chapter that many people take good communication for granted. In fact, we typically don't realize how important communication is (or how unskilled we may be at it) until things start to go wrong. Whether it's communication with your romantic partner, your parent, your boss, or even presenting speeches for this class, all of it takes WORK. No one is born a great communicator. The best communicators continually put significant time, effort, and consideration into unlocking the not-so-secret superpowers of great communication. As we mentioned at the beginning of this chapter, when you practice until it's habit, you'll begin to do it without thinking. Hopefully, you'll look at this textbook and this course as an invaluable opportunity to become your own version of a communication superhero!

Communication Areas and Opportunities

One last factor that adds to the complexity of communication is the vast array of areas of study within communication. The National Communication Association (NCA) lists 48 different divisions or areas of study within the communication discipline (NCA, 2019). Luckily, all of them can be boiled down to six main areas. First, *interpersonal communication* examines communication that occurs between two or more parties viewed as unique and irreplaceable within the conversation (see Chapter 10). For example, it's doubtful we could simply replace your mom/dad or romantic partner (see Chapter 11) with another person and have it be the same type of conversation. *Small group communication* looks at how three or more people operate as a system (see Chapter 12). You've probably had group projects for a class more than once, so you understand how groups can be very beneficial but can also go incredibly wrong. *Organizational communication* often envelops the interworking of numerous small groups and interpersonal relationships—all within an organization's culture (Chapter 13). It can also involve the larger networks, systems, or structural communication aspects of an organized group. Whether it's a fraternity, sorority, a sports team, or even your workplace, each organization you're a part of has its own unique culture. *Mass media* looks at how technology is used to reach a large audience. It can include the study of media such as newspapers, television, radio, and even social media (see Chapter 15). Increasingly, researchers are examining how mass media influences all other areas of communication study. For example, if someone's social media feed has ever influenced how you perceive them, it could also affect your interpersonal communication with them. Next, *intercultural communication* examines how individuals from different cultures communicate with one another (see Chapter 14). The first type of culture you probably think of involves race and ethnicity. But as we mentioned earlier, a culture is any group of individuals who share a system of beliefs, values, rites, rituals, norms, or other similarities that shape their identities such as age, religion, gender, sexual orientation, and many others (Holliday, 2010). Finally, *public speaking* or *rhetoric* is the act (or art) of performing or delivering (see Chapter 4) a speech to an audience. Although most people think of public speaking as being one-sided communication, we hope you'll begin to see public speaking as an enlarged conversation that involves careful listening and recognizing that your audience plays an important role in what and how you present.

Because there are so many different areas of communication, no one communication scholar can truly be an expert in all of them. Therefore, one of the key features that sets this textbook apart from others is the fact that we recruited experts from across the Communication Studies discipline (perhaps even your own instructor!) to write each chapter in this book. Every chapter is written by a professional scholar in his or her own area of expertise, giving you insight into the latest research and ideas in our discipline.

Although your authors admittedly are biased and think communication is pretty amazing, we hope you, too, will find at least something in this book that sparks your interest. Perhaps it's even a possibility to become a communication major or minor at your school. Then, you'd get a chance to explore some of these concepts even further, equipping you with what can be an incredibly marketable and flexible degree. Maybe you're interested in a career such as television, radio broadcasting, or public relations? Do you dream of being a social media mogul for yourself or another company? Or, maybe you're more interested in the personal side of communication? Some of the best sales reps and those who work in nonprofits are/were communication majors. They know how to connect with and adapt to their audience/clients. Communication also opens doors to jobs in human

© julymilks/Shutterstock.com

resources and management. A simple search online will give you many lists of jobs like these—ones you can do if you specialize in communication. That's why instead, on page 6, we listed some of the more fun, unique jobs you may not have considered—ones that prioritize hiring people with excellent communication skills. Even though this is just a small selection of the numerous jobs for which a degree in communication can prepare you, remember, you can have all the knowledge in the world, but your ability to connect with others and effectively share your knowledge is what will set you up for success—in your own life and for making a difference in the world around you.

References

Aristotle. (1853). Peri hermeneias: de interpretation. *The organon, or logical treatises of Aristotle* (O. E. Owen, Trans.). London, UK: John Childs & Son. (Original work published in antiquity).

Association of American Colleges & Universities. (2018). *Fulfilling the American dream: Liberal education and the future of work: Selected findings from online surveys of business executives and hiring managers.* Retrieved from https://www.aacu.org/sites/default/files/files/LEAP/2018EmployerResearchReport.pdf

Baumeister, R. F., & Leary, M. R. (1995). The need to belong: Desire for interpersonal attachments as a fundamental human motivation. *Psychological Bulletin, 117*, 497–529. doi:10.1037/0033-2909.117.3.497

Berlo, D. K. (1960). *The process of communication.* New York, NY: Holt, Rinehart & Winston.

Bok, S. (1984). *Secrets: On the ethics of concealment and revelation.* New York, NY: Vintage Books.

Bok, S. (1999). *Lying: Moral choice in public and private life.* New York, NY: Vintage Books.

Dunbar, N. E., Gangi, K., Coveleski, S., Adams, A., Bernhold, Q., & Giles, H. (2016). When is it acceptable to lie?: Interpersonal and intergroup perspectives on deception. *Communication Studies, 67*, 129–146. doi:10.1080/10510974.2016.1146911

Dwyer, K. K., & Davidson, M. M. (2012). Is public speaking really more feared than death? *Communication Research Reports, 29*, 99–107. doi:10.1080/08824096.2012.667772

Floyd, K., & Deiss, D. M. (2012). Better health, better lives: The bright side of affection. In T. J. Socha & M. Pitts (Eds.), *The positive side of interpersonal communication* (pp. 127–142). New York, NY: Routledge.

Hallo, W. W. (2004). The birth of rhetoric. In C. S. Lipson & R. A. Binkley (Eds.), *Rhetoric before and beyond the Greeks* (pp. 25–46). Albany, NY: SUNY Press.

Hartley, R. V. L. (1928). Transmission of information. *Bell System Technical Journal, 7*, 535–563. doi:10.1002/j.1538-7305.1928.tb01236.x

Hayakawa, S. I. (1972). *Language in thought and action* (3rd ed.). New York, NY: Harcourt Brace Jovanovich, Inc.

Helmreich, R., & Collins, B. E. (1968). Studies in forced compliance: Commitment and magnitude of inducement to comply as determinants of opinion change. *Journal of Personality & Social Psychology, 10*, 75–81. doi:10.1037/h0026282

Holliday, A. (2010). Complexity in cultural identity. *Language and Intercultural Communication, 10*, 165–177. doi:10.1080/1470847093267384

Jay, T., & Janschewitz, K. (2008). The pragmatics of swearing. *Journal of Politeness Research, 4*, 267–288. doi:10.1515/JPLR.2008.013

National Communication Association. (2019). Interest groups. *NCA Website.* Retrieved from https://www.natcom.org/about-nca/membership-and-interest-groups/nca-interest-groups

Pearson, J. C., & VanHorn, S. B. (2004). Communication and gender identity: A retrospective analysis. *Communication Quarterly, 52*, 284–299. doi:10.1080/01463370409370198

Pennebaker, J. W. (1989). Confession, inhibition, and disease. In L. Berkowitz (Ed.), *Advances in experimental social psychology* (Vol. 22, pp. 211–244). San Diego, CA: Academic Press.

Pennebaker, J. W. (1993). Overcoming inhibition: Rethinking the roles of personality, cognition, and social behavior. In H. C. Traue & J. W. Pennebaker (Eds.), *Emotion, inhibition, and health* (pp. 100–115). Seattle, WA: Hogrefe & Huber.

Salsbury, John of. (2013). *Metalogicon* (J. B. Hall & J. P. Haseldine, Trans.). Turnhout, Belgium: Brepols. (Original work published 1159).

Schramm, W. (1954). How communication works. In W. Schramm (Ed.), *The process and effects of communication* (pp. 3–26). Urbana, IL: University of Illinois Press.

Schwartz, G. E., & Russek, L. G. (1998). Family love and lifelong health? A challenge for clinical psychology. In D. K. Routh & R. J. DeRubeis (Eds.), *The science of clinical psychology: Accomplishments and future directions* (pp. 121–146). Washington, DC: American Psychological Association.

Stryker, S. (1994). Identity theory: Its development, research base, and prospects. In N. K. Denzin (Ed.), *Studies in symbolic interaction* (Vol. 16, pp. 9–20). Bingley, UK: Emerald Group Publishing.

Tardy, C. H. (2000). Self-disclosure and health: Revisiting Sidney Jourard's hypothesis. In S. Petronio (Ed.), *Balancing the secrets of private disclosures* (pp. 111–122). Mahwah, NJ: Erlbaum.

Tefft, B. C. (2018). Acute sleep deprivation and culpable motor vehicle crash involvement. *Sleep, 41*(10), zsy144. doi:10.1093/sleep/zsy144

Teng, F., Poon, K.-T., & Yang, Y. (2016). Does social protest shake people's justice beliefs?: It depends on the level of group identification. *Basic and Applied Social Psychology, 38*(5), 269–275. doi:10.1080/01973533. 2016.1210518

Watzlawick, P., Beavin, J. H., & Jackson, D. D. (1967). *Pragmatics of human communication: A study of interactional patterns, pathologies, and paradoxes* (pp. 48–71). New York, NY: W. W. Norton & Company.

Wynter, A. (1854). The electric telegraph. *Quarterly Review, 95*, 118–164.

Rapper Nas wasn't the first person to say we fear what we don't know (go to the video for the actual lyrics); a version of this has been circulating since well before Nas made it popular in his *Hate Me Now* lyrics. And this sentiment is true, particularly when it comes to public speaking. (FYI, the opening pic/video and this paragraph serve as my **attention-getter**, or way of grabbing my audience, making them want to listen.) As Chapter 1 mentioned, some people fear public speaking similarly to death (Dwyer & Davidson, 2012), but this fear/hate is largely due to not *understanding* public speaking or the process. Simply put, **public speaking** is the spreading of a message with a specific purpose in a way that influences a particular audience's knowledge and/or views. Countless people use public speaking to advocate for social justice, inspire change, or help people better understand a subject. Although it may not fit your traditional notion of public speaking, music and videos have the power to shape an audience's

My attention-getter: Here's the controversial music video: https://www.youtube.com/watch?v=dKSJN3WWR3E

© Jamie Lamor Thopmson/Shutterstock.com

perception and influence their behavior. The inspiration for Nas's *Hate Me Now* video was the controversy in New York City over a Black, male actor playing Jesus (Serpick, 2007).

When you think about public speaking, you probably think less about Nas and imagine the best and most inspirational speakers in history, like Dr. Martin Luther King, Jr. (MLK). His poignant speech at Cornell College on October 15, 1962 (see King, 1962 for full transcript) attempted to answer: Are we making any real progress in race relations? As part of his answer, he stated:

> I am convinced that men hate each other because they fear each other. They fear each other because they don't know each other, and they don't know each other because they don't communicate with each other, and they don't communicate with each other because they are separated from each other.

Dr. King discussed making connections between races so the unknown becomes familiar (i.e., we're more alike than different), ultimately easing racial tensions. Like Nas, he stressed the sentiment that it's harder to fear something you know well. So, if you're feeling some trepidation about public speaking, let's get to know it well.

Even if you don't become famous, you'll use public speaking skills in your everyday life as a newly acquired superpower. (And just so you know, this is my **rationale**, or reason you should listen/read further, which we'll discuss later.) You can reduce your (possible) hatred of public speaking by increasing your understanding of its fundamental parts, and you'll be better able to USE those components to make effective connections with your audience. (This is my *thesis* statement or main argument, which we'll also cover later.)

Why should you listen to ME talk about THIS subject? I like to think I'm an expert in both the academic study and practice of public speaking, or *rhetoric* (a fancy schmancy word for the art of effective or persuasive speaking or writing). I have my Ph.D. in Rhetoric and Culture and my master's and bachelor's degrees in Interpersonal and Public Communication. I've been teaching courses in basic and advanced public speaking as well as in argumentation for over 21 years. I'm also a former speech and debate competitor (8 years—both high school and college) and coach (21+ years), with numerous trophies to prove it. (And, THAT paragraph was my *credibility statement*, or reason you should listen to/respect me. I also try to build credibility throughout this intro by referencing other credible sources—something I'll discuss shortly.)

MLK's influence extended beyond the United States, as seen in a Yemeni postage stamp.

© catwalker/Shutterstock.com

As Dr. King, Nas, and so many others have demonstrated, speaking to the public is a powerful endeavor, and one worth doing well. So, to help you better understand public speaking, I'll first demystify it. Second, we'll examine why and how to analyze your audience. Finally, we'll discover how to use those first two steps to design a speech that both you and your audience are happy with. (That's my *preview statement*, setting listeners up for what to expect.)

Why People Hate Learning About and Doing Public Speaking

It's *easy* to fear public speaking like it was death. Thinking about our own mortality AND fearing it usually only happens in rare moments, but public speaking, on the other hand, happens ALL THE TIME! It's NOT just the kind of intimidating public speaking you're imagining—the auditorium full of strangers staring at you while you tremble beneath anemic florescent stage-lighting clutching a podium in your best professional clothes and sweating through your deodorant. *That* very formal, public speaking doesn't happen often, and yeah, that is nerve-wracking.

Most public speaking you'll engage in during your lifetime is a lot more casual. It's equally important, but less intimidating: in your senior capstone class presenting your final project; as a representative of a student organization convincing administration to start composting; hell, even playing World of Warcraft trying to convince a guild to let you join them so you can build experience. If we think of public speaking in this way, we can see that it's really more like an enlarged conversation, and we already engage in public speaking all the time. GOOD NEWS: Because it happens often, you already have more skill than you know. BETTER NEWS: Enhancing your public speaking skills creates superpowers you didn't even know were possible across all areas of your life, in and out of the classroom. BEST NEWS: All chapters in this book cover diverse areas AND highlight how to apply their topics to public speaking.

Additionally, many don't hate public speaking because they fear it but because they think they *already know it.* They think it's going to be boring, they think they already learned everything they need to know about it in high school, and they aren't convinced they'll use it outside their classes. And, some of it IS boring (#sorrynotsorry). The fact is, when you break *anything* down into its fundamentals, it's kind of boring: "Okay, duh, I have to use quality evidence. Okay, duh, I have to organize my thoughts so they don't come out like a rendition of Lewis Carroll's *Jabberwocky* (which makes a great poem, not a great speech). Okay, duh, I have to make eye contact with my audience." GOOD NEWS: You can already recognize some components of good public speaking, and you probably use some of these regularly. BUT, this isn't the same as knowing how to give a great presentation, nor does it mean that you can do it well every time; it's kind of like Sex Panther math: "Sex Panther Cologne: 60% of the time, it works EVERY time" (Osborne, 2008).

Think of it this way: Playing a game of basketball might be fun, but rarely does someone just run out onto the court and begin *slaying* it. To be able to run complicated, effective plays against your opponents, you have to break it down into fundamentals (dribbling, passing, shooting) AND you have to practice those fundamentals until they're committed to muscle memory (remember overlearning from the last chapter?). Furthermore, knowing and doing are two separate things. Almost anyone in the arena at a game could point out some of the fundamentals of basketball; this *doesn't* mean they can play it. Furthermore, if your body isn't taken care of, you might be an "expert" and *still* play a lousy game. There are many reasons for this, but let's just sum it up by saying: It isn't just about your knowledge and understanding; it's about making connections among all the factors involved. Doing nothing but passing drills all practice long = BORING . . . but EFFECTIVE in the end. Learning about public speaking = same.

Greek philosopher Aristotle, credited as the first public speaking teacher. His work, *Rhetoric*, was a list of his teaching notes ca. 358 B.C.E.

Analyzing public speaking's intricacies should help you understand several things. It's normal to have this fear, but most people are NOT scrutinizing your every move and judging every single thing you do/say. And, even if you learn ALL the fundamentals and perform them admirably, you might still fail to reach some audience members. Even the best basketball players make mistakes despite years of dedication. Perfection is impossible, so when it comes to public speaking, teach yourself to lower the bar (just a little). It'll never be perfect, but it can be effective—just like all those passing drills.

Public speaking has been studied since the days of Aristotle and Plato. Luckily, much of our understanding of what makes up the fundamentals hasn't changed in 2300+ years (Bizzell & Herzberg, 2001). And yet, every public speaking situation is different because the audience and context are different. We can master the fundamentals of public speaking (e.g., eye contact, evidence, organization). We can also practice the "dynamics"—the principles of good audience analysis and adaptation. But, because they're dynamic (always in flux), we won't always hit our mark, but we can do our best to get onto the target.

Laying It Down So the Audience Can (Mostly) Pick It Up

Stone of Hope by sculptor Lei Yixin at MLK, Jr. Memorial, located in West Potomac Park next to the National Mall, Washington, D.C.

© Jack Nevitt/Shutterstock.com

Younge (2015) reported that on the night before the "I Have a Dream" speech, MLK Jr.'s aides advised him not to use the saying because it was overdone; he'd used the "I have a dream" line in several rallies already. Yet, August 28, 1963 would be King's debut to most of the American public. Three TV networks (back when there *were* basically only three) were covering the event. To say it was a big deal would be an understatement of epic proportions. King went to sleep in the wee morning hours after working all night with his advisors drafting his history-altering speech that did NOT include the phrase "I have a dream" (Younge, 2015).

They expected around 100,000 people to show up—they got about 250,000. You can imagine the mood of the crowd on that hot August day (87°F, sunny, humid) on the National Mall. King was the 16th speaker scheduled and had to follow the president of the American Jewish Congress, Joachim Prinz, who'd witnessed the rise and fall of Hitler—a tough act to follow. Witnesses say that although the speech was going well, it wasn't living up to King's legend.

So, in the middle of this speech that he'd spent all night prepping, King set his prepared notes aside and decided just to tell the audience about his dream. The most famous speech from

Sean Astin, a total crush of mine, also played Daniel "Rudy" Reuttiger in *Rudy* (1993), a great movie for inspiration—like when you need a pep talk before a speech or to get "in the zone" or your "game face" on for a performance.

one of the most famous public *orators* (fancy schmancy word for public speaker, usually a good one who's trying to persuade you) wasn't wholly spontaneous, but it wasn't wholly planned either! Experts named it *the greatest speech of the 20th century* (Lucas & Medhurst, 2008).

How does one achieve that level of cool, calm, and collected poise—where reading the crowd and just *rolling with it* goes without a hitch? MLK was a BOSS. Most of us will not achieve this level of public speaking genius. However, we can ALL learn from him. Notice that this G.O.A.T. wasn't perfect. *But, that isn't what people remember.* Witnesses say until the "I Have a Dream" section, the speech felt like a lecture, but he turned it around. King had the presence of mind to pay attention to the feedback he was getting from his audience.

He was prepared enough and knew his purpose and his subject so well that he could "go off script" to fit the demands of the situation. What can be learned from MLK's example? Never get complacent. Prepare; get and keep your game face on, keeping *the goals* of your speech (not yourself) in focus for your audience—from picking your initial topic to thoroughly analyzing the people who will hear you. Let's explore these concepts further.

Choosing a Topic

Like MLK, when picking a speech topic, pick something you're passionate about. If you don't care about what you're saying, why the hell should your audience be interested? Sincerity and passion go a long way. Audiences are a lot more forgiving of mistakes when you're clearly interested in the message you're sending. Plus, if you're going to spend weeks working on something, it might as well be something you enjoy.

As you pick your topic, don't squander this invaluable opportunity to speak on something you're passionate about. Don't let fear or misunderstanding stop you. People fought for the freedom of speech and the privilege to speak their mind. Don't squander it; it isn't available everywhere in the world. When I judged a debate competition in China, I discovered the Chinese students weren't allowed to criticize the government. The word "democracy" was even banned from Internet chat rooms there! Public speaking is a special opportunity where people listen to YOU speak about something that matters. It is an OPPORTUNITY, not a BURDEN.

Find an *exciting* AND *purposeful* topic! When trying to find a topic to talk about, create a mind map and use guidelines for good brainstorming (see Rules for Brainstorming box below). ***Mind maps*** are a brainstorming tool that allow you to show how subjects connect (Genovese, 2019). There are no "rules" here, but a good practice is to start by writing on a blank piece of paper (however you do it, make sure to record it somehow—good records will be crucial later!) things that you (a) have experience in, (b) already know a lot about, (c) are passionate about/matter a lot to you, and (d) may not know much about yet but that interest you. It's okay to branch off and create new categories from these. Just make sure you keep *yourself* (e.g., what you know, your passions) and the *speaking situation* (e.g., audience, time limit, technological resources available) in mind. Considering yourself and the situation, you might need to narrow down your topic (there's no way you can effectively address everything about music in one speech, but you might be able to cover Nas's career) or, you might find your topic is entirely too narrow to find enough credible research (see Chapter 3) to fill your time and make a strong argument. Keep all these factors in mind as you refer back to your notes.

Public Speaking Power: Rules for Brainstorming

- ***Start early***. Don't do your brainstorming the night before your presentation—MLK was *editing* his speech the night before; he wasn't coming up with a topic or new idea; it was all very familiar to him and stuff he'd spoken about many times. Plus, like I said, he was a BOSS. Give yourself time to get to that status before you try ALL his methods.

- ***Set a time limit***. There's nothing like deadline-pressure to get mental synapses firing. Set a 3-minute minimum timer for each category. If you go over time, no big deal, but don't STOP that category *until* time's up. You have a timer on your computer or phone—no excuses.

- ***Quantity is your initial goal***. Don't be a Judgy McJudgerton! If you edit as you go, you won't get anything written down. Self-censor during brainstorming and you'll run the risk of missing out on piggybacking. Sure, the first thing you write might be crap, but it might spark another idea and another and another, and one of THOSE ideas might be gold. ANYTHING goes during those 3 minutes! After you're all done brainstorming, you can go back and ask yourself: "Given my audience, purpose, and speaking time-limit, which of these topics wouldn't work?" Cross those out. Then, go back and rank-order what you have left to get to your best option. Quantity first, *then* quality.

- ***Teamwork makes the dream work***. If you can, brainstorm with someone else. They'll think of things you don't, bringing piggybacking to a whole new level—the whole "2 heads is better than 1" thing. Make sure they follow the same guidelines.

Contributed by K. Scholten

Your topic will also be largely driven by your *general purpose*, or main goal of your speech. There are three general purposes possible, to: *inform*, or educate in a specific manner; *persuade*, or change attitudes, beliefs, or behaviors; or *entertain*, or cause an emotional reaction. Sometimes they overlap (you can be funny while informing someone about a new technology), but usually, one purpose takes center stage. Which one is primary is determined by your speaking assignment's parameters.

Once you have your general purpose and topic, you should determine your *specific purpose*, or what *you* want your audience to do or understand by the end of your speech. Going to the grocery store without a list takes more time, involves getting things you didn't plan, and ends up costing you more. DON'T FORGET YOUR LIST! Having a specific purpose ("I want my audience to [list . . .] by the end of my speech") for your audience makes your time spent researching more effective because you'll only include things that aid your speech goals.

Even if you're incredibly passionate about your topic and have a clear, specific purpose, it doesn't mean your audience is going to listen or care. Without knowing your audience (and tailoring your speech to your audience), you'll have no impact, and you'll waste everyone's time. So, let's figure out who that audience is!

Analyzing Your Audience: Becoming *Their* Kind of Hero

Effective public speaking is finding the intersection between what YOU care about/believe and what THEY care about/know. Good public speakers, like good basketball players, anticipate moves ahead of time. They watch the video of their opponents. They have to adapt to the unexpected in the moment, but they've also mentally and physically prepared for the *specific team* they're about to face. All speech content and delivery should be guided by two overarching principles–good audience analysis and this ethical rule: Always treat your audience the way you would want to be treated. (BTW: that's a *minor preview*, which prefaces what's to come in just this section.)

First, at the most basic level there are two categories of audience analysis you'll want to do: demographic and psychological. Use the Audience Analysis Guide box on the next page as a worksheet to help you figure out your audience, and then, apply that information to craft your speech to best connect with your audience. For example, if you're doing a speech on the opioid crisis and want to make the argument that this is *not* a problem merely "happening to someone else," you might find research that discusses addiction rates among 18 to 25 year olds (or whatever age group your audience is). You might even go a step further and discuss opioid addiction in your state or city within that age group. After presenting the stats, you might discuss a true story of a college student (very similar to them) suffering from this addiction. This helps the audience understand the frequency of addiction and shows how it affects real people, people *like them*. This is the concept of *identification*, the art of creating affinity between you and your topic and audience.

Public Speaking Power: A Guide to Analyze Your Audience

1. **Demographic → Psychographic Analysis:** Take what you already know about your audience and what you can discover (through quick research) to make educated guesses about them. First, identify their demographic characteristics. Then, use those to assess their knowledge, values, beliefs, and attitudes. What do you know about them that seems relevant to your speech and why?

   DEMOGRAPHICS *(identify audience & how each might affect how they see your speech)*
   Age
   Sex and Gender
   Sexual Orientation
   Race/Ethnicity/Cultural Background
   Religion
   Group Memberships *(political affiliations, hobbies, sports, etc.)*
   Geographical Location *(where they're from AND your speech's location)*
   Socio-Economic Situation
   Education
   Other demographic categories important to consider for this speech? *(explain those)*

   NOTE: Not all will be relevant to your *specific* purpose, but you should still note where your audience falls on each of these, putting N/A for nonrelevant categories.

2. **Situation → Psychographic Analysis:** Take what you know about the time frame, physical setting, and surrounding context *(news, events, other happenings relevant to your topic/audience)* to make educated guesses about your audience's psychological state.

   What are their biggest concerns in life right now?
   Where do they stand on your topic?
   How strongly do they hold that stance?
   What do they already know or believe about your topic?
   Anything happen recently *(in news or on campus)* **that would affect their mood?**
   What's likely on their mind when you give your speech? *(Lunch? Finals?)*
   How will these things affect the content and delivery of your speech?

3. **Analyses → Application:** How will you accomplish your specific purpose *(adaptations to "speak their language")*? HOW will ALL of these things (demographics, situation, psychology) affect your speech content, organization, and delivery?

All of these things and more shape audiences' interests, values, experiences, attitudes, and knowledge about you and your subject. Don't assume you know everything about them based solely on categories 1 and 2. The more info you get, the better; even then, your analysis will be incomplete.

Consider some of these categories on a scale—not as binary, either/or options. The more rich, detailed, specific your audience info, the better you'll be at picking a topic you're BOTH into. Even if you already know your topic, analysis helps you choose examples, metaphors, statistics, definitions, and anecdotes that speak to *them*—that translate your topic, your knowledge, your ideas into *their language*.

Don't assume they think like you, know the same stuff, or have the same values. But don't assume they're totally against you, either. Your speech should address commonalities *and* differences. Knowing what these are goes a *long* way toward reaching your audience effectively.

Contributed by K. Scholten

Second, there are many lessons about ethics. In fact, ethics is its own discipline; you can take whole semesters of communication ethics classes and still have stuff to learn. I can't cover it all; therefore, *at the broadest level*, here's the ethical golden rule in public speaking: TREAT OTHERS LIKE YOU WOULD WANT TO BE TREATED. You know what that means. Don't lie, cover things up, leave things out that you know hurt your case, or otherwise be smarmy. Don't get all your info from one source. Don't use words that are likely to hurt people's feelings. Don't talk down to your audience as if you're superior, and they know nothing. This doesn't mean you should "dumb it down" for them. It just means being sensitive about the evidence, words, and visual aids you use. Ask yourself, am I being fair? Considering all relevant perspectives? Treating them like I'd want to be treated in an audience? If so, then you're ready to begin designing your speech.

Activism Hero: Your Anti-Guru for Social Change

Abbie Hoffman, a controversial activist for change in the 1960s, can teach us a lot. First, he shows us that protest can help the world, and it can be done through public speaking. He also demonstrates how sometimes people try to get heard among all the noise by startling their audience with threatening "facts" (today, we refer to these as "fake news" or misinformation). For example, it probably wasn't a great idea to tell organizers of the 1968 Democratic National Convention that he was going to put LSD in the water supply. It may have gotten attention, but it didn't get Chicago to grant a petition to protest peacefully in the park. Telling national TV that he and his "Yippies" would levitate the Pentagon, the American public may not have understood his intentionally being ludicrous to draw attention to the "political theater that is U.S. politics." Instead of rallying people to his cause, he alienated them.

Use Abbie Hoffman as your anti-guru—not only for your own arguments but also to publicly question others'. If a speaker—whether in speeches or conversations—doesn't give a verifiable source for their claims and/or your own verification process doesn't check out—assume their "facts" are false. Although it's always a speaker's responsibility to support their claims, it's *our* burden to judge the *value* and truth of statements we hear. Perpetuating falsehoods makes us almost as culpable as those who started the lies in the first place!

Today, we're so accustomed to people in power blaring out blatant falsehoods that we've almost given up believing anything anyone says. But, it doesn't have to be that overwhelming! You'll learn more about this in Chapter 3, but for now, check out Zimdars's (2016) viral list of smarmy news sources and her strategies for spotting fake news. She got hate mail because of it, showing how averse some people are to any challenge of ANY information stated as factual. No one ever said changing the world would be easy. Take a stand like she did by (kindly) challenging *everyone*—even those you trust—and their claims. Simply asking, "Who says?" may be the most direct way to make change in the world around you.

Contributed by K. Scholten and J. Eckstein

<u>Speech Design: Making a Meal Even Batman Will Devour</u>

You've gone to the grocery store with your clearly formed list (i.e., *general purpose* and *specific purpose*) in mind. You have the materials you need to make that list a reality (i.e., evidence and ideas, discussed in Chapter 3). Now, you need to put those ingredients together into something tasty. The dour Batman is a notoriously joyless eater, eating only when he has to. But, there are three ingredients that can make even the Dark Knight want to devour what you're laying down: organizational patterns, intros and conclusions, and transitions.

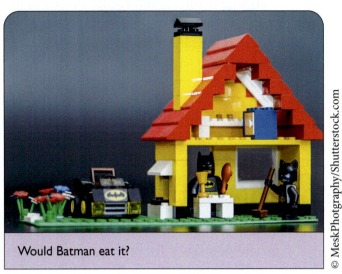

Would Batman eat it?

© MeskPhotgraphy/Shutterstock.com

Organizational Patterns: The Plating

First, you need a method, something we call an ***organizational pattern***, for putting your research and preparation into a pleasing form the audience will want to devour. It helps your speech make sense. Even with what might seem like a mish-mash of ingredients at first glance, with careful planning, you can make something delectable. Public speakers have been using several tried-and-true organizational patterns through the millennia, and your professor might assign a very specific pattern to use. I'm going to talk about the most common here, *but this isn't a complete list*. Your chosen pattern should be a conscious choice. Given your options, ask yourself what makes the most SENSE (*not* what's most *convenient*) for your purpose/topic.

Speeches to Inform

When you want the audience to understand something new or unfamiliar (what's chaos theory and why does it predict social behavior?); explain a complicated phenomenon (how do Earth's magnetic poles flip?); or teach how to do something (how to build their own Batcave?), it's an informative speech. Here are the big four informative patterns:

The ***chronological pattern*** is organized according to a unit of time. This could be specific dates, seasons of the year, times of day, or steps in a process—it all depends on your goals. For example, if my goal is to introduce myself using an object important to me (like a volleyball) and how it represents the course of my life, I might use chronological organization:

Point 1: This volleyball represents my past because I've been playing competitively since I was in elementary school. *[Then, I'd talk about my experiences, provide anecdotes, and detail awards I won back then.]*

Point 2: This volleyball represents my present because I'm currently the captain of my college team. *[Similarly, fill in info about my current volleyball activity.]*

Point 3: This volleyball represents my future because I'm currently enrolled in the Sports Communication major with a goal of a career in collegiate volleyball. *[Here's what I want to do with my life.]*

TIPS: Good rules to follow regardless of the pattern you choose, the following are especially important with this pattern. First, be consistent. Don't start using specific dates ("I started playing volleyball in *2001*") but then later switch to eras ("In the *future*, I want to play for the competitive team"). Next, make your time-unit obvious because SUBTLETY DOESN'T WORK IN PUBLIC SPEAKING! Most audiences don't pay attention closely. So, bombard them with your unit of time; use keywords to clearly indicate your units. Repetition = remembering.

A **spatial pattern** is organized according to space-unit like geography or physical space, and it only makes sense for certain topics. For example, if I talk about all the historical sites I visited in Rome over the summer, I'd use a spatial pattern (locations of each site in Rome and in directional relation to each other). On the other hand, I could talk about how the parts of an internal combustion engine are physically connected to each other and how that physical connection leads to a working car:

Point 1: To understand how a car's engine works, we need to start at the start (ha ha!)—how the starter engine turns a crankshaft when you turn that key in the ignition. *[Add detail & further explain. Back it up by sources, probably lots of diagrams].*

Point 2: Now that we understand how the starter motor makes the pistons move inside the engine, "turning it over," let's talk about how those moving cylinders draw in air and fuel. *[More explanation, more diagrams, maybe even a video].*

Point 3: To complete our understanding of how a car engine works, we need to discuss how the air- and fuel-drawing cylinders connect to the spark plugs, combusting fuel, which eventually turns into exhaust. *[I could even break this up to have four points, labeling each according to the components of a four-stroke engine. I did three here to help envision the process as starting with the turned-key action that starts the physical process. Neither way is better; they just serve different purposes. My way is more noob-friendly; the other may be better for a car-loving audience.]*

FOUR STROKE CYCLE ENGINE

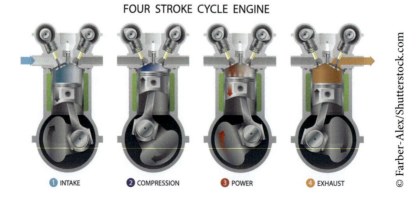

1 INTAKE   2 COMPRESSION   3 POWER   4 EXHAUST

© Farber-Alex/Shutterstock.com

MORE tips: As always, let the subject guide you. Think about where to start. With spatial patterns, there might be a natural starting place, a *physical beginning*, like with the car-starter. Or, you might start from center, moving outward; start at left, moving right; top to bottom; north to south; or vice versa. Just make the physical connection "locations" clear. Next, it's *particularly* important you don't jump around (literally and figuratively) when discussing how things physically connect. If you start at center, methodically work your way outward; don't jump from center to periphery or wherever. Audiences are easily confused—not because they're stupid but because you're competing with a lot of noise in their heads (remember all those distractions discussed in Chapter 1?) AND because they can't flip back through your speech—they only get to hear it once. Finally, clear graphics are important (see Chapter 3) —they always are but more so with this potentially complicated pattern where you're discussing something *physically manifesting itself in space* and how its parts relate to each other *within that space*.

A **topical pattern** just divides your speech by its logical divisions or subtopics. For example, in that speech about me and my volleyball, I could instead divide that into how my volleyball represents different characteristics of my personality. It'd still be a speech about me, but it'd be more about my identity than about how I got where I'm going. Both are valid; they just serve different purposes.

Point 1: This volleyball represents my athleticism. *[Discuss physical accolades I've accomplished through the sport in my lifetime.]*

Point 2: This volleyball represents my tenacity. *[Discuss obstacles I've overcome in order to play this sport I love—hopefully, while telling specific stories full of vibrant detail so you "see" my journey—not just talking about what tenacity means in general but proving to you, through examples, that I have it.]*

Point 3: This volleyball represents my connection to my family. *[Discuss family members with volleyball connections and how they influenced my own experiences.]*

TIPS: Don't choose this pattern out of convenience or just because you don't want to work at thinking about a better way to explain your topic. Choose this IF it makes sense for your topic because natural subtopics emerge. Like if I wanted to talk about the branches of government, there are three branches—natural subtopics. Also, we haven't talked about transitions yet, but make sure your **transitions** are *bridges* that look both backward and forward and tie your topics together. You can do this with any topic or pattern. Look at my car engine example to see this done intentionally. It's especially important to BRIDGE with topical patterns because it isn't always an obvious connection (like a date or a physical relationship) between subtopics, so you need to work harder to flow from one to another.

Finally, a **comparative pattern** is where you explain your topic by comparing and contrasting it to something else. Use this method to show how two things are alike and different—how they relate to one another. For example, inform the audience about two different medications claiming to help people quit smoking by comparing and contrasting the benefits and drawbacks of each. Or, use this pattern to explain an unfamiliar subject in relation to something the audience is familiar with, discussing similarities/differences between the two. For example, 90% of people in the U.S. celebrate Christmas a particular way (Pew Research, 2017), but it's celebrated differently elsewhere in the world:

Point 1: Many cultures around the world celebrate the Christmas holiday with some version of Santa Claus, but they aren't all the same. *[Then, I pick two other versions of Santa, compare-contrast those with the U.S.-jolly old man version.]*

Point 2: Many cultures around the world also give gifts during the winter season, but they don't all come under a Christmas tree. *[Then, I may contrast different cultures' gift types or how Europeans put gifts in shoes vs. under trees/in stockings.]*

Point 3: Many cultures around the world also have their own barrage of holiday-themed songs, but maybe not as annoying as the gems we hear in U.S. department stores. *[You get the idea, and now probably have an annoying Christmas jingle in your head. Also, notice my **parallelism**, each point worded similarly, giving a rhythm easier for the audience to remember. Look back—I did this in all my patterns.]*

TIPS: As always, no matter the pattern, *let the topic and speaking situation guide you*. How much time do you have (e.g., how many comparison points can reasonably be explained before you run out of time)? What's important for the audience to know to meet your specific purpose for them? If trees are used similarly for Christmas around the world, is that still the most interesting comparison point? Maybe it is—if the reason for that similarity is important for the audience to know or if it'll teach them something interesting and new. Maybe they already knew the tree thing, so other subtopics and comparisons make more sense to include. Again, *the audience is the key* to your public speaking success. And finally, use this pattern to compare/contrast two policies or solutions. It works really well for this! The smoking-cessation medicine example mentioned earlier is one example; another is if you're trying to educate about different presidential candidates' stances on fixing social security. You wouldn't try to persuade the audience to choose one over another—just inform them of all the ins and outs (Of course, you *could* make it persuasive IF that's what the situation calls for). In persuasion, it's called a **comparative advantage** pattern; I won't detail it here, but you'd place two options side by side, systematically arguing one is *more* advantageous (or has *fewer* weaknesses) than the other.

Speeches to Persuade

Persuasion is used to convince your audience to strengthen or change their attitudes, values, beliefs, or actions. For example, maybe you need to convince them to place *more value* on environmental health. Maybe you know they think recycling is already prevalent but want to convince them more needs to be done on campus (*change belief*) OR that options are available but you want them to actually partake in the cafeteria's composting option (*change action*). Here are three ways you might organize your persuasive speeches in order to accomplish your goal:

A ***problem-solution*** (or problem/cause/solution) ***pattern*** works to establish that a (past or present) harm is bad. Then, you establish what's causing this problem to occur, and finally, you propose a solution to remedy it. Good solutions can be something done on a larger (perhaps national) level OR (and this is usually better) smaller things your audience can actually do:

Point 1: Machinery and practices of humankind have led to an abundance of harmful CO_2 emissions with a devastating impact on the planet and its people. *[Using a variety of reliable sources, explain how humans and industry lead to rising CO_2 and how it's harmful to humans. To drive it home, discuss specific problems seen locally that've resulted from rising emissions.]*

Point 2: CO_2 emissions are relatively unchecked in the United States due to powerful business lobbies drowning out voices calling for stricter regulations. *[Explain why things are the way they are—the barriers to overcome to change this.]*

Point 3: There's a rising development of carbon-capturing technology that works to remove CO_2 from the air and limits its harmful effects on the planet, but we need to find ways to let this technology flourish. *[Describe how this technology works, the difference it'll make on current problems, and how we can encourage its growth (e.g., listen to new voices instead of continuing business as usual, encourage them to reach out to local environmental organizations or contact congresspersons).]*

TIPS: You can make this pattern informative by describing a problem and then several possible solutions (without advocating for one over another) or by describing a problem and discussing all of the reasons (causes) this problem exists—so the audience gets a more nuanced understanding. On that note, *there can be multiple causes*; you need to be aware of them so you can justify why you're only focusing on certain causes/effects. If you don't do this and the audience knows, it hurts your reputation. Finally, *make sure there IS actually a clear relationship between the variables* you're discussing *that you can back up with reliable evidence.* Your audience isn't stupid, and it's unethical to treat them as such. It's likely at least one audience member will know you've left something out (if you do).

Second, ***criteria satisfaction*** leads your audience to your solution by first outlining criteria or qualities a good solution should meet and then showing how your solution meets those criteria. You'd use this pattern primarily when the audience *already knows and agrees* there's a problem. For example, if you were attempting to persuade your audience to choose tacos for lunch, you would first establish the criteria for what makes a good lunch. Then, you would use each of these criteria as a main point and build arguments within each one of how tacos meet each quality, therefore, becoming a good, appropriate solution. Of course, this organizational pattern can be used with far more serious topics (although picking tacos is clearly important), such as voting for a particular political candidate.

Point 1: Tacos are cheap. *[Discuss how inexpensive ingredients are to make your own and/or costs at a local food truck.]*

Point 2: Tacos are versatile. *[Explain the many possible taco-filling options (e.g., vegetarian, meat options, even breakfast or dessert tacos) that mean they'll never get tired of tacos.]*

Point 3: Tacos are nutritious but satisfying. *[Discuss various healthy options and average calorie count.]*

TIPS: First, it's important to pick criteria your solution actually meets. For example, tacos can be particularly messy (ever try eating a crunchy taco while driving?), so "neatness" wouldn't be the best criteria to pick. Next, other solutions will likely meet your criteria (e.g., salad could meet the taco criteria I used above), so it's your job to demonstrate why your solution is the BEST one via clear, supporting evidence (stay tuned for Chapter 3).

Finally, **Monroe's Motivated Sequence** is a five-step pattern using human psychology to encourage audiences' behavior change (Monroe, 1943). Of course, not all topics fit neatly into this pattern, but for the ones that do, it's powerful—it's the ruler of all persuasive patterns because it plays off the way humans think.

Isaiah Mustafa, actor in the infamous "The Man your Man Could Smell Like" commercial: www.youtube.com/watch?v=owGykVbfgUE

© Kathy Hutchins/Shutterstock.com

Step 1: **Gain attention.** *(We'll further discuss this next with intros; for now, just note it's important to hook the audience, making them want to hear more.)* You're competing for their attention. You need to grab them before they decide it's not worth listening. As a lesson in how to use this pattern, watch one of my go-to commercials: "The Man Your Man Could Smell Like" (Old Spice, 2010), noted in the caption on your right. It's funny, ridiculous, and worth a look just for its subtle cultural sexism. It grabs attention with a half-naked, attractive man stepping out of the shower with a bold "Hello, ladies!" The target woman is asked to compare her man to him—hinting that her man might be flawed in ways she's never considered. Are you intrigued?

Step 2: **Establish need.** Is there something they're missing that'd really benefit them? Or, something harmful they need to stop? Commercials do this all the time. They try to convince you there's a problem in your life their product can solve. You might not even be aware of the problem, but they convince you of a NEED to take care of it. Old Spice does this, arguing men need to avoid "smelling like a lady."

Step 3: **Satisfy.** After showing something great you're missing or something horrible you can/should avoid, the speaker provides a solution to satisfy that need, describing specific steps to a solution and how each works to take care of the problem. In our Old Spice commercial, it's a manly-smelling body wash, helping you avoid smelling feminine, and thus (somehow) leading to happy relationships.

Step 4: **Visualize.** The goal here is to vividly describe EITHER the solution in action OR what'll happen if we fail to enact your suggestions. The Old Spice man is fit and confident, set against various idyllic scenarios (hoity toity horse-riding, posh boat scenes, diamonds, adventure)— visual elements that create an impression of better life from smelling like an "Old Spice man". Paint a picture associating all good outcomes of the proposed solution. Or, use this tactic to show negative consequences of failing

Watch the full "flower girl" TV ad (via Library of Congress): www.youtube.com/watch?v=riDypPIKfOU

© Romolo Tavani/Shutterstock.com

to satisfy the need, like the famous 1964 "flower girl" commercial, showing the desolate, mushroom-cloud annihilation of a world without Lyndon B. Johnson as President (see Mann, 2014 and the link above for more on the infamous ad). Paint a picture—positive or negative, with words and/or actual images—so the audience "sees" results and *feels* connected to your proposed fix.

Step 5: **Call to action.** Finally, challenge them to do something *and* detail what that is. How can they personally/physically get involved to satisfy your solution? Sign a petition? Donate time/resources to an organization? Change an everyday behavior? The call to action should be realistically *doable* and it should be *specific* to them. Even better is something they can do right then/there so they're invested and more likely to continue. With Old Spice, it's "Anything is possible when your man smells like Old Spice and not a lady. I'm on a horse." It could be spelled out more specifically ("go buy Old Spice!"), but the message is still clear. Moreover, ending with "I'm on a horse" is seemingly ridiculous but is also an *active* pose that reinforces the message: All good things come from this one action.

Overall Organizational Tips

Some final tips for organizing your main points in ANY speech pattern you choose: First, *keep main points distinct and parallel.* Hopefully, you noticed in each pattern I kept the subpoints related but clearly different/separate too. You have limited time, so you must make every point work! Parallelism is wording your tag lines similarly. Think of the first sentence of each point as a kind of headline—something catchy and memorable. Keeping the wording and sentence structure similar helps do this. I won't attempt to teach outlining structure here (#headache), but even with the examples I've given, you can see how larger ideas are divided into smaller ideas and then laid out in a way that flows easily.

Next, *keep main points balanced*. If it's a main point, then it should take roughly the same amount of time as the other main points. This helps give each point the time, dedication, and credit it deserves. Spending similar time on each main point is psychologically pleasing to an audience because then it *feels* like a main point and not a side-note.

Finally, *cover the right amount*. Having too many or too few points can cause problems. Not to beat a dead horse (#toolate), but think about your audience and the speaking situation. What do they NEED to know for you to accomplish your goals? What can you reasonably accomplish in the time you have? Too many points and the audience is overwhelmed and might not be able to follow. Too few and they might not get enough depth. So, how DO you know when enough is enough? You might ask yourself if you're covering the 5W/1H (Who, What, Why, Where, When, and How) somewhere in the speech. This won't make sense for every topic, but it can be a starting place to think about whether or not you're giving them enough depth. Go back to your audience analysis and your specific purpose. What do they already know? Don't waste their time on this! What do they NEED to know? Focus here!

Now that we have the main course/main points, let's talk about how to start and finish your speech. After all, appetizers set the tone for the main course to come, and desserts leave a lasting impression (sometimes a great meal can become so-so if the dessert is lackluster).

Intros and Conclusions: Apps and Desserts

Introductions

IN A WORLD WHERE INTRODUCTIONS ARE LIKE TRAILERS . . . an intro is like a commercial for upcoming TV/movies. It tries to create hunger for what's coming, giving just a taste to set the tone (like a great appetizer) so you know what it's about and are eager for it. I highlighted mine at the beginning of this chapter, so you already saw an example. An intro has five parts:

1. Attention-getter
2. Reason to listen to the topic (rationale)
3. Reason to listen to *you* on the topic (credibility statement)
4. Central idea or thesis statement
5. Preview of main points

With the exception of 1 and 5, these can be moved around, and sometimes you can accomplish two of them with the same idea.

An ***attention-getter*** creates information hunger; it makes an audience want to hear more. It does this by overcoming their internal distractions. Common attention-getting techniques include, but are not limited to: questions to the audience (rhetorical or actual), startling facts, entertaining or interesting stories, appropriate jokes, and poetic quotations. Note that none of these include saying your name and your topic. The first words out of your mouth count as your attention-getter. So, if your first words are "My name is . . ." that was a pretty pathetic attention-getter (unless you're

Does your attention-getter make them hungry for more?

Eminem, I guess). Similarly, you don't say "my topic is" because that's lame—and because it comes later in your thesis statement.

A ***rationale*** is a reason to listen to the topic. One way to make them eager to hear more is to convince them the subject is relevant to their lives. How will it affect them? Get them something they want? Help them avoid some danger? Why will they be better off knowing what you're about to tell them? You need to justify the topic, and your topic must relate to EVERYONE in your ***target audience***, the group you've intended to reach. For example, even in a speech on breast cancer, you'd point out that not just females get breast cancer; not only are males susceptible too, they also have moms, sisters, and friends. Mention how it connects to everyone you're trying to reach.

A ***credibility statement*** gives the audience a reason to listen to *you,* in particular. It can be as simple as, "I've done a lot of research on this subject." You can also detail any first-hand experience you have in the subject. In a speech about horses, mention if you've been riding for the past 15 years! Or, if you've taken a class on your topic or read a bunch of books about it, tell the audience. This is also where you can stress your passion about or involvement with the topic.

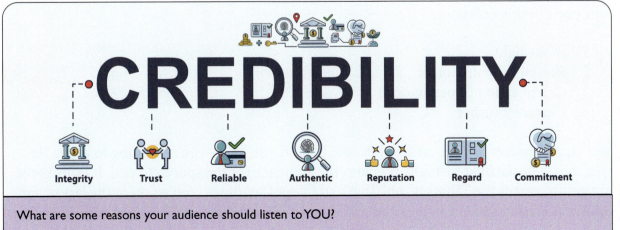

What are some reasons your audience should listen to YOU?

Your central idea, the *thesis statement* is derived from your specific purpose and sums up your speech in one, simple, declarative sentence. If they remember nothing else, they should remember your thesis. Your specific purpose (e.g., "To inform my audience of the role that volleyball has played in shaping who I am today") may not show up in your intro specifically, but your thesis statement should be a division of that purpose. It's what your audience needs to understand or believe in order for you to accomplish your purpose (e.g., "Volleyball isn't just a pastime; it's who I am."). Although the thesis statement does cover your main points like an umbrella, it shouldn't necessarily spell them out. A common misconception is that the thesis statement talks about the specifics of what you're going to cover. Nope—that's the preview! Be sure your thesis is a clear, one-sentence, overarching argument about your topic.

The final part to your introduction should be a *preview statement* listing your main points *in the exact order you'll discuss them*. Once again, some people think their central idea can act as their preview statement. In my experience (and all the professors in this book—with 250+ years combined professional and competitive public speaking experience—agree!), you should have them both, and they should be distinct. One reason is because they do two different things (i.e., prepare and organize). Another reason (which you'll learn about in Chapter 9) is because people forget about half of what they hear almost immediately— unless they're taking good notes . . . and chances are they aren't (International Listening Association, 2019). Repetition equals remembering. Summing up what the speech will be about in a central idea and then laying it out specifically in your preview will enhance the likelihood the audience will remember at least some of your speech.

These five parts must happen in a very short time. Oratory guru Lucas (2019) suggested an intro take 10% to 15% of total speech time, maximum. Remember, your intro sets the entire speech tone.

Conclusions

This is even shorter than the introduction (taking 5%–10% of your time, according to Lucas, 2019) but is no less important. The *conclusion* is the last thing your audience hears, so it *has to* end memorably, impacting them! Your main course might be life changing, but you don't want it to be lost on a disheartening dessert. Your conclusion should have three to four parts in this order:

1. Brake light
2. Review of main points
3. Call to action (if persuasion)
4. Closure/clincher

You tap the brakes in your car to let people behind you know you're coming to a stop. In speeches, a *brake light* mentally prepares the audience for the speech to end. It leads them out gently, versus the "That's it" or "That's all I've got" endings. You've spent the last several minutes creating a grand impression and doing a ton of work—don't ruin it with a horrible ending (I'm looking at you, *Game of Thrones* Season 5!). The most common brake light is "In conclusion . . ." It may be cliché, but it gets the job done. You can be more creative, as long as the audience can tell you're winding down.

Similar to the preview of points in your introduction, your **review statement** crystalizes in the audience's mind what you talked about and why it's important. Repetition = remembering. Say your points in the *exact* order discussed in your speech; do this in your preview, the body, and in the review. Keeping it consistent helps audiences stay on track.

Next, you can skip this in informative speeches, but for persuasion, you should reiterate a **call to action** to remind the audience what you persuaded them to do. Do this for any persuasive speech, not just motivated sequence patterns. What can they do right now to be a part of the solution? Remind them how they can personally get involved, and they're likely to actually do it.

Finally, a memorable last line, called a closure statement or a **clincher**, makes the audience remember you and what they learned. A good clincher ties full-circle to your attention-getter. If you started with a story, end with a few more details of that story. Began with a startling fact? Remind them of that fact. The clincher must clearly end the speech and resonate with the audience. And then . . . say nothing else. Just as your first words/noises are your attention-getter, your last words/noises are your clincher. So even if, after your actual clincher, you say "Thank you" or "I'm done" or run off in tears crying, "I'm so, so sorry!" (trust me, it's *never* that bad)—*that* is what will count as your clincher . . . not very effective. If your clincher is strong, you should be able to end with it, pause, and walk off (mic drop).

Finish like a BOSS!

© ArtHeart/Shutterstock.com

Transitions: Smooth Table-Service

Although the appetizer and dessert round out a meal, the table-service plays a key role in how your meal is received. *Transitions* are words, phrases, or other devices that act like table-service (a good waiter or a prix fixe menu), letting an audience know where/when you move to (and from) in your speech. There are major transitions and minor transitions or signposts.

Major Transitions

Used to indicate you're moving from one big idea (e.g., main speech points) to the next, *major transitions* accomplish a couple things. Looking back at the organization patterns from earlier, there are clearly logical places to put major transitions (between Point 1 and 2 or between Point 3 and the Conclusion). One type to use (especially as you begin) is the **forecast statement**, telling what's coming (e.g., "Today, I'll talk about effective classroom technology use.").

In between main ideas, you'd use transitions that are **bridges** connecting two ideas (e.g., "Now that I've discussed the developing technology of driverless cars, ←BRIDGE→ I want to move on to discuss the pragmatic and ethical problems with these cars."). A bridge shows

us where we've been and where we're going. Most effectively, I'd further my organization and my audience's understanding of where I am by following up that bridge with a FORECAST→ "I'll start first with pragmatic problems."

I've said it before, and I'll say it again: Your audience *doesn't* have your speech memorized, they *don't* have a script to follow, and if they get lost, it's unlikely they have previous knowledge of your subject. They only get to hear you *once*. Your speech must be structured and easy to follow. So, in addition to an effective organization pattern, use as much transitional language as you feel necessary to help them listen and understand your subject.

© photo-denver/Shutterstock.com

Minor Transitions

Also called signposts, **minor transitions** are words, phrases, and even behaviors that indicate to your audience where you are or where you're going next in the speech. They're usually not sentences. Words like "additionally," "therefore," "thus," "first," "second," "also," "furthermore," "finally"—all are signposts. A rookie mistake is using the same one over and over. In my public speaking classes, I see students repeat the word "also" a lot; it doesn't make you a failure, but there are better transitions. Repeatedly using the same signpost is like repeating "um"—either audiences count its frequency or they *anticipate* it, ultimately paying more attention to *that* than to actual messages you try to send. Use a variety of signposts to avoid this.

Finally (see what I did there?), preview and review statements are actually forms of transitions. When used in your intro/conclusion, your preview/review statements serve as "major" previews and reviews. But remember, you must guide your audience to follow along and understand what you're talking about throughout your speech. If a main point is complex, has many components, or is about something you KNOW your audience doesn't have a lot of knowledge on, then you should consider having minor previews/reviews too.

That's All, Folks!

"We've got some difficult days ahead." MLK said this in Memphis on April 3, 1968 (Carson, 2001). He was talking about the large-scale sanitation worker strike in that city, but I'm talking, of course, about our continued work to improve our public speaking skills. Don't fret, though—we've covered a smorgasbord of topics, and you're well on your way to being bloated with public speaking knowledge. Being an effective public speaker isn't easy—but that doesn't mean it isn't worthwhile. (BTdubs, that's my brake light signal; the end is near.)

We've FINALLY reached the end of this public speaking banquet! First, we chewed on public speaking hate in order to lessen its power. Then, we tasted how audience adaptation should inform topic choice and be led by analysis. Lastly, we munched on effective design with organizational patterns, effective introductions and conclusions, and maintaining flow between all of those components. (This whole paragraph was my main-point review, FYI.)

On that day in 1968, MLK talked to an overflowing crowd eager to hear his calls for unity and nonviolent means of protesting the years of poor pay and dangerous working conditions for hundreds of mostly Black workers. King originally stayed at his hotel that day, complaining of a sore throat; he asked Ralph Abernathy, a close friend and civil rights leader, to speak instead. However, at the crowd's disappointment, Abernathy called King and urged him to come speak. The 39-year-old civil rights leader delivered his last inspirational speech. The next day, he was assassinated on that hotel's balcony (see I've Been to the Mountaintop, n.d.).

King did many awesome things during that speech (see Eidenmuller, 2019 to listen to the whole speech)!

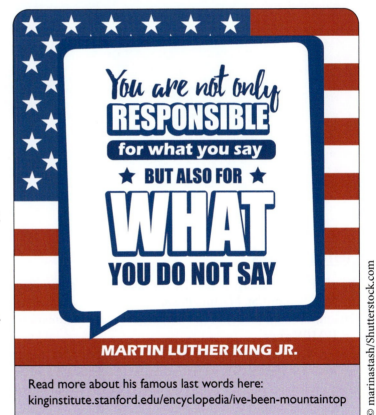

You are not only RESPONSIBLE for what you say ★ BUT ALSO FOR ★ WHAT YOU DO NOT SAY

MARTIN LUTHER KING JR.

Read more about his famous last words here: kinginstitute.stanford.edu/encyclopedia/ive-been-mountaintop

© marinastash/Shutterstock.com

He talked of the bleak trials and tribulations faced by Black people. He empathized with the plight of the sanitation workers, establishing identification. He used rhythm and repetition to discuss his near fatal stabbing by "a demented black woman" in 1958, using the phrase, "If I had sneezed, I wouldn't have seen . . ." over and over, building up how happy he was that God let him to live to see all their victories—giving the audience hope that this issue would be resolved as well. His energy and vocal qualities built to a crescendo in his ending where, almost prophetically, he articulated he was no longer afraid to die:

It really doesn't matter what happens now . . . Because I have been to the mountaintop! Like anybody, I would like to live a long life . . . but I'm not concerned about that now . . . I have been to the mountaintop and I have seen the promise land. I may not get there with you, but I want you to know tonight that we as a people will get to the promised land! . . . I'm not worried about anything; I'm not fearing any man . . . Mine eyes have seen the glory of the coming of the Lord! (Carson, 2001)

"Promised land" wasn't only Biblical but also a reference to the promises made by the U.S. Constitution to protect all of its citizens.

© Billion Photos/Shutterstock.com

Our last words are important. They're what stick in the audience's mind. Studying King's speeches teaches us many lessons: lessons about satisfying audience expectations and lessons about the kind of legacy we'll leave behind. Mentioning MLK in my conclusion ties us full-circle to my introduction, where I talked about MLK—*meaning* that I've employed (hopefully, effectively) a technique of bringing closure to my speech, and ending memorably. I am not as poetic, eloquent, or inspirational as King, but I do hope that you carry some of the lessons in this chapter with you into your future endeavors.

References

Bizzell, P., & Herzberg, B. (2001). *The rhetorical tradition: Readings from classical times to the present.* Boston, MA: Bedford/St. Martin's Press.

Carson, C. (Ed.). (2001). *A call to conscience: The landmark speeches of Martin Luther King, Jr.* New York, NY: IPM/Warner.

Dwyer, K. K., & Davidson, M. M. (2012). Is public speaking really more feared than death? *Communication Research Reports, 29*, 99–107. doi:10.1080/08824096.2012.667772

Eidenmuller, M. E. (2019). Top 100 speeches. *American Rhetoric.* Retrieved from www.americanrhetoric.com/top100speechesall.html

Genovese, J. (2019). *Learning fundamentals.* Retrieved from learningfundamentals.com.au/resources/

I've Been to the Mountaintop, event. (n.d.). In MLK, Jr. Research & Education Institute (Ed.), *The King encyclopedia.* Retrieved from kinginstitute.stanford.edu/encyclopedia/ive-been-mountaintop

International Listening Association. (2019). *Listening facts.* Retrieved from www.listen.org/Listening-Facts

King, M. L., Jr. (1962, October 15). An address by the Reverend Dr. Martin Luther King, Jr. *Cornell College.* Retrieved from news.cornellcollege.edu/dr-martin-luther-kings-visit-to-cornell-college/

Lucas, S. E. (2019). *The art of public speaking* (13th ed.). New York, NY: McGraw-Hill.

Lucas, S. E., & Medhurst, M. J. (2008). *Words of a century: The top 100 American speeches, 1900–1999.* New York, NY: Oxford University Press.

Mann, R. (2014, September 7). LBJ's mad men. *Politico Magazine.* Retrieved from www.politico.com/magazine/story/2014/09/lbjs-mad-men-110642

Monroe, A. H. (1943). *Monroe's principles of speech.* Chicago, IL: Scott, Foresman & Co.

Old Spice. (2010, February 4). *The man your man could smell like* [Video file]. Retrieved from www.youtube.com/watch?v=owGykVbfgUE

Osborne, G. (2008, November 18). Sex Panther Cologne. *Basenotes.* Retrieved from www.basenotes.net/perfumenews/2571-20081118-sex-panther-cologne

Pew Research. (2017, December 18). *5 facts about Christmas in America.* Retrieved from https://www.pewresearch.org/fact-tank/2017/12/18/5-facts-about-christmas-in-america/

Serpick, E. (2007, November). Nas' "greatest hits": A track-by-track journey. *Rolling Stone.* Retrieved from www.rollingstone.com/music/music-news/nas-greatest-hits-a-track-by-track-journey-85627/

Younge, B. (2015). *The speech: The story behind Martin Luther King's dream.* London, UK: Guardian Books.

Zimdars, M. (2016, November 18). My fake news list went viral. *Washington Post.* Retrieved from www.washingtonpost.com/posteverything/wp/2016/11/18/my-fake-news-list-went-viral-but-made-up-stories-are-only-part-of-the-problem/?utm_term=.179329d57d7f

Chapter 3:
Verbal and Visual Support

Contributed by
Dr. Beth Ribarsky
Mr. Russell Luce
Dr. Jessica Eckstein

You spent the last chapter learning about picking topics, developing main points, and putting them in an organized pattern. This is all incredibly important, but now what are you going to fill your actual speech with? Even though you have plenty of your own experiences (first-hand information) to draw from, ideally, to increase your own credibility, you'll rely on second-hand knowledge, which largely will come in the form of verbal and visual evidence from other sources. Your verbal and visual evidence essentially becomes the meat on the bones of the speech skeleton you just created.

Creating Credibility Through Verbal Evidence

Each of your textbook authors was asked to write a chapter because they're an expert on their particular subject. Many of them even tell how/why they're an expert in their particular field. For this chapter, between us combined, we have over 40 years of speech competition experience—all winning national awards, 12 years coaching competitive speech and debate, and over 50 years teaching public speaking. We like to think this goes a long way in building/establishing our credibility. And, we know you're only a few chapters into this book, but did you notice the authors all do something else? They cited research (as will we). If one person tells you a movie is great, do you believe them? Maybe. But, if 10 people tell you a movie is great, you probably are even more likely to believe them! Think of your research as those nine other people backing you up. As you get invaluable opportunities in your course to make an entire audience listen to you, it's probably best we teach you a bit about making them not just listen to you but also *believe* what you have to say.

Sorry, Bobby—even a star on the Walk of Fame doesn't mean you know everything!

© Kathy Hutchins/Shutterstock.com

Why Your Research Matters

Even if you think you know your topic inside and out, research matters. Dr. Beth loves watching the Food Network. One of her favorite shows is *Beat Bobby Flay*; it's only 30 minutes and watching arrogant Bobby Flay lose (the few times he does) warms her heart just a bit. That's the thing about Bobby Flay—he's a world renowned chef, has numerous cookbooks, several TV shows, restaurants, the whole kit and caboodle. He has room to be a little arrogant. He's an expert. BUT, that's the whole premise of the show. Other chefs from around the world come to compete against Bobby, often challenging him on a dish he's typically not as familiar with (desserts are his weakness, in case you ever end up on the show). So, even though he's an expert, it doesn't mean he knows it all, and even if you know your topic inside and out, you still don't know it all and have potential weak spots. And, even for the stuff you *do* know, having evidence to back you up will make your arguments even stronger . . . creating your own army of evidence superheroes to defeat even the skeptics.

Hopefully, you've taken Dr. Scholten's advice (Chapter 2) and picked a topic you're passionate about. However, that doesn't always happen. Sometimes you might be asked by your instructor or even boss to speak about a topic you don't know a lot about. Even if you're completely unfamiliar with a topic, having good and solid research can allow you to not only be informed and confident to speak about your topic, but by showing the audience you've done your research, you gain credibility even about topics you're unfamiliar with.

Research also establishes our credibility by having the full story. Do you have one of those friends/family members who is quick to fall for "fake news"? Or, perhaps someone who makes claims with nothing truly credible to back them up (we're looking at you flat-earthers!)? A quick search can reveal how blatantly false a story/statement might be. Using research is what can set you apart from the hundreds of other people who speak on the same subject but fail to use evidence to support their claims (Levitin, 2016). It basically sets you up as Captain Marvel in a world of Hawkeyes.

Sometimes, even through the process of doing research, we discover what we thought was right was actually wrong the whole time (or perhaps just new/better research has come to light). Think about when you were a child and your parent or grandparent made you put on a coat, justifying it by saying you would "catch a cold" by being exposed to the cold weather. A quick search online will tell you that you don't catch a cold simply by being cold. We get sick more frequently in the winter because we tend to stay indoors more often— being inside where heaters create dryer air (in which germs more easily reproduce and float; Ikäheimo et al., 2016). Also, the cold stresses our bodies and lowers our immune systems, making us more susceptible to viruses (Foxman et al., 2015). Did your parents purposely lie to you? Probably not. They just didn't know any better (and perhaps you didn't either until you read this just now). So, doing research is important for making sure that what we think we *know* is, in fact, factual.

Chocolate does NOT cause pimples. What other "facts" have you found to be untrue?

© ShotPrime Studio/Shutterstock.com

Types of Verbal Support

Verbal support, or the "data" for your speech, can come in numerous forms (LeFebvre, 2017). It's important to use a variety of forms because different types can cause people to be engaged in different ways (Allen & Preiss, 2017), so by using a variety of support types, you're covering all the bases. First are *examples*, or brief illustrations to provide evidence, which lend credibility to your speech by showing your audience the reality of your argument. Even as you read this textbook, you'll see numerous times where your authors write, "for example . . ." These are added as a way to further clarify concepts. Examples work incredibly well because they're brief and are able to get your point across quickly while also adding vitality to your speech. Your examples might be real, but a hypothetical example can also be useful. Oftentimes, hypothetical examples encourage the audience to think about/imagine themselves within a particular scenario. For example (see what we just did there), if you're doing a speech about CPR, you might say, "Imagine you're in class and the person next to you collapses and quits breathing. What do you do?" By having the audience place themselves in an imagined scenario, it creates greater relevance and applicability of your speech and topic.

Another type of verbal evidence includes *stories*, or extended examples, which are a fundamental way people have connected to others throughout history (Fisher, 1984). As Dr. Scholten said (Chapter 2), stories are great because they draw us in and, again, they add a bit of life to your speech. However, stories and narration tend to be longer, so they're something you should use sparingly. Otherwise, you'll spend all your time on a story and not as much time actually developing your speech or arguments. The best places to use stories, again, are in your attention-getter and then referring back to your story in your clincher.

Next, *comparisons* allow us to measure similarities and differences between concepts and ideas. So, for example, you might compare your college (because you're using an illustration the audience is familiar with, right?) to another campus, perhaps by population, the amount of majors available, or even the physical size of the campus. An off-shoot of comparisons is *analogies*, which link concepts we're familiar with to those we may find more obscure. For example, many of us have never used a dialysis machine (thankfully). However, most of us have probably seen or (hopefully) used a vacuum at some point in our lives (if you needed a reminder to run a vacuum through your room, there you go). Now, as different as both of these are, they work in similar ways. Both vacuums and dialysis machines filter out things that are unhealthy or not needed and then let loose the things that need to be re-implemented (into the air or the bloodstream). By linking the familiar with the unfamiliar, you're able to further the audience's understanding.

Testimonies or *expert opinions* provide outsider, first-hand experience with/knowledge of your subject. Think of a commercial for a dental product. Oftentimes, users explain what their experience was like and how much they love the product. These are great in building evidence in your speech showing others might share the same opinion as you. Further, you might notice in some dental commercials, there's an actual dentist, who serves as an *expert opinion* (information from individuals with a professional link to the topic). However, with both of these types of evidence, it's important to keep biases in mind. If somebody works for (or is being paid by) a particular company, they might have an opinion about a product different from unpaid spokespersons. Although some expert opinions might be testimonies, not all testimonies are expert opinions. For example, Michael Jordan has been a spokesperson for the Hanes Company (Rosenthal, 2019), but what does Michael Jordan know about underwear that you don't know? Probably not much. We might be drawn to his opinion as a celebrity, but he's not an expert and is likely to have been (at least a bit) biased due to his multi-million dollar paycheck from Hanes.

Speaking of numbers, that brings us to *statistics*, which provide strong evidence for a speech by summarizing a large amount of information into numbers applicable to the audience. Statistics is a word that invokes fright because, too often, they're presented in overwhelming or difficult to understand ways (see Huff, 1954). Indeed, using too many

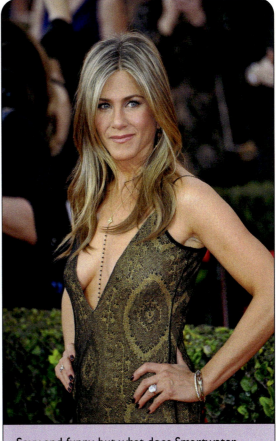

Sexy and funny, but what does Smartwater spokesperson Jennifer Aniston know about water? Check your source bias!

© Jaguar PS/Shutterstock.com

numbers can be confusing and get a bit boring for the listener. But, there are a few key things you can do to make statistics work for you—especially considering the limited time you have in speeches.

© Jakub Grygier/Shutterstock.com

Stats can make anyone feel overwhelmed! A good speaker makes data understandable.

First, only provide the *key* numbers. Rather than providing the percentages of all religious affiliations in the United States, you might only list the percentages for the top 3 largest religions. Look for the numbers that are most important and most relevant to your speech and your argument. Second, round off your numbers. It makes them much easier for the audience to understand/remember and typically is easier for you to say.

For example, rather than saying 1,113 people were saved by Captain American last year, you might say, just over 1,000 people were saved by him. Third, link your statistics to a *frame of reference* that allows the audience to feel a more personal connection to the numbers. According to the National Cancer Institute (2018), over 38% of people will be diagnosed with cancer in their lifetime. Although this is an alarming number (and a great example of a startling statistic to use as an attention-getter), you can personalize it even more by saying, "Look to your left. Look to your right. If neither of those individuals gets cancer, then, it's likely to be you." By personalizing the number, it has an even larger impression and connection. Finally, consider using a visual aid for your statistics (we'll talk about how to construct a great one in a bit). Having a visual representation of the numbers, such as a pie chart, graph, etc. makes it easier for the audience to digest and remember.

Public Speaking Power: How to Make Your Argument!

You need to give the audience a reason to believe in your information; you must justify it as an idea people should listen to by making an argument they should believe. There are very few facts in this world that are unconditionally "true" without question, so make your argument a good one with solid information and support. Just remember the acronym A-R-E—as in, ARE you connecting the dots for your audience (Toulmin, 1950)?

A = Assertion

An assertion is a claim you make: "The sky is blue" or "Someday soon, 3D printers will be able to print human organs for transplantation." Within speeches on these overarching topics/claims, you'll have sub-claims you'll need to make. For example, in "The sky is blue" speech, you'd have to explain light refraction and what makes up the particles of the air. No matter how much work needs to be done, you always start with an assertion. The more succinct and declarative the language, the clearer that assertion will be.

There are many claims we take for granted—that is, we assume we don't HAVE to provide a lot of support or explanation for them because we presume our audience is already on-board with them. Other claims aren't already widely believed and, thus, need more work. Just remember: **There's no such thing as common-knowledge**; EVERY claim needs backup!

R = Reasoning

Argumentation scholars have identified many different kinds of reasoning. You can see different kinds of reasoning at inpraiseofargument.squarespace.com (Heinrichs, 2019) and ways it can go wrong at yourlogicalfallacyis.com. For your speech, it's enough to know that this step in an argument includes your *reasons* why the audience should believe and/or support the claim you made. Reasoning is the "because" step. "The sky is blue because . . ." or "We're close to printing 3D organs because . . ." Reasons can

(Continued)

be further claims that need further reasons—again, it just depends on your purpose for the audience and what they already know versus what they need to know about your topic. As long as you're providing some kind of "because" statement(s), you're providing some reasoning.

E = Evidence

We talked a little about evidence already (in Chapter 2), and you're learning more in this chapter. A complete argument must provide some kind of support. You've read that support can be many things—anecdotes, stories, statistics, and so on. The kind of support you need is dependent *on your audience*.

Here's an example of an argument, including all the ARE parts (You'd say all the non-bold parts out loud in the speech):

> **Topic:** K-12 teachers should be allowed to use corporal punishment.
> *This is the OVERALL assertion; use other claims in an attempt to support and prove it.*
> **Assertion:** Morale is higher amongst schools that use corporal punishment.
> **Evidence:** According to an article published in the *Wall Street Journal* on June 17, 2006, "The ratio of student morale to corporal punishment has been positively correlated for the past 17 years, suggesting that students who are paddled respect and appreciate the school system."
> *The Wall Street Journal did some reasoning already (sooo nice of them). Also, the reasoning and evidence are switched around, which is totally fine if it makes sense to do so.*
> **Reasoning:** *Because* common sense tells us that morale is necessary for good teaching and for good learning, it's reasonable to believe that corporal punishment in schools is a good thing.
> *You'd want to know where your audience stood on this issue in order to know just how much evidence and reasoning you'd need to convince them. For example, do you need to include a definition of morale? Or to establish a better connection between morale and education?*

If you think of your whole speech as a chain, each link represents one of these components. When you walk someone through your reasoning chain, you're connecting the dots for them, showing how you got from points A to Z. People are more likely to trust info when they can see how you got there, versus blindly trusting it. You can think of crafting an argument as a series of statements that begin with the following: "I think" = Assertion, "because" = Reasoning, "and there's proof . . ." = Evidence. You can certainly be more eloquent than that, and you can, of course, have more than one reason or more than one kind of support for a claim. But, if you get in the habit of making sure these components are present, your speeches will be both more organized and more compelling.

Contributed by K. Scholten

Finding Your Verbal Support

There are endless places you can find support for your speech. When you're searching for support, believe it or not, a great place to start is online through your library's website or Google Scholar. But, just because you found something through a "reputable" location doesn't mean the actual source/content is great.

Questioning Source Quality

When first beginning, you're apt to feel a little overwhelmed with all the material available. So, you have to make some choices to decide what information is best for your speech.

Some critical issues to keep in mind as you look at your research are: Is this information recent? Is it relevant? Is it biased? Is it primary or secondary?

Recency. The easiest thing to figure out first to narrow down your search is to ask, "Is this recent?" It's possible the info could've vastly changed over the years . . . or even weeks! For instance, if we were looking at something like social media usage rates, they're going to be very different just 1 year ago versus last week. Using the most recent info makes your argument stronger *and* helps you look like a more competent and credible speaker.

Relevancy. Is what comes up relevant to your speech? You'll find a TON of info on your topic, but there's no way you can present it all in your allotted time. Choices must be made. Just because something is fascinating doesn't make it the most relevant to your speech goal (remember Chapter 2!). For example, did you know Fabio had a clothing line developed specifically for Sam's Club (Choi, 2004)? Fascinating? Yep! But, it wouldn't add to your speech on why buying in bulk at Sam's is good.

Fabio is also an Old Spice model. Again, interesting but not the most relevant, unless you're doing a speech on Fabio.

© Joe Seer/Shutterstock.com

Bias. We argue that ANY research has some level of bias in it—whether in *what*, *how*, and even *if* it's presented (see Habermas, 1984). Even if they're unaware of it, people can always be advancing a particular agenda (Levitin, 2016). Hey, even this textbook is advancing a particular view of communication and speeches! So, it's necessary for you to consider some compounding factors in bias. First, was the research collected/compiled ethically or were there nefarious methods involved? If it's a study, you want to make sure the research used is valid and not tainting the results in any way (Brann, 2017). Second, was it recorded and/

or interpreted accurately or taken out-of-context? Someone may be quoted in an interview, but if an interviewee was being sarcastic and reported as sincere, that's not really truthful material. If material is misquoted, misused, or misapplied, you're risking perpetuating inaccurate info if you use it in a speech. Finally, does the author have a clear reason to be biased? If your dentist is getting a nice kickback from a dental company, they're more likely to promote its products. It's up to us as writers and speakers to determine how accurate/credible our sources are—it's called due diligence!

Primacy. *Primary source* material is when the author/s is/are the ones who obtained the information they're writing about first-hand. Did the author of a study in a journal article actually collect the data

Peel back the layers and see what's at the heart of your research!

they're analyzing? Then, it's primary. *Most* information out there, however, is secondary (Levitin, 2016). *Secondary source* material is when the author of a piece is writing about or presenting something they didn't themselves experience or collect. Popular press articles or websites that report what researchers or organizations found, Wikipedia, personal website opinions on things people have "heard" circulating, and even textbooks (yes, like this one)—all of these are secondary source materials. That's not to say you shouldn't use them. But, nothing is as good as a primary source you can check yourself. So, what type of materials make the best resources?

Material Types

What to search. Source materials range in how rigorous they are and how easy they are for "anyone" to get published and distributed. We'll start with the least rigorous, easiest to get published—websites. Anyone can put anything on the internet, so you must be extremely careful looking at the information you find and where it's coming from. Blogs, for example, often are filled just with opinions, and even if there is good info in there, most likely it's secondary information and is lacking quality sources to back it up. Some companies and organizations host their own webpages as well. But, obviously, these are apt to be very biased (see info on biases, above). However, you might find the official website of a product or group helpful to get the latest information on their company. For example, if you wanted to do a speech about Ben & Jerry's Ice Cream, you should definitely seek out www.benjerry. com, their official website, for all the latest product info.

Next lowest in rigor, but a little harder to get published are newspaper and magazine articles or online news sources. Some newspapers, magazines, and televised reporting *can* provide usable content; they're typically grounded in research and often receive some level of review from an editor—deeming the content "worthy" of publication or airing. However, there's obviously a big difference in getting your information from *Scientific American* versus

Cosmopolitan (which isn't to say magazines such as *Vogue* wouldn't provide valuable insight if your topic involved current fashion trends). But, rarely are magazines or newspapers (online or in print) a primary source because they often pull material from other sources (e.g., reviewing studies published elsewhere) and are putting their own "spin" on it in their report.

Anyone can be an author from anywhere nowadays. Be sure your author is qualified to write on your subject.

© BlueSkyImage/Shutterstock.com

Books require a bit more dedication to finish and also tend to receive an even greater level of scrutiny or oversight as to their content because they require greater time and financial investments. However, in an era where self-publishing has made it possible for anyone to produce a book—in hard copy or online, you should still be wary about authors and the quality/accuracy of their book's content. If the book includes information the authors collected or experienced themselves, it's possibly a primary source. But, look to see who published it. Is it a reputable company or just an e-pub? When it comes to textbooks, the authors' job is to compile info from others, so that makes it a secondary source. So whereas textbooks (like Wikipedia pages or other websites) are great places to find information to start your search, you don't want to solely rely on them for your primary source material (because they aren't) if you can help it.

Although their reach might be smaller, trade journals are extremely rigorous in terms of technicalities. If you're writing for an audience of experts (the people who usually get the trade journals), then you better not only use their lingo but also be up-to-date on everything going on in the field/industry. Trade journals can be a great resource for detailed, recent, and relevant information.

Academic journals often receive the highest level of review, and therefore, often are seen as the most credible. They also tend to be the hardest to publish in. Top journals often have an acceptance rate of lower than 10% (Cabell's, 2019) because they *generally* include original research studies that have undergone a peer-review or blind peer-review (where the reviewers do not receive any of the author's identifying information) by experts in their field of study. Knowledge in scholarly, peer-reviewed journals is also expected to be current.

Although you can do a search online for journal articles, oftentimes you cannot access the full article/book (it's a way the publishers ensure they make money). However, a lot of authors post versions of their published work in PDF form on their own sites or academic sites. Better yet, your library is likely to have a vast array of databases that let you access all of these sources. You're already paying student fees for the library, so you might as well make use of those monies! Please, never pay for an article online; there's always another way to access it—talk to your local librarian.

How to search. Speaking of your local librarian . . . hopefully, you've visited your library at least once. Maybe at least their webpage? If not, you should! Your college's library probably is a lot cooler than you think. At many universities, the library has comfy seating with both social and quiet areas, a library of things (board games, kitchen appliances, cameras, etc. you can check out), and a selection of the most recent movie releases you can check out for FREE (well, you pay the fees, but again, use them!). And, if that's not enough incentive, you should know your librarians are an invaluable resource for ALL your classes. Many offer sessions to teach you research tips and tricks (which databases to use or how to find the right search term), and even if you don't attend those, they're usually more than happy to schedule individual sessions. They know the ins and outs of source- or background-research. If you have an issue with your car, unless you're a trained mechanic, you likely take your vehicle to an auto shop, as they're experts in that field; they've extensively trained to diagnose and repair vehicles. Similarly, librarians train to help you locate research and enjoy helping others in their endeavors. You'll save time, energy, and effort by reaching out to your librarians to assist you in your research-finding efforts.

But, chances are the first place you thought to search for research on your topic was NOT the library. Instead, you probably hopped onto Google. Remember, *anyone* can publish *anything* online. This means there's a lot—and we do mean A LOT—of inaccurate information out there! But, that doesn't mean it can't be a valuable source; it just means we need to be more conscientious consumers of the information we're getting (see Chapter 15 for more on this). Unless you're using Google Scholar, the best information is probably NOT the first site that pops up on your search.

"To infinity and BEYOND..."
 - Abe Lincoln

S. M. TINSLEY &

Seeing shouldn't be believing!

Source: David McCracken

You probably learned that the more reliable sites are websites that end in .gov, .org, or .edu, but these signifiers don't guarantee primary source materials; instead, view these as great places to start your research—then, go to the actual *primary* sources they reference. Wikipedia.org is a great example of this. It has come a long way since it began and is a great resource (notice, we said *resource*, not *source*) for beginning your hunt

The moment your instructor hears Wikipedia...

© Ollyy/Shutterstock.com

for material. But, we've yet to find an instructor who thinks this is a valid source. Please, don't give your instructors (in any course) a reason to think you're an idiot—DON'T USE WIKIPEDIA AS A SOURCE! As you probably know, Wikipedia is an open source, meaning anyone and everyone can contribute or edit information. As an example, Mr. Luce once had a friend list himself there as the third funniest person in the greater Kansas City metro area (It's not that he wasn't funny, but he certainly wouldn't make the top 10 list in any major city.); it was months before it was finally removed from Wikipedia! Beyond mere fraudulent information, Wikipedia is also notorious for presenting only particular versions of issues that are in keeping with dominant norms (Gauthier & Sawchuk, 2017).

We like to think we can easily spot false information online. However, even if it's not blatantly false, there's a lot of misleading information out there. Take, for example, the website www.dhmo.org. Everything on this site is factually accurate. However, it's presented in a way to lead the audience to an incorrect conclusion—that we should ban products with dihydrogen monoxide. Guess what? "Dihydrogen monoxide" is another term for water.

But, with a little work and planning, the internet can be an effective research tool. Which search engine you use can make a difference. Although Google currently retains over 90% of the search engine market (Desjardins, 2018), there are other options available to widen your net for material that doesn't pop up easily on Google. Infotopia is a search engine designed in consultation with academics and librarians to provide you with more qualified/credible search results. And, even Google Scholar and Google News often produce different results.

Whether you're using Google or your library's databases, one of the keys to finding your information is using the right search term. Take the topic of self-defense, for example. Simply typing in "self-defense" (not to mention without the hyphen or as one word) will give you tons of information related to that topic. Trying to sort through all that information can be like trying to drink from a firehose. Narrow down your search (and also your topic). Recognizing there are other perspectives on self-defense, you might try new search terminology such as "technology and self-defense" and "self-defense at home". Notice how we put those terms in quotation marks? By putting quotation marks around your terms, it ensures you're searching for those EXACT terms (in that exact order). Ultimately, not only does this narrow down your search, but you're also likely to find some more information beyond the stuff everyone's already heard of. If you have a hard time coming up with synonyms or other ways to search on your topic, consider using Google Keyword Planner.

One last source you may not have thought of is interviews. Of course, please see if your instructor considers interviews an appropriate source for your speech requirements. An interview can allow you to get more in-depth information and answer very specific questions (Lindlof, 1995). But, *who* you interview matters. As much as you might love your roommate, they probably aren't the best person to interview for information about the latest dental technologies. And, even if they love superhero movies, there are much better and more credible sources out there on the evolution of superheroes (don't you love all the speech topic ideas we've been giving you???). Even though you're not a professional interviewer, just be sure to come prepared with good open-ended questions to make the best use of both your and the interviewee's time (Tenzek, 2017)!

Without carefully narrowing down your search terms, you might find yourself flooded with information.

© a katz/Shutterstock.com

Being Ethical With Your Information

As with any communication scenario, presenting your research in a speech involves ethics (Hamilton & Mueller, 2010). The first major ethical issue is presenting information correctly. Just as you need to make sure your sources actually interpreted *their* material correctly (always go to the primary source!), you also need to be accurate in how you present your material. Consider this statement: "If you depend solely on reality TV for your information, you're likely to believe catfishing is a significant problem in online dating." Taken as it is, this statement suggests catfishing is exaggerated on reality TV. But, what if we just used the end part: "catfishing is a significant problem in online dating"? It might say what you want it to say for the purposes of your presentation, but it doesn't actually reflect the true/full sentiment of the writing/source. As easy as it might be to pick and choose what we're looking for, it's not ethical.

Second, imagine you spent hours writing a paper and someone stole the file from your computer to turn it in for credit with their name on it. You'd probably be pretty pissed. When you fail to cite your sources verbally *and* in writing, you're doing the same thing. It's essential you cite your sources—from both ethical and legal perspectives. From a legal perspective, plagiarism is on the same level as copyright infringement or intellectual

Don't steal people's ideas and work!

© Rudie Strummer/Shutterstock.com

property theft (Kopaczewski, 2017). People have been sued, lost their jobs, and lost their reputation over plagiarism. So, it shouldn't be surprising that you can fail a course or be expelled from your school for plagiarism. Claiming you didn't know it was plagiarism is never an excuse (Park, 2003). It's ultimately your responsibility to make certain that you properly cite your sources.

A lot of people think if they have their source written (e.g., in the outline or on a presentation slide), that's all they need in a speech. But, you're expected to cite your sources in written *and* verbal forms. After all, how can a listener know you had the source in your material unless you TELL them!? Any time you use info that's not readily known, you should be citing a source. It's not just direct quotes; *any information* you put in your speech (even if you "know" it yourself) should have a source cited to back you up (otherwise,

it just looks like you're spewing your opinion). Further, any time you use more than 4–5 words in a row from a source, it needs to actually be quoted (i.e., be in quotation marks) in your outline or manuscript.

In your paper or outline, be sure to check which citation style your instructor requires for your course. Most communication professors will prefer APA (American Psychological Association), though some may use MLA (Modern Language Association) or another style. So, check first! The ONLY 100% correct reference for citing using APA is the *APA Manual* (APA, 2020). But, if you refuse to buy the manual, check out the Owl Purdue (2019) resource page listed in this chapter's references; it's the *closest* you'll find to the actual manual. There are tons of automated sources and helpers to create your reference pages, but we've yet to find one that's perfect. Even the automated citations you might try to pull from your library's page are apt to be wrong. Therefore, we suggest continuing to do them the "old-fashioned" way.

But, citing your sources in your paper or outline isn't enough. Remember, your audience won't have a copy of your speech in their hands, so they need to *hear you say* your sources. By citing your information, you're enhancing your credibility by showing others you can back up your ideas (Wieman & Walter, 1957)! At a minimum, you should tell your audience *where* and *when* your information is from and the author's last name. Also, be as specific as possible with dates. For example, if you're using a *USA Today* article, you might say, "According to an article by [author] in the May 17, 2018, *USA Today*, …." Newspapers are typically published daily, so it's important to include a month, day, and the year. Magazines are published weekly or monthly, so you'd include the week/month and year. Books are much less frequent, so you'd simply include the year. Citing the author in addition to where and when your source is from increases the credibility of your information and, thus, YOU!

Presentational Aids

Although verbal support is incredibly important, visual support often provides another level of understanding and vividness to your speech (Petty & Cacioppo, 1986). You've heard the saying, "A picture is worth a thousand words"? It truly is; frankly, someone can vocally describe to you—until they're blue in the face—how to properly swing a golf club, but unless they actually SHOW you the process, you're probably not going to get the full picture (pun intended). As Dr. Scholten mentioned in Chapter 2, your audience has a lot on their minds (plus, they're probably listening to several speeches in one day in your class), so a good visual aid not only helps your concept to make sense but also to stick out in your listeners' minds. I bet you'd remember if a student plugged in a clothes iron and illustrated how to make grilled cheese in your dorm room. Dr. Eckstein still remembers speeches from students almost 20 years ago who used visuals like a plunger (history of toilets) and a life-sized horse mannequin (used to show rodeo moves).

Types of Visual Aids

Like verbal support, visual support comes in many forms. First, *models* or *objects* are literal representations of your topic. They give a clear, visual image to support your argument. For example, for a speech instructing how to make homemade pasta, it'd be great to bring in a pasta machine to demonstrate how to thin the dough and eventually cut the dough into noodles. However, keep in mind many models/objects might be too small for your audience to see. If you're demonstrating how to sew a button, it'd be impossible for even people in the front row to see what you're doing. It's vitally important to consider your model/object's size-appropriateness for the room.

Second, graphs provide visual representations of numbers/statistics and are one of the best ways to present complicated statistical information (Huff, 1954). There are three major types of graphs. Use *line graphs* to show changes in amounts over time, *bar graphs* to compare different amounts, and *pie charts* to display percentages—like how big a piece of pie an amount might take up. See just *some* of your graph/chart options on the next page!

Third are lists. These are admittedly not always the most exciting visual aid, but they can be useful, depending on your topic; you can always "jazz them up" a bit too. For example, if you're doing a cooking demonstration speech, you might outline all the major steps. Or, rather than verbally telling your audience all 54 current Ben and Jerry's ice cream flavors (Ben & Jerry's, 2019), you might simply show a list of all of the various flavors.

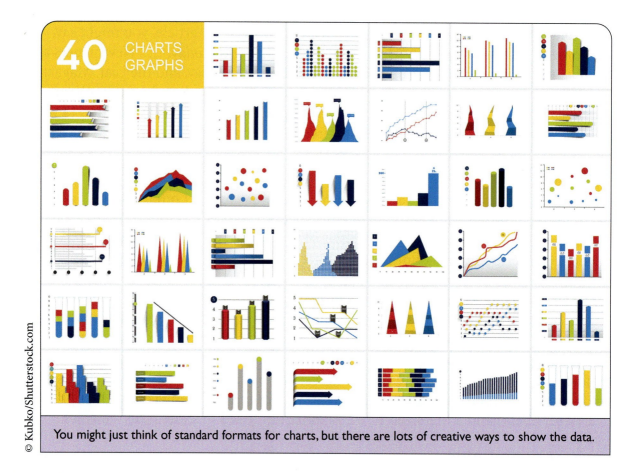

You might just think of standard formats for charts, but there are lots of creative ways to show the data.

© Kubko/Shutterstock.com

Next, photographs are a way to show the REAL item rather than a representation of it. The problem most people run into with photos, though, is that unless you use appropriate technology, they're much too small. We cannot count how often students have tried to show an audience pictures on their phone from the front of the room. When they do decide to pass the phone around for everyone to see, there are a slew of additional problems that occur. If you're going to use a picture, make sure you can project the image—something as simple as pasting it onto a PowerPoint slide.

Fifth, maps also make great presentational tools—especially for spatially organized speeches (remember the patterns from Chapter 2). Maybe you want to talk about the "big 5" sites in Rome. By showing your audience a map of where those sites are located in relation to one another (plus, pictures of the sites), your audience gets the best understanding of their accessibility. Or, perhaps you want to inform your audience about the progression of the Civil War? You might show how the opposing sides conquered more or less areas over time.

Finally, there are people. Yes, this is a bit odd, but people can be especially helpful for a demonstration speech. For example, if you're giving a speech about braiding hair, it might be good to have someone to actually do the braids on (but don't forget to supplement it with another visual because braids are small!). Or, way back when Dr. Beth and Mr. Luce were undergrads together, Russ had Beth come in and hold a wooden board for his speech on how to break a board because Beth knew how to properly hold a board (if it's not held properly, it's quite easy to break your hand rather than the board). If you're going to use people, make sure you have their permission. In other words, don't walk up to give your speech just assuming someone will volunteer to help you. Even if you have their permission, people can be tricky. As much as you love your roommate, there isn't a guarantee they're going to show up to be your visual aid unless you physically drag them to your speech. Or, sometimes your person-prop isn't the professional you'd hoped for, and they end up goofing around to become the center of attention. Along a similar line, live animals might be just as unpredictable as your roommate. Plus, you might end up sparking others' allergies or fears. Three minutes into a speech on snakes, Dr. Beth's student pulled a live python from his sleeve. Not only were we left wondering if he had that snake up his sleeve for the entire class (and how weird that was), but several students went running for the door.

Presentational Aid Technologies

Practically speaking, there are two types of presentational aid technologies. ***Physical aids*** are tangible: objects, handouts, posters, whiteboards, etc. ***Digital aids*** require technology such as a projector, a computer, and/or speakers. Each comes with numerous benefits and drawbacks.

Physical Aids

There are several physical aid mediums you might use. First, your classroom probably has some form of a chalkboard/whiteboard. The best feature of this medium is it's readily available, so there's NO doubt your visual aid will be there for your presentation. A whiteboard would be perfect for teaching your audience how to draw a giraffe, for example. However, a whiteboard/chalkboard is not necessarily the best/easiest to use. If you're like us, your handwriting might not be the most beautiful (don't you hate when you can't read what your instructor wrote?). Or, as your nerves heighten, suddenly your ability to spell even the most basic terms disappears, which significantly lowers your credibility and competence. And, as you turn your back to write things, suddenly you lose eye contact with your audience and your voice becomes muffled—a major way to lose your connection with them.

Even if you have incredible handwriting or drawing skills, writing on a chalkboard/whiteboard has many possible problems.

© Helder Almeida/Shutterstock.com

Next is the good old-fashioned poster board/foam board. Both tend to be easy to transport, and you can prepare the visual aid ahead of time. But, if they're

Sorry—even if you're super cute, a poster board won't work in a large room.

© De Repente/Shutterstock.com

not prepared well, they can end up looking rather unprofessional (we'll give a few tips to make them look better in a bit). You also have to think about how you're going to display the board. If you've ever tried to put a poster up on the ledge of a chalkboard, you know how even a sneeze can send it flying to the floor—creating a distraction for your audience and sending you into a panic. And, although posters can work for smaller classrooms, larger lecture halls are going to make seeing your visual aid nearly impossible for those beyond the first few rows.

You also might consider handouts. Of course, please consult with your instructor to determine particular visual aid requirements for your speech and if handouts might fulfill those. Handouts can be great for the audience to have a take-home (e.g., How to Register to Vote) or to follow along with your speech if it's an instructional activity (being given a piece of paper to learn how to fold an origami swan). But, handouts really need to be used with caution. If you hand out your handout during your speech, it becomes a distraction as your audience is either waiting to get theirs OR they become distracted by looking through your handout. If you're doing the origami speech, for example, be sure everyone has their paper before you start. For the Register to Vote speech, it might be best to indicate during your speech that handouts with the information will be available after you're done with your speech.

Activism Hero: Do the Legwork for Them

You want people to do something? The simpler the change, the more likely they are to do it. Use visual aids to jump-start that change and to make it as appealing as possible. This works both for public speaking and our daily encounters with people. For example, if you're trying to get an audience to register to vote, give them a handout with information on where they can do it online or provide them with actual voter-registration forms. Want them to consider a more plant-based diet? Bring in some vegan food to sample after your speech. If they're able to taste that a product is better than they'd anticipated (and closer to something they already eat), they'll be more likely to consider purchasing or ordering more plant-based meals. As compelling as your evidence might be, sometimes your audience needs an extra push to get them on board.

Contributed by B. Ribarsky

© barbaliss/Shutterstock.com

Digital Aids

Although physical aids can be incredibly useful, sometimes a digital aid is more effective *and* easier. There are numerous advantages to using a digital aid such as PowerPoint or Prezi. First, simply knowing how to use it WELL is a skill you'll want to have in your future career. Second, using a projector helps ensure your entire audience sees your visual aid, even in a large lecture hall. Digital presentations can be dynamic yet also keep both the speaker and audience organized. They're easy to prepare and provide smooth transitions between visual aids (more about this in a minute).

But . . . chances are you've seen HORRIBLE PowerPoint presentations—likely from both other students and instructors (but, of course, not your instructor for this class). The first mistake many people make is turning their PowerPoint presentation slides into giant notecards. In other words, they end up turning their back to their audience and simply reading what they wrote on their visual aid. This ends up being *incredibly* boring—their voice is muffled with their back turned, they've lost eye contact with the audience, and no longer are they *talking with* the audience—they are *reading to* the audience. Because they're using it as a giant notecard, they probably put entirely too much on their slides, making it difficult for the audience to read (tiny print trying to fit it all). Or, they've taken advantage of one too many features of their software. Have you seen the awful presentations where the slide transitions make noises or do weird flips? Dr. Eckstein remembers a giant "DWEEEOOOP" horn sound coming in for every single bullet point on one girl's speech about the very serious topic of cancer. Poor girl had about 30 of these noises throughout her presentation! Remember that simple is better.

In addition to PowerPoint, which can be used on both Macs and PCs (and easily saved online), Prezi is a free and popular alternative offering a spider web style presentation. It can be downloaded but can only be edited online. Although visually stunning if used properly, it's easy for presenters to get lost or push too many buttons. Another source, Sway, allows you to share a URL link with other users so they can view your presentation on their phone, tablet, or laptop. It can also be downloaded as a PDF but can only be edited online. These are just a few options available to use. Ultimately, you need to think about how you want to present your information to your audience and what works best for YOU as a presenter.

Public Speaking Power: Audible Support

Beyond visual aspects to aid your speech, you might even consider an audible aid if it's topic-appropriate. These, too, can make your speech memorable. Everyone remembers jingles from commercials—did you know the Pillsbury Doughboy's giggle is trademarked (U.S. Patent and Trademark Office, 2014)? We bet without even having to look it up, you could think of the signature "hoo-hoo." What topics might lend themselves to an audible aid? Whether you choose to use a visual element, an audio element, or a combination of both, by using them correctly, they can have tremendous impact on your audience.

Contributed by R. Luce and B. Ribarsky

You also might consider using a video as a digital aid. Quick videos can be interesting and add a great level of vividness. But, showing a video does not constitute completing a speech. Numerous times throughout our teaching careers, we've seen students try to get away with showing a 3-minute video during their 5-minute speech. Not only does this most likely violate your instructor's requirements, it also takes away from valuable time to make YOUR argument. Trust us, your audience wants to hear YOU speak—not just watch a video. Ultimately, your digital aid is meant to help you (and your audience), not to hurt your presentation.

Tips and Tricks for Visual Aid Use

Although we've talked about numerous tips already, there are some key pointers that can make both physical and digital visual aids more impactful. These pointers fall into three major categories: selection, design, and use.

Don't make a monkey out of yourself! Pick the right type of visual aid.

Selection

The first key to selecting your visual aid is easy—have a reason to use it. We realize many of your instructors require you to use a visual aid (possibly even a PowerPoint presentation) for at least one of your speeches, but *that* should not guide your choices. Remember, your visual aid is there to AID you and your audience. So, use it to reinforce statistics or make a concept clearer or more gripping.

Second, think about the level of sophistication of the visual aid, and if the medium you choose is going to be appropriate for both the physical environment and your audience. Again, a poster board isn't very effective in a large lecture hall. And, although a hand-designed poster board might be perfectly acceptable for a group of kindergartners, it probably wouldn't be a good idea for presenting to your university/college president.

Preparation and Design

We shouldn't have to mention the first rule of preparation and design, but apparently (because it's happened in so many classes), we must: Your visual aid shouldn't be illegal or offensive! You might want to give a speech about winemaking, but for many campuses, it's illegal to have alcohol on campus (or at least in classrooms). Dr. Beth and Dr. Eckstein have both had students bring guns into class for their speeches; even if disassembled, it's obviously still dangerous and likely illegal on your campus. On the other hand, some controversial/offensive images might be interesting if they add to your argument. Just remember, it's easy to lose your audience if they can't look at your visual aid or if they get extremely offended. As much as people fear public speaking, the anxiety experienced at the sight of blood may be just as bad. So choosing to dissect a cow's heart in front of the audience (another real example from our classes) might not be the best choice. To this day, Dr. Beth remains traumatized by a video a student used (for a speech about why you should adopt an animal); it showed animal control euthanizing numerous dogs by cramming them into a small box, gassing them to death (the whines, whimpers, and cries were horrific!). Numerous students were crying! Did it make a point? Yes, but at the cost of traumatizing the audience. If you find yourself even beginning to question if your visual aid is appropriate, then the answer is "NO!". However, we encourage you to talk with your instructor if you have any questions or concerns.

Second, size *does* matter. Everyone in your audience needs to be able to see your visual aid. Again, this is one of the reasons using a digital aid and projecting it can be great. But, this does NOT mean a poster board or demo objects can't work in an appropriately-sized room.

Third, color is far more important than you might think. Just plain black and white is boring. On the other hand, too many colors (you know the rainbow font we're talking about) is distracting. Whatever color scheme you choose, make sure there's a clear contrast in colors so that it's visible to your audience—blue/purple writing on a black background is impossible to read. A group of students presenting on Coca-Cola decided to use the company's colors for the presentation: red, white, and black. Red lettering on a black background and white lettering on a red background could not be easily read by the audience. In theory, it was a novel idea to use the color scheme associated with Coca-Cola. In practice, it was a disaster. And, even if the colors clearly contrast—it still doesn't guarantee it's visually appealing. In general, try using three or fewer colors throughout your slideshow. Keep your background color the same throughout. Additionally, you may want to think about what colors you select and how that may send a message to your audience. Blue tends to have a more calming effect while red creates greater arousal (Wilms

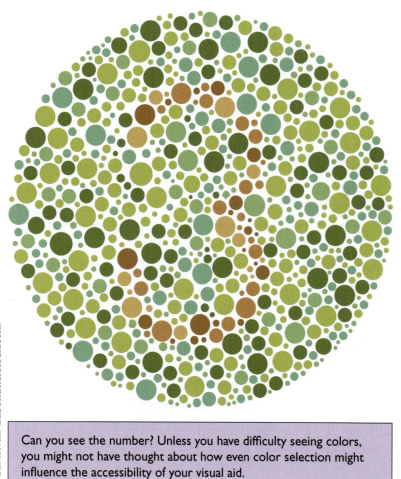

Can you see the number? Unless you have difficulty seeing colors, you might not have thought about how even color selection might influence the accessibility of your visual aid.

& Oberfeld, 2018). Finally, recognize some audience members may not be able to see certain colors and how this might affect your content.

In addition to simple colors, make sure your visual aid is simple too. Duarte (2008) argued you should practice design, not decoration. All those extra flowers and smiley faces aren't necessary. But, you can make it visually appealing and still easy to read. First, regardless of the software/medium you use, you need to consider the design of your presentation. Avoid clutter. Try following the 6×6 rule to emphasize just your main points: At most, use six lines of content with six words per line. If you have seven words, it's not the end of the world. But, too much text on the screen will cause people to read from your slide rather than listen to you speak (people read faster than we talk, so they'll read ahead and then get bored), and you may be more tempted to use it as a giant note card. When it comes to font selection, using Comic Sans doesn't make you funny. It's acceptable to go with a bold font, a plain font, or a practical font. Although there's no clear consensus regarding which one to use, your font represents your style of delivery. Also, don't letter things vertically, as it's remarkably difficult to read. If you're using poster board, consider printing out (rather than handwriting) your text to paste onto the board—which'll also help a bit with spell-checking. Have you ever talked to someone when you noticed they had spinach in their teeth or a booger in their nose? Once you noticed, did you still pay attention to what they said? In a similar fashion, your audience will focus on slide or poster board errors and ignore the content you present.

Finally, a good visual aid needs a title or descriptor. You might have a visually stunning graph, but if your audience doesn't know what it's representing, it's pretty useless. Even if you show a picture on a PowerPoint slide, for example, be sure to clearly label or caption it to explain what the audience is looking at. And remember, any image that you didn't take/make yourself needs to be sourced—otherwise, it's plagiarizing!

Visual Aid Use

Now, even if you have an amazing visual aid, its impact largely depends on how you use it. First, plan for your digital presentation aid to fail because at some point, technology will fail your instructor, your classmates, or even you. Projector bulbs burn out unexpectedly, the internet randomly stops working, YouTube regularly removes videos. Does this mean that you need to have paper copies of your aid for everyone? No, of course not. But, having something to use as a backup is always a good idea. You can minimize the impact a technological fail will have on your presentation. Make sure that you have your presentation stored in at least three separate locations. Email, a USB drive, and a website like Google Drive or OneDrive are good options. When possible, download material rather than rely on hyperlinks to websites. Hyperlinks take additional time to load and take away from your presentation time or smooth, quick transitions between speakers. Come into the room you're speaking in a bit before class (if possible) and load up your presentation, check to be sure the projector is working, and the sound (if applicable) is at an appropriate level (we've all been blasted nearly to death with some ill-planned sound). Be sure all the technology you planned on using is there *and* functioning properly.

Next, only show your visual aid when you're speaking about it: Don't show it until you're ready. Put it away when you're done. The ASPCA commercial is familiar to many of us. The images of distraught kittens and puppies pulls on the heartstrings of the viewer. This could be an effective image for your audience if shown for a brief amount of time. But, if left up during your entire presentation, your audience may become too focused on the aid and miss the content of your speech. With a physical aid, you might have your poster board flipped to a blank side or you

It's hard enough to read this page without thinking about this dirty, skinny, homeless dog. How do you expect your audience to pay attention to YOU?

might have your object out of sight until you need it, and then, put it back out of sight or flip it over when you're done talking about it. With a digital aid, you should use a blank slide or a blank screen, whichever is most convenient, before and after you show your visual aid.

Next, you MUST practice with your presentational aid. If it's a physical object, you'll want to practice where you'll place it while speaking. If you hold onto the object, you're likely to play with it, and it'll be distracting to your audience. If using technology, you need to make sure you're comfortable using the software you utilized. See the next chapter (Chapter 4) for more great tips on this!

Also, it takes additional time to use visual aids because any good visual needs to be explained. Don't just flash the visual aid and move on. Explain what the graph is showing us. Or, for example, if you're showing a video, tell us what we should be watching for. It's incredibly frustrating, for example, when an audience is shown a video clip, but it's never discussed or explained. Practice with your visuals so you have an idea how long your presentation will last AND you'll become more comfortable using your visual aid.

Finally, and we've already alluded to this, don't talk to your visual aid—talk to your audience. Eye contact maintains your audience's attention and creates rapport (more to come in Chapter 4). Speaking to the aid gives the impression you're not prepared and that you lack confidence. Practice what we call the "Vanna White" by standing to the side, gesturing toward the visual aid while maintaining eye contact with your audience.

Tying It All Together

Remember, your verbal and visual support ultimately become the meat of your presentation. So, think carefully about what you choose (or don't choose) to use. What's appropriate for your speech/occasion? What's most appropriate for your audience? And, what's best for you? You have an invaluable opportunity to make an impact—let your choices help, not hurt, your presentation.

References

Allen, M., & Preiss, R. W. (1997). Comparing the persuasiveness of narrative and statistical evidence using meta-analysis. *Communication Research Reports, 14*, 125–131. doi:10.1080/08824099709388654

APA. (2020). *Publication manual of the American Psychological Association* (7th ed.). Washington, DC: APA.

Ben & Jerry's. (2019). *Ice cream pints*. Retrieved from https://www.benjerry.com/flavors/ice-cream-pints

Brann, M. (2017). Research ethics and social values. In M. Allen (Ed.), *The SAGE encyclopedia of communication research methods* (pp. 1441–1443). Thousand Oaks, CA: Sage.

Cabell's. (2019). *Journal metrics*. Retrieved from https://www2.cabells.com/metrics

Choi, C. (2004, December 4). A no-frills thrill: Fabio teams up with Sam's. *The Orlando Sentinel*. Retrieved from www.orlandosentinel.com/news/os-xpm-2004-12-04-0412030414-story.html

Desjardins, J. (2018, April 23). How Google retains more than 90% of market share. *Business Insider*. Retrieved from www.businessinsider.com/how-google-retains-more-than-90-of-market-share-2018-4

Duarte, N. (2008). *Slide:ology: The art and science of presentation design*. Beijing, China: O'Reilly Media.

Fisher, W. R. (1984). Narration as human communication paradigm: The case of public moral argument. *Communication Monographs, 51*, 1–22. doi:10.1080/03637758409390180

Foxman, E., Storer, J., Fitzgerald, M., Wasik, B., Hou, L., Zhao, H., . . . Iwasaki, A. (2015). Temperature-dependent innate defense against the common cold virus limits viral replication at warm temperature in mouse airway cells. *Proceedings of the National Academy of Sciences of the United States of America, 112*, 827–832. doi:10.1073/pnas.1411030112

Gauthier, M., & Sawchuk, K. (2017). Not notable enough: Feminism and expertise in Wikipedia. *Communication and Critical/Cultural Studies, 14*, 385–402. doi:10.1080/14791420.2017.1386321

Habermas, J. (1984). *The theory of communicative action: Reason and the rationalization of society*. Boston, MA: Beacon Press.

Hamilton, J., & Mueller, A. (2010). Ethics simulations as preparation for public discourse. *Communication Teacher, 24*, 1–8. doi:10.1080/17404620903433416

Heinrichs, J. (2019). *figarospeech.com*. Retrieved from inpraiseofargument.squarespace.com/

Huff, D. (1954). *How to lie with statistics*. New York, NY: Norton & Company.

Ikäheimo, T., Jaakkola, K., Jokelainen, J., Saukkoriipi, A., Roivainen, M., Juvonen, R., . . . Jaakkola, J. (2016). A decrease in temperature and humidity precedes human rhinovirus infections in a cold climate. *Viruses, 8*, 244. doi:10.3390/v8090244

Kopaczewski, S. (2017). Plagiarism. In M. Allen (Ed.), *The SAGE encyclopedia of communication research methods* (pp. 1256–1258). Thousand Oaks, CA: Sage.

LeFebvre, L. (2017). Data. In M. Allen (Ed.), *The SAGE encyclopedia of communication research methods* (pp. 336–337). Thousand Oaks, CA: Sage.

Levitin, D. (2016). *A field guide to lies: Critical thinking in the information age*. New York, NY: Dutton.

Lindlof, T. R. (1995). *Qualitative communication research methods* (Vol. 3). Thousand Oaks, CA: Sage.

National Cancer Institute. (2018). *Cancer statistics*. Retrieved from www.cancer.gov/about-cancer/understanding/statistics

Owl Purdue. (2019). *Research and citation resources*. Retrieved from owl.purdue.edu/owl/research_and_citation/resources.html

Park, C. (2003). In other (people's) words: Plagiarism by university students–Literature and lessons. *Assessment & Evaluation in Higher Education, 28*, 471–488. doi:10.1080/02602930301677

Petty, R. E., & Cacioppo, J. T. (1986). *Communication and persuasion: Central and peripheral routes to attitude change*. New York, NY: Springer/Verlag.

Rosenthal, P. (2019, March 11). Michael Jordan and Hanes mark 30 years together—And consumers get the trading cards. *Chicago Tribune*. Retrieved from www.chicagotribune.com/sports/bulls/ct-spt-michael-jordan-hanes-anniversary-trading-cards-20190311-story.html

Tenzek, K. E. (2017). Field notes. In M. Allen (Ed.), *The SAGE encyclopedia of communication research methods* (pp. 564–566). Thousand Oaks, CA: Sage.

Toulmin, S. (1950). *An examination of the place of reason in ethics*. Cambridge, UK: Cambridge University Press.

U.S. Patent and Trademark Office. (2014). *Listen to soundmarks*. Retrieved from www.uspto.gov/kids/sound.html

Wieman, H., & Walter, O. (1957). Toward an analysis of ethics for rhetoric. *Quarterly Journal of Speech, 43*, 266–270. doi:10.1080/00335635709382245

Wilms, L., & Oberfeld, D. (2018). Color and emotion: Effects of hue, saturation, and brightness. *Psychological Research, 82*, 896–914. doi:10.1007/s00426-017-0880-8

Contributed by
Ms. Jessica Cherry
Dr. Jessica Eckstein

So far, in this text, you've learned how to create awe-inspiring speeches, but another significant aspect of public speaking is the actual speaking part! This chapter covers *delivery*, or the vocal and physical presentation of your speech. In addition to the major speech types, we'll discuss how you can become a more effective speaker in terms of delivery. Your delivery IS important because of how much it affects your audience's perception of you as a speaker, which in turn affects how your topic is received and remembered once your speech is over.

We tend to worry about delivering our speeches, but it's important to remember—as you prepare and practice—you're always improving. Even as you research and become more familiar with your topic, you'll begin to feel more comfortable presenting the content. As we continue to improve our comfort in front of an audience, we're perpetually finding our voices as public speakers. This chapter will include many tips to help you get through any nerves or hiccups you might encounter when giving your speech.

Types of Speech Delivery

In your course, you may be required to give not only several types of speeches (remember general purposes in Chapter 2?) but also to deliver those speeches in different ways. Each comes with its own set of benefits and challenges. Going in order from most-planned/least spontaneous or flexible to least-planned/most spontaneous or flexible, there are four major types of speeches you should understand: manuscript, memorized, extemporaneous, and impromptu.

Manuscript

Manuscript speeches get used a lot when interpreting literature.

First is a *manuscript speech*, which is obviously delivering a speech directly from a script. Most of us have had to sit through a class, meeting, or some other situation where someone read right off the paper to us. So, you already know just how mind-numbing and boring this type of speech can be if it's not delivered well (and it's usually not, by the way). It's often hard for these speakers to make eye contact because they're reading. This, then, makes it nearly impossible to build rapport with the audience.

Ever watched the show *Friends*? In one episode (one of Professor Cherry's favorites, in fact), the character Ross, hired as a guest instructor, practices his lecture with his friends as his audience. Ross proceeds to read off his note cards in a VERY monotone voice and never looks up. Even though he's rehearsing to

Remember how boring it was to listen to book reports?

friends, they can't stand listening to him! One friend jokes that listening to him is what will kill her, while another jokes that he's "never seen anyone stare so hard at a piece of paper that didn't have naked chicks on it." Check it out to get a good example of a poorly done manuscript speech; it also highlights just how much your audience *looks* to the speaker for eye contact and *listens* for vocal variety so they can connect with them. We'll touch on the importance of eye contact and vocal variety a lot in this chapter because it makes all the difference in your speech delivery. Although a teleprompter can create the illusion of effective eye contact during a manuscript speech, it still may not facilitate enough rapport to truly connect you with your audience.

Although manuscript speeches can be dull and appear unnatural (think high school book reports), there are some advantages to using a manuscript. When you've put a lot of effort into focusing on your exact phrasing/wording, then this style is one you might consider. For example, if you've spent time crafting a lot of witty phases or have very specific terminology you wish to provide, you wouldn't want to skip over these or forget them altogether. This type of speech also can be beneficial if you're anxious about forgetting those elements you've worked so hard to put together. You won't forget anything because you'll have every aspect of your speech right in front of you. Additionally, manuscripts allow for better control over the time-length of the speech by providing the exact wording—making you less likely to remove or add information. So, overall, a manuscript speech does have some benefits, but it can appear unnatural and should only be used if you need to have full control over your speech—and if your instructor allows it.

Memorized

A second type of speech, the *memorized speech*, is what it sounds like: You memorize that manuscript we just talked about, and present it to your audience. Like the manuscript speech, you

"Of course you're allowed to have stage fright. As soon as your talk is over."

have a lot of control over the timing and wording of your speech. But, you also won't have to worry about looking down at notes, so you'll be able to make more eye contact (than with the manuscript speech). You'll appear very confident and prepared.

This speech has all the positives of a manuscript speech, but now, you have to remember everything on that paper, without the actual paper. If you're gifted with a great memory, this type of speech might be a cinch to do. Nonetheless, memorization takes a significant amount of time and energy. Even with every word memorized and the confidence of Iron Man, sometimes words simply escape us, especially as our nerves get the best of us. Many of us experience moments like this at one time or another in the form of *stage fright*, which is the fear that washes over you when performing for an audience; *communication apprehension*, specific to giving speeches, is another form of this (Sawyer & Behnke, 2002). But, it doesn't just occur when you're in front of an audience; it can also be felt as you prepare for a performance. Most of us have heightened nerves (either anxiety or good adrenaline) before a speech (Eckman & Shean, 1997), but this rush of energy can be problematic with the added pressure of having to remember every single word, action, and citation included in your speech (Bodie, 2010). It takes a lot of confidence (and rehearsal!) to be able to present a memorized speech well.

Public Speaking Power: Stop Saying You're Nervous & Start Saying You're Excited!

You might fear public speaking, but fear isn't a hindrance. If you care about something, you might feel butterflies. But, those butterflies aren't just nerves—they're energy. For this reason, you don't want to actually eliminate your "excitement" but rather manage it so your adrenaline funnels into passion and vitality. Taming those butterflies all starts with mental preparation and positive mental talk.

If you mentally tell yourself something is going to suck, it *will* actually suck (see Chapter 6 for more on self-fulfilling prophecies). If you think you're going to fail a speech, you just might because you're not going to put the time or effort into it. Pessimists not only notice the things that already confirm their negative perspectives but often encourage (consciously or subconsciously) them to happen. So, Step 1 in taming those butterflies can be as simple as taking a more positive outlook and repeatedly saying to yourself (perhaps silently, if you're in class), "I've got this!"—even if you don't quite believe it yet. This brings us to Step 2: "Fake it 'til you make it." This old adage has actually been proven to work (Carney, Cuddy, & Yap, 2010). It's a physical and cognitive restructuring (Ellis, 1963) based on activating a *growth-mindset* (believing you can grow your brain/abilities as opposed to thinking you've learned all you need/want to; Dweck, 2016). Putting on a smile, throwing your shoulders back, and acting like you've got this in the bag can trick your brain (and in turn, YOU) into confidence. Science supports your success!

Contributed by K. Scholten & J. Eckstein

Extemporaneous

An *extemporaneous speech* requires preparation and practice, but you get to use limited notes to present your speech, allowing for greater flexibility in delivery. You *need* to plan ahead, but you're not expected to reiterate every little detail like with a manuscript or memorized speech. This is most likely the type of speech you'll be required to deliver in your classes. It's the preferred speech for your communication classes because it has many of the advantages of the manuscript and memorized speeches but allows you to adapt to the situation.

Extemp speaking is ideal—the best of all types!

© fizkes/Shutterstock.com

After crafting an amazing outline using the ideas from Chapters 2 and 3, you'll have great content like in manuscript and memorized speeches. Then, through rehearsal/practice, you'll become comfortable enough with that material to be able to use just brief notes to present. You'll definitely want to rehearse A LOT! It's well-documented that the more you practice, the less performance anxiety you'll have (Menzel & Carrell, 1994; Rubin, Rubin, & Jordan, 1997). Through effective practice, you'll be able to make good eye contact with your audience—a crucial part of extemporaneous speeches that allows you to connect with them. Your eye contact and interaction with your audience let you react to their nonverbal signals (like their smiling at certain concepts, examples, or jokes) and respond to those.

Because you'll only be using brief notes, each time you present your speech will be slightly different, but your intro and conclusion (see Chapter 2 for a refresher) should remain consistent. You might even consider memorizing your intro and conclusion sections to help you avoid missing these essential elements and hopefully put some of those additional nerves to rest! But, don't worry—if you can't memorize anything, the solution comes in the form of great notes (we'll discuss these soon).

Impromptu

Have you ever been asked a question and had no idea what to say but had to answer anyway? Let's say your instructor asks you how your speech prep is going, but you haven't even thought about it yet. (I'm sure this'll never happen to anyone reading this, but let's pretend.) You know your professor is expecting to hear more than "I haven't started it yet." In that moment, you formulate a response that's semi-organized and shows them you have some idea where you'll begin. You basically just gave a mini impromptu speech.

The *impromptu speech* is spontaneous, without any rehearsal. We're expected to do this type of speech much more frequently than we realize in life; you probably just didn't have a name for it before. You don't get very long to prepare (about 1–2 minutes, if even that) or to present (2–3 minutes) these speeches. The lack of preparation and the short amount of prep time make impromptus very different from the other speech types.

Now, even though an impromptu speech is just speaking "off the cuff," your speech should still be well organized. In other words, any impromptu speech should still contain the

necessary components of any speech, including an intro (with attention-getter, thesis, preview statement), transitions, and a conclusion (thesis, review statement, and clincher). You might wonder, "Why do I need to think about this type of speech outside of class?" We guarantee there *will* come a time when you're required (outside of class!) to give an impromptu speech, and you'll need to adapt to deliver it with confidence (Ladegaard, 1995). Practicing "in the moment" speeches in your classes not only helps you develop more confidence but also teaches you to adapt and develop the skills needed to become a more

Don't worry; impromptu topics will always be provided for you—in life and in class.

effective public speaker overall. If you forget where you're going in your speech, learning to think more effectively on your feet will help you recover more quickly.

Professor Cherry once found herself having to deliver an impromptu speech at her grandfather's funeral. The priest had finished speaking, everyone had gone up to say "goodbye" and returned to their seats, and then . . . no one moved! After what seemed like 5 minutes (but was probably more like 1–2), she realized everyone needed to know what was happening next. But, who wants to be the first one to talk or leave right after a funeral service? So, being the superhero communicator she is, she went up front, introduced herself, thanked everyone for coming, said a few things about her grandfather, thanked everyone for coming again, and invited them to the banquet that followed. She couldn't tell you now everything she'd said (because she doesn't remember), but it was quick, organized, to the point, and did the trick (Dr. Eckstein was there and was so impressed with her poise in this impromptu speech while grieving)! The point of this anecdote is not to bum you out but to demonstrate that you never know when you may have to deliver an impromptu speech and why knowing how to do one well is so important.

Let's Talk About Notes, Ba-by!

Now that we've gone through the different types of speeches, let's talk about how to get the most out of your presentation notes. When delivering an extemporaneous speech (and occasionally, an impromptu speech), you most likely want to have notes with you, so you need to consider how to create them most effectively. Our tips apply not just to typical notes; you can also create "notes" for yourself within your presentation software. For example, the "Notes" section at the bottom of each slide can be viewed during Presentation Mode view in PowerPoint and makes a great tool if used effectively.

The type of speech (e.g., informative, persuasive) and the amount of time you have to present it will determine just how many note cards might be necessary. Your instructor might even have a required number of note cards and collect them after your speech is completed. Other times, it's up to you to decide how many note cards are needed, depending on the type of speech and your topic (we'll cover this in a bit). For example, if you're presenting a topic you know really well, you might not need as many reminders. Once you have an idea of how many note cards you might need for your speech, a few key elements will help you create useful ones; these tips might seem insignificant, but they'll make all the difference when you present. Just remember the five Card Cs: clarity, conspicuousness, color, charting, and content.

Is he holding those notes so high because he needs glasses?

© Bronwyn Photo/Shutterstock.com

Clarity

Whether you use actual note cards or the "Notes" section in a PowerPoint as you present, there are a few things to consider. First, for both methods, remember that your slides themselves are not giant note cards! It's SO obnoxious when someone presents standing in front of the slides, with their back or side toward the audience while they read them to us like we're a bunch of kindergartners! Remember, we can read (Carver, 1992) and process information (Carver, Johnson, & Friedman, 1971) faster than you can talk— so don't give us the opportunity to jump ahead and get bored waiting for you to catch up speaking. To avoid writing out a lot on your slide, follow the 6 × 6 rule from Chapter 3 and put longer info on your note cards or in the "Notes" section of PowerPoint. These notes show up on the computer monitor when your slides are in Presentation Mode, which means you'll be able to see them, but your audience won't because they're not projected on the screen. You can see how this looks to a presenter at the top of the next page.

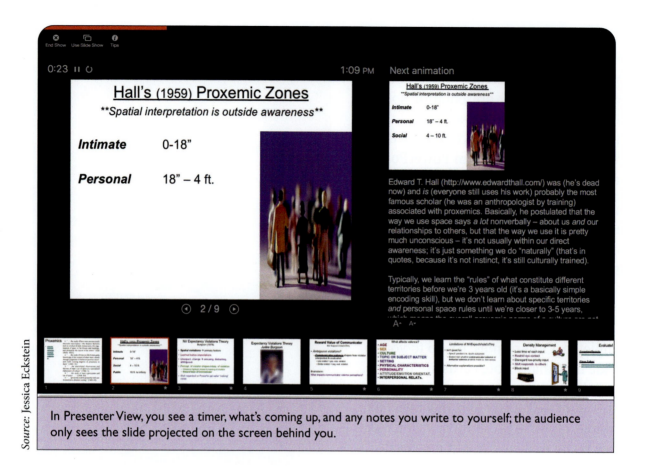

Source: Jessica Eckstein

In Presenter View, you see a timer, what's coming up, and any notes you write to yourself; the audience only sees the slide projected on the screen behind you.

Next, whether you use notes within PowerPoint or decide to go with "old-fashioned" note cards, you must still consider legibility—for yourself! If you're like us, you might sometimes have a hard time reading your own writing, so don't forget you can type up and print off your own note cards. But, you don't want to be standing in front of the audience with your eyes tied to your note cards (or leaning over to look at the computer screen) as you present, so don't use font only Ant-Man could read. Make that font on your notes as big as you need to! And, make sure to bold, underline, and/or italicize, certain terms, phrases, or words to make it easier for you to see while presenting. This will also help you remember what aspect(s) of the presentation you really want to drive home to your audience. The whole point of notes is to reference them quickly, not to lose time trying to read them. So, you see, size really does matter, and it comes up again in note card choice as well.

Conspicuousness

When presenting with notes, you want them to seem nonexistent. The easiest way to accomplish this is to use the "Notes" function in your PowerPoint. But, if you do decide to use physical note cards, they shouldn't be a focal point or distract from the audience paying attention to YOU and your visual aids. Keeping your notes subtle also makes you *appear* more prepared and confident when presenting your speech—like you know it so well, you're not relying on anything, which is a common assessment of students' speaking abilities (see

Iberri-Shea, 2017). To accomplish this, keep the cards small and the font big! The standard note card is 3 × 5″, which is just small enough to keep inconspicuous during your speech.

You should also think about the type of paper you want your note cards to be. Card stock doesn't make as much noise or visible commotion as regular paper does when your hands shake (which happens not only when you're nervous but just excited on adrenaline too!). Card stock also reduces how conspicuous your notes are when you flip to a new card. Trust us, notes cut from regular paper have a different sound than harder/thicker paper. Test it for yourself!

Well, at least she won't lose her notes!

© Olena Chukhil/Shutterstock.com

Color

Another way to keep your notes hidden is to avoid choosing cards that come in any funky colors. We understand wanting to add some color and flare to your notes. When you use those fun-colored cards, your NOTES (not YOU) are saying to your audience, "Here I am! Notice me!" Further, it's a bit more difficult for speakers to read off of colored note cards. If you want to add color and funky flare to your notes, use colored pens/pencils/markers (yay for Sharpies!). Write your notes using different colors to represent ideas to highlight, or choose a different color for any notes to yourself about your delivery.

For example, if you have a hard time maintaining eye contact with the audience, you could write in red: "MAKE EYE CONTACT" or "LOOK AROUND THE ROOM" as reminders to yourself (see the example "delivery notes" on p. 87). You could also use different colors to make your sources and quotes stick out so that you remember these important supporting resources. Finally, color-coding for each speech section would help keep track of where you are in your speech, remind you to transition from each section and/or main point, and maintain organization of your notes.

Charting

It should be obvious, but we have to say it: Making sure your notes are organized can be a lifesaver during your speech. If your cards aren't charted according to your delivery, you might lose track of where you are in your speech, skip a section or main point, lose time finding your place again, and overall decrease how credible and competent you seem to your audience. So, how do we keep everything organized?

First, write on only one side of the note card. You may want to use as much blank space as you can, but writing on both front and back can cause a lot of confusion. During your speech, you can forget which side you need to focus on, or which ones have been flipped and which ones haven't. If you lose your place, you then end up fanning yourself with your cards, flipping them back and forth until you find your place again. You should especially use only one side if you wrote in those fun colors. It'd be pointless to use white cards to avoid attention when the audience can see your bright pen or pencil and read everything you've written!

Next, numbering your cards also keeps you organized. Hopefully, it'll help you avoid any confusion if a few of them happen to be placed in the wrong order. If you fear you might drop them and aren't sure numbering will get you back in order fast enough, you could also punch a hole in the corner, and tie them together with a string or even get fancy with a keyring or carabiner. No matter how many times you drop them, they're guaranteed to be in order.

Finally, if you use PowerPoint Notes (or an equivalent), it's important to keep notes limited. This is because, first, as mentioned before, you don't want to be stuck in front of your computer screen in order to read your notes. Further, if you include too many notes in your "Notes" section, you'll have to physically scroll through them while presenting the same slide, which can, again, make you too tied to the computer. If, during your rehearsals, you find this happening, create a new slide altogether that corresponds with your notes or try to reduce the number of notes for that slide. How do you know what you should remove from your notes? To answer that question, you'll need to consider what exactly needs reminders while speaking, or the content of your notes.

Content

You have a lot of options for what to put in your notes, but remember, make sure everything you include is *important* to you and *necessary* to help you get through the presentation. An excellent place to start is with a draft of your note cards. You already have an idea of what you want to include and how you'll structure your speech thanks to your outline (see Chapter 2). Use it to create your first-draft of your note cards. As you practice your speech, you'll find you know some things better than others, so you can make several drafts of note cards before you create a clean, final set. Rehearsing the speech doesn't just build confidence; it also helps you prepare by creating the best version of your notes to keep your presentation in order (Allen, 1990). All of this practice can earn you a higher grade (Pearson, Child, & Kahl, 2006).

Because you're doing an extemporaneous (*not* a manuscript!) speech, make sure to use keywords only—so you're not tempted to read directly off your notes. Notes are just a guide; you don't want to constantly be staring at them, using them as a crutch when presenting. There are a few exceptions to the "keywords only" rule for notes, though: direct quotes from other sources and reference names with pertinent details (e.g., date, source) that you need to verbally SAY. Only put a brief amount—just enough to remind you of what you wanted to say in that moment—on each note. And, *rehearse* because you want to limit the number of notes you need! Using fewer notes makes you look more competent and credible when speaking.

Dr. Eckstein's speech notes. Can you tell which delivery issues she was trying to work on for a manuscript speech she gave at 8 years old!?

Source: Jessica Eckstein

Remember, they're not only useful for remembering key information; notes also improve your delivery! First, not being prepared is a key source of the anxiety many people feel about public speaking, so reducing that anxiety through preparation will only help once you actually do it (Daly, Vangelisti, Neel, & Cavanaugh, 1989)! Second, it helps delivery to rehearse with draft cards because once you know what some of your challenges might be (because you've rehearsed and practiced it many times before this, *right*?), it can be helpful to leave little reminders to yourself for when you present. Do you need reminders to make eye contact? Smile? Clarify certain words? Speed up more? Slow down? Include whatever you think will help you deliver a more effective speech!

Practice

You should always prepare your speech as soon as possible—pretty much as soon as it's been assigned so you have enough time to make any adjustments. As you rehearse, you'll discover that you present it a bit differently each time, especially using an extemporaneous method. So rehearse in many formats/venues. Although you might make fabulous eye contact with yourself in a mirror, nothing beats practicing with an audience of your family, friends, classmates, or even attentive pets. As painful as it can be to watch, reviewing a video of yourself can help you catch a lot of delivery issues you probably didn't even know you had. No matter where you are, keep running through your speech in your head to become ever more comfortable with the material (the shower is a great time not to be interrupted). However, the majority of your practice should occur aloud (to obviously practice vocal delivery) and on your feet (to practice physical delivery). You might think reading your speech on your couch is good enough, but trust us . . . it's NOT. Practicing aloud and on your feet will not only make you more prepared and comfortable for speech day, but you're also likely to find it takes longer to present this way—forcing you to be even more conscious of your time requirements. Speaking of which . . . time your speech. Always aim for the middle of your allowed time range, as you might find on speech day that you speak a little faster, shortening your time OR you begin to add in a bit of extraneous information, going over time (both common results of nerves). It's nearly impossible to practice your speech *too much*, so KEEP PRACTICING! Just like every other aspect of communication, practice is the ONLY way to improve your superpowers!

We emphasize practice so much in this text because frequently rehearsing your speech makes you more comfortable with the material and delivery, helping you calm your nerves (Phillips, 1986) *and* improve (Berger, 1997). Another thing to calm your nerves is to start thinking about your speech as a conversation with your audience, rather than just speaking AT the people staring out in front of you. Not only does this frame your speech as simply an enlarged conversation but also makes you much more relatable to the audience. Have you ever sat through a lecture where the professor is simply talking AT you versus WITH you? It makes a huge different in if/how you connect with the material.

Vocal Delivery

One way to create this enlarged conversation is through effective vocal delivery. You want to show enthusiasm and engagement in your speech, just as you would if speaking with a friend. Again, this helps you connect with your audience *and* makes your message that much more memorable (Zhang, 2014). At this point in your Intro Course, you've probably gotten to know some of your classmates. Think about how you'd talk to them normally. *That's* how your speech should sound too. There are few things worse than a monotone, mechanical, boring, read-out-loud speech that puts you to sleep 2 minutes after the person starts (PLEASE make it stop!). To accomplish effective vocal delivery, remember the six Vocal Vs: variety, volume, velocity, verbalization, vernacular, and vocalizations and verbal fillers.

Variety

If you've ever sat through a monotone speech, you know just how unbearable it can be. Assuming you want (we hope) to keep your audience interested, rather than help them nap, many vocalic aspects can get you variety. With **pitch**, which is how high or low our voices are, it's important to find a balance. Higher pitched voices are easier to hear and understand (think screaming child versus bellowing rhino) but may hurt your credibility—because our sexist society equates vocal depth with rigor or dominance (Glenn, Glenn, & Forman, 1989; Stel, van Dijk, Smith, van Dijk, & Djalal, 2012). Have you ever seen the movie *White Chicks*? Although otherwise problematic, this movie is a great example of pitch variety. The movie's main Black, male characters have naturally deep voices and must try to impersonate young, White females (hence, the title); they accomplish this by imitating the stereotypical "Valley Girl" high-pitched voice.

The Valley Girl voice is also tied to *tone*, or the (up/down) emphasis on a sound scale that a speaker puts on particular words within a phrase or sentence. The Valley Girl voice is very distinct because it puts an "upward?" emphasis at ends of sentences, creating a higher tone, resulting in what sounds like a question. It's also referred to as "uptalk" or "upspeak" and reduces perceptions of credibility because it makes you sound unsure of what you're saying (Burrell & Koper, 1998). When presenting, it's also important to adjust your tone according to the mood of your

Elle Woods in *Legally Blonde* had a stereotypical Valley Girl voice.

© Featureflash Photo Agency/Shutterstock.com

speech at a particular moment. For example, you don't want a chipper, happy, perky voice when you're describing something horrible or serious; the communication must meet the demands of the situation at hand (Spitzberg & Brunner, 1991). See the John Oliver (2019) link in our References for a great example of even professional speakers (news anchors) failing in this regard. Their energetic tone is uncomfortably the wrong inflection for the moment.

Ross really is "FINE!": www.youtube .com/watch?v=T55vZAlTLI8

© Kathy Hutchins/Shutterstock.com

Finally, putting it all together, *vocal inflection* is how differently we use emphasis (and tone, pitch, and other things like volume) to convey particular feelings (Krauss, Apple, Morency, Wenzel, & Winton, 1981). For example, if someone asks how you're doing and you respond with, "Oh, I'm great," they can tell from your inflection if you're truly doing well or just being sarcastic. In another good example of vocal inflection from *Friends* (yes, again; Ms. Cherry is *obsessed* with this show), Ross tries to communicate to his friends that he's OK with something he just witnessed. His vocal inflection in the scene clearly demonstrates to his friend is that he is not, in fact, "fine."

Research shows that when we use vocal variety, listeners are much more receptive to our message (Rodero, Potter, & Prieto, 2017). In fact, your vocal variety will also increase the audience's perceptions of your effectiveness and their own interest/arousal, attention to you, immediate recall, and recognition of information later (Rodero et al., 2017). Another way to accomplish this vocal variety is by moderating your volume.

Volume

It'd be easier for him to just practice speaking from his diaphragm.

When speaking, you need to become conscious of your **volume**, or how loud or soft-spoken you are. You'll want to account for the size (and acoustics) of the room in which you'll be speaking. Obviously, you don't want to shout at your audience, but it's possibly worse to speak too softly because then no one can hear you. Practicing your speech in front of (but far away from) others or recording yourself are effective ways to evaluate a correct volume. If possible, practice your speech in the actual room (or one very similar to it) where you'll be presenting—another proven technique for reducing speech anxiety (Menzel & Carrell, 1994).

If you're someone who might be naturally soft-spoken or you just need to learn to project a bit more, try some deep breathing exercises. Our volume is largely controlled by projecting from the diaphragm. If you've ever done choir, meditation, or yoga, you know the type of breath we're talking about; basically, focus on breathing from your "belly" rather than your chest to control your volume. Here's an easy practice to see where you're *really* breathing from: Lay on your back. Place one hand on your chest and the other on your belly. Take several deep breaths and notice if it's mainly your upper chest rising or your lower rib cage/belly rising. By breathing from your belly, you're learning to use your diaphragm, which projects your voice more. Plus, almost any breathing exercise can help you settle your nerves!

Demosthenes was an ancient Greek orator who initially struggled to speak loudly enough to be heard—and this was back when thousands of people would gather in outdoor public forums to hear people speak. His solution? He'd go to the ocean where waves crashed against the rocks and deliver his speech at the roaring sea! If you live near an equally loud source, try something similar. Or, try speaking over a hand-dryer or hairdryer. Remember, the key

Perhaps he's just practicing like Demosthenes?

(even while practicing) is not to shout; that'll strain your vocal cords—and annoy your audience. Simply project your volume from a different body part, making it resonate more and sound louder/fuller, and ultimately, more powerful (Stel et al., 2012).

Velocity

One of the more common speech struggles is speaking *rate*, or speed/pace. If you're presenting your speech like an enlarged conversation, you'll likely be speaking at a fairly quick clip, which will keep the audience engaged. We generally perceive people who speak faster (as long as we can still understand them!) as more competent (Smith, Brown, Strong, & Rencher, 1975), potent, and credible (Scherer, London, & Wolf, 1973) than slower speakers. Think about it; do you even know how quickly (or slowly) you speak? Most people don't know until someone tells them. However, once adrenaline kicks in, you might find you're speaking even faster than usual.

You can learn to manage your speech rate through practice (are you sensing a trend?). Consider asking the audience you practice in front of how quickly you speak or use an online rate tracker to measure yourself. But remember, if someone isn't a native speaker of the language you're using, if you have an accent, or if you have trouble articulating, mumble, or slur, you'll have to slow down—regardless of people's info-processing abilities. Competent communicators are efficient *and* effective (Spitzberg & Brunner, 1991).

Verbalizations

Once you have your volume and rate under control through practice, practice, practice, it's time to work on pronunciation and articulation. It's important to know how words are *meant* to sound, which is the power of **pronunciation**. Some words have multiple pronunciations, but some are considered more "correct" than others, which is why so-called "correct" pronunciation is highly tied to perceived social status of the speaker (Trudgill, 1974). Ms. Cherry once had a grade-school teacher named Mr. Shorepenis. Clearly, there are a few ways you could pronounce this name. If you're like her and her classmates, you read his name as SHORE-pee-niss. After her instructor clarified, they learned it's pronounced Shore-PEN-is. What a difference the correct pronunciation makes! Work out ahead of time how to say any terms essential to your speech or an author's name you find hard to pronounce.

Luckily, in addition to looking up words' phonetical spellings, you can also access audible pronunciation guides in online dictionaries. For proper names, if you can't get clarification from those around you, look it up online; you can probably find a video of someone saying their name. If you can't track it down, it's likely the audience won't know it either, so just roll with it. Admitting you don't know how to say something almost immediately *lowers* your credibility. So, be sure to practice tricky words as much as possible! Look like you know what you're talking about and avoid confusion or misunderstandings by speaking correctly *and* clearly; it's one of the first things people use to evaluate our competence (McCroskey, 1982).

Articulation is verbal precision attained by sharply enunciating syllables or consonants. How do you master articulation? By this point, you can probably guess: Practice! Ever try talking with your mouth full? It can actually be helpful! Believe it or not, the ancient orator Demosthenes (of roaring-sea volume-practice fame) also mumbled (poor guy had a lot to overcome; he's also reputed to have lisped and stuttered). So, he worked to overcome these issues with another easy trick—he put a

Marshmallows and gummy bears—the key to articulation?

bunch of little rocks in his mouth when practicing. It's kind of nasty (who knows what dog peed on them!?), but the idea is good. Like Demosthenes, try putting an obstacle (try gum or caramels) in your way during practice. It'll force you to work around it and overemphasize your articulation. But, please do not add any additional obstacles (gum, mints, cough drops, or newly pierced tongue-ring) on your actual speech day. Trust us— just your tongue alone can seem like an obstacle sometimes.

Speaking of which, you can do a few simple things to make your body less of an obstacle to a great speech. Sufficient sleep and drinking fluids (both the day before and the day of) help you avoid tripping over your words due to exhaustion and that unpleasant, dry, cotton-mouth feeling, respectively. Cotton-mouth interferes with proper articulation and pronunciation. Don't drink too much water right before class (otherwise you'll have to pee!)—just enough to keep you hydrated. Fluids, however, are anything that *hydrates* you. Many of us view caffeine as life, but it can have adverse effects on your body during speech day; it can make it hard to speak clearly if it heightens your anxiety.

Vernacular

Some words are necessary to emphasize, but others should be avoided. Any words unnecessary to your speech, too difficult to say, or that you stumble over should be used sparingly or not at all. Use synonyms to replace terms you can't pronounce! It's also important to orient your language to the audience in front of you. It isn't *wrong* to use jargon or slang in your speech; it just depends on your audience. If you do use abbreviations or slang they might be unfamiliar with, be sure to explain them to your audience.

Speaking like your audience and using common language connects you with people (Giles & Smith, 1979). But, don't go out of your comfort zone; there's nothing worse than trying to be the "cool dad/professor" (or whatever) by speaking "the kids' lingo" ("Fo shizzle, my nizzle," anyone?). Obviously, avoid anything offensive or vulgar—*even if* you think it connects with your audience more. Being too casual decreases speakers' credibility. It's a fine balance, where "appropriate vocabulary" and "optimally effective language" each matter; it's possible to do one well and not the other, so consider both separately (Iberri-Shea, 2017).

© Constantin Stanciu/Shutterstock.com

Vocalizations and Verbal Fillers

We're all prone to *vocal fillers*, or unintentional verbalizations, in our speeches—especially when nervous. These come in two main forms: *Vocalizations* are nonlanguage sounds like "ahh," "uhh," or "umm" whereas *verbal fillers* are actual words such as "like," "you know," or "sooo . . ." (Miller & Hewgill, 1964). We use them all the time in normal conversations but tend to do them even more (because we're more nervous) when giving speeches. Fillers are incredibly distracting and hurt your credibility because they tend to project a lack of confidence (Corley, MacGregor, & Donaldson, 2007). When people use these too often, we start tallying how many times it happens and fail to listen to what they're actually trying to say.

The best way to rid yourself of fillers is to realize just how much you use them (Berger, 1997). Becoming filler-conscious helps remove them from your speech (Christenfeld, 1996), and there're a few different ways to do this. While you practice giving your speech in front of others (perhaps even the whole class), whenever someone makes ANY vocal filler (verbalized or vocalized), have everyone in the room yell out "NOPE!" or make an obnoxious buzzer sound. Dr. Eckstein has them throw popcorn pieces (popped, of course) or small paper "spit" balls (without the spit) every time the speaker uses a filler.

After hearing these horrific sounds or getting bombarded by little white things, you'll become more conscious of your fillers and even notice more yourself while speaking.

Silence is the alternative to fillers. We can guarantee that while you're presenting, the amount of time you don't speak seems two to three times longer to you than it does to the audience! Your perception is skewed while eyes are on you (McRaney, 2011). Replace vocalizations and verbal fillers

© Francesco Losenno/Shutterstock.com

SILENCE SPEAKS WITH POWER

with "meaningful pauses" instead. Silence is a great way to add vocal variety; pauses add emphases to your speech. Your audience may even *need* you to pause because it helps them process and recognize that the point you just made was probably important. Listen to famous speeches, and you'll notice *many* pauses at key points that add to the speech. There's NO reason to feel awkward pausing in front of an audience. Practice this skill, but you can also write "PAUSE" reminders on your notes—just one more delivery tip you can prepare ahead of time.

Body

Our body movements, just like our voice, show our audience exactly how we're feeling and can go a long way in projecting (even if you're faking it) confidence. We physically work hard during speeches, starting from our body's top: eyes, poise, gestures, stance, and feet.

Eye Movement

Mentioned many times already, eye contact is an essential part of delivery—it helps your audience feel engaged with you. But, eyes as "windows to the soul" may explain why many people experience stage fright or speaking anxiety. It's not just having to look AT people; it's the fact that people are watching *and* we must connect eyes with them (McCroskey, 1977). If you struggle with this under normal circumstances, it'd seem even more impossible during speeches!

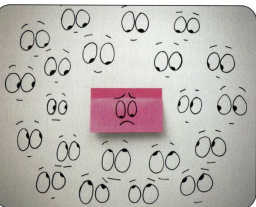

© Jess Rodrigues/Shutterstock.com

Try to strike a balance between staring and avoiding. First, don't keep your eyes constantly moving and darting around the room because it makes you look nervous. You want to gradually cover the entire room (don't forget the front and back corners!), looking at someone for a brief second before moving on. Don't hold the gaze for too long. If someone looks away, you know you've looked at them too long (Kendrick & Holler, 2017)—so move on! Otherwise, it's really creepy! Trust us; we know because students tend to stare *a lot* at their instructors (as though trying to "prove" their eye contact to us) while presenting. So, don't creep out your teacher! However, if making eye contact with your instructor or friends helps calm you, look at them to regain your composure, and then, continue on to the rest of your audience.

This is how you look to us if you maintain eye contact too long!

© Paul Vasarhelyi/Shutterstock.com

For those with the opposite problem, difficulty looking people in the eye, there are ways to address that too. If it's reeeally bad for you, then, depending on the quality of your vision, you might be able to play around with your glasses or contacts. Assuming you can still see your notes, removing your eyewear makes the audience blurry (so you don't see them looking at you). However, this trick only works for the nearsighted. You can also try looking at people's foreheads or directly behind their head rather than their eyes. Trust us, they won't notice you're not looking directly in their eyes. Finally, you can practice eye contact with someone or something like a poster hanging in your room, an actor on (paused) TV, or even your pet! Ms. Cherry's pups love it, so they always give their full attention.

Leo & Turbo, Ms. Cherry's captive audience!

Source: Jessica Cherry

Poise: Head, Neck, and Shoulders

Clenching or stiffening your upper body isn't just uncomfortable, it also challenges your confidence and audience interaction. Overall, try to be as fluid as possible to avoid looking like The Thing from *Fantastic Four*. Where you stand affects your neck and shoulder movements and how stiff you appear. Being too close to the audience forces you to twist your head to include your entire audience in the far corners of the room (because you're making eye contact with *everyone*, right?). Stand far enough away from the front row that you can see the front two corner seats comfortably. This has the added benefit of saving your audience from spit (because a good articulator *should* have spit flying!) while also maintaining your engagement with them.

Note cards give you flexibility with where you stand, but if you use PowerPoint Notes (with the monitor displaying your notes), adjust to where the computer is by standing roughly parallel to the screen so you can simply glance over to see your notes. And, adjust the positioning of the monitor too! You don't want to be going behind the desk to look at the monitor or every time you need to advance a slide. The monitor moves; take advantage of it! Again, think about how close you have to be to the audience and computer to accomplish this. Once you've established the right location, you pretty much stay there or keep coming back to it during certain spots during your speech.

Gestures

Even if you're standing in one spot, it doesn't mean you're not (or shouldn't be) moving—you're hopefully gesturing. Gestures are harder to control "in the moment" because they're more likely to be unconsciously used (Ekman & Friesen, 1972). **Intentional gestures**, though, are planned, specific hand movements to help the audience visualize something (e.g., illustrating how big/small something is) or to emphasize emotional points (e.g., pointing at someone; or saying "When you put that all together . . ." while gesturing putting something together).

But, there are "bad" ones (no, we're not talking about flipping the finger). Uncontrolled gestures, or ***nervous gestures***, usually come to the audience's attention because they're done in a way indicating nerves or anxiety. Also known as adaptors, we use these unconsciously to regulate our emotions or feelings of discomfort (Ekman & Friesen, 1972). More obvious nervous gestures include biting or picking your nails, clenching and releasing your fists, using a "claw hand," cracking your

Pointing can work sometimes, but don't be obnoxious!

© Your image/Shutterstock.com

knuckles, gripping the podium (we'll get to this later), putting your hands in your pockets, or pulling/flipping hair (pull it back to avoid the temptation). Although it's not terrible to just let your hands hang naturally at your side, not using any gestures *at all* becomes a problem if it makes your body looks stiff.

Just remember: For anything to "count" as a gesture, it must be made ABOVE the waist. Anything BELOW the waist is a nervous fidget—not a gesture. So, bring those arms up before gesturing! Also, avoid repetitive gesturing. We've seen students look like they're trying to karate chop a log over and over and over again. Gesture with purpose.

Further, avoid gesturing with your note cards. Remember, your notes should seem invisible, so gesturing with them works against this. Dr. Eckstein always advises students to pretend their note-holding arm's elbow is tied to their waist with a loose string, creating a built-in card stand. Once it's holding your notes, that hand shouldn't be doing anything else. If you're afraid you'll use nervous gestures, it *is* better to hang your (non-note-holding) hands loosely at your sides.

And, although you might not traditionally think of it as a gesture, your face also speaks volumes. We generally find smiling people more approachable (and easier to connect with), so be sure as you practice (yep, we said it again) that you check yourself out in the mirror or record yourself. Yes, we know resting bitch face is a legitimate problem and a simple smile can help this. But, remember a smile isn't *always* appropriate. Like those newscasters with inappropriate tone, you don't want to be smiling while saying, "Because of the car crash, he would never walk again." Although it's one more thing to remember, think about what your face is doing.

Stand With Power

Positioning isn't just about where you stand but also *how* you stand. One bodily movement to be conscious of is your leg positioning, or your ***speech stance***. Whenever possible, make your body visible to your audience; don't hide! An "open" body position may project

Podiums are really a crutch, in any form . . .

confidence, trustworthiness, and competence to those watching you (Cashdan, 1988). So, avoid closed positions like crossed arms, shifting away, or leaning on anything in the general presentation area. Most instructors know that furniture is used as a speech-crutch, so they'll move nearby objects (e.g., podium, desk) to remove temptations to lean or hide while presenting. Standing behind anything makes you look scared (you may be but shouldn't look that way!) and leaning makes you look uninterested, lazy, or *too* relaxed. Being relaxed is great but not at the sacrifice of actively engaging your audience; if *you* look bored during your speech, why should *we* listen?

If you do have a podium option, realize you don't have to use it just because it's there. We know people who've gotten jobs largely *because* they were the only candidate to come out from behind the podium provided for them; they actually engaged the people, not the furniture! If you DO rely on the crutch—er, podium, put your notes on it (thus, freeing your hands for more gestures and your body for more walking), using it as "home base" for your speech.

The most common improper stance across speakers of all ages is sometimes called the "teen stance" because it makes you look like the stereotypical teenager hanging around the mall. It's when you place more weight on one hip or side of your body than on the other, sometimes with a slightly bent knee. And, rarely do people keep the position—they shift their weight back and forth throughout the speech, unconsciously rocking themselves in a self-soothing technique. Dr. Eckstein has had people sway so much, she's gotten motion sickness! Even if you hold the teen stance still, without moving, it looks ridiculously unprofessional and weak or passive (Carney et al., 2010)! One way to avoid the rocking stance is to put your feet in-line with your hips and shoulders while pushing your heels into the ground. This not only gives you a confident posture but also prevents you from crossing your feet, tapping them, or crossing/uncrossing your legs as though you really have to pee.

Gotta pee? Or, just a nervous speaker?

Dr. Eckstein competed in forensics (i.e., speech competitions) and enjoyed it but would (and still does!) get a surge of adrenaline causing her hands to slightly tremor (that's how she knows the card-stock > paper note cards tip from earlier) and her legs to visibly shake. She wasn't actually nervous, so to avoid looking like she was, she'd lock her knees whenever standing in one place. Temporarily locking your knees has the added benefit of controlling nerves. Put it on your notes, then lock your knees until you walk the room.

Now, when we instruct people to do this, there's always someone (usually from the military or marching band) in class who says, "but you're not s'posed to do that 'cause it restricts blood flow and you'll pass out!" Guess what? In band, you're holding a huge instrument and walking sometimes miles! You're not a soldier marching cross-country; you're giving a 5–8 minute speech in a classroom. Lock those knees *when stationary* to avoid teen stance!

Feet Movement

As long as you don't encroach on the front row by moving too close or vigorously near them (Burgoon, 1978), it's perfectly fine to move around the "stage area" at the front of the room. Walking around or otherwise moving our bodies serves several functions including regulating our speech flow (e.g., speed up movement at an exciting part), maintaining an audience's attention, and emphasizing certain parts of our speech (Scherer, 1980). So, moving around in CONTROLLED fashion engages different parts of the audience directly (e.g., "working the room"), keeps their eyes moving (and interested), and emphasizes transitions or major sections of your speech (remember physical transitions from Chapter 2?). But, notice how we said controlled? Nervous energy sometimes manifests itself in the form of pacing, which makes you appear more nervous, can be distracting, and adds miles of wear and tear to your shoes.

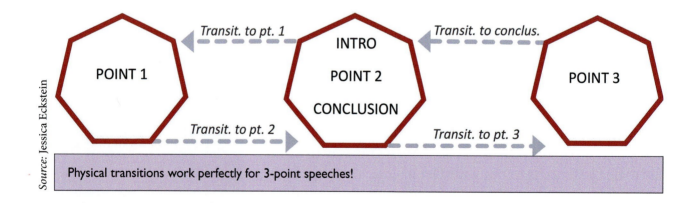

Source: Jessica Eckstein

Control your movement by walking only at certain points in your speech: each time you transition from your intro, each main body point, and conclusion (use the above image as a guide). These also happen to be times during your speech when it'll appear "natural" to move—even if it *was* rehearsed—so it works in your favor. Coming full circle, in a speech with three main points, moving only at each major transition puts you back to center by the end—a perfect bodily conclusion (see what we did there? hee, hee).

Speech Day Is Here! How to Prepare

Well, you got there—you did all the practice (right? RIGHT?). The day is here. Dr. Scholten, who coaches *many* competitive public speakers (and wrote Chapter 2), compares speech preparation to an athlete getting "in the zone" or putting on their "game face." Music to pump you up, stretching your joints/muscles, eating the right food—all these things (though corny-sounding) ensure you give your physio-mental activity (that's the speech) the same attention a superior athlete would leading up to the big game. To dive into the action, just remember these three As (as in, the speech grade you want to get): attire, active ingredients, and allies.

Attire: Suit Up Like Superman!

Your instructor may have given you specific guidelines for what to wear, but if not, a good rule of thumb is to dress at minimum in *comfortable* business casual (e.g., nice pants/jeans and a nice shirt; or dress). Now, depending on your speech topic, dressing the part might mean something different. For example, if you're delivering an informative speech on Marvel Comics, dressing up as your favorite character or wearing a Captain America t-shirt would probably *add* to your speech. Outside this context, however, wearing these items might look like you don't care about your speech. It shouldn't be surprising that we're immediately judged by others based on how we look—a large part of which is what we wear (Howlett, Pine, Cahill, Orakcioglu, & Fletcher, 2015). Just as your notes shouldn't be the center of attention, you also don't want people focused on your clothing or revealed body parts (Gurung, Brickner, Leet, & Punke, 2017) rather than on YOU, your words, and visual aids. Find something simple that you feel good in because it fits you well.

First, avoid excessively "busy" attire. Loud or busy patterns; graphic or text-based shirts; flashy or noise-making jewelry; uncomfortable or limiting shoes (e.g., super-high heels); or extra accessories like hats, earphones, or sunglasses all distract from you as a speaker. Plus, hats and sunglasses cover your face— what your audience wants to see to connect with you. And, don't forget, what you're wearing *before* you even arrive on speech day can affect your presentation. If your feet are killing you from walking around in painful (yet super cute!) shoes all day, you might walk a little funny. Similarly, a hat worn earlier will give you hat hair for your presentation. And though we, as teachers, wouldn't care at all, it could very easily make you self-conscious, affecting all the other parts of your speech.

Comfort is key!

© pathdoc/Shutterstock.com

If your clothes fit, you don't need to touch yourself!

© andriano.cz/Shutterstock.com

Next, if you can, try to wear something that fits. Excessively baggy or tight clothing is the most common thing that causes people to fidget while they adjust their clothing during the speech, revealing an obvious form of anxiety to the audience. Observing many fashion changes across the past 20 years of judging/grading speeches, Dr. Eckstein has noticed (sadly, because she despises *any* generalizations across the sexes!) one enduring trend. The most common unconscious fidget for "guys" remains the crotch-adjust or pants-tug and for "gals" is still the shirt-adjustment: pulling down the too-short shirt-front to cover their tummies, then pulling it up to cover their cleavage, then down again and so forth.

Finally, wear something that makes you feel good. We all know that looking good makes us feel good (Taggart, Ozolins, Hardie, & Nyhof-Young, 2009) *and* makes people perceive us more credibly (Patzer, 1983). Harness this to give yourself a confidence boost during your speech. Wear something you've worn before and feel great in. Even if you just bought a fabulous new outfit, this isn't the time to test the waters with how it performs. Whatever you wear, dress the part for your speech, making sure your clothes do your speech justice and give you confidence! Once you've prepared your outward appearance, you should start thinking about prepping your body internally.

Active Ingredients: Imbibing the Foods of the Gods

Eat a *bit* of something *plain* before you get to class (e.g., granola bar, banana, toast). You need the fuel! This helps you avoid becoming light-headed while speaking, eliminates potential hunger-headaches, and reduces any embarrassing tummy-grumbles your audience hears. Although you want to stay hydrated, you should also avoid too many liquids in the hour before you speak so you don't need the Fortress of Solitude (aka, bathroom). However, it's fine to down some water right before you go up to present to avoid cotton-mouth. You might already be shaky and nervous about presenting your speech; don't add hunger- or caffeine-shakes.

You don't want to have the *wrong* things in your mouth, either. Remove *anything* in your mouth that could negatively impact your well-practiced, articulated vocal delivery. It's probably common sense to avoid speaking with gum in your mouth, but you also want to avoid retainers, using cough drops, or sucking lozenges as well. These things might help your nerves, but they're more nervous fidgeting, so suck away . . . right up until you present. After all the hard work you put in to make sure your speech would be clear to your audience, don't sabotage it! Further, a well-articulated speaker might have some spittle coming out, but you don't want to add projectiles to it when your gum/lozenge comes flying out of your mouth accidentally.

Another thing to avoid eating? Your body parts. Yep, common nervous habits that tend to come out during presentations include nail biting, lip/mouth chewing, or hair chewing (Dr. Eckstein just about gagged typing that). Nail-biters can keep one hand full of note cards and use the other one to gesture; unless you're Dr. Octopus, this will eliminate all access to your nails. Lip/mouth chewing is solved by keeping a quick pace (discussed previously) and using *active* breathing (covered shortly); the speed at which air and words come out of your mouth prevents your teeth from edging to your tasty cheeks/gums. Finally, hair-chewers can put their hair up. Yeah, that one's an easy fix and should probably be done by everyone anyway because it lets us see your face clearly! Even if you're prone to nervous habits, simply relaxing your body (instead of eating it) actually brings positive affect in the form of internal allies.

Allies: Recruit the Positive Energy Team!

Finally, on the day you speak, you want people to believe you're just "going with the flow." As for so many other things, the key to making this happen is something you do already—breathing. Of course, you want to practice mindful breathing ahead of time, but doing it in the minutes right before you speak has especially profound results because by simply making that relaxed, confident pose with your body (that breathing brings about), you'll be actually *feeling* more powerful by the time you speak, too (Carney et al., 2010). Physiologically, mindful breathing calms our internal organs, centering us in a way that actually affects our thoughts/perceptions as well as our bodies!

Still feeling that nervous energy surge? Take it out on something else. Tension-release exercises often reduce anxiety and improve functioning (Scogin, Rickard, Keith, Wilson, & McElreath, 1992). Practice some covert tension-release exercises while seated: Pushing your feet into the ground, tighten your leg muscles, hold for a few seconds, then release. Tighten your core muscles for a few seconds, then release. Squeeze the sides of your seat, tightening your hand and arm muscles, and release. These exercises use up some of that extra energy.

She's calm, centered, and ready to present!

© kornnphoto/Shutterstock.com

As you prepare in the moments leading up to your speech, recruit positivity as an ally! See the Activism Hero box on the next page for more on this. Remember, the worst is NOT going to happen, and we're likely to be embarrassed by things that no one else notices or cares about but us (McRaney, 2011)! If you *do* say something wrong or stutter a bit while speaking, just take a nice "meaningful breath," pause and proceed; no one will notice or care but you (Gilovich, Medvec, & Savitsky, 2000). Chances are you're not the only one presenting that day, so your audience is not only nervous waiting for their own turn to speak, but are also "in it" with you, as a team. So, rely on your very own Justice League!

Activism Hero: Confidence Is Key!

Confidence is key during speeches, but it also plays a huge role in getting people to believe us, rely on us, and ultimately look to us for guidance (Haiman, 1949)—all tools that can be harnessed if you want to advance a particular social agenda in your world. Beyond positive self-talk, you can employ **positive visualization** (Stampfl, 1966), in which you picture yourself going through the steps to achieve your goals. This process can bring about both short-term (e.g., speech) and long-term (e.g., social change campaign) goals (Phillips, 1986). It's a tool used successfully by many athletes. Michael Phelps, the most decorated Olympian *ever* (at the time of this publication), methodically incorporates this practice into his training. By imagining every part of a successful race—from starting block to celebration, he creates his own "mental DVD" to replay over and over again.

You can do the same for your speeches: Imagine a very enthused, engaged audience; your slides working without a hitch; and you delivering your speech like a pro. This technique also works for long-term success (Kelly & Keaten, 1992). Envision your audience eating up every word of your message and becoming part of the change; being written up in the local paper, which further publicizes your cause; attracting the notice of lawmakers and celebrities, who ultimately decide to pass laws and recruit others to help your cause! Replay these mental recordings several times in the days leading up to an event, at each stage of accomplishing your social-change goals.

Contributed by K. Scholten & J. Eckstein

© barbaliss/Shutterstock.com

Final Thoughts

Keep the tips and tricks from this chapter in mind, practice as much as you can beforehand (you didn't think you'd get away without another reminder, did you?), use your relaxation techniques before you get up to speak, and you'll emerge kicking butt! Even your final speech isn't your "final" product; each presentation is merely dress rehearsal, a chance to improve your skills for future encounters, like a superhero training camp. Start your prep work today!

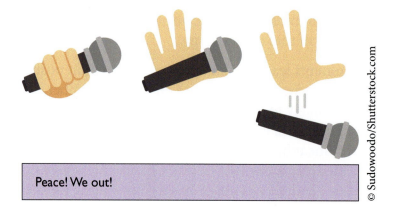

Peace! We out!

© Sudowoodo/Shutterstock.com

References

Allen, T. (1990). *The effect of imagined interaction & planning on speech fluency & message strategy selection.* Unpublished doctoral dissertation, Baton Rouge, LA: Louisiana State University. Retrieved from https://digitalcommons.lsu.edu/gradschool_disstheses/4968

Berger, C. (1997). *Planning strategic interaction: Attaining goals through communicative action.* Mahwah, NJ: Erlbaum.

Bodie, G. D. (2010). A racing heart, rattling knees, and ruminative thoughts: Defining, explaining, and treating public speaking anxiety. *Communication Education, 59,* 70–105. doi:10.1080/03634520903443849

Burgoon, J. (1978). A communication model of personal space violations: Explication & an initial test. *Human Communication Research, 4,* 130–131. doi:10.1111/j.1468-2958.1978.tb00603.x

Burrell, N. A., & Koper, R. J. (1998). The efficacy of powerful/powerless language on attitudes and source credibility. In M. Allen & R. W. Preiss (Eds.), *Persuasion: Advances through meta-analysis* (pp. 203–217). Cresskill, NJ: Hampton Press.

Carney, D., Cuddy, A., & Yap, A. (2010). Power posing: Brief nonverbal displays affect neuroendocrine levels & risk tolerance. *Psychological Science, 21,* 1363–1368. doi:10.1177/0956797610383437

Carver, R. (1992). Reading rate: Theory, research, & practical implications. *Journal of Reading, 36,* 84–95. Retrieved from www.jstor.org/stable/40016440

Carver, R. P., Johnson, R. L., & Friedman, H. L. (1971). Factor analysis of the ability to comprehend time-compressed speech. *Journal of Reading Behavior, 4,* 40–49. doi:10.1080/10862967109546974

Cashdan, E. (1998). Smiles, speech, and body posture: How women and men display sociometric status and power. *Journal of Nonverbal Behavior, 22,* 209–228. doi:10.1023/A:1022967721884

Christenfeld, N. (1996). The effects of a metronome on the filled pauses of fluent speakers. *Journal of Speech and Hearing Research, 39,* 1232–1238. doi:10.1044/jshr.3906.1232

Corley, M., MacGregor, L., & Donaldson, D. (2007). It's the way that you, er, say it: Hesitations in speech affect language comprehension. *Cognition, 105,* 658–668. doi:10.1016/j.cognition.2006.10.010

Daly, J., Vangelisti, A., Neel, H., & Cavanaugh, P. (1989). Pre-performance concerns associated with public speaking anxiety. *Communication Quarterly, 37,* 39–53. doi:10.1080/01463378909385524

Dweck, C. (2016). *Mindset: The new psychology of success* (5th ed.). New York, NY: Random House.

Eckman, P., & Shean, G. D. (1997). Habituation of cognitive and physiological arousal and social anxiety. *Behaviour Research and Therapy, 35,* 1113–1121.

Ekman, P., & Friesen, W. V. (1972). Hand movements. *The Journal of Communication, 22,* 353–374. doi:10.1111/j.1460-2466.1972.tb00163.x

Ellis, A. (1963). *Reason and emotion in psychotherapy.* New York, NY: Lyle-Stuart.

Giles, H., & Smith, P. (1979). Accommodation theory: Optimal levels of convergence. In H. Giles & R. N. St. Clair (Eds.), *Language and social psychology* (pp. 45–65). Baltimore, MD: University Park Press.

Gilovich, T., Medvec, V. H., & Savitsky, K. (2000). The spotlight effect in social judgment: An egocentric bias in estimates of the salience of one's own actions and appearance. *Journal of Personality and Social Psychology, 78,* 211–222. doi:10.1037//0022-3514.78.2.211

Glenn, E. C., Glenn, P. J., & Forman, S. H. (1989). *Your voice and articulation* (2nd ed.). Englewood Cliffs, NJ: Prentice Hall.

Gurung, R., Brickner, M., Leet, M., & Punke, E. (2017). Dressing "in code": Clothing rules, propriety, & perceptions. *Journal of Social Psychology, 158,* 1–5. doi:10.1080/00224545.2017.1331991

Haiman, F. S. (1949). An experimental study of the effects of ethos in public speaking. *Speech Monographs, 16,* 190–202. doi:10.1080/03637754909374974

Howlett, N., Pine, K. J., Cahill, N., Orakcioglu, I., & Fletcher, B. (2015). Unbuttoned: The interaction between provocativeness of female work attire and occupational status. *Sex Roles, 72,* 105–116. doi:10.1007/s11199-015-0450-8

Iberri-Shea, G. (2017). Adaptation and assessment of a public speaking rating scale. *Cogent Education, 4*(1), 1287390. doi:10.1080/2331186X.2017.1287390

Kelly, L., & Keaten, J. (1992). A test of the effectiveness of the reticence program at Pennsylvania State University. *Communication Education, 41*, 361–374. doi:10.1080/03634529209378898

Kendrick, K., & Holler, J. (2017). Gaze direction signals response preference in conversation. *Research on Language & Social Interaction, 50*, 12–32. doi:10.1080/08351813.2017.1262120

Krauss, R. M., Apple, W., Morency, N., Wenzel, C., & Winton, W. (1981). Verbal, vocal, and visible factors in judgments of another's affect. *Journal of Personality and Social Psychology, 40*, 312–320. doi:10.1037/0022-3514.40.2.312

Ladegaard, H. (1995). Audience design revisited: Persons, roles & power relations in speech interactions. *Language & Communication, 15*, 89–101. doi:10.1016/0271-5309(94)00017-7

McCroskey, J. C. (1977). Oral communication apprehension: A summary of recent theory and research. *Human Communication Research, 4*, 78–96. doi:10.1111/j.1468-2958.1977.tb00599.x

McCroskey, J. C. (1982). *An introduction to rhetorical communication* (4th ed.). Englewood Cliffs, NJ: Prentice Hall.

McRaney, D. (2011). *You are not so smart: Why you have too many friends on Facebook, why your memory is mostly fiction, & 46 other ways you're deluding yourself.* New York, NY: Gotham.

Menzel, K. E., & Carrell, L. J. (1994). The relationship between preparation and performance in public speaking. *Communication Education, 43*, 17–26. doi:10.1080/03634529409378958

Miller, G., & Hewgill, M. (1964). The effect of variations in nonfluency on audience ratings of source credibility. *Quarterly Journal of Speech, 50*, 36–44. doi:10.1080/00335636409382644

Oliver, J. (2019, February 24). *Last Week Tonight* – And now this: Oh no, that is the wrong tone for the story you're reporting [Video file]. Retrieved from www.youtube.com/watch?v=yFsiFUvChXo

Patzer, G. (1983). Source credibility as a function of communicator physical attractiveness. *Journal of Business Research, 11*, 229–241. doi:10.1016/0148-2963(83)90030-9

Pearson, J. C., Child, J. T., & Kahl, D. H., Jr. (2006). Preparation meeting opportunity: How do college students prepare for public speeches. *Communication Quarterly, 54*, 351–366. doi:10.1080/01463370600878321

Phillips, G. M. (1986). Rhetoritherapy: The principles of rhetoric in training shy people in speech effectiveness. In W. H. Jones, J. M. Cheek, & S. R. Briggs (Eds.), *Shyness: Perspectives on research and treatment* (pp. 357–374). New York, NY: Plenum.

Rodero, E., Potter, R. F., & Prieto, P. (2017). Pitch range variations improve cognitive processing of audio messages. *Human Communication Research, 43*, 397–413. doi:10.1111/hcre.12109

Rubin, R. B., Rubin, A. M., & Jordan, F. F. (1997). Effects of instruction on communication apprehension and communication competence. *Communication Education, 46*, 104–114. doi:10.1080/03634529709379080

Sawyer, C. R., & Behnke, R. R. (2002). Reduction in public speaking state anxiety during performance as a function of sensitization processes. *Communication Quarterly, 50*, 110–121. doi:10.1080/01463370209385649

Scherer, K. (1980). The functions of nonverbal signs in conversation. In R. St. Clair & H. Giles (Eds.), *The social & psychological contexts of language* (pp. 225–244). Hillsdale, NJ: Erlbaum.

Scherer, K., London, H., & Wolf, J. (1973). The voice of confidence: Paralinguistic cues & audience evaluation. *Journal of Research in Personality, 7*, 31–44. doi:10.1016/0092-6566(73)90030-5

Scogin, F., Rickard, H., Keith, S., Wilson, J., & McElreath, L. (1992). Progressive and imaginal relaxation training for elderly persons with subjective anxiety. *Psychology and Aging, 7*, 419–424. doi: 10.1037/0882-7974.7.3.419

Smith, B., Brown, B., Strong, W., & Rencher, A. (1975). Effects of speech rate on personality perception. *Language and Speech, 18*, 145–152. doi:10.1177/002383097501800203

Spitzberg, B. H., & Brunner, C. C. (1991). Toward a theoretical integration of context and competence inference research. *Western Journal of Speech Communication, 55*, 28–46. doi:10.1080/10570319109374369

Stampfl, T. (1966). Implosive therapy: The theory. In S. Armitage (Ed.), *Behavior modification techniques in treatment of emotional disorders* (pp. 12–21). Battle Creek, MI: VA Hospital.

Stel, M., van Dijk, E., Smith, P. K., van Dijk, W. W., & Djalal, F. M. (2012). Lowering the pitch of your voice makes you feel more powerful and think more abstractly. *Social Psychological and Personality Science, 3,* 497–502. doi:10.1177/1948550611427610

Taggart, L. R., Ozolins, L., Hardie, H., & Nyhof-Young, J. (2009). Look Good Feel Better workshops: A "big lift" for women with cancer. *Journal of Cancer Education, 24,* 94–99. doi:10.1080/08858190802664594

Trudgill, P. (1974). *The social differentiation of English in Norwich.* Cambridge, UK: Cambridge University Press.

Zhang, Q. (2014). Assessing the effects of instructor enthusiasm on classroom engagement, learning goal orientation, and academic self-efficacy. *Communication Teacher, 28,* 44–56. doi:10.1080/17404622.2013. 839047

One of the best ways to understand a new concept is through a story. Let me invite you into a story from some years ago . . .

As I waited on the screened-in porch to interview Ellie, a farmer's wife, I could see a small sparrow seeking refuge from the summer heat in a thicket of milkweed plants growing through the farm's field-fencing. I watched as the bird delicately perched on the firm milkweed pod and then disappeared into the tall grasses. It was on this day, nestled in by acres of tasseled corn, I met Ellie on the back porch of her farmhouse. There were dogs at my feet, kittens all around, chickens in the yard, and then a rough, cracked, and dirty hand was extended. "Hi, my name is Ron." We exchanged pleasantries, but he quickly picked up on my outsider status. By this point, I'd become used to being told, "You don't sound like you're from here—You from the city?" He meant Chicago, Illinois. He was inquisitive about the kinds of questions I would be asking his mother and how her responses were of interest to me. Luckily, Ron, a short, rather gruff-looking man, remembered me. Years ago, my mother-in-law and I came to their home to visit his mother Ellie to purchase two hand-raised parakeets. Ron's mom and his brother are known in the area for raising domesticated birds and for taking in orphaned animals, too. "Oh, yeah, you're the gal from the city," he said. "I remember you." And, just like that, the ice was broken. Ron's untamed beard jiggled as he laughed about my standing on his back porch.

In fact, we both laughed. In a way, I felt like I had to laugh. By laughing at my own *positionality* (my social position in relation to others) as someone from the "city," I made myself vulnerable to Ron and allowed him to see I was a human being, too. Honestly, I knew I needed him to trust me; otherwise, he wouldn't invite me in the home to see his mother. After all, I do not belong to the area, let alone his neighborhood. Neighborhoods are peculiar in the rural Midwest countryside, especially for an outsider, because they violate all of the traditional conceptions of how one from the city would imagine a neighborhood. The houses are few, the spaces are wide-open, and the only sounds are from livestock, tractors in the fields, and sometimes the sound of a car coming down the gravel lane. After a few moments, Ron yelled, "Ma, she's here!" And just like that, I realized I had crossed the threshold as an outsider into a protected space for insiders.

Source: Stevie Munz

View from Ellie's back porch

From this short vignette, you're introduced to the power and importance of perceptions in everyday interactions. You're also reminded of the complexity of identity in communicative interactions (see Chapter 6 for more on this). My presence on Ellie and Ron's back porch failed to match their expectations in this rural countryside both in how I dressed (wedge sandals, linen pants, flowy top) and in how I verbally communicated—with a Chicago accent (e.g., pronouncing "th" sounds in words like "this" or "that" with a "d" sound, as "dis" and "dat" or saying "tt" as a "dd" as in little/liddle or bottle/boddle). I was perceived as an outsider to the community, which in this case was quite accurate.

Perception is the process of gathering information about others and situations based on what we observe and how that information may or may not fit our ideas/beliefs. Our perceptions often influence how we interact with others, and fortunately, our perceptions are not fixed. Ron's perception of me changed once he remembered our prior interaction, which resulted in him trusting me, and he also altered his communication style. Notice how he became friendlier once his perceptions of me changed. Through this chapter, you'll learn about the role of perception in the communication process.

Building in Warren County, Illinois

Source: Stevie Munz

The Perception Process

Take a look at this image of the building in Warren County, IL. What do you see? You likely see a dilapidated building, tall uncut grass, and some trees. What else did you see? Did you notice the tombstone on the right side? Did you try to read the signs on the front of the building? Did you start imagining a story for the building or the space? From something as simple as a picture, there are so many cues we must process. Although our perceptions are influenced by society, it's an individual/unique process, which means that what you focused on in that picture, thought about, or tried to make sense of was different from everyone else. It doesn't make it right or wrong. It's just unique to you! Our perceptions build, challenge, and reinforce values, ideas, and beliefs as well as permeate and influence how we interact with others. But, what do you choose to pay attention to and how does this influence how you see or interact with others? Ultimately, the perception process can be broken down into four steps: selecting, organizing, interpreting, and remembering.

Selecting

Even a mundane experience is overwhelming if we try to perceive everything!

© Kwangmoozaa/Shutterstock.com

As we move about our social worlds, we are inundated with messages. Think about the last time you went to the grocery store. It should be a pretty simple task, right? But, consider how many stimuli you experienced through your five senses during your trip. Visually, you probably saw other shoppers and staff. What were they wearing? How were they acting? Did you check out the vivid colors of the produce? Auditorily, did you hear the sounds of plastic bags slide and rip off the rolls? Did you become curious when you heard a conversation about a local event? Was your store playing some hip tunes or soothing music? What about smells?

Did you smile when you smelled fresh-baked bread in the store? Think about touch. Did you pick up an oddly sticky package? Did you carefully examine each piece of fruit for bumps and bruises before you selected one to purchase? Did you rush through the freezer section because you got goosebumps? Did you sip a coffee while you shopped, or are you guilty of tasting every sample available? These weren't the only things you experienced, but they might be the only ones you noticed. There is no way we can pay attention to every message with the same attention or diligence, so we have to engage in *selection*, or a process of paying attention to some messages/stimuli and disregarding others. The ability to be able to handle so many stimuli should be considered a superpower in itself. There are several factors that influence which stimuli we notice or select, including selective attention, selective exposure, mood effects, and variations.

Selective Attention

Selective attention is the process of *choosing* to focus on one aspect of an environment or context. We engage in this process every day and so often throughout the day, it's engrained in how we move about the world. Take, for example, a common occurrence in a classroom: Your professor is discussing the intricacies of communication and a classmate is texting—*ding . . . ding . . . ding . . . ding.* Others are flipping through books and some are taking notes by hand and on keyboards—*scratch . . . click click click click . . . click . . . scratch.* Another classmate begins to unbox a slice of pizza. You smell *roasted garlic* and *sweet tomatoes* and hear the *crinkle* and *crunch* of the box opening and closing. In this moment, you see, hear, and smell aspects of these different experiences, but what you pay the most attention to is your professor talking (of course you do, pat yourself on the back). All of these sounds and smells are embedded in the environment, but you *choose* to pay attention to your professor. It's important to remember that if we're paying attention to one event or experience, this means that we're ignoring others.

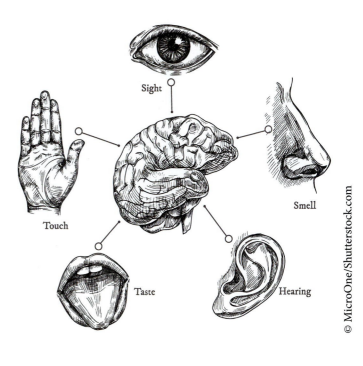

© MicroOne/Shutterstock.com

Selective Exposure

When we choose to open ourselves only to particular messages or experiences, our perceptions are shaped by ***selective exposure***. We typically use this strategy to select messages that align with our beliefs, values, and ideas. Although selective exposure can happen through face-to-face encounters, it can also happen through the media you encounter. Many social media websites and streaming services have algorithms that adjust the messages you receive based on your engagement with the website. Believe it or not, each day back in 2007, an individual saw an average of 5,000 advertisements (Story, 2007); think how much higher that amount must be today! There's no way you can see and process all of the ads, so as you scroll through your social media accounts or browse shopping websites, you engage in selective exposure. Some social media outlets like Instagram allow you to "like" users' content, which curates the messages you receive. It's important for us to be mindful (or aware) of how selective exposure may contribute to us reinforcing already held ideas, values, or beliefs. For example, actively choosing to read/watch news outlets that challenge your political beliefs can broaden and test your understanding; however, we have to *select* to expose ourselves to these messages. By broadening the types of messages we receive, we're more likely to understand the perceptions of people who are different from us.

Mood Effects

When people are sad, they tend to choose to listen to sad music (Van den Tol & Edwards, 2013). So, even our mood can cause a form of selective exposure. Our mood changes not only what we expose ourselves to, but also what we notice. Have you ever found yourself being ticked off by things you'd typically let slide because you were already in a bad mood? You might usually just walk by your roommate's socks on the floor—not even noticing

Admit it! Even you listen to sappy music sometimes.

© Phatthida Chinnawong/Shutterstock.com

them, but you had a bad day at work. So, all of a sudden you're yelling at your roommate for something that typically doesn't bother you. Your bad mood caused you to *select* (and attend to) a negative stimulus. Conversely, if you're feeling happy, you tend to notice pleasant or cheerful objects/interactions and blow off the negative ones. You did an amazing job on your speech (because you read your textbook and implemented our suggestions, of course) and got an A. Being pretty pumped about the situation, you didn't even notice the cashier at the cafeteria being rude to you.

Variations

Sometimes we choose to select stimuli because they're different—so they stand out. For example, your typically boisterous friend is remarkably quiet today. This variation in their behavior might cause you to pay attention to this stimulus. Some of my field-research has brought me to spaces that were largely unfamiliar to me—like interviewing farmers' wives in Western Illinois (Munz, 2019). As someone who did not grow up on a farm, I found myself surrounded by people who lived in similar, yet distinctly different ways. So, I sometimes picked up on things that varied from my typical day-to-day interactions, just as I posed a

Where does your focus go to when looking at this picture? That's selection due to variation in action.

© nukeaf/Shutterstock.com

significant variation to the individuals I was interviewing and interacting with. Remember the story at the beginning? My Chicago accent was much different from what Ron was used to hearing around the countryside and caused him to select/focus on my variance.

Organizing

Once we've engaged our stimuli-selection superpower (it *is* something we do without even thinking about it!), we then begin the next stage of the perception process: organization. *Organizing* is a superspeed brain-process of arranging information in a way that makes sense. This might seem simple, but it's actually quite complicated! We organize perceptions through **schemas**, which are mental categories based on our past experiences that we use to understand and respond to interactions (Macrae & Bodenhausen, 2001). There are four different types of schemas: prototypes, personal constructs, scripts, and stereotypes.

Prototypes

A *prototype* is an image, example, or model we have for a particular person, item, or situation. When you hear the word "professor", what do you think of? Do you imagine a gray-haired, White male wearing a sports coat with suede elbow patches? The image or idea that comes to mind is based off your previous experiences and interactions—from your life or even what you see in the media. You use prototypes such as the one you have for "professor" to help you organize your observations of how something does/doesn't fit with your category. You have prototypes in your mind for everything from the most mundane object (e.g., coffee cup) to more complicated experiences like romantic relationships. One of the most important aspects to understanding the prototype concept is to remember that it's subject to change and modification as you engage in more interactions. Although your instructor may fall within the described prototype, most likely they don't. Because prototypes aren't fixed or stable, we can change them with critical thinking or further exposure to new experiences and begin to develop more flexible prototypes and constructs.

Who did you imagine teaching your class?

Personal Constructs

Whereas prototypes are boxes/mental files we might try to put our observations in, *personal constructs* are essentially mental yardsticks/continuums we use to judge/rate a person/observation. These "ratings" include ranges such as: lazy to hardworking, smart to dumb, generous to stingy, pleasant to unpleasant, etc. As we interact and engage with our social world, we develop our own personal constructs, and in turn, use them to organize what we expect of individuals and situations we've selected to perceive. It's important to remember that all of this is based off your experiences. So, what you might consider lazy could be vastly different from what someone else perceives.

"Of course, since it's Tuesday, that cow only gets two scoops, for obvious reasons."

Cognitive complexity: Recognizing people are never just one thing.

© studiostoks/Shutterstock.com

Further, this means that some of us have more simple constructs, whereas others have more complex and sophisticated constructs for understanding their world. Here's what's really neat: As we mature and have more social interactions, our constructs can change (i.e., get more complex) too! Have you ever been around small children? You probably noticed how they have simple ways of understanding or perceiving the world (Hewer, 2017). Little kids have constructs like "friends = good, liked" and "not friends = bad, not liked" whereas, adults (at least those with higher cognitive complexity) understand they can still be friends with someone who might have flaws or still like someone who's otherwise bad. This is known as *cognitive complexity*, which refers to increased ways of thinking about others and interactions and having a variety of terms or mental files to access to identify/organize these experiences (Burleson & Samter, 1990). In other words, as we have more life experiences and develop more personal constructs with greater levels of complexity (or notches on our mental yardsticks), we're better able to distinguish intricacies and have greater depth to our organizational process.

Scripts

Although we use prototypes and personal constructs for people, places, and things, *scripts* provide an expected sequence of events and behaviors (Schank & Abelson, 1977). They allow us to organize events/situations based on our past experiences and exposure to media depicting these interactions. Think back to the grocery store example at the beginning of the chapter and what you do when you check out. You might place your items on a conveyer belt. Your cashier is apt to ask how you are as she or he scans your items. Perhaps an individual bags your groceries for you while you pay. Your script for the grocery store helps you understand how to process the information within the context. At every step in the process, you engage your script to decide what to do next. The more frequently you participate in a social environment, like a grocery store or restaurant, the more familiar you become with the expected "rules," so it becomes a relatively established script. Therefore, as we are in various situations and interactions, we attempt to organize what we observe based on how it does or doesn't fit our scripts.

You might be wondering, "What happens in unfamiliar situations?" In these situations, you rely on scripts from similar experiences that you feel will work well for the new environment. For example, Aldi has become the fastest growing grocery store chain in the United States (Tyler, 2018). Despite being a grocery store, the rules/scripts for checking out at the store are quite different from most chains. First, you have to bring your own quarter (i.e., a "cart deposit") to get a grocery cart—something not common in the U.S. but popular in Europe. Cashiers are known to be exceedingly fast to keep lines short (some patrons even race the cashier to get all their items on the belt before the cashier catches up!). The cashier places your items into a different cart than the one you used during your shopping. After payment, you switch out

Insert a quarter—Unlock a shopping adventure.

© Holli/Shutterstock.com

your now empty cart for the one your items are in and then go to a separate bagging area to bag your own groceries (with bags you're expected to bring yourself). After you're done with your cart, you return it to the cart corral to get back your "cart deposit." For a lot of people, their first Aldi's experience can be overwhelming. It's a grocery store, so the typical shopping script should fit, right? In some ways, it does, but there are also differences that cause disruption in your script. Each subsequent time you're in a new environment, you'll start **script scaffolding** (or building) for the experience and become better able to organize your experiences based on these new and improved scripts.

Stereotypes

Finally, let's talk about stereotypes, but let's get this out of the way first: The word "stereotype" has been misused in media and education! It isn't inherently bad! A **stereotype** is a generalization or assumption for an entire group of people, situation, or interaction based off the characteristics or traits of a few individuals in the group. Our brains use stereotypes to intentionally oversimplify and generalize an entire group of people, situations, or experiences (Stangor, 1988). They allow us to process information quickly without having to construct an entirely new mental file/box (prototype or construct) for every single thing/person we encounter. That would get exhausting!

For example, you see a woman wearing a Kurta (a collarless, loose-fitting, long garment) and assume she's from India because Indian women often wear Kurtas. When you engage in this stereotyping, it allows your brain to make superspeed classifications based on prior experiences. However, this speed comes with a sacrifice; you fail to recognize the nuance and complexity of what you might be perceiving. The woman could be from any number of nations and backgrounds. We develop stereotypes for all types of social interactions and environments based on our previous experiences, the media we've been exposed to, how we were raised, and myriad other factors. Although stereotyping (as a process in our heads) is not actually a "bad" thing on its own, there are major problems IF we use it to categorize/organize and then treat individuals as if they embody all of the qualities and characteristics of the stereotype. In other words, if we use them as a hard, fast rule/truth, not a mental, organizational guide, we get ourselves in trouble.

One problem with how we *use* stereotypes (the stereotypes themselves are NOT *bad*) is that they may be based on inaccuracies and/or assigned to entire groups, so we miss out on individuality. For example, what stereotypes do you have about women? Yes, I know you might be uncomfortable saying you have stereotypes about anyone, but you do have them! We all do! It's impossible NOT to have them because it's a natural, automatic brain process! In your mind, is a woman caring? Does she have children or want them or, at the very least, is good with children? Does she like shopping and the color pink? If we place a stereotype on how all women perform gender, their identity, or relationships, we'll be left with an understanding that is inaccurate and may result in both inappropriate and ineffective communication.

Now, because you were probably mis-taught that stereotypes are bad, let's talk about what people actually mean when they incorrectly use this term. The concepts that are actually considered "bad" as you know them include prejudice, discrimination, and biases that can lead to microaggressions. *Prejudice* is an emotional reaction to a stereotyped group or to an individual who belongs to the group (Hecht, 1998). Sometimes prejudice can include positive emotional responses if your stereotype for the group is positive. For example, if you're thrilled because a Chinese student is assigned to your math workgroup, that's a "positive" prejudice because it assumes all "Asians" are good at math. Or, in the case of *benevolent sexism*, we "put women on a pedestal" and "worship" them as "refined" beings (well, some people do). In the long run, neither of these "positive" prejudices is really *positive* as they both attempt to put concrete standards on unique and evolving beings. More often, prejudice is clearly negative and results in disgust, anxiety, anger, fear, or negative feelings (Allen, 2010).

Is this discrimination or prejudice?

©fizkes/Shutterstock.com

If a person acts or communicates differently with an individual from a stereotyped group, this is known as *discrimination* (Kurylo, 2013). For example, a company might discriminate by offering a lower wage to a female employee who is doing similar work as a male. Another example is whenever young, Black youth in a store, who have been stereotyped as criminals, are followed by employees (because they're believed to be shoplifting) or forcibly removed from the store. As illegal and just plain infuriating as these behaviors are, they're unfortunately a common occurrence.

Finally, *blatant bias* is a conscious decision to discriminate or otherwise enact prejudicial behaviors or communication, whereas *subtle bias* is the unexamined and unconscious decision to let our prejudice guide our actions or communication (Fiske, 2019). Although many of us do not engage in blatant bias and intolerance, we may engage in subtle bias and intolerance more often than you might think—which can influence how we talk to individuals and may result in microaggressions. *Microaggressions* are everyday comments or actions that intentionally or unintentionally communicate hostility or negativity toward another individual (Sue, 2010). For example, a message like: "Wow, you speak English really well" received by an Asian American woman implies that she is "foreign." Or, "Is that your real hair? Can I touch it?" is a message frequently received by Black women and suggests their hair is an exotic object to be questioned (e.g., wig or their own "real" hair). These comments may not have been explicitly chosen to make the other feel uncomfortable. Nonetheless, whether intended as hostile or not, these messages not only say something about your perceptual categories for others but influence how others perceive you.

Stereotyping allows us to quickly organize stimuli we select, but communication taken to the level of prejudice or discrimination is harmful, damaging, and makes life difficult, especially for members of minority groups. Remember, stereotyping is not inherently negative or bad—it's what we do with these organizational categories. How we verbally and nonverbally communicate with others is what matters. The key is to become *aware* of our perceptions and how they influence our interactions.

Interpretation

The third step in the perception process is *interpretation*, or assigning meaning to what we observe. Again, this is a step that usually happens so fast we don't even know it (we "jump" to conclusions); bet you didn't realize how many innate powers you really have! There are many influences on our interpretations of people, contexts, social interactions, and messages. And to understand this better, an important theoretical perspective for you to be aware of is *Attribution Theory*, which asserts that we make causal inferences about why people behave the way they do (Heider, 1958). You

Why is she falling? Are your attributions internal or external?

© fotoliza/Shutterstock.com

saw someone trip on the sidewalk. Why did they trip? They're clumsy? The sidewalk is in disrepair? You probably didn't even "think" about it—you just made a quick, snap judgment/assumption, or attribution.

Our *attributions* (perceived motives for behavior) are either internal or external associations about people/things (Heider, 1958). An *internal attribution* is when we assume someone's behavior is reflective of "who they are inside." Consider this example: Someone is taking too long to order at a restaurant, so you assume the person is stupid and

Activism Hero: Perception-Checking for Change-Makers

There are so many biases that can influence our perception process. So, what do we do to actually counteract some of these things and make change in the world around us? Well, you've already taken the first step—simply starting to be aware of them, challenging yourself to overcome biases in your daily life. Remember, bias isn't "bad"—we all have it; it's what makes us human. But, if you want to strive to conquer your own cognitive kryptonite, consider the critical-thinking skill of **perception-checking**—a three-step process you can go through any time you want to counteract the role of biases in your communication and to make the unconscious process of perception into a *conscious*, activist process of analysis.

Step 1: Describe behavior—Figure out what behavior triggered your perception process. Ask yourself (out-loud, if necessary), "What exactly am I perceiving/attending to— what behavior or language or visual cue is leading me to feel or think certain ways?" For example, maybe I'm feeling positive toward someone because they're wearing glasses. By doing this, you're isolating specific things that led to your brain *selecting* cues to focus on. This is usually the most challenging step.

Step 2: Form possible interpretations—Force yourself to come up with *at least* two possible, different interpretations for the behavior. WHY did the cue occur? For my liking someone because they wore glasses, it may be because (a) I think everyone with glasses is smart so I liked them *or* (b) I wear glasses and assume they're similar to me and so I liked them. But, even these explanations are similar, positive beliefs, so I have to challenge myself on how valid they are and why I might have them. Is everyone with glasses really smart (and what are my biases/background for thinking that? Society? Culture? Media? Personal Experience?)? Does wearing glasses mean they're similar to me? How many people wear glasses who are NOT like me? Can I think of specific examples to support it—like people I hate who wear glasses? In other words, critically evaluate your *own* interpretations.

Step 3: Get clarification—If you can, always go directly to the source. Ask the person questions, get to know them, and maybe, in some cases, even directly ask them things that your brain stereotyped—to see if you're right/wrong. In situations where you can't ask the person directly for clarification, you can always ask around about them, look online, and/or just find examples of other instances where your perceptions are accurate AND times when they're inaccurate. By doing this, you're making sure you have an outside source, who might help you check yourself before you wreck yourself.

MOST people RARELY, if EVER, do these steps. But, good activists or change-makers do! And that, my fellow bias-monkeys, is why biases, injustice, rudeness, and ultimately unfounded hate exist in this world. It's a simple fix we can do to begin to address difficult problems!

Contributed by J. Eckstein

indecisive. If, however, you perceive the person is taking too long to order because they can't hear the server speak or it's too dark to see the menu, then you're practicing *external attribution*, or assigning their behavior as caused by environmental or outside factors. The assertions we make about people's behaviors are part of the process of interpretation—making sense of what we perceive.

But, why did your mind jump to the conclusion that someone behaved the way they did? We each have a unique lens through which we perceive the world around us, and in turn, interpret what we perceive. Your lenses through which you make your interpretations are often influenced by culture, media, and personal experiences.

Culture

Have you ever thought about *all* of the different cultural groups you belong to? Take a moment to write down as many as you can; you should be able to easily identify at least 20 quickly! We belong to specific religious communities, nationalities, racial or ethnic groups, national heritages, social movements, gender identities, and socioeconomic backgrounds—just to name a few (see Chapter 14)! The cultural groups we belong to may be majority or minority groups and therefore also have differentiated levels of power and influence in society. And, although you'll read more about your *self* in Chapter 6, right now it's important to know how our cultural background influences the ways we understand and interpret the world.

You may live among people who look, communicate, and live their lives in ways similar to or different from you. Differences can be visible, like a Muslim woman wearing a hijab, or invisible, like a domestic violence survivor who has depression and anxiety. According to *Standpoint Theory*, because of our unique cultural backgrounds, we each have a particular lens through which we see and interpret the world (Harding, 2004). Our standpoints shape our views, perspectives, outlooks, and positions, and in turn, influence our communicative behaviors. Think back to Ron at the beginning of this chapter. As a White male in his 50s to 60s from and living in rural Illinois, he sees and interprets the world differently than me, a White female in her 30s from Chicago and living in Utah. How does YOUR standpoint influence your perceptions? I want to encourage you to appreciate the ways your cultural groupings shape

Standpoints are multiple and complex.

© Jesus Sanz/Shutterstock.com

and influence your perceptions and interpretations. Even if you have an identical twin, your standpoint is unique because of your lived experience and will ultimately result in perceptions and interpretations different from everyone else's.

Media

As you're reading this chapter, you are likely being inundated with dings, bings, and chimes. These familiar sounds indicate you're connected to modern media, such as social platforms, news outlets, email, and video streaming services. Whether connecting with friends, browsing international news stories, or watching a favorite superhero movie, we experience digital, audio, and print channels that influence our interpretations of what we've selected to perceive. From magazines to billboards, they all create and reinforce our understanding of our social world in terms of beauty ideals, gender and family role expectations, and cultural values. For example, according to the Centers for Disease Control and Prevention (2017),

Thin or thick, wrinkles or not—You're still beautiful.

the average American woman is just over 5′3″ and weighs 170.5 lbs. How do these stats compare to the average model you see in advertisements? Whether we like it or not, the media often shapes our interpretations of something as good or bad, pretty or ugly, etc., so it's essential that we critically examine and evaluate these messages (you'll learn more about this in Chapter 15) in order to become aware of how they influence our perceptions.

Personal Experiences

Unless you have amnesia, it's impossible to enter a communication interaction without being influenced by previous personal experiences. Think of these previous experiences as a backpack you carry with you everywhere you go; it might be filled with positive or negative encounters, and together, they shape our perceptions and interpretations as we move through social interactions and contexts.

For example, maybe you're the person who's never had a cavity, so going to the dentist is a breeze for you. Your interpretation of the dentist's behavior is likely neutral or positive. However, if your dentist appointments have been filled with torture, it's unlikely you'll interpret dentists' behaviors in positive ways—even if they only have the best intentions. Our past personal experiences also influence whether we decide to remain open or closed-off to people or interactions. Imagine you dated someone from a particular fraternity or sorority but discovered he or she was a horrible person. Your personal experience is not only apt to encourage you to interpret others from that sorority/frat as horrible but will also keep you from even selectively exposing yourself to interact with them in the first place (thus, confirming and reinforcing any biases you may have construed due to lack of more encounters that could change your mind). But, as ethical communicators, we should think critically about how our past experiences are influencing our own perceptions and behaviors—and challenge ourselves to overcome them.

Public Speaking Power: Habituation & De-Sensitization

When giving a speech, it's common to think the audience notices every little mistake we make or stares at some perceived flaw on our bodies. But, nothing could be further from the truth! Unless your audience contains a true sociopath, no one is delighting in your failures or hoping you'll fumble. When you start to believe things are worse than they are, your perceptions are being overrun by something called the *spotlight effect*, which makes you paranoid people are judging you. To address common cognitive barriers in our perceptions, here are some facts (i.e., supported by numerous studies over the years! See Chapter References for some researched examples) about speaking you should know:

- Almost everyone gets nervous or anxious before public speaking; it's *normal* to have surging adrenaline in these times! But, guess what? Research suggests even though public speaking may *feel* horrible for some people, it DOES NOT AFFECT THE OUTCOME QUALITY. Even if you're one of the few people with extreme speech anxiety, realize that if you do your planning ahead of time (see Ch. 2) and practice (see Ch. 4), your anxiety won't likely hurt your grade. People typically won't even know you're nervous or you made a mistake unless you tell them! It's all in YOUR perception!

- For most people, psychological and physiological anxieties related to speeches are highest in the minute right before you start speaking, and they go away within the first minute. So know that once you start, it only gets BETTER (this is called *habituation*). **Just begin, and you'll be closer to feeling more confident already!**

- For those people who *actually have* (and don't just *feel* like they do) diagnosed speech anxiety, the process of *sensitization* (or how "difficult" the task is framed/perceived to be before beginning) is what makes this particularly bad for them. Luckily, there are two ways to deal with this:

  - Your professors have likely already addressed one way for you, by making the simpler speech assignments the ones you start with. Starting with the easiest stuff makes it easier to progress your way to the more complex assignments. This process is called *de-sensitization*.

  - Another way YOU can make things easier is to continually expose yourself to the problem—repeatedly *do* the thing you're afraid of. Soon, you'll likely see it's not that bad. Yes, this is *supported* by research when it comes to public speaking. In fact, one of the things that actually *contributes to* people's speech anxiety is avoiding speaking! So, quit fretting about it and just do it!

Contributed by J. Eckstein

Memories and Remembering

A final part of the perception process includes memories and remembering. People recall everything from the most mundane to fantastic of experiences, which all color our lenses and how we perceive the world. We have so many experiences and as a result, so many memories, that to be able to handle them all, our brains engage in **selective memory bias**, a cognitive "trick" where our biases enhance or impair our recall of memories (Fletcher & Fitness, 1996). The information we retain from our interactions is selective because it always involves remembering, forgetting, and sometimes even fabricating. That's right, sometimes, we unknowingly "make up" aspects of our memories which influence our perceptions! I bet you didn't even know you had the abilities of Metamind!

Our memories are relational, dynamic, evolving, creative, and fragile; they're not perfect copies of actual happenings. It's messy! Even as we share stories about our experiences, our memory of those moments changes based on our current feelings or relationships with the people embedded in the story (Jackson, 2005). Simply put: We may remember an experience in a more positive way if we have a good relationship with the person related to the memory, or the memory itself may be influenced by a strained or stressed relationship. Let's say you're in a romantic relationship, and everything seems to be going fine until one day your partner stops texting and talking to you. You're completely in the dark about what happened (i.e., you get "ghosted"). Because of your negative feelings toward your former partner, the way in which you recall even happy events in that relationship can be clouded with a negative affect. And, what you remember of your experiences in a romantic relationship can continue to shape expectations for current and future encounters—which then shape your likelihood of attending to certain "cues" in the future—bringing us back to the beginning stage of perception once again . . .

Summary

In this chapter, you were introduced to the complexities of perception. It's a lot to absorb and understand! Nonetheless, it's important as ethical human beings that we each consider *how* perception influences our interactions, interpretations, and ultimately our sense of self (covered next in Chapter 6). Look around the space you're in while reading this chapter, thinking about what you've paid attention to and what you might've ignored. Perhaps now, you'll also question some of your memories. Hopefully, relationships and interactions will look different to you because you'll think about them more carefully . . . becoming more cognitively complex. And, *that* is yet another superpower you can work on developing!

© Rawpixel.com/Shutterstock.com

References

Allen, B. J. (2010). *Difference matters: Communicating social identity* (2nd ed.). Long Grove, IL: Waveland Press.

Beatty, M. J. (1988). Situational and predispositional correlates of public speaking anxiety. *Communication Education, 37*, 28–39. doi:10.1080/03634528809378701

Behnke, R. R., & Sawyer, C. R. (1998). Conceptualizing speech anxiety as a dynamic trait. *Southern Communication Journal, 63*, 160–168. doi:10.1080/10417949809373086

Burleson, B. R., & Samter, W. (1990). Effects of cognitive complexity on the perceived importance of communication skills in friends. *Communication Research, 17*, 165–182. doi:10.1177/009365090017002002

Centers for Disease Control and Prevention. (2017, May 3). *Body measurements.* Retrieved from www.cdc.gov/nchs/fastats/body-measurements.htm

Fiske, S. T. (2019). Prejudice, discrimination, and stereotyping. In R. Biswas-Diener & E. Diener (Eds.), *Noba textbook series: Psychology* [online copy]. Champaign, IL: DEF Publishers. Retrieved from http://noba.to/jfkx7nrd

Fletcher, G. J. O., & Fitness, J. (1996). *Knowledge structures in close relationships: A social psychological approach.* Mahwah, NJ: Psychology Press.

Gilovich, T., Medvec, V. H., & Savitsky, K. (2000). The spotlight effect in social judgment: An egocentric bias in estimates of the salience of one's own actions and appearance. *Journal of Personality and Social Psychology, 78*, 211–222. doi:10.1037//0022-3514.78.2.211

Harding, S. (2004). Introduction: Standpoint theory as a site of political, philosophical, and scientific debate. In S. Harding (Ed.), *The feminist standpoint theory reader: Intellectual and political controversies* (pp. 1–16). New York, NY: Routledge.

Harris, K. B., Sawyer, C. R., & Behnke, R. R. (2006). Predicting speech state anxiety from trait anxiety, reactivity, and situational influences. *Communication Quarterly, 54*, 213–226. doi:10.1080/01463370600650936

Hecht, M. L. (1998). *Communicating prejudice.* Thousand Oaks, CA: Sage Publications.

Heider, F. (1958). *The psychology of interpersonal relations.* Hoboken, NJ: John Wiley & Sons.

Hewer, M. (2017). Perception and play: How children view the world. *APS Observer, 30*(5). Retrieved from www.psychologicalscience.org/observer/perception-and-play-how-children-view-the-world

Jackson, S. (2005). Touchable stories and the performance of infrastructural memory. In D. Pollock (Ed.), *Remembering oral history performance* (pp. 45–66). New York, NY: Palgrave Macmillan.

Klonowicz, T. (1987). Reactivity and the control of Arousal. In J. Strelau & H. J. Eysenck (Eds.), *Personality dimensions and arousal* (pp. 183–196). New York, NY: Plenum Press.

Klonowicz, T., Zawadzka, G., & Zawadzhi, B. (1987). Reactivity, arousal, and coping with stress. *Personality and Individual Differences, 8,* 793–798. doi:10.1016/0191-8869(87)90132-2

Kurylo, A. (2013). *Inter/cultural communication: Representation and construction of culture.* Los Angeles, CA: SAGE Publications.

Macrae, C. N., & Bodenhausen, G. V. (2001). Social cognition: Categorical person perception. *British Journal of Psychology, 92,* 239–255. doi:10.1348/000712601162059

Mineka, S., & Thomas, C. (1999). Mechanisms of change in exposure therapy for anxiety disorders. In T. Dalgleish & M. J. Power (Eds.), *Handbook of cognition and emotion* (pp. 747–764). Chichester, UK: John Wiley & Sons.

Munz, S. M. (2019, in press). Oral histories: Stories from the farmer's wife in western Illinois. *Women & Language, 42*(2). Forthcoming at www.womenandlanguage.org/

O'Donohue, W., & Krasner, L. (1995). Theories of behavior therapy: Philosophical and historical contexts. In W. O'Donohue & L. Krasner (Eds.), *Theories of behavior therapy: Exploring behavior change* (pp. 1–22). Washington, DC: American Psychological Association.

Sawyer, C. R., & Behnke, R. R. (1999). State anxiety patterns and the behavioral inhibition system. *Communication Reports, 12,* 34–41. doi:10.1080/08934219909367706

Sawyer, C. R., & Behnke, R. R. (2002). Reduction in public speaking state anxiety during performance as a function of sensitization processes. *Communication Quarterly, 50,* 110–121. doi:10.1080/01463370209385649

Schank, R. C., & Abelson, R. P. (1977). *Scripts, plans, goals and understanding: An inquiry into human knowledge structures.* Oxford, UK: Lawrence Erlbaum.

Stangor, C. (1988). Stereotype accessibility and information processing. *Personality and Social Psychology Bulletin, 14,* 694–708. doi:10.1177/0146167288144005

Story, L. (2007, January 15). Anywhere the eye can see, it's likely to see an ad. *The New York Times.* Retrieved from www.nytimes.com/2007/01/15/business/media/15everywhere.html

Sue, D. W. (2010). *Microaggressions in everyday life: Race, gender, and sexual orientation.* Hoboken, NJ: John Wiley & Sons.

Tyler, J. (2018, August 19). 13 things you never knew about Aldi, the German grocery chain that's coming straight for Walmart and Kroger. *Business Insider.* Retrieved from www.businessinsider.com/aldi-store-facts-2018-8

Van den Tol, A., & Edwards, J. (2013). Exploring a rationale for choosing to listen to sad music when feeling sad. *Psychology of Music, 41,* 440–465. doi:10.1177/0305735611430433

Wolpe, J. (1995). Reciprocal inhibition: Major agent of behavior change. In W. O'Donohue & L. Krasner (Eds.), *Theories of behavior therapy: Exploring behavior change* (pp. 23–57). Washington, DC: American Psychological Association.

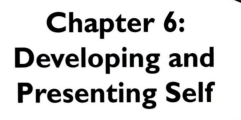

**Chapter 6:
Developing and
Presenting Self**

**Contributed by
Dr. Jessica Eckstein**

Communication is central to everything that makes us human (or animal, for that matter). On the one hand, *what* and *how* we say and do things forms our ***self-concept***, or who we feel we are or want to be. That self-concept combines with internal and external attributes of ourselves, like our ideas and experiences, to make up our ***identity***. On the flip side, identities do their own part to shape what we say and how we communicate things to ourselves and others. Put another way, communication influences who we are over time; but also, because our identity informs how we communicate, it's a constant, reciprocal, mutually influential process (Burke & Reitzes, 1981).

These interacting factors of self-other-communication are why we study self/identity in an intro communication class. In this chapter, we'll first see the different processes that go into how we become who "we are" to ourselves and others. Then, by looking at the different types of identity that come out of those processes, with some often-studied examples of each, we'll be able to see how our identities and communication are inseparable from the world around us. Finally, by discussing examples of identity aspects that tend to influence us most, we'll examine the actual ways identities affect our communication and ultimately, how these superpowers can be used by *you*, as an activist, for good and for evil.

Identity Processes

You already know our identity is made up of not just how we view ourselves but is constantly shaped by how others see us as well. ***Self-presentation*** involves all of my behaviors I do to communicate my identity to other people. It's what I do as a type of performance to present myself—what I choose to say, how I say it, what I wear, and other things—to act toward you based on the role I want to take on and how I want you to treat me. My communication to you shapes how I see myself and vice-versa. Goffman (1959) talked about these things as though we're all actual performers; he likened life to Shakespeare's line that all the "world is a stage, and all the men and women merely [actors who play] . . . many parts" (Act II, Scene VII, Lines 139–143).

On the flip side, ***altercasting*** is what I do to show you what I think should be *your* identity; my communication shapes what I want from you or want you to be (Weinstein & Deutschberger, 1963). In other words, how I treat you affects how I see myself as well. If I view myself as a nice person, then I'd better be nice to you; if I'm disrespectful to you, it means I view your identity as worth less than mine; and if I flirt with you, it indicates I view you as an attractive person who's apt to be receptive to my flirty communication. My communication toward you tells you how I see you *and* also shapes both our ideas of your identity. I'm *casting* you (alter means "the other") in a role as another character in my play on the stage of life.

And, we don't just do these things in face-to-face interactions with others. We use social media to self-reinforce identities; we rely on how others treat us to determine how we feel. For example, if someone's always leaving mean comments about me, over time I may begin to feel I'm deserving of them; they have cast me into the part of someone who's not worth nice treatment. Or, individuals start depending upon "likes" to justify their self-worth.

Looking at ego-needs (like how we want others to treat or altercast us) and identity fulfillment (like how we self-present), Toma and Hancock (2013) found people's social media feeds reinforced who they felt they were to others (duh!); more importantly, after a blow to their egos, people were more likely to go look at their feeds "in an unconscious effort to repair their perceptions of self-worth" (p. 321). They were hoping they'd find

Does social media impact how you view yourself? Do you present yourself a particular way online?

more nice messages altercasting them positively to offset the blow they'd taken to their self-esteem. So basically, it sucks—for us *and* for the interpersonal interaction—when our own self-perceptions (especially good ones) aren't reinforced by others.

When our perceptions *are* reinforced, however, it can be fantastic! So, we're all kind of like walking *self-fulfilling* (sometimes, *self-defeating*) *prophecies* when we act in ways that unintentionally make things true that might not otherwise happen (Merton, 1948). Magneto thinks mutants are oppressed by humans, so he acts like a dick to people, who then just react by oppressing him, thus proving his original discrimination theory (even though *he's* the one who brought it about by altercasting humans as the evil oppressors)! By acting these ways, we confirm and reinforce both our self-presentations and the ways others have altercast us. In other words, not only can we prophesize our own behaviors and identities but also others'.

Beyond these prophecies, we also figure out who we are in a way described by *Social Comparison Theory*, which in its simplest form says we judge ourselves against others, often within our peer group, to determine our worth. In an era when selves are not only in-person but also online, it's not unusual for us to compare ourselves to what others are presenting. But, that's the key . . . presenting. What you or others put online is still a presentation of self, and often, this presentation is simply a show. How often do you think people actually post the first selfie they take? One without a filter? Yeah, thought so. Even knowing that, we engage in comparisons with these images; perhaps because of this, some research finds a link between higher social media usage and higher rates of depression (Brunborg & Burdzovic, 2019). Whether online or offline, sometimes these comparisons can cause negative feelings ("I didn't get as good a grade as she did, so I'm obviously not very smart"), but we also might use them to feel better about ourselves (Festinger, 1954). We do this in two main ways. First, if we feel bad about ourselves, we often make *downward social comparisons* by looking at those worse off than us so we feel we're different/better than them: "Thank Krypton I'm not so weak as these mere mortals," thinks Superman. We also make **upward social comparisons** when we try feeling like we're one of the elite or part of the dominant group in order to feel inspired: "With my new Spidey-senses, I'm totally gonna be one of the Avengers," thinks the young Peter Parker.

Because others influence us over our lifetime just as much as (or more than) we influence ourselves, we end up having two main types of self. And no, this isn't a multiple personality thing. Goffman

Do we present our perceived self?

© pathdoc/Shutterstock.com

(1959) talked about our "selves" in terms of performing our identity in "front of curtain" and "backstage" areas. Our **perceived self** is who we believe ourselves to be deep down inside, or how we act "backstage" when no one's viewing us, and we don't have to be "on" for anyone. Whereas our **presenting self**, sometimes overlapping with a **Looking Glass Self** (or how we think others are viewing us, like in a mirror), is who we want others to believe we are (Baumeister & Hutton, 1987). This presenting self is usually based on what we think the socially approved image is for the context. So, it's like us reciting the right "lines" for our role when we're "on stage" (Goffman, 1959); another way to view this is in terms of social scripts (discussed in Chapter 5). Basically, our presenting selves are governed by social norms, or what we believe society (the audience) wants us to do and look like.

However, how we perceive ourselves and how we present ourselves do not always coincide with one another. I happen to believe I'm an extreme introvert, but because my job depends on it, I have to present to others as an energetic extrovert while teaching. When this mismatch happens, all hell breaks loose. Okay, not really. But, constantly contradicting them may cause discomfort for us when we feel we're never being "true" to ourselves. That begs the question, what is our "true" self?

Types of Identities

Our true identity is plural; we have identities or "selves" rather than one self. But, here's the thing: Different aspects of ourselves are more important (or *salient*) to us at certain times than at others. Not every single part of our identity plays a role in every moment of our life. Different self-aspects come out in different ways while communicating with different people at different times. So obviously, I'm not going to perceive myself (and thus, act/behave) the same way with my romantic partner as I would with my brothers. Those are completely different roles. And also, it would be rather skeevy to treat lovers like brothers or mothers (despite what John Mayer sings).

© Mikhail_Kayl/Shutterstock.com

Are these siblings or lovers? How can you tell?

© 4 PM productions/Shutterstock.com

Because identities both shape and are shaped by communication with other people, an ideal way to look at them is in terms of social interactions with others. The cool thing is that, to *some* extent, we get to decide how we want to be perceived. Tracy (2002) created a model that looks at the different things that affect our various identities. The figure at the top of the next page shows how variable our identity is. The *stable, preexisting* aspect refers to things that don't usually change unless we have some major life event like surgery or a huge trauma, whereas the *situational, negotiated* aspects are those that vary according to each person/encounter we interact with. The other continuum deals with how widespread something is, or how unique it makes us compared to others around us. The *social group* refers to features people share and that societies tend to categorize or group together, shown in things like census forms, social media groups, or categories that marketers target, whereas the *personal features* are those specific to individuals, like tastes or preferences that are unique to us.

This diagram shows how the two axes work together to form quadrants, which result in four main identity types Tracy (2002) called Master, Personal, Interactional, and Relational. I'll cover each of these types by discussing examples that most often come up in our daily lives when we communicate with others.

Personal Identities

If you have some aspect of yourself that'll stay pretty much the same over time (*stable/preexisting*) and is also specific to you as an individual (*personal*), it's called a **personal identity**. First, although we grow and change over time, much of us remains the same. Tastes in music types, types of food we like/dislike, kinds of hobbies we tend to enjoy—I can make changes to any of these things in my life, but overall, they'll remain relatively similar over time. For example, I might decide to take up knitting as a new hobby, but it's in keeping with my long-term preference for activities I can do with my hands and not think about—which are the types of things I enjoy and already do (like mindless iPad games or eating in front of TV).

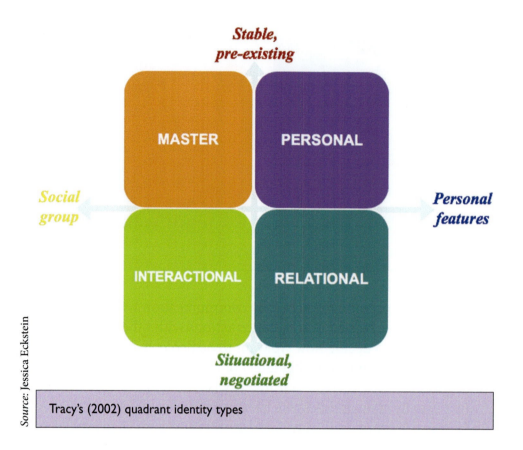

Source: Jessica Eckstein

Tracy's (2002) quadrant identity types

The second aspect, the specific to *you* part, means other people might form a club to share the interest with you, but there aren't set cultural expectations for how those people "should" communicate just because they're members of that club. A country-music lover might wear cowboy boots and jeans or they might wear sweatpants and sandals. Either way, they don't usually get socially judged for being a country-music lover *because* they also wear one or the other—they get to like music in whatever way they like it.

Beyond tastes and hobbies, another main way personal identities tend to affect us in life are through personalities. Do you (or others) consider yourself to be a Positive Pollyanna or a Debbie-Downer? An Honest Harry or a Lying Leonard? Team Edward or Team Jacob? Given a choice, I tend to be a pretty big introvert; most days, I'd prefer to stay home with my dogs and read a book while I'm deep in the middle of the woods. And though there are days when I like to go out with pals or when I'm forced to go to work and interact with many people, my personal identity as an introvert still is going to shape the majority of my interactions.

Master Identities

Master identities are unlikely to change (*stable/preexisting*) and entail things for which we're usually grouped with expectations by society (*social group*). For example, I was called a girl/female at birth because of the genitalia the doctors saw and decided to label me.

And based on that classification, people in my society communicate with me (and I with them) in certain ways (e.g., asking me if I need help putting air in my car tires . . . yeah, seriously). My status as a "female" is not likely to change unless I undergo some pretty serious operations or drug treatments. Additionally, there are social expectations for how people in the "girl" (versus "boy") group act or should look. When I was about 6 years old, I was wearing a super 80s (big ruffles, plastered in flowers) dress and cute little girly shoes to a new church when the pastor came out and said in a big, gruff voice, "And, how are you doin' today, son?" Would it make more sense (or be more acceptable) if I told you I also had really short hair then? This old guy was basically choosing one cue to read my master identity rather than looking for congruity among all the cues. In his old-school view, boys = short hair and girls = long hair, and that's all there was to it.

Other examples of master identities (and expectations that go with them) would be age groupings (e.g., old/young or teen/adult/child or Baby Boomer/Millenial), race (e.g., White/Black/Latinx), and average-for-my-age height (tall/short). We have very clear societal expectations for each of these groups as opposed to others—so much so that marketers even sell the same product in different ways (and for different amounts!) to different master categories! This is something called the "pink tax" and includes any product or service that costs more *because* it's marketed to women.

THE PINK TAX

The same product at different prices: Pink tax is based on Master identities

© astel design/Shutterstock.com

Further, although we can sometimes technically "pass" as a member of a master group we weren't assigned to, it's extremely difficult to do so—which has implications for people across their lifetime. Assuming people get to "choose" all their identities doesn't recognize that some of these categories are imposed on us and/or applied (e.g., pink tax) in ways that can be coercive, constraining, and have political consequences (Kroskrity, 2000). It means there are often some things society assigns to (or expects from) our groups that we have no control over. This is particularly true in what's considered the most fundamental "division" or group-categorization in society—sex, and its assumed-accompaniment, gender.

Sex, the physical and chromosomal category you're placed into at birth (although usually, this lifelong assignment is made much more simply by some dude just looking at your baby penis/vulva and calling it as they see it), is one of the most basic aspects of people's identities. Some say it's THE fundamental *master status* identity around which everything else is determined! Despite its importance (or lack thereof!), words we use to describe this

Master identity status can be hard to change.

particular master status identity are often thrown around so loosely in our culture, we've actually mistaken some key terms. So first, we need to clarify them.

Sex refers to your biological categorization and in our society is usually given the label *male* or *female*. This is itself problematic because a good number of babies are born *intersexed*, possessing ambiguous or both "male" and "female" characteristics. It happens more than you probably think (you just don't hear about it because their sex was chosen *for them* in the hospital)!

Gender, on the other hand, only refers to the way people enact or communicate their identity to others, usually combining some levels of both *masculinity* and *femininity*; it ranges on a spectrum from one extreme to the other but shifts situationally. Unfortunately, people almost always use the term "gender" incorrectly nowadays—to refer to male/female (sex) instead. The reason for this is largely because, historically, we've equated masculinity with males and femininity with females . . . which is obviously problematic. You're assigned (without much choice in the matter) to a sex-group. You have somewhat more choice when it comes to your gender performance. In other words, sex is a master identity, whereas gender, or *how you communicate/interact with others*, is more of a relational identity, which we'll cover shortly.

Consider some established trends: Vulgar language is more acceptable when said by males than by females (Jay & Jay, 2013); females are more likely to be raped and susceptible to abuse from intimates than are males (Breiding et al., 2014; Desmarais, Reeves, Nicholls, Telford, & Fiebert, 2012); and females, on average, still make less money for the same job as do males (American Association of University Women, 2019). Each of these facts mean that if I was biologically assigned by doctors as a female (and that's recorded in my government records across society), I can *try* to live and "pass" as a man, but my assigned femaleness will mean that I'll always still be susceptible to the benefits and challenges that affect others in this master identity category to which others decided I belonged.

Interactional Identities

Some of our identities change depending on who we're interacting with (*situational/ negotiated*). When these situational identities also have certain expectations/attributions in a given culture (*social group*), they're known as ***interactional identities***. So whereas a male can be a dad, only his biological sex assignment is a master status. The fathering part depends on what he's done and how he behaves, or his ***role***. And, you'd only call a man with kids a dad if you're referring to his role in relation to those kids. Otherwise, in other contexts, he's something else: romantically, husband or boyfriend; with his grandkids, a grandpa; at work, an employee/worker; in medical/health contexts, a middle-aged male.

We definitely expect people in these "group" categories to behave certain ways. But, different from master roles (where we expect that behavior constantly, in every situation), we only expect interactional identities to behave appropriately in those particular contexts. So, for example, you expect that when I'm being a professor, I won't show up to class drunk, wearing sweatpants and flip-flops. But, I wouldn't be judged for drinking a beer (Bud Light with orange slices is my "shitty beer" of choice) and dressing casually when I'm on vacation, out at a bar.

We all have multiple interactional identity roles.

© In The Light Photography/Shutterstock.com

Sometimes, our interactional roles conflict. At some schools, for example, professors (and students) aren't allowed to drink alcohol—in any context—while they're on the job. When those profs take their students on trips to conferences, the fact that they're still in "teacher" mode may conflict with the fact that conferences are also a place where faculty frequently relax and hang out with their own friends. Seeing your "teacher" act like a "real" human being with their own peers may be disconcerting. That's because you may expect them to be embracing an interactional identity role they aren't playing at the time.

Relational Identities

Finally, if an identity is different for every circumstance (*situational/negotiated*) AND also unique (*personal features*), it's considered a **relational** status. These are the types of things that can change over time, vary according to people, and/or differ by mood. That means they're highly dependent on which person and context we're communicating with. Although there are no specific social group expectations at a culturally prescribed level (like for sex roles) for these identity types, they nonetheless can affect our communication (and vice-versa). That's because *which* relational identity we choose to communicate (i.e., self-present) to someone tells them how we view him or her and our relationship to them (Watzlawick, Beavin, & Jackson, 1967). Relational identities both *self-present* and *altercast* expectations to others with whom we come in contact.

One of my own relational identities is being a "Diet Pepsi-from-bottles drinker" when I eat chocolate or sweet foods. But, in a different situation, when I'm eating salty foods or only have access to can- or fountain-drinks, my personal preference is for Diet Coke (and yes, I expect my "relational" partner to know these things about me when he's making us dinner!). These are relational identity characteristics because they're idiosyncratic traits, meaning there are no overall cultural or social expectations for how Pepsi or Coke drinkers can drink their pop. Notice also that I used the word "pop" here (because I'm a Minnesotan), embracing both my master identity (being born in Minnesota can't change, and people expect certain things of us, like "niceness" and Canadian long-ohs like in *Fargo*—which is in North Dakota, by the way!) and my relational identity as *similar to* other Midwesterners. I also use the word "pop" whenever I'm back in the Midwest. But, when I'm in Connecticut (where I live now), I maintain my master identity, while shifting the presentation of my relational identity because I'd be "different" for saying pop. So, I say "soda" when I don't want to be perceived as a Midwesterner when I'm talking to East Coasters (because I don't want a whole discussion; I'm thirsty and just want my damn pop!).

Activism Hero: Sex, Gender, & Essentializing

How often do *you* use the word "gender" to describe male/female (which is "sex")? We see it on surveys (incorrectly) all the time, and I've even had students say to me, "Well, my doctor said it's supposed to be gender"—as though that settles it. It's verrrry interesting how certain terms—and their accompanying meanings—can get ingrained into particular cultures just because "everyone else says" it must be that way. Some of you may respond, who cares? They're basically the same thing, right? Well, are you always masculine or always feminine? Do you always fit into the stereotypes? Probably not—and that's a good thing.

Despite knowing we're not 100% masculine or 100% feminine all the time, we engage in *essentializing*, which is assigning people into groups based on their "essential" (or at least, *believed to be essential*) characteristics. It's when you say everyone who is X does Y. And, you only put them into the X group in the first place based on some arbitrary thing. One of the most common ways we essentialize is based on sex and gender. For example, if a male perpetrates violence, an essentializer would then say, "All men, more so than women, have the potential to be violent"—which some people have actually said/believe. So, it's like an *ism*—racism, sexism, and so on. It's saying just because you're a member of this arbitrary grouping, you're this way too. And, it doesn't always have to be "bad" things. Ever hear that women are *supposed* to be more "nurturing"? That's essentializing.

Although you're not always responsible for things you're raised/trained to believe as "fact," you *are* responsible for continuing to perpetuate these incorrect and/or harmful beliefs once you've been exposed to them as such. So now, because you've just read this, ignorance is no longer an excuse for you using the term "gender" when you mean "sex"! Hold yourself (and others) accountable for communicating correctly! It's the first step in beginning to reshape cultural understandings (and someday, treatment) of men and women. Simple words YOU choose to use on a daily basis have the power to change nations!

Contributed by J. Eckstein

So relational identity, or how we view others *in relation* to us, can be thought of in terms of contrast—those similar to and different from us personally. You might see a man as similar to you one day because you both ordered the same thing at the same restaurant for lunch, but then see that same man as different from you later when you find out he voted for someone other than you did for President. If you search for "Dancing Twin Babies" on YouTube, there's a great example of how perceived similarity can reinforce our own

behaviors. Notice that most of the time these two babies, side-by-side in their highchairs, are joyously looking at their dad playing the guitar. But then, there's a slight break where one sibling pauses in dancing. That baby picks right up again, almost intuitively, without too much thought, and resumes dancing when it sees its twin doing so again. It forms its impression of "what I'm doing right now" based on what its twin is also doing—almost like they have one, single body. That's a relational identity really in action!

Noted previously, sex and gender are where this gets tricky. Sex, as you know, is a master identity category. Even though cultures believe certain sexes should act in certain *gendered* ways, that's just forcing people in one type of master identity to also do a particular type of relational identity. Basically, assuming sex is the same as gender (i.e., all males = masculine, females = feminine) is pretending you have no choice in your relational identity (due to a particular master identity you had no choice in)—which just isn't true! And, it's a big con we've submitted to in society for quite a while now. The way we *do* our gender—the way we communicate it to others—shows who/what we feel our relational identity is *and* who we feel someone else is too (*altercasting*). This performance can start to affect not only how others treat us interpersonally but even the emotions we personally feel, as you'll see shortly.

Gender, which you choose on a daily basis HOW to enact—according to your own personal preferences *and* each situation (that's why it's a relational type identity)—is based on whatever YOU want to do with it, and however you want to communicate it. Gender is also not binary even though we have these two labels (masculinity and femininity). Everyone does some masculine things sometimes and some feminine things other times. But, just because we all make choices for how to DO our gender (Butler, 2006) doesn't mean we won't get judged. Just like any other identity you decide to exhibit, you risk others judging you for it. And, it seems most of us aren't as bold as we'd like to think in exhibiting our freedom to do relational identities, particularly ones society tells us should be fixed and tied to master categories.

Back in the 1970s, researcher Sandra Bem started to measure Western culture's view of gender expression. The Bem Sex Role Inventory looked at **sex roles**, or the *gender* expectations society has for different *sexes* (Bem, 1981). She called the variables in her scale **masculine sex role** (or masculinity), **feminine sex role** (or femininity), and **androgyny** (considered "just human" and not specific to one or the other). Her initial theory was that androgynous people (not highly masculine *or* feminine) would be happier overall in life and have better well-being because they didn't feel the need to "fit" into any norms. But, her hypothesis was wrong! What she actually found was that people who were either *highly masculine males* or *highly feminine females* were the ones who had better overall well-being. In other words, people who followed society's instructions to make their master identity match their culturally typical relational identity knew what was expected of them in a particular setting; they knew the "norms" they were expected to communicate based on their sex, and they were OK with living those roles. In contrast (perhaps sadly), it was the androgynous people who had a harder time fitting in because they either didn't know or want to act how they were expected to (according to society, just because they had certain genitals).

So, to recap, we have "set"/static or changing/optional identities that are also personally specific or socially grouped. These result in personal, master, interactional, and relational types of identities. We are complex beings! And, that complexity means we need to be aware of our tendencies and personal options for enacting them all. Such an awareness matters because research suggests we're much more likely to accomplish our goals if they "mesh" with what we think about ourselves. So, our identities actually play a big role in what we'll be able to get done—like making change in the world around us (or not). Put another way, *self-concordant* or self-consistent goals are more likely to be achieved than ones that go against who we feel we are inside (Milyavskaya, Nadolny, & Koestner, 2014). Finally, it's important to understand that we don't communicate identities based on the situations we're in but rather on our *perceptions* and *interpretations* of those situations. Our outlook (shaped by and shaping our identities) is what determines our communication.

Why Self *Matters*: Working Consensus

We've already established *what* and *how* we say and do things performs our self-concept, which makes up our identity. And because those identities, in their various forms, in-turn shape our communication, we must study self-identity in order to figure out how to communicate better—especially in a world where we're all working from different "fields of experience" and frames of reference! To really harness these alter-egos, we must understand our superpower choices in terms of situational salience, implied expectations, and endless possibilities.

Situational Salience

First, we pick whichever aspects of ourselves are *most* salient (i.e., crucial and relevant) in each encounter we have. We have so many different identities—so many possible in each of those quadrants!—that we're sometimes forced to privilege some of them over others in particular situations. I can't be a "dog-mom" in every encounter, for example (as people would get pretty sick of constantly hearing about my fur-babies while checking out groceries or peeing in the bathroom stall next to me).

Identity salience is one of the most important things we use to determine how we'll communicate with other people! It's *so* important, in fact, that the situation (i.e., which identity we feel is most "right" to do at that time) has been found to have *more* influence on our performance choices than even our overall self-concept (Onorato & Turner, 2004). So even though they seem to get the most attention in society, master identities (e.g., race, sex) may become secondary to our priority to emphasize interactional (e.g., mother) or relational (e.g., "being one of the guys") identities. And knowing which identity to prioritize as most salient is key to a **working consensus**, or fit between perceived (by others) and expressed (by self) identities (Goffman, 1959).

Why would I want to leave my house with a face like this?

Source: Jessica Eckstein

One major cognitive challenge to a working consensus is the *self-serving bias*, which privileges our views in ways that reinforce our various identities. The upward and downward social comparisons (from Social Comparison Theory at the beginning of this chapter) we do are examples of this. Also, when we attribute (see Chapter 5's coverage of Attribution Theory) reasons for communication, we're more likely to give ourselves the benefit of the doubt than we do for others. In other words, we're likely to believe our expressed identities and ideas are correct for the situation/other person; so this bias may lead us to maintain an incorrect self-presentation. You probably already know that lots of conflicts don't get resolved because of people's tendency to assume their own (or their group's) version of events is correct. This happens because while we're privileging those who're similar to us, we're simultaneously *essentializing* (see Activism Box for a definition; usually negatively) those who are different from us.

Saguy and Halperin (2014) saw how the salience of *which* identity type is prioritized influences perceptions in conflict situations. They did this by looking at one of the most entrenched identity conflicts in history to-date: Israeli Jews and Palestinians. Most of us have no problem seeing how master identities play a role in conflicts. But, in this study, people's decision to focus *instead* on the situationally relevant relational identities is what actually affected outcomes! Using multiple experiments, researchers looked at how the two groups (Israelis and Palestinians) would respond to others' opinions in an interpersonal conflict situation. They found that Israelis who heard Palestinians criticizing other Palestinians were more likely (because those Palestinian criticizers held beliefs *similar* to the Israelis') to then be more open to those same Palestinians' versions of the conflict. Put another way, even if my master identity status is violently opposed to yours, if I hear you communicating views I agree with (meaning we have a similar relational identity status), I'm more likely to agree with other stuff you say, too. Thinking we're similar in some beliefs or attitudes makes me more likely to agree with you/like you/listen to you about other things (Kaplan & Anderson, 1973; Montoya, Horton, & Kirchner, 2008).

Our desire to get a working consensus is one of the reasons we may adjust which identity shapes our communication. This is even more surprising when you consider there are so many more ways to get situationally based identities "wrong" in any situation—because expectations for what is the "right" identity at the right time *and* the "right" way to enact it appropriately are rarely made obvious to us.

Which self-presentation is right for the situation?

© GoodStudio/Shutterstock.com

Public Speaking Power: Creating Shared Identities

Research suggests people are more likely to like, and thus be persuaded by, us if they affiliate with us (Kaplan & Anderson, 1973; Montoya et al., 2008). This is important because finding small similarities (even in the face of glaring differences!) works to connect people. You can use this to your advantage when speaking to ANY audience. Even if you seem very different from them, simple things can make them feel more connected to you—that you all have *something* in common. Here are some simple identity-connectors you can use in ANY speech:

- Say "we" and "us" instead of "I" or "you" when referring to any groups of people.
- Insert statements that appeal to basic human characteristics like a desire to be treated decently and respected.
- Use positive or negative stories or examples about family and positive ones about animals—although there are some people this won't connect to, the overwhelming majority of people come from some form of family and have experienced good and bad moments of this. Similarly, no matter how they feel about them, animal antics always make for a personal experience most people can connect with, or at the very least, understand.
- Finally, reference the shared experience of the particular moment you're in. This could be the weather, climate, room, or class speech-giving situation. There's a reason people "chit chat" about these things with strangers—it's because not only are they "safe" topics, but they are implicitly guaranteed to be *shared* because they're happening to both of you in that exact moment.

Contributed by J. Eckstein

Implied Expectations

Next, we don't always know what other people expect from a particular identity role because those expectations are usually implicit, not explicitly stated. Most people don't go around verbally saying, "This is how I expect you to act as a young, White, female professor," and if they did, I'd probably have a huge problem with it. But as a result of these things being implicit, we may violate others' expectations and "do" the identity wrong, or at least differently from what they expected.

One major way we know if we've acted inappropriately according to others in a given situation is through *stigmatizing* behaviors directed at us. Goffman (1963) explained that we know if we've followed social rules and/or fulfilled our expected identities with other people through this process of **stigma**, which involves communication intended to "discipline" us either through indirect (e.g., being ostracized or rejected) or direct social punishment (e.g., being yelled at or other hostilities). So, for example, if I walk into my grandma's funeral wearing a bright pink miniskirt and have my iPod blaring in my ears, I'll know it's inappropriate because I'll either notice people whispering and giving me dirty looks and/or

I'll be physically escorted from the church to stand outside. But, it would really suck if the only way we ever knew we were "correct" in our identity performance was through stigma.

We need both the stick *and* the carrot, so to speak. So when we do something good, people tend to make that known to us as well—in both indirect and direct ways. Indirectly, I might gain acceptance or access to others who accept me and involve me. Dr. Strange doesn't get to live in the Sanctum Sanctorum or access the "secret" library's Forbidden Knowledge until he proves himself worthy by completing the most difficult training to act appropriately. Directly,

There are various ways we're "told" to conform to social norms.

© 9'63 Creation/Shutterstock.com

I'll receive ***confirming responses*** that show me my perspective is valued because I'm enacting the correct identity in the right way for the situation and people with whom I'm communicating (Watzlawick et al., 1967). Captain Marvel isn't accepted by the Avengers until they see she's "one of them" and Thor expresses his acceptance through the understated confirming response, "I like this one."

But, as good as it is to feel loved and confirmed, lots of studies suggest we tend to be more affected by the "bad" or punishing behaviors (even just the threat or possibility that we might get stigmatized!) that society uses to keep us "in line" to communicate our identities appropriately (Baumeister, Bratslavsky, Finkenauer, & Vohs, 2001). This is an outcome-based way of shaping us to fit into society: If we do it right, we're rewarded; if we do it wrong, we're punished. Unfortunately, because we often (a) don't get told ahead of time what to do or how to communicate and (b) don't find out if we're wrong/right until we try it out, combined with the fact that (c) there are billions of unique experiences we'll encounter in life, the potential to succeed or fail in communicating effectively and appropriately is never-ending.

Endless Possibilities

Finally, we have to consider that because so many identities aren't "defined" in society (some are, though), we have a million and one options for how we can choose to enact them. I can enact my professor identity by teasing, joking, and having fun with students in the classroom; or I can be authoritarian, critiquing, and strict with students; or I can be some combination of both. The point is that even when put into certain categories—by ourselves, through choice, or as assigned by others—there's still a degree of flexibility in how I can communicate that identity "correctly" and even a choice to behave "incorrectly" on purpose.

Because of these three things (situational salience, expected inference, and endless options), we need to work harder than you might think to establish an initial working consensus with other people when we enact our identities with them. Luckily, we learn how to do this as we grow up and interact with others, particularly our family members (Dailey, 2009), so we don't often have to think too much about all the work we're really accomplishing (i.e., the superpower seems like it's just natural and easy) until we encounter something out of the norm that shakes things up.

How Self Matters: Face Management

We've now seen how identity exists, or the different ways it can play out and why that's important to our communication. Now, we'll look at the ways we manage our identities—the actual *specifics* of how we adjust and/or portray them to other people. The main way we "manage" our identities in social interactions is by managing our *face*, or the overall image we present to others. According to Goffman—the theater analogy dude—(1959), face has three main components that affect our communication with others: It's social, situated, and must be claimed.

Social and Public

Face is social; it's something that *only* happens *in interactions with other people* (Goffman, 1971). We make our self-presentation of face based on what's expected socially and accepted culturally. Also, it's public, which means it's the presenting self (remember, at the beginning of this chapter?) we put out there to others. This is why Goffman (1959) framed our lives as performances on a stage.

By gauging what we think others want to see or what we think is socially acceptable, possibly based on what they altercasted to us, we focus on doing what will get us positive, confirming responses. And then, we attempt to control our face through *facework*, which involves the communication used to manage our self-concept simultaneously with external forces and others' altercasting communication (Brown & Levinson, 1978; Ting-Toomey, 1988). Goffman explained this is the theater equivalent of knowing the "right" lines/dialect, wearing the "right" costume, and acting in the "right" way.

Face isn't based on idiosyncratic preferences; we use larger social norms to shape our presentation. In case you forgot, I'm a total introvert. But because outgoing, extroverted personalities are typically seen as more effective in the classroom (Martin, Chesebro, & Mottet, 1997; Zhang, 2014) and being a successful teacher is important to me, I'm willing to step outside my "cozy shell" when I'm at work. My *ability* and *willingness* to do this are tied to a form of identity management called *self-monitoring*. Each of us differs in how much we (a) care about what image we present and (b) our ability to put on a good show (Duvall & Wicklund, 1972). And because scholars like to group everybody based on levels and scales, there are two main groupings of this: high and low self-monitoring.

Paying attention to every little thing around you and noticing how your behavior affects others' reactions is called *high self-monitoring*. Although some people are better at this than others, it's something we're capable of switching on/off and getting better at over time and with training. Being able to tell how they're being perceived, high self-monitors can (and most often *do*) adjust their communication to create desired impressions in others. Like Mystique changing herself to be whatever the mutants need/want, high self-monitors can and want to adapt to what they perceive others in the interaction want to hear/see and how they altercast them.

High self-monitors are good "people readers" and know how to adjust their communication to many contexts in different ways. Being sensitive to the *dis/confirming messages*—both direct and indirect—around you has obvious benefits. The perks of high self-monitoring are that you can work at creating an identity you want, and you're so good at reading people that you're

Do you have Mystique-like adaptation powers?

rarely challenged on that identity (in other words, you're a great actor). This allows you to handle social situations really well and put other people at ease with little effort.

Low self-monitoring, on the other hand, is a tendency to just express whatever you're feeling or thinking without worrying about what impression it creates. Although some people simply can't "read" people or situations well (a common occurrence for those with autism), others may be perfectly aware of the effect their behavior has on others and simply not care. For whatever reason, *low self-monitors* are the ones who don't adapt to what the situation or another person expects as appropriate.

Low self-monitors tend to be less "superficial," so that with them, what you see is usually what you get. This is because they're more focused on who/what they want to be (in some cases, they also tend to be really self-assured and in touch with who they are). They tend to be straight-forward communicators who don't bother sugar-coating things in socially appropriate ways.

However, it's important to remember neither high nor low self-monitoring is ideal. There are pros and cons to both. So once you figure out what you personally are (or want to work toward being), it's good to (a) embrace it (be in control of your own choices, of course) but also know that (b) there are times/places where it's good to be flexible and roll with the opposite "type" too. And *that* ability—to both *know* and *enact* what is both effective *and* appropriate—is the superpower known as **communication competence**. This is why, ultimately, we may prefer to be one way, with a particular identity aspect prioritized all the time, but we *can* all switch if we have/want to, based on the social needs at the time, which are largely . . . situated.

Situated

A second aspect of face is how the rules for it aren't standard or the same all the time. Rather, it happens in certain ways based on particular contexts. Even though we usually rely on cultural norms to guide how we present to others, we still have other identity aspects we pick and choose to show the *particular person* in a certain encounter. Overall, our face depends on *which identity role* we take in a particular encounter with someone. Because it's so dependent on the people/situations around us, when managing our face- or identity-needs through communication, we must be careful to avoid cognitive and social biases.

One major cognitive perceptual bias we have is known as ***self-handicapping***, which involves communication or behaviors outside our awareness that we put in place to protect our perceived self later on. You might also know it as self-sabotaging. It can take the form of a self-fulfilling or self-defeating prophecy (discussed at the beginning of this chapter) where we create conditions for failure ahead of time in order to protect our ego or self-concept with excuses should we fail. A common example of this is someone who's always sick. You may simply view them as a complainer or a hypochondriac but realize it's a tool they may be using so that if something isn't of superior quality, they can just say they didn't feel well. As McRaney (2011) described:

> You might wear inappropriate clothes to a job interview, or pick a terrible character in *Mario Kart*, or stay up all night drinking before work; you're very resourceful when it comes to setting yourself up to fail. If you succeed, you can say you did so despite terrible odds. If you fall short, you can blame the events leading up to the failure instead of your own incompetence or inadequacy. (p. 228)

Self-handicapping is a risk for everyone.

© photoschmidt/Shutterstock.com

And it's not just in situations when we're feeling "down" on ourselves or un-positive that we do this "backwards" way of protecting our face; in fact, the opposite is true. One study started by testing people's verbal abilities (Alter & Forgas, 2007), after which they were put into groups and told either they had great verbal test scores or that they sucked (actual scores didn't matter; groups were randomly assigned)—so researchers boosted/deflated their egos. Those two groups then watched either a good-mood-inducing movie (e.g., British comedy) or a bad one (e.g., cancer documentary). After the movie, everyone was told they'd take another test but were first given the choice of two different teas to drink; one was sleepy-tea, the other was caffeinated energy/focus-tea. And *this* was the point of the study. Alter and Forgas (2007) wanted to know if people who were likely to self-handicap (identity aspect) would be even more likely to do it (i.e., pick the drowsy tea) when they were sad (situation). What they found was unexpected!

People with positive identities (told they had great verbal abilities) who were in a good mood (watched comedy) were *much* more likely to choose the drowsy tea than those who did well but saw the documentary (i.e., positive identities in bad mood situations). To make sure this wasn't just a fluke, Alter and Forgas (2007) re-ran the study a bunch of times in different ways (i.e., checking to make sure they were self-handicapping, eliminating and adding diverse variables) and found the same thing: The happier situation you're in, the more likely you'll be to pick ways to delude yourself into maintaining your rosy outlook on life (self-confirmation bias, social comparisons, etc.) and to explain away any failures in your own abilities. This is but one example of how our desire to maintain our identities in the context of *face threats*, or any challenges to our self-concept, may depend on the situation at hand.

Claimed

Finally, in order to actually matter to people (i.e., affect their self-concept), Goffman (1963) noted face must be claimed by the people communicating. Because we're working based off moment-to-moment self-presentations that can change with any incoming cues in the interaction (think of an improv show performance), little things can make us change how we do or communicate our face. It also means if we're not paying attention, we might miss an important cue that'd adjust how we present ourselves appropriately.

There are two types of face: *not* wanting bad things that challenge our presented identity and *wanting* good things to reinforce our presented identity (Laing, 1961). Despite their names, both are healthy and good things for each person to have. The first one, **negative face**, is akin to respect. It's the desire we have to perform our identities unimpeded, to be free from constraint, or to *avoid* having our self-concepts challenged. Negative face is basically our desire to avoid stigma and disconfirming messages. A face-threat to my negative face is anything that embarrasses or demeans me, such as falling on my ass on a slippery sidewalk or hearing criticism about my driving. I'm perfectly capable of walking and driving, so anything that takes away from this presentation/part of my self could be a negative face threat. The second one, **positive face**, is closer to liking. It's the desire we have to be approved of, to have our self-concept positively reinforced, or to have our positive identity aspects reaffirmed by others. Face threats to our positive face needs include not getting enough confirming/affirming responses from others that they like or need us (see Chapter 10 for more on this). We all have both negative and positive face needs, and both need to be met for a person to feel good about their self-concept and accompanying identities.

But—and this is important—face threats only apply to our *claimed* identities, or the ones we actually feel are central to our perceived or presenting selves (Goffman, 1971). Communication to address my negative and positive face needs only affects me if I personally view (i.e., claim as part of my own self-concept) something as threatening an identity I actually feel I have. Back in the day, when I was a teenager, some guys were trying to make girls feel un-ladylike by telling them they'd heard the girls snoring. These boys assumed snoring would be considered a face threat to girls trying to flirt and maintain feminine-style identities; for most of the girls around me, they were right and these "ladies" all squealed in horror and shame. Even though I didn't actually snore back then, I turned it on them by not being embarrassed. I pretended I *knew* I snored and was *proud* of it. I was only able to do this, though, because I didn't care; it wasn't important to my "feminine" identity to be a non-snorer; I simply didn't view that as something "women" were supposed to avoid. I didn't "claim" stereotypical femininity as part of my identity, so having it threatened didn't bother me. Today, students say they can't read my handwriting or that my stick-figure drawings don't make sense. If I considered myself an artist, this might bother me and threaten my negative face needs. But I don't, so it doesn't.

Both positive and negative face needs can be challenged with face threats, so most people's goal is to make sure they get both needs met, or at least *not* challenged. When I'm teaching in class, I'd prefer to not fart loudly or fall on my face because that damages my credibility as a smooth-operating, professional teacher able to function with grace and independence (or so I like to believe). That's my desire to maintain my negative face needs. Simultaneously, I also want students to learn concepts, tell me they understand and apply what I'm teaching, and usually enjoy coming to my class because they like me—all to reinforce my "good teacher" identity. Those are ways I seek to maintain my positive face needs. And because I do claim an identity as a

There are many ways to show respect, meeting people's negative face needs.

teacher who both cares and wants to be liked *and* respected by her students, having these aspects of my "teacher" identity threatened would certainly bother me!

These threats may work in different ways across our identity types. For example, I might have a face threat to my master identity that does or doesn't apply to my relational identity; so it matters which is most salient to me at the time. Because our communication is more affected by dominant norms (i.e., others' communication) than we think, even acting outside that norm risks a threat to our face needs.

Conclusion

Let's end with a final illustration of how everything we've learned in this chapter actually comes together. Because so many people assume a particular gender (i.e., a relational identity) must go with a particular sex (i.e., master identity), this is one realm where we get competing face needs. McCarty, Kelly, and Williams (2014) looked at how people experience emotions (typically tied to our perceived selves) in gendered ways; they hypothesized it'd be harder for people to process and show emotions that weren't in line with their sex-gender pairing (e.g., harder for females to think clearly while showing anger/ aggression, which is considered masculine) because it "should" take more cognitive effort to exhibit an emotion "counter-stereotypic" to corresponding identities (i.e., they assumed master identity females would all want to be relational identity feminine). To add a twist, they also expected this effect to be even more pronounced in public settings, as opposed to in private—because we're presenting to others based on what they expect from us.

What did they find? People had worse cognitive focus when they experienced counter-stereotypical emotions in public. In other words, having to think about the "right way" to act (according to gendered prescriptions for their sex) meant they had less brain power to devote to other tasks. Interestingly, the gender counter-stereotypic emotions didn't affect performance at all in the private condition—people who didn't have to put on a show for others could just be real with their relational-master identities' contradictions and not worry about doing gender "correctly" (McCarty et al., 2014). Basically, females asked to be angry/aggressive and men asked to be weepy/sad in public had a hard time doing so—it took a lot of effort on their part. But in private, kind of like their personal backstage, there were no problems for anyone to exhibit any of the emotions.

We need to ask ourselves what this means in terms of public performance and so-called "innate" differences between men and women. Clearly, it lends credibility to an idea that—at least in our culture, where women are expected to be feminine and men to be masculine—both are expected to publicly portray gender (a relational identity) "correctly" when it comes to extreme behaviors like aggression and sadness. Unfortunately, as McCarty et al. (2014) noted, this leads to the perpetuation of essentialized expectations in the communication of men and women, who are then actually *emotionally* and *cognitively* affected when they do/don't live up to those norms.

So if we put this all together . . . we have multiple identities, so we're always trying to figure out when/how to present our identities appropriately. Sometimes we present ourselves automatically without thinking because our communication habits are so ingrained, whereas other times, we consciously present a deliberate image to others. But because these ways of presenting can vary and are collaboratively coordinated with others based on their reactions, it gets potentially confusing—for us and others. But, never fear; this can be potentially fantastic because it means you have a ton of flexibility and room to grow and exhibit your communication superpowers in every single experience throughout your life! We're works in progress, ever-percolating to activate our most phenomenal selves!

References

Alter, A. L., & Forgas, J. P. (2007). On being happy but fearing failure: The effects of mood on self-handicapping strategies. *Journal of Experimental Social Psychology, 43,* 947–954. doi:10.1016/j.jesp.2006.07.009

American Association of University Women. (2019). *The simple truth about the gender pay gap: Fall 2018 edition.* Report retrieved from https://www.aauw.org/research/the-simple-truth-about-the-gender-pay-gap/

Baumeister, R. F., Bratslavsky, E., Finkenauer, C., & Vohs, K. D. (2001). Bad is stronger than good. *Review of General Psychology, 5,* 323–370. doi:10.1037/1089-2680.5.4.323

Baumeister, R. F., & Hutton, D. G. (1987). Self-presentation theory: Self-construction and audience pleasing. In B. Mullen & G. R. Goethals (Eds.), *Theories of group behavior* (pp. 71–87). New York, NY: Springer.

Bem, S. L. (1981). Gender schema theory: A cognitive account of sex typing. *Psychological Review, 88,* 354–364. doi:10.1037/0033-295X.88.4.354

Breiding, M. J., Smith, S. G., Basile, K. C., Walters, M. L., Chen, J., & Merrick, M. T. (2014). Prevalence and characteristics of sexual violence, stalking, and intimate partner violence victimization—National Intimate Partner and Sexual Violence Survey, United States, 2011. *Morbidity and Mortality Weekly Report, 63*(8), 1–18. doi:10.2105/AJPH.2015.302634

Brown, P., & Levinson, S. C. (1978). Universals in language usage: Politeness phenomena. In E. N. Goody (Ed.), *Questions and politeness: Strategies in social interaction* (pp. 56–311). New York, NY: Cambridge University Press.

Brunborg, G. S., & Burdzovic, A. J. (2019). Increase in time spent on social media is associated with modest increase in depression, conduct problems, and episodic heavy drinking. *Journal of Adolescence, 74,* 201–209. doi:10.1016/j.adolescence.2019.06.013

Burke, P. J., & Reitzes, D. C. (1981). The link between identity and role performance. *Social Psychology Quarterly, 44*(2), 83–92. doi:10.2307/3033704

Butler, J. (2006). *Gender trouble* (3rd ed.). New York, NY: Routledge.

Dailey, R. M. (2009). Confirmation from family members: Parent and sibling contributions to adolescent psychosocial adjustment. *Western Journal of Communication, 73,* 273–299. doi:10.1080/10570310903082032

Desmarais, S. L., Reeves, K. A., Nicholls, T. L., Telford, R. P., & Fiebert, M. S. (2012). Prevalence of physical violence in intimate relationships, part 1: Rates of male and female victimization. *Partner Abuse, 3,* 140–169. doi:10.1891/1946-6560.3.2.140

Duvall, S., & Wicklund, R. A. (1972). *A theory of objective self-awareness.* Cambridge, MA: Academic Press.

Festinger, L. A. (1954). A theory of social comparison processes. *Human Relations, 7,* 117–140.

Goffman, E. (1959). *The presentation of self in everyday life.* Englewood Cliffs, NJ: Prentice Hall.

Goffman, E. (1963). *Stigma: Notes on management of spoiled identity.* New York, NY: Simon & Schuster.

Goffman, E. (1971). *Relations in public: Microstudies of the public order.* New York, NY: Harper Colophon.

Jay, K. L., & Jay, T. B. (2013). A child's garden of curses: A gender, historical, and age-related evaluation of the taboo lexicon. *American Journal of Psychology, 126,* 459–475. doi:10.5406/amerjpsyc.126.4.0459

Kaplan, M. F., & Anderson, N. H. (1973). Information integration theory and reinforcement theory as approaches to interpersonal attraction. *Journal of Personality and Social Psychology, 28*, 301–312. doi:10.1037/h0035112

Kroskrity, P. V. (Ed.). (2000). *Regimes of language: Ideologies, polities, and identities*. Santa Fe, NM: School of American Research.

Laing, R. D. (1961). *The self and others*. London, England: Tavistock Publications.

Martin, M. M., Chesebro, J. L., & Mottet, T. P. (1997). Students' perceptions of instructors' socio-communicative style and the influence on instructor credibility and situational motivation. *Communication Research Reports, 14*(4), 431–440.

McCarty, M. K., Kelly, J. R., & Williams, K. D. (2014). The cognitive costs of the counter-stereotypic: Gender, emotion, and social presence. *Journal of Social Psychology, 154*, 447–462. doi:10.1080/00224545.2014.933160

McRaney, D. (2011). *You are not so smart*. New York, NY: Gotham Books.

Merton, R. (1948). The self-fulfilling prophecy. *The Antioch Review, 8*(2), 193–210. doi:10.2307/4609267

Milyavskaya, M., Nadolny, D., & Koestner, R. (2014). Where do self-concordant goals come from?: The role of domain-specific psychological need satisfaction. *Personality & Social Psychology Bulletin, 40*, 700–711. doi:10.1177/0146167214524445

Montoya, R. M., Horton, R. S., & Kirchner, J. (2008). Is actual similarity necessary for attraction?: A meta-analysis of actual and perceived similarity. *Journal of Social and Personal Relationships, 25*, 889–922. doi:10.1177/0265407508096700

Onorato, R. S., & Turner, J. C. (2004). Fluidity in the self-concept: The shift from personal to social identity. *European Journal of Social Psychology, 34*, 257–278. doi:10.1002/ejsp.195

Saguy, T., & Halperin, E. (2014). Exposure to outgroup members criticizing their own group facilitates intergroup openness. *Personality and Social Psychology Bulletin, 40*, 791–802. doi:10.1177/0146167214525475

Shakespeare, W., & Dusinberre, J. (Ed.). (2006). *As you like it*. London, England: Arden Shakespeare.

Ting-Toomey, S. (1988). Intercultural conflict styles: A face negotiation theory. In Y. Y. Kim & W. B. Gudykunst (Eds.), *Theories in intercultural communication* (pp. 213–238). Newbury Park, CA: Sage.

Toma, C., & Hancock, J. T. (2013). Self-affirmation underlies Facebook use. *Personality and Social Psychology Bulletin, 39*, 321–331. doi:10.1177/0146167212474694

Tracy, K. (2002). *Everyday talk: Building and reflecting identities*. New York, NY: Guilford Press.

Watzlawick, P., Beavin, J. H., & Jackson, D. D. (1967). *Pragmatics of human communication*. New York, NY: Norton.

Weinstein, E. A., & Deutschberger, P. (1963). Some dimensions of altercasting. *Sociometry, 26*, 454–466. doi:10.2307/2786148

Zhang, Q. (2014). Assessing the effects of instructor enthusiasm on classroom engagement, learning goal orientation, and academic self-efficacy. *Communication Teacher, 28*, 44–56. doi:10.1080/17404622.2013.839047

I remember going on a date at a local restaurant. As we were eating, she said, "I just love the décor in this place. It is quintessential American Southwest." So many things crossed my mind as she used the word *quintessential*. First, I often hear designers on those home remodeling shows use this word. Maybe she's one of those people obsessed with those shows. Or, maybe she knows I'm a professor and wants to use unique words to impress me. Or, maybe she's just really smart and has a sophisticated vocabulary. All of these questions crossed my mind in an instant, just with the word "quintessential."

Language is inherently tied to not only our identities but also how we make sense of others' identities. And, we do this all the time. We often judge people by the words they use—whether it's cursing in public (they're vulgar), using a word incorrectly (they're uneducated), using the same slang as us (they're connected to us), or using complex terminology (they're intelligent). Further, we often get a sense of the emotional state of a speaker simply based on word selection. For example, imagine a man describing his new colleague to his wife. He describes this colleague as amazing, brilliant, beautiful, and funny. How might his wife interpret his praise? Why would he use "beautiful" to describe a co-worker? Perhaps the wife assumes he's attracted to his new colleague. In another example, the husband might say his new colleague is "fine." Here, she may assume he has no opinion on his new colleague, or, maybe he's hiding something (or, if we're using the modern version of the word that she's *wink* "fiiine").

Great communicators—those who've really harnessed their superpowers—use language to connect with others. They have the power to create a sense of community and understanding. They use words to establish empathy and caring. Their carefully selected words create a visage of the ideal character. But, language can also create havoc. One of my students started his speech using the word "Fuck" in his attention getter. The rest of his speech was wonderful. He had amazing sources, his organization was superb, and the flow and logic of his argument were some of the best in the class. Yet, when his peers turned in their evaluations, all they seemed to be able to focus on was him using a curse word in the attention getter. One word!

In this chapter, we'll dig into language and its complicating factors. But, before we begin, let's do a little experiment. Get on your phone or computer and text a friend or family member. Make your message particularly kind—something like, "Hey, you're such a brilliant and thoughtful friend." Note what they say in return, as we'll revisit this at the close of our chapter.

Well, it certainly grabs their attention!

© Pranch/Shutterstock.com

Language Defined

Language is much more than words. Yes, dictionary definitions are important for someone learning language, but language is much more complex. Though there are quite a few specific definitions of language, for the purpose of this chapter, *language* is a culturally symbolic system of behaviors, sounds, and signs used to exchange and organize meaning in an interaction. To better understand this complex concept, let's break down this definition.

Language and Culture

On the surface, the connection between culture and language seems self-evident: If you grow up in an English-speaking culture, you'll likely speak English. But, they're also connected in a more sophisticated, complex way. If we define culture as "an accumulated pattern of values, beliefs, and behaviors shared by an identifiable group of people with a common history and verbal and nonverbal system" (Neulip, 2017, p. 16), we can see culture includes numerous other groupings and inherently influences the way we see and interact in the world—including how we look at language. Some have even argued that language is one of the best tools we have to understand our own cultures (Neulip, 2017).

One theory that's often cited in the language–culture discussion is the **Sapir-Whorf Hypothesis**. This proposal suggests our understanding of reality is influenced by how we think *and* how we think is influenced by the language we use (Brown, 1976). As such, the hypothesis—which is more or less impossible to test in reality—argues our language influences our perceptions of reality (and vice-versa). The best example of this theory is color. If you know or are an art major, you might know what I'm talking about. When I look out the window, I see a blue sky. An artist, however, might see something much more subtle. They may see shades of blue (e.g., steel, periwinkle, powder, Turkish) or the layering of the clouds I didn't even pay attention to. And, if they're effective communicators and have a mastery of the artistic cultural language, the artist could provide a vivid and detailed description of the same sky. To me, it's simply blue. Because I'm not part of the

An overused Sapir-Whorf example: The many Inuit words for different snows. Kaktovik, AK: What a village looks like today.

© Reimar/Shutterstock.com

artistic culture, my language is limited, and I can't provide such vivid descriptions.

The Sapir-Whorf hypothesis also argues our environment influences the type of language we use. People who live in colder, icier climates have a larger vocabulary for types of ice (*sleet, slush, glaze*) than people from warmer climates. People who live in areas hit by tornados may have more words for types of tornados (*twister, tube, trough*). People who grow up on a farm have more descriptors for dirt types (*loam, topsoil, peat*). Our cultures often develop sophisticated language to survive and thrive in our specific environments.

Language Is Symbolic

Try this activity. Repeat the word "family" aloud (or in your mind if you don't want your roommates to think you're crazy) over and over 20 to 30 times. If you're like me, the word starts sounding weird. It starts feeling like random sounds with no meaning. That's because language is ***arbitrary*** and based only on a generally agreed-upon definition as established by a culture. Simply put, the letters "F-A-M-I-L-Y" only connect to your family because we all agreed that those symbols (e.g., letters created from lines on a page), when put together, would refer to your relatives. If our culture decided that "F-A-M-I-L-Y" was an offensive term to describe rotten sushi, then it'd have nothing to do with your annoying sister.

We often have two different types of meanings associated with language (Ogden & Richards, 1923). ***Denotative meaning*** refers to the dominant, agreed-upon meaning of the word. I often think of the denotative meaning as the dictionary meaning. The denotative meaning of "F-A-M-I-L-Y" (*symbol*) is "a group of individuals who share a common ancestry" (*referent*). And whereas, for the most part, we can agree on this, we know that family is much more than that. When I think of family, I think of the loving bond between my children and I, and the dedication and devotion my mother has in caring for me. I also sometimes consider my students as part of my academic family. My football team in high school was a family. These alternative meanings are examples of connotative meanings, or the *reference*/thought in the Triangle of Meaning.

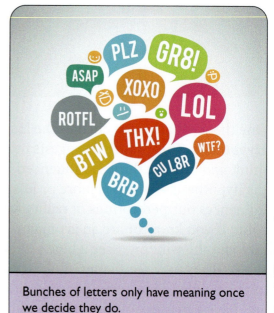

Bunches of letters only have meaning once we decide they do.

© Hermin/Shutterstock.com

Connotative meaning refers to the emotional connections individuals associate with words. So, denotative meanings are "agreed upon" definitions, but connotative meanings are unique for everyone.

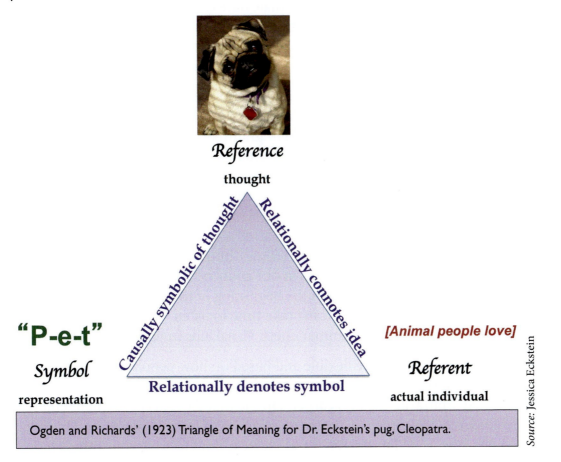

Ogden and Richards' (1923) Triangle of Meaning for Dr. Eckstein's pug, Cleopatra.

Source: Jessica Eckstein

Take the word *bitch*, for example. I was walking on my campus when I heard one female student yell to a group of women, "Hey, bitches." The women laughed and smiled. Denotatively, "bitch" has become a derogatory term, but in this context, between these women, bitch was used as an endearing term, used to affirm a positive connection. Another time, a male student started teasing another male who was clearly nervous about asking out a woman. He said, "Quit being a little bitch." In this case, "bitch" was used to challenge his masculinity and to create feelings of shame. We'll discuss derogatory words later in this chapter, but for now, it's important to understand that we all have different emotional responses to words, sometimes dependent upon the people involved or the context.

Language Is Systematic

Language relies on a set of rules agreed upon by a culture. You probably remember going through "grammar" lessons throughout elementary and high school education. We're taught early on that a subject and a predicate are necessary for a sentence to be complete. Though I'm confident you all paid perfect attention during your grammar lessons, you likely have situations where you violate those grammar rules. For example, if you're talking to your professor, perhaps asking for an extension on a paper or advice on a speech topic, you'd likely use the grammar you were taught in elementary school. Yet, when you speak to your roommate, you might communicate using grunts and incomplete thoughts . . . and still communicate effectively. That's because you and your roommate have established, over time, your own system for communicating. This isn't to suggest your grammar lessons were a waste of time. Employers want someone who can write and communicate effectively (Clokie & Fourie, 2016), which means someone who abides by the grammar rules taught to us all those years ago.

I often pose this difficult question: Which is better, to speak correct grammar or to use the language everyone tends to use? Am I a more competent communicator when I follow Strunk's (1920) guidelines (the textbook every grammar teacher bases their rules on), or am I more competent speaking the way my friends speak? Batistella (2005) proposed that our culture should often switch between prescriptive and descriptive language rules. *Prescriptive rules* suggest we have standardized rules that everyone should follow, with any variation from these rules considered "bad" language. You know you have prescriptive leanings if you obsess over grammar. I once played a YouTube clip from a popular documentary, *The Canary Effect* (Davey & Yellow Thunder Woman, 2006), in an attempt to discuss the plight of Native Americans in our country. After the clip, one "prescriptive"-driven student said, "I noticed a typo in the beginning of the clip. I quit listening after that. If they can't take time to proofread, I can't take time to listen." Yikes! But, it should serve as an important reminder to spell/grammar check visual aids in your speeches.

Descriptive rules are much more flexible and based on how people actually speak. This isn't to say there aren't "rules"—just that they're based on common usage and not on rules established arbitrarily decades earlier. On the first day of class, I might enter and say, "Hello students. Welcome to Communication 100. I'm your professor, Dr. Murphy." Or, I could say, "Sup Y'all! I'm Dr. Rich, and y'all are 'bout to have your minds blown!" One is clearly more prescriptive and the other is a rather pathetic attempt to connect with students by communicating as I perceive their descriptive norms. The answer to this debate is difficult. Your ability to read the room to determine if/when professional, prescriptive communication is appropriate is important but so is trying to adapt your language to how you perceive your audience speaks. Just be careful. People can easily interpret your descriptive attempt at language use as patronizing and offensive. Be equally careful not to assume that someone speaking with "unprofessional" language isn't well-educated. Being a socially competent communicator means adjusting your language to and within the particular, relevant system.

Check out the Tribeca award-winning film *The Canary Effect*: www.youtube.com/watch?v=2R9pPZmAjp0

© Grossinger/Shutterstock.com

Behaviors, Sounds, and Signs

When most people talk about language, they're talking about words. But, what exactly makes a word? I have a 2-year old girl at home who's just learning this concept. Her ability to control sounds and behaviors is just starting to form. It's amazing how the two of us are learning together to interpret sounds and behaviors. When she wants a drink of water, she points to my bottle and says "meh" and then places her right index finger into her left palm. Despite her inability to say "Hey dude, quit watching baseball and do your job as a father," she's still able to communicate her needs through basic sounds and gestures, which can constitute language.

Public Speaking Power: Communicative Rhythm

Lucas (2015) proposed four elements of language rhythm that can help you improve your use of language in a speech. First, he suggested we use *parallel structure*, which refers to arranging similar words, phrases, and sentences. Here's an example of a nonparallel sentence: "Batman is better than Ironman because he is a skilled fighter, he has way cooler villains, and also Batman's costume is more intimidating." That sentence doesn't flow well. It seems like the three ideas are just random rantings of someone who clearly knows comic books but has problems with parallelism. Try this sentence instead: "Batman is better than Ironman because of his fighting skill, his villains, and his costume." Notice nothing in the content changed. We just made the sentence a bit more concise and organized the concepts in a similar format.

Along with a parallel structure, Lucas (2015) suggested helping your speech flow by using *antithesis*, contrasting ideas in a sentence to emphasize an idea. The best example of antithesis is Neil Armstrong's famous quote after landing on the moon, "That's one small step for man, one giant leap for mankind." Another example is "Batman slowly rose from the dark ashes of Gotham city to give sudden light to its citizens." In this case, contrasting two ideas (slowly: sudden; dark: light) helps the listener focus on specific elements and emotions.

Another concept is *repetition*, which refers to repeating the same word or set of words to unify ideas (Lucas, 2015). For example, "Batman is strong against crime, strong against corruption, and strong against bright colors." Okay, I struggled on that last one; the point is repeating the phrase "strong against" gave power and focus to the sentence (which also had parallel structure).

Finally, Lucas suggested using *alliteration*, similar to repetition, except the speaker uses words with a similar starting-sound. For example, "Batman is *i*ntense, *i*nnovative, and *i*ntelligent." Look at the sub-headings in the upcoming "Language Obstacles" section. Alliteration draws attention to concepts, making them easier to remember.

Contributed by R. Murphy

Signs refer to direct-representations of something else. In language, the most common signs are letters of the alphabet. The letter "B" represents a specific sound. So, as you read this text, your mind quickly identifies the sign (the letter "B"), translates it in your mind as a sound, then, interprets the sound within the context. The letters are often combined into words, which your mind also translates into a meaning-sound.

Together, these sounds, behaviors, and signs are interpreted by the receiver and translated into meaningful language. Because we've been doing this since we were born, we rarely think about the sounds, behaviors, and signs we use to create language. We only really start to notice these things when we hear or see unexpected behaviors, sounds, or signs. When someone makes a weird sound or odd behavior, we become keenly aware of it and struggle to place meaning on it. Just for fun, sometime today while talking to someone, make a weird sound in a sentence. Say, "It's hot today. I'm feeling florphen." Watch their expressions! It illustrates how we often take behaviors, sounds, and signs for granted.

Language and Organizing

To be effective at whatever task you're doing, you have to know the language of the job. When I first enlisted in the Air Force, I didn't know a crescent wrench from a screwdriver. Once I learned my tools and the airplane parts, I became an effective mechanic. Language helps us organize and understand our world.

There are, of course, problems with this concept. We label everything—and not always in the same way or even accurately. In my research with military students, one of the things people in my study often said was that their behaviors were frequently labeled as posttraumatic stress disorder, or PTSD (Murphy, 2009). PTSD is a severe mental diagnosis common among combat soldiers who have several symptoms, such as depression and withdrawing from society. I remember one soldier saying he just wanted to watch TV. He'd been deployed for over a year and just wanted to have a weekend to watch TV and relax. I can relate; when I teach for a week, *I* want to do that! But, he said his wife labeled his behavior as PTSD and continued to push him to get treatment, though he hadn't even seen combat and was never actually diagnosed with PTSD. By labeling his behaviors prematurely, his wife started seeing things that never really existed. This phenomenon I've just described is referred to as *totalizing*, or oversimplifying characteristics about people (Miller & Metcalfe, 1998).

It's important we're careful in what we label and how we label things. We use language to organize and label individuals for efficiency, but often we let that label totally represent who they are. My participant's wife focused on the "combat veteran" label instead of viewing him in terms of his many other experiences and labels. When we totalize, we home in on one "label" and disregard the idea that we have many different labels for people, places, things, experiences, and so on.

Language and Meaning

The final element of the language definition is related to the exchange of meaning. We communicate so that we can share our understanding of the world with others. A student once told me he really liked my class because it was easy. In his mind, calling my class easy was a compliment. He meant that I taught clearly and made learning fun and effortless. But, at that exact moment, I thought he meant that my class was a joke, wasn't challenging, and was a "blow-off" class. Luckily (for me, not him), I often have problems controlling my facial expressions (my face got red, and I scowled at him), and he was able to adapt by clarifying what he meant. As you might remember from Chapter 1, just because you encode a message a particular way doesn't guarantee that's the meaning your receiver infers. We must work toward being clearer in how we communicate to best develop shared meaning.

If I were to say, "Ashley is really old," how old would you say she was? If I were to say, "Addie did well on her SATs," what was her score? Your answers likely vary because the descriptors in those sentences are too ambiguous. Hayakawa (1964) presented the "ladder of abstraction" to describe language. At the bottom of the ladder, he places words that are very direct and typically have very literal meanings shared by most people. These *concrete* words evoke very specific images in our heads. For example, Ashley is 95-years-old. The more general or abstract a word is (the higher up the ladder you go), the more likely it is to have multiple meanings, due to differing perspectives. Thus, words around the upper-middle of the ladder—like *smart*, *old*, *edgy*, and *easy* can be not only more **abstract** (i.e., indicating more idea-based conceptions—providing us also the ability to talk about things not physically in front of us), but also **ambiguous**, or intentionally used (because of their wide range of possible interpretations) to indicate a variety of meanings. If someone asked you if you liked their new outfit and you didn't want to hurt their feelings, you might say, "It's different" or "It's interesting." The ambiguity of those terms makes it intentionally difficult for the receiver to determine your meaning.

Abstract terms like "old" are also ambiguous.

What's "easy" for a senior communication major could be incredibly difficult for a first year biology major. What's "old" for my 9-year-old daughter (she says 60) isn't necessarily that to my mother (who views "old" as 90 and over). Everyone calls my 2-year-old daughter "smart" when she asks to brush her teeth in the morning, but "smart" takes on new meaning when applying to graduate school and competing with 4.0 GPA students from around the world (which is why I'm teaching my 2-year-old SAT vocab right now; just wanting to brush her teeth won't get her into a good school!). As we become more specific or concrete with our words, we reduce the likelihood of misinterpretation. Language allows us to engage properly in exchanges with others. But, as with other parts of our definition, this meaning-exchange isn't without problems, which I discuss next.

Language Obstacles

Imagine you took over your department's social media account. Your professor says she wants you to be edgy and innovative. So, being edgy and innovative, you take your phone to the tailgating event at your school where you live-stream interviews with current and former (and sober and non-sober) students from your major. Some of the students drop F-bombs and say a few controversial things. But hey, your professor wanted edgy content. That evening, you notice your access to the social media account has been cut off, you've received an email from your

Bypassing at its finest . . .

© Andre Adams/Shutterstock.com

professor saying your content was inappropriate, and you've been fired from your social media manager position. What happened? This phenomenon is called **bypassing**, miscommunication that occurs when two people think they left an interaction fully understanding each other, but in fact they didn't (Sullivan, Kameda, & Nobu, 1991). Bypassing is a natural result of the symbolic nature of language. As competent communicators, it's *our* (i.e., the *sender's*) job to communicate our message in ways that can be accurately received. To make sure that happens, we need to avoid some common pitfalls by focusing on a variety of language techniques. We need to work to make sure our language is clear, concise, familiar, and direct.

Creating Clarity

In the social media manager example, "edgy" is a **vague** concept, or one higher on the ladder of abstraction (Hayakawa, 1964) with various possible connotative meanings. To the professor, edgy probably meant a few funny memes and informal language use. To the social media manager, edgy might've meant no rules. Either way, expectations were violated in that situation despite the fact both communicators thought they were clear. A primary contributor to bypassing is lack of clarity.

We've all had that course where we just felt lost. For me, it was Astronomy. The professor walked into class, started talking about apparent magnitude and globular clusters, and boom, I was lost. We've all communicated with people who appear really intelligent and seem like they know what they're talking about, except . . . we can't follow what they're saying. So, no matter how intelligent you think you are, if you cannot clearly communicate your knowledge, your intelligence is useless (and questionable). Even among actually intelligent speakers, bypassing often occurs because we're too obscure or vague in our language use. If we want to avoid bypassing, one technique we can adopt is to be more concrete (and less vague or ambiguous) when we communicate (see Activism Box on the next page).

Commanding Conciseness

Every time I assign a paper for a class, someone inevitably asks me "How many pages should this paper be?" I always hesitate in answering this question. I get so many papers that are filled with "fluff" or unnecessary language used only to stretch out the paper. Add to this the use of large margins, Courier fonts, and a little extra space between paragraphs (yes, we know ALL the tricks!), and you can turn a 3-page paper into a 5-pager! Sadly, some people attribute the length of a paper to quality. I often overhear students compare their paper sizes. As a professor, I typically give higher grades to students who are concise, to the point. Students who add filler or overly complicated language (see the clarity tip!) don't do as well. I promise you: In the case of language, length does not matter . . . until it's *too* long! Quality matters over quantity.

Let's look at an example to illustrate this point. Which of the following sentences is clearer and easier to understand?

> *In today's society, people of the male sex often expend an innumerable number of hours and money engaging in the process of betting their wages on football games played by athletes who are in places of post-secondary education.*
>
> *Today, men often spend time gambling on college football.*

Did you get anything extra from the first sentence that you couldn't get in the second? No! And further, the first sentence is easy to get lost in.

I have three reasons why you should focus on smaller, more concise sentences. First, it's easier to confuse your listener with longer sentences. In my example, I could imagine a listener spending time trying to determine if you're talking about college football athletes, or perhaps semi-pro players who are also enrolled in college courses. Second, you often only have a limited time to communicate your message. Imagine you're in an elevator and your celebrity crush steps in and presses the 19 button. If you want to talk to them, you only have a very short time to introduce yourself and sound interesting. So, be ready to tell Scarlett Johansson that her portrayal of Black Widow was life-changing. And, whether it's the limited time you have to give your speeches or making an impression on your new boss, make it brief, powerful, and concise! Finally, focus your message on the meaning, not the writing. You may craft a long, eloquent, poetic sentence to introduce your idea. But, if the listener is focused on how eloquent, poetic . . . and long your sentence is, she's likely not paying attention to your actual message.

Activism Hero: Speak Their Language

We generally understand things at three levels (Smith, 1992). The lowest level is *intelligibility*, where we decipher if we can recognize the words or not. Next, is *comprehensibility*, where we figure out if we know what the word even means (denotatively, usually). Finally, we determine *interpretability*, where we figure out if we've understood the connotative meaning intended by the speaker. If you aren't using clear language, you're preventing people from ever getting to truly understand you and your message, preventing you from making the change you desire.

Most people understand and process info at a 6th to 8th-grade level. That means if you really want to reach people, you shouldn't sound like an ass-hat. Instead, keep things concise and simple. First, go through your sentences and ask yourself, what's the point of the sentence? Then, take out any unnecessary adjectives, adverbs, or phrases that don't add clarity to your sentence. Next, look for any clauses or phrases that can be reduced. For example, could "athletes who are in college" be reduced to "college athletes"? Could "people of the male sex" be shortened to "males"? Finally, can you convert long sentences with multiple ideas into two smaller, more concise sentences? Not only are shorter sentences easier for people to understand, but they also provide a natural place for you to take a breath. These simple steps can help you be clearer in your communication *and* more effective getting your message across—ultimately, making a difference in the world around you.

Contributed by J. Eckstein & R. Murphy

Framing Familiarity

Picture this: You walk into a class, and the teacher assumes you're all graduate students in the discipline. But, you aren't. The professor starts using big words with which you're unfamiliar. Now imagine you're with a new group of students, and *they* all start using words and phrases you've never heard before. Finally, imagine it's your first day on the job: Your supervisor asks you to do a task you've never heard of. Ideally, in all of these situations, you'd simply ask what the terms mean. But, that can be intimidating! One of our biggest kryptonites is a fear of appearing stupid. You don't want the professor to think you're not prepared for college. You don't want your classmates to think you're a loser. And, you certainly don't want your boss to think you're incompetent. As communicators (during speeches and in everyday life), it's essential to avoid language that's unfamiliar to your audience, such as idioms, jargon, and slang.

Let's begin with ***idioms***, which are sayings used within a culture that have meanings commonly understood to be different than their denotative meanings. Most likely, if you're from the United States, you know the phrase "dime a dozen" (as in, "guys like that are a dime a dozen") suggesting an opportunity is common and not particularly special. This phrase gathers its meaning through culture (see Chapter 14), so it can be difficult to interpret for the listener if they aren't part of the culture. Because it references money, you might think someone's trying to "sell" you some men. Or, imagine someone locking herself in her room because it's "raining cats and dogs."

And, these are just idioms about cats! I wonder what this says about our culture . . .

© BlueRingMedia/Shutterstock.com

Specialized cultures within mainstream cultures often create distinctive adaptations of common language unique to their group. For example, professionals in certain fields develop ***jargon***, or "technical" language understood only by individuals in that particular co-culture. When I was in the military, I learned a lot of jargon used by all military folks, including PT (physical training), mess hall (where you eat), and the field (war zone). As an Air Force avionics mechanic, I also learned sorties (flight plans), cannibalizing (using interchangeable parts from other vehicles), and JP8 (jet fuel). This can be incredibly intimidating (or even dangerous) for someone new or not familiar with military culture. Jargon is important, however, for the professions. Medical doctors, for example, have developed jargon to carefully communicate medical procedures to work safely and efficiently. Consider your audience! Overusing medical jargon in a speech, for example, could confuse them. However, if you're speaking to doctors or nurses, you'd improve your credibility (and perhaps conciseness) by using medical jargon.

Like jargon, some specialized cultures develop *slang*, or informal language modifications typically understood only by members of/in that specific culture (Dumas & Lighter, 1978). Every year, I ask my students what new slang "the kids are using"—a question always met with silence. I guess younger generations aren't aware that some of their language is slang (or they're just stupefied that the old guy's trying to be hip). They quickly recognize their terms are slang once someone outside their culture begins using them. Once, I asked, "What does the term 'thirsty' mean?" After some uncomfortable giggles, one of my students said, "Dr. Murphy, just don't *ever* use that term again." I later learned it derogatorily refers to a female (typically) who posts online hoping for good responses (to put it mildly), or a sexually desperate person.

Whereas jargon is typically used to make communication more efficient and safe, slang is commonly developed to unify co-cultural identities. When I was a kid, I grew up in a small river town in central Illinois. We often called each other "River Rats" as a term of endearment. To someone outside my little town's culture, calling someone a "rat" is likely insulting. But to us, it was an acknowledgement of our co-culture. But, if out-of-towners called us "River Rats," we took it (and they meant it) as an insult. However, the problem is, after slang becomes part of the mainstream, it no longer unifies a culture, and thus may not be used by the culture to create unity. For example, when nerdy guys like me start saying "totes," "guac," and "check out my crib," it's no longer slang. And, that seems "lame" to me, #facepalm. Should we use slang in our communication? It depends on the audience. If you believe the audience is part of *your* co-culture and will understand the slang, and if you actually *are* in that co-culture, it works well to connect with others.

Donning Directness

A *euphemism* intentionally substitutes one term for another to lessen the emotional impact of a powerful phrase (Neaman & Silver, 1985). In using a euphemism, the true meaning is often obscured and can cause significant miscommunication. For example, when I was a kid, my parents informed me that my German Shepherd, Duke, had to be "put to sleep." My folks used this phrase because, as a 6-year-old boy, the term "euthanized" was a bit too harsh. As a kid, I remember being quite confused. Was my dog just sleeping until they found a cure? Like idioms, euphemisms can be problematic because their language may confuse someone unaware of the expression or from another culture. Think about how many terms we have for sexual intercourse. If you're talking to your friends, I doubt you'd call it intercourse, coitus, or copulation. Rather, you might call it "doin' it" or "sleeping together." And although these terms might work for your friends, someone outside your culture might not understand these terms mean what you intend. There's a big difference between sleeping together and having sex. Again, understanding your audience can help you determine if a euphemism is appropriate.

A particularly problematic version of this is referred to as doublespeak. Euphemisms may reduce harshness of the connotative meaning of a word/phrase, but *doublespeak* is the deliberate manipulation of words or phrases to distort the actual meaning of the word. For example, the term "collateral damage" refers to innocent civilians killed during a military operation. Politicians often implement "revenue enhancements," which sound much more pleasant than "tax increases." Of course, if you failed a speech, just tell your friends you experienced "Communicative Evaluation Infection" (I just made that up; you really should've practiced your speech more). By purposefully distorting the seriousness, it's less focused on concern for the listener and more on how the speaker is viewed. So many public figures rely on this that there's even a Double Speak Award given annually by the National Council of Teachers of English (see NCTE, 2018)! Unsurprisingly, winners include many politicians (Donald Trump even *before* he was President, Bill Clinton), media members (Kellyanne Conway, Rush Limbaugh), PR-threatened companies (Exxon, NRA), and the military (Defense Department, Oliver North).

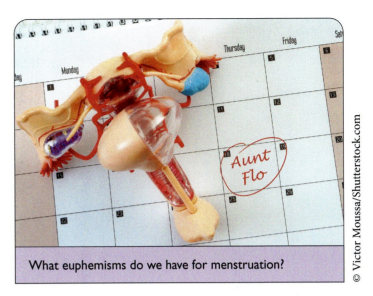

What euphemisms do we have for menstruation?

© Victor Moussa/Shutterstock.com

In sum, we need to be conscious of our words. Although we can strive for clarity, conciseness, familiarity, and directness, *not* having these language features won't (usually) cause an apocalypse. But, there are some features of language we *do* need to worry about.

"Bad" Language: Releasing the Kraken!

If you care about being an effective *and* appropriate communicator, you need to be concerned about what people consider "bad" language. In the following sections, we'll look at trigger words, profanity, and sexist and racist language.

Trigger Words and Warnings

Before we jump into specific bad words, it's important to remember that words' connotative meanings vary from person to person, group to group. For example, some people, due to their upbringing or past experiences, may be troubled by language referring to sex in casual or aggressive ways. *Trigger words* are words that evoke an emotional (often negative) response. Too often, people believe others are being *overly sensitive* and feel it's merely "political correctness" to worry about these expressions; that is *hardly* the case! It's important to remember that the effects of this speech aren't imagined; they're based on real-life, negative encounters the triggered persons have actually experienced. For example, for many people, the word "cheap" may not seem negative. However, some Jewish people experience bullying and even violence based on a belief that Jewish people are rich and stingy with money. Thus, "He's being cheap" may trigger strong emotional responses.

Triggers are based in reality for those who experience them.

© Master1305/Shutterstock.com

Sometimes it's not just the words themselves but the subject the words are describing. In my speech classes, I ban the topic of abortion, not because I have strong opinions about it but because it could be a potentially triggering term for someone who may have personal experiences with abortion. In his research on trigger words, Boysen (2017) argued using trigger warnings, letting them know they're approaching a potentially emotionally triggering topic, is important for instructors to accommodate students. It's equally helpful in everyday life. With any potentially triggering words or topics, it's important to proceed with caution.

Just because you aren't emotionally responsive to these words or phrases doesn't mean they aren't trigger words. As with all communication, understand your audience before jumping into these and other forms of potentially troubling language.

Profanity

The Chicago Bears were losing to the Indianapolis Colts in Superbowl XLI. I was sitting in the living room, where my then-toddler son was crawling around on the floor. Peyton Manning threw another touchdown, and I threw my hands up in the air and sighed. My son looked at me, then at the TV and exclaimed, "SHIT!" It was then I realized he probably learned this from me . . . and that I may be a bit too invested in watching sports. When I was a kid, Tipper Gore and colleagues started the Parents Music Resource Center, whose main purpose was to add a "Parental Advisory: Explicit Lyrics" sticker to music selling "inappropriate" content. For me and many of my friends, this sticker made the album *more* desirable. Why are some words considered inappropriate or offensive? Who decides what's explicit or inappropriate?

Profanity is any term a society determines to be "obscene" or off-limits. This means that different groups across different cultures or different times will consider different things to be profane. For example, it's highly offensive to say "fag" in the U.S. (Pascoe, 2005), whereas "fag" simply refers to a cigarette in England. This means some people within

© igorstevanovic/Shutterstock.com

each social structure *decided arbitrarily* to label certain things this way—a process often tied to who was in power (Ardener, 1975). Because they're so tied to what we've been taught is "morally" wrong, we tend to auto-respond emotionally to curse words.

Consider: Why is the phrase *making love* more "appropriate" than *fucking* in the context of sexual intercourse? In 1873, the Comstock Act banned sending certain materials through the U.S. postal service. This included materials with obscene language such as shipment of books, toys, or anything related to sexual acts; sending condoms and even birth control informational pamphlets was punishable with imprisonment (Gordon, 2002). This, then, made the publication and sale of texts with the word "fuck" incredibly difficult. The Act was later overturned, but the impact of the legislation gave the word emotional power.

Pinker (2007) noted five ways we use curse words. First, curse words are used *descriptively*. Instead of saying, "Man, that guy is mean," we instead say "What an asshole!", which is far more emotionally charged, to accurately reflect the speaker's emotional state. Next, curse words are used *abusively* to hurt, attack, or intimidate the receiver. Because of the emotional power of words, calling someone "unintelligent" isn't quite as intense as calling them "dumb-ass." If we really want to hurt someone, we use curse words. Curse words also *emphasize*, or draw attention toward an idea. For example, as I write this chapter, I'm drinking good coffee. But, if I were to go to the coffee shop down the road, I'd be having "damn good coffee!" By arousing emotions in the receiver, I'm emphasizing my point. A fourth way we use curse words is *idiomatically*, or as a way to relate to the receiver. Often, cursing can signify a more informal setting or connection to the receiver. For example, an electrician came to my house to check on my circuit breaker panel. As he looked at the panel, he sighed, "Shit." I responded, "Yeah, this damn box is driving me crazy." By cursing, I was attempting to relate to the electrician. Also, the damn breaker panel *was* driving me crazy. Finally, Pinker (2007) said we use cursing for *catharsis*, or letting off some steam. Sometimes it just feels good to curse. And curse loudly! If I'm driving down the road and a car cuts me off, I shout "Asshole!" so I instantly feel a little better. Sure, the driver ahead couldn't hear me. I'm sure they're a wonderful person, and I wish them all the best. But, at that moment, I have pent up anxiety and anger, and shouting the curse word just feels good—frankly, much better than simply yelling "Bad driver!"

Remember that these five purposes of cursing are descriptions of what's possible. It doesn't mean cursing *will* have these outcomes. For example, you may yell a curse to feel better, but if you get written up at work for cursing in front of customers, you won't feel good. Or, if I curse in front of a new friend who's strongly opposed to cursing, I may actually create a disconnect between us. Mentioned in this chapter's intro, a curse word can be quite distracting! In other words, we have good reasons to curse, but our intended outcome may not always come to fruition. Obviously, curse words should never be used to purposefully offend or abuse someone. Remember, we all have different levels of offense (e.g., offended by "fuck" but not "damn") and differing connotative meanings associated with particular curse words.

Sexist Language

Whereas curse words are problematic in some instances, sexist language is worse and is inexcusable in every instance. Language that is **sexist** includes words or phrases that highlight and perpetuate gender-biased prejudices that essentialize a sex-group; in our culture, these typically place women in a lower status than men (Swim, Mallett, & Stangor, 2004). Sexist language—whether intentional or not—accomplishes discrimination through excluding, degrading, or demeaning others. First, sexist words *exclude* men or women, but most often women, from equality. For example, gender-specific compound words like fireman or chairman can contribute to stereotypes about who should carry certain roles in society. It's easy to think of many more of these (e.g., postman, policeman), but think of how many still used today do the opposite—exclude men. Landlady? More often, we use terms like male-model or lady-doctor, which are **gendered modifiers** that show the "regular" word-use must be changed to fit cultural understandings. Terms like "male-nurse" contribute to notions that men aren't effective nurses.

© vectorfusionart/Shutterstock.com

Second, sexist language also degrades or demeans. We're all familiar with obvious forms such as name-calling or insults like *slut*, *cunt*, or *dick*. It also takes place via **microaggressions**, which are subtle and often unintentional insults directed toward someone based on their perceived group membership (Sue et al., 2007). Recently, our culture has become more aware of the sexist microaggression **mansplaining**, which happens when someone talks down to patronizingly, or implies having better-knowledge of a woman's life-experiences (for more types, see Rutherford-Morrison, 2016). Imagine a female athlete who's worked hard in the gym with some of the best trainers to get into peak physical condition to compete at the collegiate level. Now, imagine her at her university's gym running into a male who lifts a few times a week telling her how to correct her "form" and workout technique. It's condescending (and just general douche-baggery). My favorite example of mansplaining is from a *Cosmopolitan Magazine* article (Mei, 2017; yes, I read *Cosmo*; I particularly love the surveys) where a reader observes her friend "mansplain to my roommate how to ~correctly~ pronounce her own name bc he thought she was doing it wrong." Mansplaining blatantly disregards women's status, power, or knowledge—even over her own experiences. Obvious mansplaining of this caliber happens quite often, but the subtler microaggressions can be just as problematic. For example, when men refer to non-familiar women as "sweetheart" or "honey," they're engaging in sexist language because those terms are typically used in a patronizing and condescending manner. Regardless of the type, sexist language creates problems and isolates others. Avoid it. Just, don't do it.

Racist Language

Most of us know the basics of *racist* language, which contains "racial epithets," or rude and offensive terms used to describe individuals based solely on their race. In most cases, we just don't say those words; we're not villains like Hate-Monger, after all! We know better, or at least we should. Illustrating the historic and cultural evolution of language, many groups have "reclaimed" some racial epithets and use them as a form of social unity. In the 1980s to 1990s, the group N.W.A. (Niggaz Wit Attitudes) shocked the world by celebrating the word that for centuries has been one of the most powerful epithets in the U.S. Although frequently used in hip hop music and among African Americans, the term still holds strong connotative meanings and may even be a trigger word—particularly when used by those outside the group. The difference in one tiny letter can create vastly different words/meanings!

It's hopefully obvious that racial epithets should be avoided, but many of us still practice racial microaggressions. For example, when a White speaker refers to a Black person as "articulate," it can be interpreted as code reinforcing prejudices that Black people are uneducated. The show *The League* jokes about sports announcers' terms commonly used to refer only to athletes of certain ethnicities (e.g., Latinos as "firecrackers" or "sparkplugs" and African Americans as "class acts"). Other common interracial microaggressions include making fun of name pronunciations (advisors have even told Asian foreign students to select an "American name" in order to avoid this!) or asking someone of a different race where they're "really" from.

As with sexist words, there's never an appropriate time use this language. However, some people feel avoiding racist language has led to an unfortunate side effect: the fear to engage in thoughtful discussions about race. For many, the fear of inadvertently insulting a culture or another race has led to many being afraid to discuss it all. Especially in the current social and political climate, educated discussions on race and sex are crucial. If we carefully think about the words and phrases we select and avoid being defensive when we make mistakes, we can still engage in thoughtful discussions and improve our communication at the same time.

Ice Cube (formerly of N.W.A.) performed "Fuck tha Police" as a protest against police brutality—another example of the power of profanity.

© Faer Out/Shutterstock.com

Conclusion

We've covered quite a few important elements of language. It can be overwhelming! In a speech, you try to use all the things you learned about in the delivery chapter, deal with your anxiety, connect with your audience, and now I'm asking you to think about the multiple meanings a single word can create. It could cause verbal paralysis—a complete shutdown of your superpowers! Calm down. I guarantee that, although you'll make a mistake some time in your life, you WILL be okay. I promise. The critical thing to know about language is that it's alive. It changes and melds with our culture and over time. Our language reflects our identity; just as you're not who you were 2 years ago, the language we speak is not the same. The best advice I can give is to be aware, humble, and willing to learn. Simply being thoughtful about language will tremendously grow your ability to communicate effectively. By taking ownership of our own words and realizing they have power, we can make this world a better place.

Alright, now go back to your phone. I bet you got a response to the positive message you sent when you started reading this chapter. And, you probably made the recipient smile. Our language can create stress, anxiety, jealousy, anger, and other negative emotions. But, it can also create happiness, joy, excitement, and love. So, choose your words carefully.

References

Ardener, S. (1975). *Perceiving women*. London, England: Malaby.

Batistella, E. (2005). *Bad language: Are some words better than others?* New York, NY: Oxford.

Boysen, G. (2017). Evidence-based answers to questions about trigger warnings for clinically-based distress: A review for teachers. *Scholarship of Teaching and Learning in Psychology, 3*, 163–177. doi:10.1037/stl0000084

Brown, R. (1976). In memorial tribute to Eric Lenneberg. *Cognition, 4*, 125–153. doi:10.1016/0010-0277(76)90001-9

Clokie, T. L., & Fourie, E. (2016). Graduate employability and communication competence: Are undergraduates taught relevant skills? *Business and Professional Communication Quarterly, 79*, 442–463. doi:10.1177/2329490616657635

Comstock Act of 1873, 42 U.S.C. §§ 256–258 (1873).

Davey, R., & Yellow Thunder Woman (Directors & Producers). (2006). *The canary effect* [Motion picture]. Los Angeles, CA: The Bastard Fairies.

Dumas, B. K., & Lighter, J. (1978). Is slang a word for linguists? *American Speech, 53*, 5–17. doi:10.2307/455336

Gordon, L. (2002). Birth control and social revolution. In K. Peiss (Ed.), *Major problems in the history of American sexuality: Documents and essays* (pp. 320–326). Boston, MA: Houghton Mifflin.

Hayakawa, S. I. (1964). *Language in thought and action*. New York, NY: Harcourt Brace.

Lucas, S. (2015). *The art of public speaking* (13th ed.). New York, NY: McGraw Hill.

Mei, G. (2017). 17 Absolutely infuriating examples of mansplaining. *Cosmopolitan Magazine*. Retrieved from www.cosmopolitan.com/lifestyle/a9171951/mansplaining-tweets

Miller, L. J., & Metcalfe, J. (1998). Strategically speaking: The problem of essentializing terms in feminist theory and feminist organizational talk. *Human Studies, 21*, 235–257. doi:10.1023/A:1005379625641

Murphy, R. (2009). *Family communication and the military veteran: Relational maintenance strategies of veterans returning home from military service*. Paper presented at meeting of National Communication Association, Chicago, IL.

National Council of Teachers of English. (2018). *The double speak award*. Retrieved from www2.ncte.org/awards/doublespeak-award/

Neaman, J., & Silver, C. (1985). *Kind words: Thesaurus of euphemisms*. New York, NY: McGraw Hill.

Neulip, J. (2017). *Intercultural communication: A contextual approach* (7th ed.). Los Angeles, CA: Sage.

Ogden, C. K., & Richards, I. A. (1923). *The meaning of meaning: A study of the influence of language upon thought and of the science of symbolism*. New York, NY: Harcourt Brace.

Pascoe, C. J. (2005). "Dude, you're a fag": Adolescent masculinity and the fag discourse. *Sexualities, 8*, 329–346. doi:10.1177/1363460705053337

Pinker, S. (2007) *The stuff of thought: Language as a window into human nature*. New York, NY: Viking.

Rutherford-Morrison, L. (2016, January 19). 6 subtle forms of mansplaining that women encounter each day. *Bustle*. Retrieved from www.bustle.com/articles/136319-6-subtle-forms-of-mansplaining-that-women-encounter-each-day

Smith, L. (1992). Spread of English & issues of intelligibility. In B. Kachru (Ed.), *The other tongue: English across cultures* (2nd ed., pp. 75–90). Urbana, IL: University of IL Press.

Strunk, J. (1920). *The elements of style*. San Diego, CA: Harcourt.

Sue, D. W., Capodilupo, C. M., Torino, G. C., Bucceri, J. M., Holder, A. M. B., Nadal, K. L., & Esquilin, M. (2007). Racial microaggressions in everyday life: Implications for clinical practice. *American Psychologist, 62*(4), 271–286. doi:10.1037/0003-066X.62.4.271

Sullivan, J., Kameda, N., & Nobu, T. (1991). Bypassing in managerial communication. *Business Horizons, 34*, 71–81. doi:10.1016/0007-6813(91)90084-9

Swim, J. K., Mallett, R., & Stangor, C. (2004). Understanding subtle sexism: Detection and use of sexist language. *Sex Roles, 51*, 117–128. doi:10.1023/B:SERS.0000037757.73192.06

If you've ever been called out by someone saying, "It's not what you said; it's *how* you said it!" or in a disagreement where someone yells "I'M NOT ANGRY!", then you already know the importance of nonverbals for creating meaning. ***Nonverbal communication*** is the creation or sharing of meaning without words. A wide variety of species communicate without using (what we understand as) words. In fact, animals (including humans) may have evolved to communicate

We have more in common than you'd think!

© NotionPic/Shutterstock.com

nonverbally because doing so provides an important survival advantage: the ability to coordinate effectively with others (Darwin, 1872/1965). There are many social animals who communicate nonverbally. Birds use complex song patterns (Thorpe, 1961) and bees perform a "waggle dance" to communicate the location and richness of food (Thom, Gilley, Hooper, & Esch, 2007). Humans have also developed rich, complex, and varied nonverbal communication abilities.

Why We Use It: Functions of Nonverbal Communication

Because of its unique characteristics, nonverbal communication does a LOT for us. Its symbolic nature performs many functions which work together to make the other communication types (e.g., verbal) even better. Some of these functions (there're many more, so take a nonverbal class!) include: complementing, replacing, regulating, deceiving, and identity management.

First, nonverbal communication **complements** our verbal communication by reinforcing the message. For example, it's rare that you say (and mean) "yes" without simultaneously nodding your head. Try saying "no" while nodding or "yes" while shaking your head side to side; you can do it, but you have to think for a second beforehand. Just like pointing when we give directions, nodding our head reinforces and helps convey a verbal message. And, sometimes our complementing nonverbals become so ingrained, we might not even realize we're doing it.

Next, nonverbal communication replaces verbal communication. Sometimes nonverbals are more useful than words—like when it's noisy or we're far away. This is when they become strictly symbols. Using the nodding example again, if you're asked if you want pizza (and who doesn't?), you can nod your head "yes" (without having to verbalize it), and the receiver still understands your message, even from across a busy restaurant. Our nodding has **substituted** or replaced the verbal communication.

Third, nonverbal communication plays an important role in **regulating**, or controlling the flow, of our interactions. You might nod to encourage someone to continue speaking. Or, if someone won't stop talking and you want out of a conversation, you might use ***intention movements***, codes indicating something you're preparing to do. You might look at your watch or phone numerous times; avoid eye contact; begin to lean or turn your body away, or move toward the door, hoping they get the point you're making nonverbally. In this way, we use nonverbal cues every day to regulate our interactions: to encourage others to speak, maintain our turn, indicate a turn is over, or refuse/request a speaking turn (Goodwin, 1981).

Next, we use nonverbals to be deceptive (not necessarily lying). One way we do this is by hiding what we're really feeling through ***concealment*** or masking. Have you ever found yourself "putting on a happy face" just so no one asks you what's wrong? Words are only a small part of deception, so to be convincing, we have to step up our nonverbal game. A bit of nonverbal deception can make us (and others) feel a lot better. If you go to the ER with a gory, stinking wound, a good doctor will calmly assess it, explaining treatment as they work. If the doctor

Aren't you glad you don't always know what people think? Masking can be good!

© Aaron Amat/Shutterstock.com

freaked out, you'd feel more panic, *and* it could negatively affect the doctor's competence, making you less likely to follow treatment advice, putting your health further at risk. Now, aren't you glad adults can control their nonverbals? "Masking" really does make for good superheroes!

Finally, much of our identity is expressed nonverbally. You probably wouldn't dress the same way for hanging out with your friends as for a job interview because you're attempting to play two different roles and expressing two different identities (remember Chapter 6?). Even beyond appearance cues such as clothing, jewelry, and hairstyles, we may use posture or even vocal tone to express identity. For example, do you change your voice when you answer the phone in a professional setting? Think of the voices of TV anchors, sports announcers, and radio hosts: Are some vocal qualities preferred for these professional roles? I co-host an online radio show, and I can attest that my radio voice is smoother, and I enunciate better than with my "everyday" voice.

Characteristics of Nonverbals: What Makes Them a Superpower?

There are several important characteristics of nonverbal communication that make it super powerful. Nonverbals are powerful, multi-channeled, continuous, emotion-based, ambiguous, and culturally-bound and coded.

First, nonverbal communication is powerful. Although there's debate about exact percentages, most studies find nonverbal communication carries the majority of the meaning of any communication utterance (Birdwhistell, 1970; Mehrabian, 1981). That means we rely more on *how* a message is communicated than we rely on the particular words being used. When verbal and nonverbal messages are contradictory, adults tend to believe the nonverbal messages over the verbal ones (Volkmar & Siegel, 1982). Children tend to rely more on the verbal message than on the nonverbal; this is why many children younger than 5 years old don't understand sarcasm (Dews et al., 1996). By paying attention to the words alone, they miss the irony. Still not sure of its power? Go back to the first scenario mentioned at the beginning of this chapter: When a person angrily yells at you, "I'M NOT ANGRY!", you're apt to believe their tone of voice more than their literal words.

Why don't you believe me when I say, "I'm fine"?

© Lisa Charbonneau/Shutterstock.com

Second, we tend to believe the nonverbal more because there are many more forms of nonverbal versus just words, making nonverbals harder to control and easier for truth to "leak" out. Nonverbal communication is multi-channeled, which means we use numerous channels, or parts of our bodies, to communicate. For example, at the same time we make eye contact with someone, we also have a particular facial expression and body movements, tone of voice, posture, physical appearance, and other nonverbal cues.

Third, in part due to the multiple channels being used simultaneously, nonverbal communication is continuous. In fact, the reason authors in this text keeping saying "we cannot *not* communicate" (Watzlawick, Beavin, & Jackson, 1967) is *because of* nonverbal communication—not verbal communication! Whereas verbal communication is like a light switch that can only be turned on/off, nonverbal communication is more like a dimmer switch on a light that's always on at some level but can be adjusted to produce more or less light. Because even silence is a form of nonverbal communication, there's no way to avoid communicating! Have you ever been waiting to receive a reply to a text message? It's frustrating, but it's also a prime example of how not verbally communicating still communicates meaning.

Fourth, nonverbal communication is the primary way we communicate emotion. How do you let others know you're happy? Do you explicitly state, "I feel happy"? No, probably not; that'd be weird. Rather than verbally expressing happiness, we might smile and laugh, our voice might get higher, we might get "bouncier" in our step, and we may gesture more animatedly. Our ability to express our emotions nonverbally helps us form social bonds (Darwin, 1872/1965).

Fifth, like verbal communication, nonverbal messages are ambiguous, meaning one behavior has numerous meanings. Even something as simple as crying isn't so simple. People shed tears because they're happy, sad, angry, in pain, or just dealing with allergies. Because there are so many different interpretations of a behavior, we have to develop our nonverbal decoding skills to investigate and uncover the meaning behind someone's nonverbal communication.

Sixth, nonverbal communication is largely culturally-bound, so one symbol can mean something different in another culture. You may remember when you learned that extending your middle finger at someone (also known as "flipping them the bird") has a particular meaning in our culture and provokes a response that you don't get when you extend any of your other fingers. However, the roots of that finger gesture aren't found in language; what we call "the bird" is one of many phallic gestures observed across cultures since ancient times; people insult by gesturing to mimic thrusting a figurative penis at someone (Morris, 1994). Cultures express this with a closed fist, a thumb, or even a brush of the chin (rather than a middle finger). We aren't born using and understanding phallic gestures; as is the case with all symbols, we learn their meanings from other members of our culture.

This commonly used symbol has many culturally-bound interpretations: "okay" (U.S.), "asshole" (Brazil), zero (France), money (Japan), or flipped around, "White power".

Finally, all of these characteristics stem from nonverbals being intricately coded—being signs of something else. And, these codes are arbitrary, having no necessary connection to their referent (Ekman & Friesen, 1969). We have to learn what symbols represent from other people. We're not born knowing that throwing both arms straight above our heads means "touchdown." Two ways symbols are displayed are through intrinsic and iconic codes (Ekman & Friesen, 1969).

Intrinsic Codes

We all have innate, impromptu things that "tell" other people (or ourselves!) things about us; these are *intrinsic codes*, or biologically-based behaviors. These codes rely on "external manifestations of an internal state" (Buck & VanLear, 2002, p. 525). That means they're spontaneous; we don't have to think about doing them. Sometimes these things are biologically "caused": gray hair indicating age or bodily stress, wrinkles or spots from sun exposure, or weight suggesting metabolic functions. Other times, they don't indicate as "permanent" but are temporary messages coming from our bodies.

For example, babies don't have to be taught to cry when upset or smile when happy; their behaviors (loud, shrill vocalizations; scrunched up, reddened faces; fisted hands) are natural symptoms of their internal state (being upset or uncomfortable). Babies are born with the ability to express themselves nonverbally through intrinsic codes.

Iconic Codes

Just as intrinsic codes rely on natural signs, *iconic codes* also *appear* "natural" at first glance (Ekman & Friesen, 1969). That

Intrinsic threat displays may be enough to dominate—without having to follow through—because the meaning is shared, even across species!

© lassedesignen/Shutterstock.com

means they rely on *semblances*, which look like or resemble natural signs but aren't actually the real deal. For example, at some point, we figure out that we can *pretend* to cry. When we fake cry, we make faces that resemble real, spontaneous behaviors, but

Tattoos may be both iconic (make us look "tougher") and arbitrary (whatever they symbolize/represent in pictorial form).

© zetwe/Shutterstock.com

what we're displaying doesn't match how we feel inside. Iconic codes aren't necessarily deceptive, though; they can be "social glue" holding society together through rules and politeness. You might make eye contact and smile at someone simply to appear friendly. You're not being deceptive; you're using iconic cues to indicate politeness.

Forms of Nonverbal Communication: Your Not-So-Hidden Superpowers

Hopefully, you're starting to recognize how complex nonverbal communication is and why nonverbals are so important to the communication process (and also a source of many problems). Let's dissect that complexity a bit more by looking at the many forms or channels of nonverbal communication. There are even more channel distinctions (#TakeaNonverbalClass), but for now, let's look at some of the more common ones: kinesics, proxemics, haptics, appearance, vocalics, facial expressions/eye contact, chronemics, and artifacts and environment.

Kinesics

Kinesics is the study of body movement, including posture, gestures, and mobility (Birdwhistell, 1970). As you read these words, FREEZE! Now, without moving, get conscious of your body. Are you sitting, standing, reclining on a couch, or running on a treadmill (in which case, I hope you didn't actually freeze)? Is your body tense or relaxed, formal or casual? What might someone who sees you in this position think you're feeling?

The ways we move our bodies send messages to others about our thoughts, feelings, and intentions. For example, we clearly see the difference between *threat displays* (forward lean, wide stance, shoulders thrown back, forceful hands) and *fright displays* (hunched posture, pulled-in shoulders/legs/arms, lower head; Burgoon & Dunbar, 2006). In both displays, our movement and positioning of hands, arms, feet, shoulders, and head tell others how we feel and whether we're open to approach. They mean the same thing whether communicated by people or other animals (Tiedens & Fragale, 2003); you've probably even observed your pet doing these!

Kinesics, however, is more than threat and submission displays. We often use it to display our attraction to others. When we're with someone we like, we may avoid crossing our arms, we might lean in, and we may even mimic their postures and gestures. Desmond Morris (1967), a zoologist, studied humans as "naked apes" and uncovered *mimicry*, the idea that we often emulate, or move our bodies in ways similar to the movements of our interaction partner. We often mimic the movements of others we like to show how we're similar. Once you notice this pattern, you'll start to see it all over; being able to "read" others' nonverbals is a superpower that gives you insight into the way people think and feel—and even tells you if that cute guy/gal who sits next to you in class is actually into you!

Mimicry is largely unconscious/intrinsic, but we can do it iconically to increase affiliation with others.

© little star/Shutterstock.com

Some kinesics scholars devote their entire lives to just one tiny sub-area—*gestures*, communicating by moving parts of our bodies. Gestures are typically used in four ways, as: illustrators, adaptors, regulators, and emblems.

Illustrators are gestures that visualize, emphasize, and synchronize words (Ekman & Friesen, 1969). Here in Michigan (the state that looks like a mitten), people tell where they're from via speech and gesture: holding up right hand to visually represent Michigan's lower peninsula as left hand points to a particular location. As you read in Chapter 4, illustrators are important for emphasizing or depicting concepts in speeches.

We may not suck our thumbs anymore, but there are plenty of other ways we self-soothe in public!

Next, *adaptors* are (often unintentional) movements that help us cope with problems (e.g., provide comfort) and/or manage our needs (e.g., grooming; Ekman & Friesen, 1969). Self-adaptors help cope with fear or discomfort. As you can probably guess, people use these a LOT in public speaking: wring/hold hands, stroke hair, rub arms, cross arms giving a little hug to reassure themselves, rock slightly back/forth or side-to-side to emulate being rocked as a baby—all these self-adaptors indicate anxiety; control them to exhibit competence (see Chapter 4)!

Third, you already read how nonverbals regulate speech. Gestures are a primary form of this. *Regulators* manage a conversation's flow and pace by prompting the speaker to wait their turn, speak, continue, elaborate, and so forth. Something as simple as raising your hand in class is a perfect example of a regulator. We use them so much that we're usually not fully aware of doing it—but we *would* notice their absence (try conversing without ANY).

Finally, *emblems* are learned gestures that typically have a direct verbal equivalent; in other words, they're intentional movements, usually of the hands and/or arms, that translate to a particular word or phrase; they're arbitrary codes—like *Star Trek*'s Vulcan "Live long and prosper" parted-fingers V-emblem and *Black Panther*'s "Wakanda forever" cross-armed salute (adopted by celebrities, athletes, and even school teachers as a symbol of Black pride, solidarity, and resistance; Gander, 2018). Emblematic gestures are not only cultural but also historical, with different meanings across time periods. For example, in the United States, using the "OK" gesture upside-down was part of a deliberate online hoax to get people to use it as a fake "White power" sign to troll those who'd find it offensive. At some point, the hoax caught on, and some White supremacists began using it sincerely (Anti-Defamation League, 2019): The New Zealand man who allegedly shot 50 people in mosques flashed the symbol during his courtroom appearance (Falconer, 2019). You'd need to rely on context and other nonverbal channels to accurately interpret this emblem.

© pathdoc/Shutterstock.com

Facial Expression/Eye Contact

They're both body movements, so sometimes facial expressions and eye contact are considered kinesics. However, they're important to discuss on their own because they're the primary way we express emotions. Emotional facial expressions, known as ***affect displays***, represent (as intrinsic or iconic codes) external representations of how we feel internally.

As with gestures, facial expressions of emotion involve adaptors, regulators, illustrators, and emblems (Ekman & Friesen, 1969). Facial adaptors help us cope with stressors and meet our needs; we bite or lick our lips to cope with stress. Facial regulators manage the conversation, like a mouth slightly open and inhaling to indicate you're about to start speaking. Facial illustrators complement, visualize, emphasize, and synchronize speech; examples include raising your eyebrow(s) or widening eyes for emphasis. Facial emblems can actually replace or substitute words, such as when we roll our eyes, wink, or give someone the "side eye." Again, these emblems are culturally and historically specific.

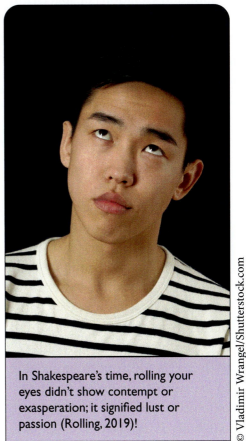

In Shakespeare's time, rolling your eyes didn't show contempt or exasperation; it signified lust or passion (Rolling, 2019)!

© Vladimir Wrangel/Shutterstock.com

Facial expressions are broken down even further by those who devote their research specifically to the study of eye communication, or ***oculesics***. This involves looking at eye contact, movement, dilation, and gaze, to name just a few areas. Eye contact, or mutual gaze, is an important nonverbal channel; it's a primary way we create and maintain ***immediacy*** (Andersen, Andersen, & Jensen, 1979), a sense of stimulation that fosters interpersonal closeness (see Chapter 10). A simple way we indicate our interest in someone (romantic or otherwise) is through eye contact. When talking with someone whose eyes stay on their phone, we don't exactly feel validated by them; we've been disconfirmed . . . all because of two little eyeballs! But, remember that even eye contact is culturally-bound, so what might appear inviting in one culture is seen as aggressive in another.

Proxemics

Edward T. Hall (1966) coined the term ***proxemics***, which is how we use space and distance to communicate. Rather than focusing on what the body's doing, proxemics looks at where the body is—how it's positioned relative to others/objects in a space. Hall (1966) described ***interpersonal distance***, or how far apart communicators are from one another, and asserted that cultures around the world have different interpersonal distance norms. These claims still largely hold up today: A study of nearly 9,000 participants across 42 countries found interpersonal distance norms vary by personal relationship, age, sex, and culture. For example, when interacting with strangers, closer interpersonal distances were kept by younger people, people in warmer cultures, and men (compared to women) overall (Sorokowska et al., 2017).

Hall (1966) broke personal distances into four "proxemic zones," which Burgoon then applied to create *Expectancy Violations Theory* (EVT) to describe, explain, and predict how people respond to violations of space (Burgoon & Jones, 1976). Since it was first created, EVT has been applied to other nonverbal norms like touch and environment, but it's most helpful for explaining how we deal with territory and distance proxemics (Burgoon, 2016) within Hall's original zones: intimate, personal, social, and public.

Intimate distance refers to the closest space (contact to 18″) around our bodies that we protect the most and reserve for intimates like romantic partners, friends, and close family. If a complete stranger enters this space without our permission, it may provoke our fight-or-flight response (Hall, 1966). EVT predicts we may even feel uncomfortable when those with "permission" enter this space if we don't have a close personal relationship with them.

For example, we allow doctors into our intimate space as they peer into our eyes, nose, and throat; listen to our lungs; and palpate our organs, but we probably feel uncomfortable while it occurs and relieved when it's over. Those in our intimate space have a high degree of direct sensory contact with us: In addition to being able to see us in close detail and hear our softest whisper, they can feel our body temperature, catch our scent, and yes, even taste us.

© Wolphgang/Shutterstock.com

Personal distance is the distance (18″ to 4′) we maintain in *most* casual encounters with close friends, family, and romantic partners. At this distance, sensory info is usually limited to sight, hearing, and limited touch. When we first meet someone, we often step into their personal space to shake hands, then step back. We still defend our personal space from strangers without permission to be there, but when violations occur, we're more apt to be annoyed and uncomfortable than to fight or flee (Burgoon, 2016).

Social distance is the space (4′ to 12′) most people are comfortable using for impersonal conversations with strangers day-to-day. At this distance, it's still easy to hear voices at normal volume and see with detail. Think of when you go to a customer service desk at a shop or airport; chances are good that you maintain a social distance from the person helping you, who's often behind a wide counter to ensure that you maintain that distance.

Finally, *public distance* is space beyond 12′. Sensory info reduces with distance, so to be heard at public distance, we often amplify our voices like public speakers, teachers, drill sergeants, and singers do. Likewise, sight becomes more limited, and we start to lose detail; to compensate, theatre actors and other performers often use exaggerated makeup, voices, and movements to make sure their nonverbal cues aren't lost on the audience. The most effective performers can make public space *feel* like intimate or personal distance.

Other theories predict that people compensate (typically, by moving away from) those who fail to meet our proxemic norms, but EVT states that we also find it rewarding if some people (those we view positively) get closer than we expect. For example, if Captain America actor Chris Evans (my favorite Marvel Chris) moves into the space I normally reserve for my closest friends or family, I'd be pretty happy about it. Who am I kidding? I'd light up social media to tell everyone I've ever met! And, that's without him even touching me!

Haptics

Haptics is the study of how we communicate using the largest of our sensory organs, touch. It's one of the most meaningful forms of nonverbal communication, especially for expressing affection, gratitude, comfort, and compassion and for creating social bonds (Hertenstein, Holmes, McCullough, & Keltner, 2009). Have you ever had someone (or perhaps you did it yourself) throw their arm across your chest when a vehicle came to a sudden stop—what is often called the "mom seatbelt"? Even a controlling form of touch such as this can be seen as an expression of care/concern. Both anecdotal and empirical evidence suggest, from the moment we're born, positive touch is essential for well-being.

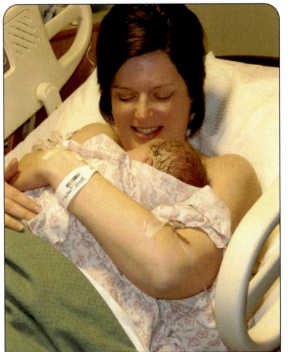

Especially moving for me: The Ogg twins were born just 14 days after I gave birth to my daughter (shown here), for whom I provided kangaroo care.

One example of the power of touch is *kangaroo care*, a technique in which newborn babies are given skin-to-skin (often, chest-to-chest) contact immediately after birth. It helps control pain, encourages breastfeeding, regulates temperature, and reduces infection and mortality rates in newborns (Campbell-Yeo, Disher, Benoit, & Johnston, 2015; Hunt, 2008). When Katie Ogg gave birth to premature twins, the girl was healthy, but the boy wasn't breathing. After trying to resuscitate him for 20 minutes, the doctors declared him dead and placed his body on her chest one last time. The heartbroken

Source: Nathaniel Lockwood

parents cuddled their baby, stroking his back and head, believing these moments to be their first and last with him. Five minutes later, they thought he'd moved, but doctors confirmed these movements were reflexive, not signs of life. But, his movements grew stronger and 2 hours later, baby Jamie opened his eyes and began to nurse, to the shock of the doctors who'd pronounced his death. Years later, Jamie Ogg is healthy; his parents tell him that though he's older than his twin sister, she's been alive longer (TODAYMoms, 2012).

Empirical evidence for the benefits of positive touch is also strong. It can be therapeutic for both body and mind— in animals and humans. It decreases stress and anxiety and positively affects "growth, brain waves, breathing, heart rate, [and] even the immune system . . . [touch is] critical for growth, development, and health" (Field, 2014, p. ix). Positive touch doesn't just help us; the absence of it can hurt us! *Touch hunger*, resulting from failure to satisfy physical touch needs (i.e., touch deprivation), can happen to *anyone* but is especially common in incarcerated individuals (e.g., immigrant children, adults held in detention centers). Just like mutant Rogue, you may even experience touch deprivation. Despite being surrounded by people all day, have you ever just needed a hug? Although there are formal touch therapies, even massage fulfills touch hunger, increases serotonin levels, and decreases blood pressure (Field, 2014).

Finally, it's important to note that not all touch is positive. Haptics express dislike or unwanted control. And, sometimes negative touch, such as physical and/or sexual abuse, can have long-lasting effects for victims—affecting how all forms of touch from anyone are experienced (Eckstein, 2016). In workplace or education settings, touch becomes problematic when people with more social status or authority touch those who don't want it. Negative touch can harm health by causing mental health issues, obesity, heart disease, depression, anxiety, and poor self-esteem (Monnat & Chandler, 2015).

Appearance and Beauty

Physical appearance refers to our bodily features, both natural and strategic, that make up the way we look. You'll learn more about these in Chapter 14, so for now I'll just highlight how appearance is *used* to communicate. We use our natural appearance to our advantage if it helps us connect with others. For example, height/weight, skin and hair color, and age all affect how people perceive and interact with us. But, if we don't like our appearance, we can change aspects of it. Getting braces, cutting your hair, even shaving are common examples. We also decorate ourselves with appearance **artifacts**, objects to express ourselves. Artifacts serve multiple functions (see Public Speaking Box) whose meanings are cultural and historic.

Public Speaking Power: Clothes Make the Wo/Man

You already know to be comfortable and competent while speaking, but beyond that, you can use appearance artifacts to shape an audience's impression of you. If you want to increase affiliation with or similarity to the people you speak to, take advantage of several communicative functions of clothing/accessories that exhibit culturally-shared meaning (Todorović, Toporišič, & Pavko-Čuden, 2014). Here are some ways we use attire and how you can adopt them on speech day:

- **Protection** (psychological or physical safety): *bulky winter coat, firefighters' gear*
  - If it's cold, wear a jacket so you don't shiver and look nervous. Or, wear your favorite sweater because it makes you feel like an invulnerable superhero.
- **Sexual Attraction** (enticing desire): *well-fitting clothes, particularly flattering colors*
  - People listen to us a lot more when we're attractive. Consider clothing to flatter your assets, but don't go overboard! You want the audience focused on what you say, not visualizing you naked; being *too* revealing lowers your credibility. Superheroes have certain colors that make them look more powerful. What do the color of your clothes say about you?
- **Persuasion** (goal-achievement): *"preppy" clothes to appear upper class to get a loan*
  - The reason we're always told to "look professional" in speeches? It increases speaker ethos so people listen to/believe us. Use it to your advantage: Be "business casual"—not too dressy because that'll separate you from your audience.
- **Status Display** (convince others of worth): *designer items, military rank medals*
  - Your appearance can convey expertise/worth. Wear something to show you're a pro, perhaps your rodeo wear for your speech on horseback riding.
- **Group Affiliation** (show membership belonging): *job or club uniform, cultural garb*
  - An affiliation artifact serves two purposes. First, it's your credibility claim. For a CPR speech, wear your EMT uniform! Second, it makes audiences feel similar to you, which increases immediacy. If there's a particular campus style, embrace it for your speech! They'll be inclined to see you as "one of them" and listen closely to what you say.

Clearly, clothing could do all of these functions at once—all creating an impression on your audience without uttering a word!

Contributed by J. Eckstein

How do you express your identity nonverbally? What biases and stereotypes do we have about certain physical appearance cues?

© CLP Media/Shutterstock.com

Image is important; within seconds of meeting, people form impressions based on how others look (Olivola & Todorov, 2010). That's not to say we're always, or even *often*, correct in the assumptions we make, but make assumptions we do! The "***what's beautiful is good*" concept** explains how/why we believe attractive people have more desirable personal qualities (Dion, Berscheid & Walster, 1972), like being smarter, college-worthy, better romantic partners, more sensitive, kinder, intriguing, more sociable (Murphy, Hussey, Barnes-Holmes, & Kelly, 2015), and less guilty in mock trials (Efran, 1974). This is a cognitive bias called **the halo effect,** and its inverse (believing unattractive people have bad personalities) is the **reverse halo effect** (Asch, 1946; Thorndike, 1920). Overweight job applicants are often seen as less conscientious, agreeable, emotionally stable, or outgoing than those who aren't overweight—despite them being no more likely to possess these traits than others (Roehling, Roehling, & Odland, 2008).

Given our attractiveness bias, researchers often study whether universal qualities exist regarding what's beautiful. Many beauty standards vary culturally and historically, but some argue there are things everyone values (Cunningham, Roberts, Barbee, Druen & Wu, 1995): straightness, averageness, symmetry, and proportionality. The **straightness principle** predicts we'll view straight (body/face) profiles as more beautiful than less straight ones. That's why people wear braces (Khalid & Quiñonez, 2015). The **averageness principle** says we'll prefer mathematically attractive averages of people who are the same sex/age as us (Langlois & Roggman, 1990). The **symmetry principle** suggests faces are beautiful when each vertical half mirrors the other. Very few of us are exactly symmetrical (e.g., one ear lower than the other, one eye slightly bigger, an arm or leg longer), but the closer to symmetrical we are, the more attractive we're

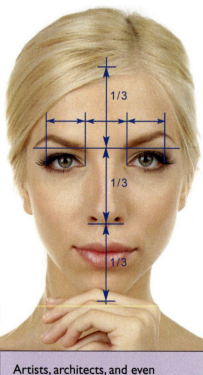

Artists, architects, and even surgeons use these principles to make their work more beautiful.

© Africa Studio/Shutterstock.com

believed to be. The ***proportionality principle*** finds faces most beautiful when they reflect the "golden ratio" (1:1.618 ratio); that's roughly 1.5× longer than wide. Surgeons have even used this ratio to create masks representing ideal faces—which are then applied to those seeking plastic surgery (e.g., Marquardt, 2002). So, which principle does the best job of explaining what's beautiful? No one yet agrees. Maybe that's because "beauty" is too often tied to other nonverbals . . . like our voices.

Vocalics

Also known as *paralanguage*, **vocalics** are nonverbal cues that accompany speech—not the words themselves but how we say them. Many vocalics accompany speech, so I'll mention just a few here: pitch, rate, volume, inflection, and accent. ***Pitch*** is the perceived "highness" or "lowness" of a voice, determined by the length and width of our vocal cords. Women and children tend to have higher pitched voices, whereas men's voices tend to be lower pitched (Poyatos, 1993), but of course, we can fluctuate our own pitch—think to when you've attempted to sound more masculine or feminine. ***Rate*** is how quickly or slowly someone speaks. Some people speak faster than others, but on average, humans speak at a rate of 125 to 150 words per minute. Our speech rate affects others' perceptions of us; for example, if instructors speak too slowly, they "risk damaging their credibility, lowering perceptions of their immediacy, and hampering student affective learning" (Simonds, Meyer, Quinlan, & Hunt, 2006, p. 193). ***Volume***, how loudly/softly we speak, can reflect our emotional state (e.g., yelling when angry) and/or need for privacy or consideration for others (e.g., whispering in library).

Combining elements of all of them is ***inflection***, also known as modulation or vocal variety. It's the rise/fall of your pitch; for example, we raise pitch at the ends of sentences to ask questions rather than statements (Poyatos, 1993). Lots of inflection is essential for public speakers who don't want to bore their audience (see Chapter 4), and it's why computerized voices like Apple's Siri or Amazon's Alexa are easily identified—they lack vocal inflection. Combined, all these vocalics change how/whether a message is received and how it's interpreted.

Vocalics also includes ***speech accents***, the pronunciations and speech sounds associated with the language of a given region, social class, or ethnic group (Moyer, 2013). Accents, together with the unique grammar, vocabulary, and language of people in an area, form ***regional dialects***. Regional dialects vary widely across the United States. When I'm in Michigan (the state

Accents aren't just regional—specific U.S. states have them too: www.youtube.com/watch?time_continue=2&v=UcxByX6rh24

© Kotin/Shutterstock.com

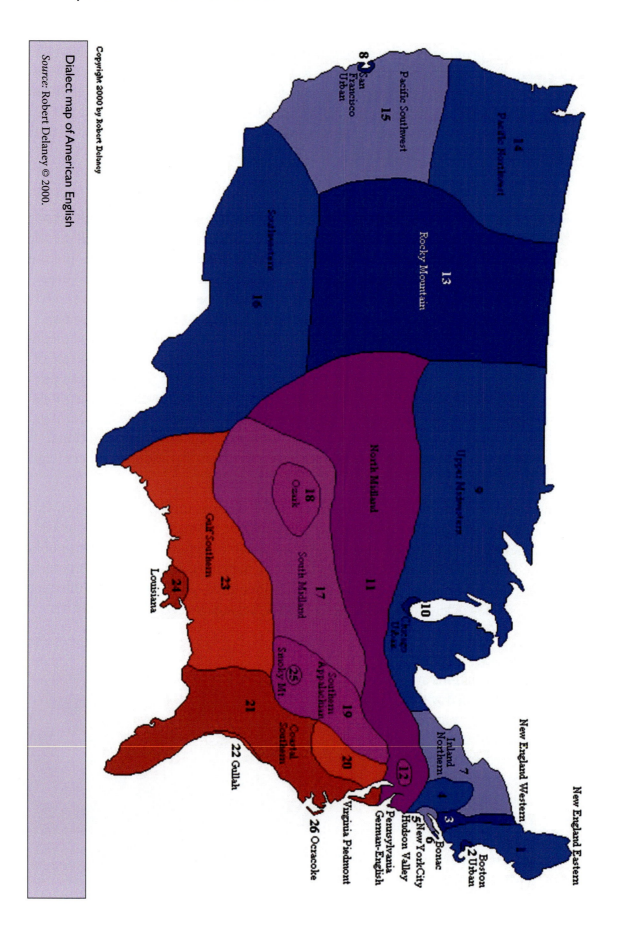

Dialect map of American English

Source: Robert Delaney © 2000.

I've adopted), "I parked my car," and when I'm in Maine (where I'm from), "I pahked my cah." We ALL have accents, and we use these vocalics to distinguish those who are like us from those who aren't (Hansen & Dovidio, 2016). Here in the U.S., regional accents are stereotyped in TV and film to be associated with particular character types. It might seem quaint or amusing to make generalizations about others based on their accent, but this bias can have serious consequences. For example, a person's accent has been found to affect eyewitnesses in criminal trials, specifically in terms of how witnesses evaluate a person's credibility, judgments of accuracy, deceptiveness, and prestige. Even more troubling, accent combined with ethnic background, influenced eyewitnesses' perceptions of the defendant's guilt (Frumkin, 2007).

As much as vocalics can be about how we say something, not saying anything at all is equally powerful and important. Sometimes silence says even more than words. Like many nonverbal cues, silence conveys multiple meanings in interpersonal communication (Bruneau, 1973); in fact, there are over 20 different meanings (see Johannesen, 1974), including disconfirmation, companionship/intimacy, and many others! We've all experienced the disconfirmation of having someone use silence to give us the "cold shoulder" to tune us out and act as though we don't matter or exist to them. In this way, silence is censure or punishment. Silence, however, can also be warm, comfortable, and indicative of relational intimacy, such as when romantic partners or close friends sit together in a "companionable silence" (see Chapter 10). If you want to test your relationship (romantic or friendship), take a long road trip (8+ hours) where you'll be silent at some point. If that silence is comfortable/natural, it may show closeness so deep that words are unnecessary. Other times, silence communicates respect (e.g., "take a moment of silence" to remember lives lost), confrontation avoidance (e.g., "biting our tongue" in response to controversial views), lack of attention (e.g., when we daydream), and not knowing what to say (Johannesen, 1974). But, sometimes just the timing of the silence speaks volumes.

Chronemics

Chronemics is the study of communication focused on "human time experiencing" (Bruneau, 2012, p. 73). Although we don't typically think of time as a nonverbal factor (as it doesn't specifically involve our bodies), our use of time communicates a lot. For example, if you have a job interview at 10:00 a.m., what time are you going to show up? One would hope you'd arrive early to convey the message you're serious about the job and dependable.

We also understand time use through two major approaches: monochronic and polychronic. *Monochronic* time use involves focusing on one task at a time, whereas *polychronic* refers to being simultaneously involved in two or more activities. Individuals, organizations, and even entire cultures differ in their orientations to time along a monochronic to polychronic continuum (Bluedorn, Kaufman, & Lane, 1992). Monochronic orientations tend to value task-focus, promptness, privacy, adhering to plans, and may even monetize time. Conversely, polychronic orientations tend to value relationship-focus, have more relaxed attitudes toward promptness and privacy, may change plans often, and allow people to run on their own schedules.

Activism Hero: Is Time on Your Side?

Cultural time orientations—how we use time to live, relate, and structure society—*enormously* shapes the world. Taken for granted ("just the way it is")—like the larger power structures (e.g., media, money, calendars) requiring us to "assimilate or be destroyed by the Borg," we rarely notice we're doing it. But, observing how our "norms" are just arbitrary (decided by those in power back in the day; e.g., Roman numerals, Julio calendar) questions how society works (particularly, at the expense of some groups). Those ancient decisions *still* affect *ALL* of us today—whether we want them to or not. If you want to begin changing the world around you, you need to understand how time influences our culture. Hall (1959) showed seven ways it does this:

1. *Ordering*—*reliance on fixed, even sequences like days of the week*: Weeks may begin on Sunday (e.g., devout Christians who "start week with God") *or* Monday (e.g., 5-day work-weeks).
2. *Cycling*—*if/when history renews*: America is highly cyclical; we begin "anew" each day/week (I'll start dieting next week!).
3. *Valuation*—*time's importance*: We may see time as "valuable" for its own sake (e.g., spend time with loved ones, live long lives).
4. *Tangibility*—*time as commodity*: Cultures *create* this shared meaning; we can't see/touch time, so we make things represent those values (e.g., "time is money").
5. *Synthesisity*—*compiled increments*: Minutes → hours → days. U.S. pays hourly (not a global practice). Even salary/contract pay is rationalized by how many hours it "should" take.
6. *Duration*—*norm for what occurs (or should) in a span*: European-based cultures standardize what happens "between" two predetermined points of time; others use characteristic event sequences (e.g., Hopi look to *when* corn's ready to harvest); others use rotations like seasons (e.g., "many moons from now" or gaming tournaments, drafts).
7. *Depth*—*predicting future*: Those who prioritize tradition or dislike uncertainty reassure themselves life is predictable (e.g., predict team win, stock value, relational success).

WHY do we value time the way *we* do? Consider how culturally arbitrary it is! Not that it's an excuse. Saying "I have a different orientation" won't let you avoid April 15th taxes; we must adapt to chronologies we live/operate within. BUT, if you figure out how *you* orient toward time, you'll see there's no "normal" or "right" way to view the world; if others have a different approach, you can cut them some slack *and* educate others about differences. Remember—being an activist isn't just about knowing (being informed); it's about doing (educating others).

Contributed by J. Eckstein

Differences in these time orientations can lead to multiple interpretations of behaviors. Imagine a couple (who each have a different time orientation) are out on a date. The monochronic person may show up early and when their polychronic date arrives later than the "scheduled" time (hey, there's no rush), the monochronic person is apt to be irritated (this was valuable time they were to spend together). There are many other elements to chronemics, particularly in terms of cultural differences (see Activism Hero box).

Artifacts and Environment

A final nonverbal channel is how we use what's around us. Sometimes, this involves *artifacts*, personal objects that communicate about our identities, or "objects invoked in the performance of identity" (White & Beaudry, 2009, p. 213). Stop and look at the material objects around you right now. How have you used artifacts to make the space (even if it's a public one) your "own"? If you were to visit my office, you'd find it filled with books, papers, and many artifacts: toys representing characters from Marvel movies, *The X-Files*, *Harry Potter*, and *Bill and Ted's Excellent Adventure*. You'd see a model replica of the ship *Serenity* and autographed photos of actors Nathan Fillion, Stephen Amell, Mitch Pileggi, and David Tennant. You'd find a framed poster of the Hogwarts castle in the moonlight and a photo of me and two colleagues on the bridge of the starship *Enterprise*. What do you now know about me, based on the artifacts displayed in my office? What can you infer from these items about my identity?

© Vectorpocket/Shutterstock.com

We communicate using artifacts to not only personalize but also claim our environment as our *territory*, which is a place, space, or area we mark as our own. We typically defend it because we meet important needs there (Becker, 1973). Think about when you drive through a subdivision and see fences around everyone's yards. Even in the vast wide-open expanses of the American West, farmers/ranchers use fences to claim their territory. But, our space isn't just about land. Sometimes we don't realize that a space is our territory *until* we feel compelled to defend it. You might not think your car is your territory, but if someone were to break into it, you'd probably feel violated, angry, or anxious to defend it.

Just like other animals peeing on things, not only do we claim and mark the spaces we own, but sometimes we claim/mark spaces we don't own! A *jurisdiction* is a space we don't own but temporarily mark as ours, usually for a specific purpose (Roos, 1968). For example, we often have a "spot" or chair in each class that we consider "ours," even though we know it's not. How'd you react to someone sitting in the seat you occupied all semester? One way we claim space is by using one or more artifacts as **markers**, or signs that communicate to others that a space is "owned" or occupied (Becker, 1973). Just watch people claim public spaces as jurisdictions: (draping jackets over) movie theater seats, (stacking books in) library study carrels, or (placing trays on) dining hall tables. You probably even do this in your classes—placing your book bag in a seat next to you to "claim" a bigger territory than your own chair/space.

Whether fences or place-markers, in the end, we're all just animals... trying to stake claim to things that aren't ours!

It's not just *which* objects we use to claim space, but also *how* we arrange them: where they're placed, whether tidy or cluttered, and the permanency of fixed/semi-fixed design features (Mehrabian, 1976). I have a big, open space in the middle of my office; my desk faces and abuts a wall so students sit right beside me to look at my computer. Against another wall is a small, round table with two upholstered side-by-side chairs. I intentionally designed this space for collaborative work and open dialogue to minimize power differences. If my desk was in the middle of the room and faced the door, I'd be sending a different kind of message. Even something as seemingly innocent as furniture arrangement can communicate power.

Following Nonverbal Communication Norms

This chapter focused on the characteristics, functions, and channels of nonverbal communication. We communicate without words in so many ways! And, this matters in so many areas of our lives! We rely on nonverbals to make interpretations about others in important ways. For example, in job interviews, we often make inferences about an applicant's personality and abilities—such as their confidence, leadership skills, motivation, interest, and honesty—based on kinesic, appearance, chronemic, and other nonverbal cues (von Raffler-Engel, 1983). Even though they're not necessarily accurate, people still perceive that they are!

In some jobs, the ability to read these cues is a skill that makes the difference between life and death. Police officers, for example, rely on kinesics and haptics to make split-second decisions about whether someone is going to submit to an arrest, flee, or attack. Mistakenly interpreting these cues can be fatal for officers, suspects, and/or others. Knowing more about nonverbals helps you see behaviors you never noticed before. You can use that knowledge to make informed, reflective choices about your own and others' communication. Plus, being aware of these perceptions gives you an advantage in those interviews so that you're not just a communication superhero but an employed one!

References

Andersen, J. F., Andersen, P. A., & Jensen, A. D. (1979). The measurement of nonverbal immediacy. *Journal of Applied Communication Research, 7*, 153–180. doi:10.1080/00909887909365204

Anti-Defamation League. (2019). *Okay hand gesture: Racist hand signs*. Retrieved from www.adl.org/education/references/hate-symbols/okay-hand-gesture

Asch, S. E. (1946). Forming impressions of personality. *The Journal of Abnormal and Social Psychology, 41,* 258–290. doi:10.1037/h0055756

Becker, F. D. (1973). Study of spatial markers. *Journal of Personality & Social Psychology, 26,* 439–445. doi:10.1037/h0034442

Birdwhistell, R. L. (1970). *Kinesics and context: Essays on body motion communication.* Philadelphia, PA: University of Pennsylvania Press.

Bluedorn, A., Kaufman, C., & Lane, P. (1992). How many things do you like to do at once?: An introduction to monochronic and polychronic time. *The Academy of Management Executive, 14*(2), 17–26. doi:10.1177/0961463X07080270

Bruneau, T. (1973). Communicative silences: Forms and functions. *Journal of Communication, 23,* 17–46. doi:10.1111/j.1460-2466.1973.tb00929.x

Bruneau, T. (2012). Chronemics: Time-binding and the construction of personal time. *ETC: A Review of General Semantics, 69,* 72–92.

Buck, R., & VanLear, C. (2002). Verbal & nonverbal communication: Distinguishing symbolic, spontaneous, & pseudo-spontaneous nonverbal behavior. *Journal of Communication, 52,* 522–541. doi:10.1111/j.1460-2466.2002.tb02560.x

Burgoon, J. (2016). Expectancy violations theory. In C. Berger & M. Roloff (Eds.), *The international encyclopedia of interpersonal communication.* Retrieved from onlinelibrary.wiley.com/doi/pdf/10.1002/9781118540190.wbeic102

Burgoon, J., & Dunbar, N. (2006). Nonverbal expressions of dominance and power in human relationships. In M. Patterson & V. Manusov (Eds.), *The Sage handbook of nonverbal communication* (pp. 247–262). Thousand Oaks, CA: Sage.

Burgoon, J., & Jones, S. (1976). Toward a theory of personal space expectations & their violations. *Human Communication Research, 2,* 131–146. doi:10.1111/j.1468-2958.1976.tb00706.x.

Campbell-Yeo, M., Disher, T., Benoit, B., & Johnston, C. (2015). Understanding kangaroo care & its benefits to preterm infants. *Pediatric Health, Medicine & Therapeutics, 6,* 15–32. doi:10.2147/PHMT.S51869

Cunningham, M., Roberts, A., Barbee, A., Druen, P., & Wu, C. (1995). "Their ideas of beauty are, on the whole, the same as ours": Consistency & variability in cross-cultural perception of female physical attractiveness. *Journal of Personality & Social Psychology, 68,* 261–279. doi:10.1037/0022-3514.68.2.261

Darwin, C. (1872/1965). *The expression of emotions in man and animals.* Chicago, IL: University of Chicago Press.

Dews, S., Winner, E., Kaplan, J., Rosenblatt, E., Hunt, M., Lim, K., . . . Smarsh, B. (1996). Children's understanding of the meaning and functions of verbal irony. *Child Development, 67,* 3071–3085. doi:10.1111/j.1467-8624.1996.tb01903.x

Dion, K., Berscheid, E., & Walster, E. (1972). What is beautiful is good. *Journal of Personality and Social Psychology, 24,* 285–290. doi:10.1037/h0033731

Eckstein, J. (2016). Factors affecting victims' preferences for love-communication from abusive partners. In L. Olson & M. Fine (Eds.), *The darker side of family communication: The harmful, morally suspect, & socially inappropriate* (pp. 175–197). New York, NY: Peter Lang.

Efran, M. G. (1974). The effects of physical attractiveness on judgments in a simulated jury task. *Journal of Research in Personality, 8,* 45–54. doi:10.1016/0092-6566(74)90044-0

Ekman, P., & Friesen, W. V. (1969). The repertoire of nonverbal behavior: Categories, origins, usage, and coding. *Semiotica, 1,* 49–98. doi:10.1515/semi.1969.1.1.49

Falconer, R. (2019, March 16). Mosque attacks suspect gives "White power" sign in Christchurch court. *Axios.* Retrieved from www.axios.com/christchuch-attacks-brenton-tarrant-1552716245-18d37895-d870-4e94-8dd6-0a56eb7a0a5e.html

Field, T. (2014). *Touch* (2nd ed.). Cambridge, MA: MIT Press.

Frumkin, L. (2007). Influences of accent and ethnic background on perceptions of eyewitness testimony. *Psychology, Crime and Law, 13,* 317–331. doi:10.1080/10683160600822246

Gander, K. (2018, March 13). Is the *Black Panther* "Wakanda Salute" becoming a symbol of Black pride? *Newsweek*. Retrieved from www.newsweek.com/wakanda-salute-becoming-symbol-black-solidarity-842294

Goodwin, C. (1981). *Conversational organization*. New York, NY: Academic Press.

Hansen, K., & Dovidio, J. (2016). Social dominance orientation, nonnative accents, and hiring recommendations. *Cultural Diversity & Ethnic Minority Psychology, 22*(4), 1–8. doi:10.1037/cdp0000101

Hall, E. T. (1959). *The silent language*. New York, NY: Doubleday.

Hall, E. T. (1966). *The hidden dimension*. Garden City, NY: Anchor.

Hertenstein, M. J., Holmes, R., McCullough, M., & Keltner, D. (2009). The communication of emotion via touch. *Emotion, 9*, 566–573. doi:10.1037/a0016108

Hunt, F. (2008). The importance of kangaroo care on infant oxygen saturation levels and bonding. *Journal of Neonatal Nursing, 14*, 47–51. doi:10.1016/j.jnn.2007.12.003

Johannesen, R. L. (1974). The functions of silence: A plea for communication research. *Western Journal of Communication, 38*, 25–35. doi:10.1080/10570317409373806

Khalid, A., & Quiñonez, C. (2015). Straight, white teeth as a social prerogative. *Sociology of Health & Illness, 37*, 782–796. doi:10.1111/1467-9566.12238

Langlois, J. H., & Roggman, L. A. (1990). Attractive faces are only average. *Psychological Science, 1*, 115–121. doi:10.1111/j.1467-9280.1990.tb00079.x

Marquardt, S. (2002). Dr. Stephen R. Marquardt on the golden decagon and human facial beauty (interview by Dr. Gottlieb). *Journal of Clinical Orthodontics, 36*, 339–347.

Mehrabian, A. (1976). *Public places and private spaces: The psychology of work, play and living environments*. New York, NY: Basic Books.

Mehrabian, A. (1981). *Silent messages: Implicit communication of emotions and attitudes* (2nd ed.). Belmont, CA: Wadsworth.

Monnat, S., & Chandler, R. (2015). Long term physical health consequences of adverse childhood experiences. *The Sociologist Quarterly, 56*, 723–752. doi:10.1111/tsq.12107

Morris, D. (1967). *The naked ape: A zoologist's study of the human animal*. London, UK: Cape.

Morris, D. (1994). *Bodytalk: A world guide to gestures*. New York, NY: Crown.

Moyer, A. (2013). *Foreign accent: The phenomenon of non-native speech*. Cambridge, UK: Cambridge University Press.

Murphy, C., Hussey T., Barnes-Holmes, D., & Kelly, M. (2015). The Implicit Relational Assessment procedure (IRAP) and attractiveness bias. *Journal of Contextual Behavioral Science, 4*, 292–299. doi:10.1016/j.jcbs.2015.08.001

Olivola, C. Y., & Todorov, A. (2010). Fooled by first impressions?: Reexamining the diagnostic value of appearance-based inferences. *Journal of Experimental Social Psychology, 46*, 315–324. doi:10.1016/j.jesp.2009.12.002

Poyatos, F. (1993). *Paralanguage: A linguistic and interdisciplinary approach to interactive speech and sound*. Philadelphia, PA: Benjamins.

Roehling, M., Roehling, P., & Odland, L. (2008). Investigating the validity of stereotypes about overweight employees: Relationship between body weight & normal personality traits. *Group & Organization Management, 33*, 392–424. doi:10.1177/1059601108321518

Rolling. (2019). In *Oxford English dictionary*. Retrieved from www.oed.com/view/Entry/167012

Roos, P. (1968). Jurisdiction: An ecological concept. *Human Relations, 21*, 75–84.

Simonds, B., Meyer, K., Quinlan, M., & Hunt, S. (2006). Effects of instructor speech rate on student affective learning, recall, & perceptions of nonverbal immediacy, credibility & clarity. *Communication Research Reports, 23*, 187–197. doi:10.1080/08824090600796401

Sorokowska, A., Sorokowski, P., Hilpert, P., Cantarero, K., Frackowiak, T., Ahmadi, K., . . . Pierce, J. D., Jr. (2017). Preferred interpersonal distances: A global comparison. *Journal of Cross-Cultural Psychology, 48*, 577–592. doi:10.1177/0022022117698039

Thom, C., Gilley, D. C., Hooper, J., & Esch, H. E. (2007). The scent of the waggle dance. *PLoS Biology, 5*(9), e228. doi:10.1371/journal.pbio.0050228

Thorndike, E. L. (1920). A constant error in psychological ratings. *Journal of Applied Psychology, 4,* 25–29. doi:10.1037/h0071663

Thorpe, W. H. (1961). *Bird-song: The biology of vocal communication and expression in birds.* Oxford, UK: Oxford University Press.

Tiedens, L., & Fragale, A. (2003). Power moves: Complementarity in dominant & submissive nonverbal behavior. *Journal of Personality & Social Psychology, 84,* 558–568. doi:10.1037/0022-3514.84.3.558

TODAYMoms. (2012, March 8). *Pronounced dead, revived by mom's hug: "Miracle baby" turning 2.* Retrieved from www.today.com/parents/pronounced-dead-revived-moms-hug-miracle-baby-turning-2-366375

Todorović, T., Toporišič, T., & Pavko-Čuden, A. (2014). Clothes and costumes as form of nonverbal communication. *Tekstilec, 57,* 321–333. doi:10.14502/Tekstilec2014.57.321-333

Watzlawick, P., Beavin, J., & Jackson, D. (1967). *Pragmatics of human communication: Study of interactional patterns, pathologies & paradoxes* (pp. 48–71). New York, NY: W. W. Norton.

Volkmar, F., & Siegel, A. (1982). Responses to consistent & discrepant social communications. In R. Feldman (Ed.), *Development of nonverbal behavior in children* (pp. 231–255). New York, NY: Springer.

von Raffler-Engel, W. (1983). *The perception of nonverbal behavior in the career interview.* Philadelphia, PA: John Benjamins.

White, C., & Beaudry, M. (2009). Artifacts & personal identity. In T. Majewski & D. Gaimster (Eds.), *International handbook of historical archaeology* (pp. 209–225). doi:10.1007/978-0-387-72071-5_12

You already know this is a chapter on listening. So, close your eyes and take a moment to reflect on how you're feeling about studying listening. Does it interest you? Do you think it's a waste of time? Are you curious? Were you even listening or paying attention to what you just read? This kind of awareness and attention to your own process is essential for listening—and, in my opinion, life in general.

Effective listening is the key to any form of effective communication. But, every person—whether expert or brand new baby—has a unique perspective on listening (Purdy, Roca, Halley, Holmes, & Christy, 2017). Throughout this chapter, I'd like you to think about how *you* listen—not just generalizations about how other people do (or don't do) it. Most of what I'll discuss isn't just ear-based; that's just *hearing*. *Listening*, on the other hand, involves the entire body and the interpersonal processes that go along with

Be curious! Start exploring/questioning all the "reality" around you.

© MVolodymyr/Shutterstock.com

that to process stimuli we hear. In other words, hearing is passive and physiological, and listening is active and psychological.

You can and *should* take entire classes on listening; this chapter just skims the surface. I can introduce you to the basics, but what matters most for you in the long run is to develop a *curious* approach to understanding communication and yourself. Throughout this chapter, we'll battle some obstacles presented by listening by asking WWBD? (What would Batman do?). We'll do this by asking (and answering): Why, When and What, and finally, How?

POW! WHAM! Batman Gets the Riddler by Knowing 'Why?'

Up until relatively recently, no one really bothered to study listening by itself (International Listening Association, 2019), let alone in classes where you also gave speeches. Communication scholars didn't even recognize it as its own area of study until the 1980s. So, why cover it now? Because of the big four: Listening is prevalent; it's a basis of all communication; it's tied to your future success; and it'll make people like you (sorta).

First and foremost, the discipline finally acknowledges how significant listening is for communication models (see Chapter 1)! How could they understand communication by leaving out half the process? We spend much more of our lives listening (24%–53%) than we do speaking (20%–23%; Bohlken, 1999; Janusik & Wolvin, 2009). We listen (in some sense) even when we sleep!

Second, if you look at communication (and hopefully, this textbook) as a tool (or superpower) for your personal life, then listening *in particular* is one of the most important parts of that! We're all guilty of zoning out sometimes ("Are you even listening to me!?"), but how do *you* feel when you think someone isn't paying attention to you? The onus is on us. You'll now be educated (after this chapter, of course) in this communication superpower to listen better and make the people in your life feel valued and respected.

Third, practically speaking, to get and be good at a job, the tips in this chapter are quite essential. You know that one student (not you, of course!) in class who always asks a question (because they weren't listening) about an assignment the teacher *just* addressed moments before? Chances are, much like every time superheroes are mentioned in this book, there's a collective eye-roll in the class—you all find it rather frustrating (or just cheesy, in the case of the heroes theme). We know most people aren't perfect listeners; we all occasionally blank out. But, as instructors, we also know these people are likely to do the same thing at their jobs, leaving similarly negative impressions on their boss. So, if anything, you should probably listen to what I (and your instructor) have to say about listening if you want to get and keep a job.

Finally, you may have already given speeches in this class (or in life), and it's a safe bet you remember some better than others. What'd the memorable speakers do to make you *want* to listen? Listening highlights the relationship between you—the speaker—and your audience. Knowing what draws you to particular speakers can help you know what to focus on in your own speaking, making it easier for others to listen to you . . . and hopefully, to like you.

Public Speaking Power: Attention Is Your Gift

Paying attention to your classmates' speeches can be an interesting opportunity to learn about listening. Come up with a list of the ways you'd like your classmates to listen to you when you present your speeches (eye contact, no yawning, sitting upright, etc.). How hard would it be for you to attend to them in those same ways? French philosopher Simone Weil (1970) said, "Attention is the rarest and purest form of generosity" (p. 18). It's a wonderful thing to give that gift to (and receive it back from) your audience.

Contributed by K. Wiss

© Orange Vectors/Shutterstock.com

Your attention may not be "real" at first, but your body will catch up with your outward displays.

© Artem Kovalenco/Shutterstock.com

Thinking about these big four reasons to study listening, be honest with yourself: How good a listener are you *really*? Are you that way ALL the time? Even if you answer, "Pretty good, I think," there's *always* room for improvement. I've taught and studied listening in-depth for decades, and I'm *still* honing my skills! So, let's delve deeper into listening's intricacies to combat one of the most lacking communication skills out there—our attention to listening.

OUCH! Riddler Punches Back by Asking 'When?' and 'What?'

I just mentioned listening is often taken for granted. Perhaps that's because it's actually a complex, varied process. Scholars differ (somewhat) on definitions, with listening models highlighting various elements (Brownell, 2016). We'll first look at a general model to understand the order in which things happen—answering the When? question. Then, I'll discuss some listening types to answer the What? question.

When Does This All Happen?

Building off Wolvin and Coakley's (1996) definition, *listening* is a process involving six elements: receiving, attending, understanding, remembering, interpreting and evaluating, and responding to stimuli. By treating each part of this definition as a stage, we see an "order" to how listening happens. Understanding each step reveals quite a bit about how we auto-process the world around us. Perhaps we should start paying a bit more attention to what we're allowing our bodies/brains to do *for* us without questioning them. We want to be active heroes—not the mindless drones they're forced to rescue. Now, realize these steps aren't strictly limited; we can (and do) revert to earlier stages as we listen, in an ever-repeating cycle. However, they *are* strictly sequential, meaning I can't advance to the next step without accomplishing the one before it. It's like a game of SuperMario; you can always go replay earlier levels but can't advance to the next one until you successfully complete the most recent one.

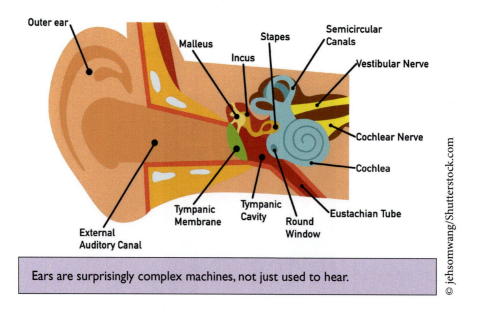

Ears are surprisingly complex machines, not just used to hear.

© jehsomwang/Shutterstock.com

Receiving

First, the most biological part of listening, *reception*, is when we receive and (begin to) process physical stimuli. We tend to think of listening as sound-related, but all our senses are involved. Heck, some people even put on their glasses to listen better! If you've ever missed what someone on TV said and backed up to watch it again more closely, you've done the same thing—used your visual senses to help your aural one.

Each of our sense organs is good at receiving something. *Hearing*, when audible, involves us physically collecting soundwaves with our ear parts, which translate them for the nervous system, which sends them to the brain for processing. Fully functional ears are masters at receiving sound vibrations and sending them to the brain. But, even those (like Deaf people)

whose ears don't function like others' can still hear/receive stimuli; they just use other senses (which we *all* do, to some extent, anyway). It's not lesser; it's just a different way of doing the same process. Although people may use "listening" and "hearing" interchangeably (even though they're not), listening encompasses a LOT more. So, as we go forward, use the term *hearing* to refer only to the first, physiological stage of listening.

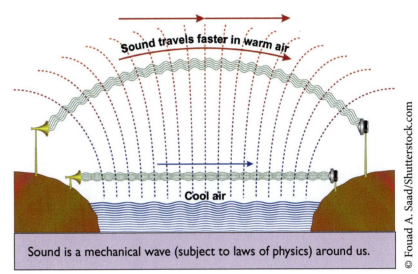

Sound travels faster in warm air

Cool air

Sound is a mechanical wave (subject to laws of physics) around us.

© Fouad A. Saad/Shutterstock.com

Receiving was touched on a bit in the perception chapter (Chapter 5), but it's much more specific in listening. Receiving is affected by numerous factors. Obviously, physical circumstances can hinder our message reception. You have difficulty hearing your instructor while the person next to you talks, or your channel interferes if your drive has a cell-phone dead zone. And, we all have different levels of visual acuity and auditory sensitivity. Even our own sensitivity varies. Remember, something as simple as a head cold or being tired makes us very poor listeners.

Attending

Next, we constantly receive messages, but our bodies (and minds) are designed not to pay attention to EVERY sound out there—otherwise, we'd overload! So, we must choose what we *attend* to, making a somewhat conscious effort to *pay attention to* the noise we hear. You know how some people need noise around them to help them focus? That's what's going on here. They're "tuning out" most of the noise they hear to focus on something else. If we choose to tune something out, then the listening process stops right there for those particular stimuli. You learned in Chapter 5 that we do this to perceive anything. But, as a stage in the *listening* process, it's even more complex. Once we hear/receive something, we decide which of those millions of stimuli we need or want to pay attention to. This process of "attending to" is a form of filtering.

From a listening approach, attending has three main qualities; it's selective, energetic, and fluctuating. First, attending *has* to be selective. Your body can't possibly deal with all the stimuli it scoops up, so your brain lets you instantaneously sort through all these stimuli and focus on a handful. Broadbent (1958), whose original attention model still largely holds up today, posited that stimuli are received and held briefly in a buffer where they're quickly scanned for relevance and analyzed for meaning. But, even this "auto" process is a choice, which is why attending is *energetic*. Even when we select what to listen to, it takes interest, desire, and effort to pay attention. It's easy to tune out repetitive noises or overwhelming smells (that awful smell didn't go away; your body chose to stop attending to it), but sometimes we can't allow ourselves to do that. Perhaps the teacher's monotone-delivery is conveying something that'll be on the test.

Even Mr. Duckworth has trouble attending to boring speakers: www.youtube.com/watch?v=SlzKyyKb9_U

Even the most motivated person deals with attending's final aspect—*fluctuating* attention. Kahneman's research (1973) suggests we can't truly pay 100% attention to more than one thing at a time; we sacrifice some attention to every new stimulus going on. To come as close as they can to multitasking, air traffic controllers must dedicate a LOT of time and effort. Even then, attention is still sequential, meaning we still pick and choose which stimulus we'll attend to first, second, and so on—something called **strategic control of attention** (Marzano & Pickering, 2010).

Everything we receive goes into our brain but competes with everything already "inside" our head and everything else around us in our environment. That's why the listening process so often fails, ending right here; we never get to the next stage, understanding what we're hearing.

Understanding

Assuming you choose to attend to something, the next step is **understanding**, or making sense of the stimuli we process; it's also known as assigning meaning. For example, if you work in a crowded restaurant or at the mall, there are a LOT of stimuli! Every now and then, the thing you pay attention to will make sense to you; your brain processes what you see/smell/and so on as a "symbol" with meaning. If I hear a word I know, that means I *understand*. If it's a language I don't speak, or maybe there's too much other noise, then I won't understand it, so listening stops right there. Yes, you actually have to "understand" to truly listen—otherwise, it's just noise (in the Chapter 1 models, the understanding stage is where you decode communication). Just like attending, it happens instantaneously, but understanding isn't actually automatic; it's not a rote process. If you've ever tried learning a foreign language (Smith, 1992), you've experienced this—you must *actively try* to understand. And sometimes, we don't really understand the symbols or stimuli we should know (e.g., words we aren't familiar with spoken in the same language). That's because so much relies on *how* we assign meaning. But, before we get to that, something else seemingly auto-happens in our bodies first.

Remembering

After we sort what we've heard/attended/understood, our brain moves to *remembering*, or the storage of stimuli. Many listening researchers currently subscribe to a three-part memory system (Baddeley, 2001). The first part is called *immediate memory* or the sensory register that serves as our auto-processing port. When you perceive a sound, for example, you're able to recall it for 3 to 4 seconds. After that, you'd have to choose to focus on it, or it vanishes.

If you do focus on it, that stimulus goes to your *short-term memory*, the "working memory" that allows us to have social interactions. Perceptions you attend to stay in your memory for about 20 to 60 seconds before they're lost. Your short-term memory is what helps you make a sandwich in the right order—not the recipe itself (that's the next type of memory) but the sequencing of having completed one task before moving onto the next. This helps us remember what was *just* said so we respond appropriately to people. That's why people who have some kinds of traumatic brain injuries—the kind that affect short-term memory—struggle with conversations and thus interpersonal relationships.

If you rehearse and attend to stimuli in your short-term memory, they eventually find their way to your *long-term memory*, which is infinite (i.e., we'll never reach full capacity in our brains) and stores most of your experiences and impressions. Long-term memory forms the basis for all our future perceptions on which we base our communication. Things may get to our long-term memory *passively*, like how you probably know what your mother usually says when you leave the house ("Be safe, honey") without ever having actively tried to remember it; it's based on patterns. Generally, though, it takes more effort to *actively* get ideas and experiences into your long-term memory. That's because we may dismiss (unwittingly telling our brain not to store anything irrelevant to us) stimuli we don't interpret as important or necessary.

Interpreting and Evaluating

You may technically "understand" a word you hear, but the split second we comprehend what someone's saying (i.e., understand and recall/remember), our brain starts *interpreting*, figuring out what's meant, using our own world-views and life experiences. And, without even consciously doing so, our minds also quickly *evaluate*. They ultimately tell us what to pay attention to and how to make sense of what we perceive.

You know that "I love you" said sarcastically between longtime friends means something different than when a mother says it to her child. Assigning meaning—which we begin in the understanding stage of listening—is very much a social process. It's shaped by our life experiences, our culture, and those we interact with. Because we each have our own ways of seeing and being in the world, we also each have our own ways of interpreting and evaluating stimuli (Rajadurai, 2007). Think about your favorite comedic movie. One of mine is *Harold and Maude* (Ashby & Higgins, 1971). I took a friend to see it; she was highly offended and didn't find it funny at all. Although you might be seeing, listening to, and understanding the same movie, it doesn't guarantee you'll interpret it in the same way. Luckily, simply becoming aware that we're interpreting life through certain lenses (and that others have different lenses) already makes us better listeners. If you make it

Like *Harold and Maude*, everyone interprets this couple differently.

© AJR_photo/Shutterstock.com

this far in the listening process (remember, *most* stimuli don't get so far), your brain then says "this fits (or doesn't fit) here" as it interprets and evaluates.

Responding

To "complete" (although it never really ends) the listening process, we **respond** or react to the stimuli. In the context of listening, responding refers only to how we use our interpretations and evaluations to process and react to the info we listen to. We have very little control over the instantaneous reactions our body makes. For example, if we smell something funky, we scrunch our noses; if we think something's funny, tiny little micro muscles in our faces indicate that. Our responses aren't necessarily obvious to others—we can *try* hiding or not display it, but it's there nonetheless—at least for a moment. To count as a response, there must be SOME verbal or nonverbal, overt or covert reaction to some stimulus. In other words, just thinking about a response doesn't count as one.

This step-by-step way of looking at when each stage occurs "views listening as a system comprised of . . . interrelated processes [that] function together" with each "involved to some degree in every listening encounter" BUT "different purposes and types of listening require emphasis on different listening processes and behaviors" (Brownell, 2016, p. 52).

What Types of Listening Are Possible?

There are many, varying reasons people listen. We do some of the common ones naturally as we go through life or choose to develop them as superpower skills to be even better communicators. Others, we commonly do (but shouldn't) as ineffective types.

Common Listening Types

Just because they're "common" doesn't mean they're not important. The stages of the listening process describe necessary steps to complete/accomplish **comprehensive listening** or general,

© Daxiao Productions/Shutterstock.com

Always alert, attentive, caring, and concerned . . . the ideal therapeutic listener?

standard listening—the kind we do in our daily lives without much thought. Sometimes, people talk about informative listening as a distinct listening type, but really, listening for information is something we just do as part of the overall comprehensive listening process. Typically, listening scholars don't consider this a distinct type.

Other types of listening, though, can be some of the most *thought-full* processes in interpersonal communication—and often take the most work! For example, *therapeutic listening* is done for social support purposes. We do this in our own lives with informal relations, like listening to friends/family when they're troubled. It also occurs in formal contexts, like when professional listeners (e.g., counselors, HR, therapists . . . even teachers) do it as part of a job.

In contrast, *appreciative listening* is for pleasure or enjoyment. Some people listen to the sound of trees in a forest, their pet snoring, or just leave the TV or radio on in the background. Personally, I listen to a lot of podcasts, audiobooks, and a variety of radio shows for enjoyment. While I'm doing this, it may overlap with informative listening because I listen to podcasts for the purpose of understanding and remembering info I hear.

We can do appreciative listening anywhere.

© stockfour/Shutterstock.com

Finally, *evaluative* or *critical listening* is what we do to assess the value or truth of a statement. The term "critical" doesn't mean negative. Rather, we are critical in carefully evaluating what we've listened to, distinguishing among facts, inferences, and opinions. For example, if you've ever listened to a commercial or a sales pitch in general, you'll critically evaluate the cost, function, and if you really need the product. We'll talk about some tips to do this better in a bit. But, now that we've seen some of the useful types of listening, let's look at some ways it can all go very, very wrong . . .

Poor Listening Skills

It's always more fun to talk about anecdotes of things we see people doing wrong . . . so, let's get to it. Remember, we're *all* guilty of some of these at some time, but that doesn't make them OK. Some common traps include: pseudolistening, stage hogging, selective, insulated, defensive, ambush, and insensitive listening.

First, *pseudolistening* is when people pretend they're listening but really aren't. They may even make "active" listening noises or nonverbally nod their head (i.e., to fake the *responding* step). The stereotype here is the guy who's supposedly listening to someone while reading the paper or watching TV, going "Uh, huh. Uh, huh" and nodding; you could probably say anything, and he wouldn't really process it—making the speaker feel quite disrespected.

Listening shouldn't be just about YOU! Don't be a stage hog!

© Ron Leishman/Shutterstock.com

Stage hogs are the people who make everything about them. There are two types of stage hogs: those who want to be (a) the center of attention and/or (b) in control all the time. Both types of stage hogs tend to interrupt other people a lot. The first type tends to shift all topics/responses to themselves so that we're always focusing on them, saying things like, "Well, when that happened to me . . ." The other type may have the same goal, but they typically also/instead use interruptions to make sure they're dominating the interaction or the other person.

Selective listeners pay attention only to things that concern them—it's very egocentric. They tend to focus on (a) stuff that applies to them personally, and/or (b) things that interest them. So, they may get bored and begin to zone out if you talk about something they're not interested in. But, they're not necessarily affected by whether or not the info is good or bad; as long as it concerns them personally, they'll typically listen even to bad info. For example, in a budget cuts meeting, a selective listener would tune out when their own group isn't discussed.

Similar to selective, but a bit different, are the *insulated listeners*, who will avoid hearing anything bad. These people focus on (a) good stuff that doesn't contradict their beliefs, and/or (b) things that confirm their view of reality. They'll essentially ignore anything that challenges their identity or worldview. The distinction for insulated listeners is the good/bad part. Whereas selective listeners focus on either as long as it applies to them personally, insulated listeners avoid anything bad or contradictory to their beliefs. In that same budget cuts meeting, the insulated listener would avoid most content (cuts = bad), being very unfocused the whole time.

Fifth, *defensive listeners* typically interpret everything as a personal attack. These are highly combative people who believe the world is out to get them. Someone says "Nice haircut," and they say "What's wrong with it?" or someone says "New pants?" and they respond, "You think I look fat in them, don't you!" Clearly, there's something going on for these people in the interpreting/evaluating stage of listening that *isn't* going on for other people. Stage hogs, selectives, and defensives are all egocentric—just in different ways.

Sixth, *ambushing listeners* are *technically* very "good" listeners. They'll complete the whole listening process successfully, show effective listening skills in response, and be very invested in learning/reflecting. In fact, they could probably repeat back (with almost photographic memory) the words *and* feelings conveyed by the speaker—and that's also the bad part. They remember it all and are only using the info to get people to trap themselves—either in the current conversation or later on down the road. They are essentially planning their attack. Their "So you're saying . . ." (usually an effective, active listening technique, covered in a bit) is really an interrogative, strategic move.

Finally, *insensitive listeners* also may look like great listeners on the surface because they, too, could repeat back to you verbatim the exact words you told them. BUT, they wouldn't be able to actually *reflect* back to you the meta-message—the emotions/gist/feelings you're trying to convey. They lack truly reflective, active listening skills in that context. This allows them to avoid becoming emotionally invested and can be incredibly frustrating for listeners! Frankly, any of these types aren't great for the other person encountering them, which is why we should discuss how to get better!

WHACK! BAM! BOOM! Batman Beats Riddler by Learning 'How?'

Whether we engage in common listening types or are guilty of those poor listening skills, there are ways to improve or upgrade and listen better to people around you. Remember, even great listeners have room for improvement!

Upgrade Your Utility Belt, Batman!

There are many places people struggle along the steps of the listening process, but some tend to happen more than others. We usually don't struggle as much to receive (our five senses are pretty automated), understand (it either fits an existing "brain box" or it doesn't), or interpret or evaluate (again, our past experiences almost drive this car *for* us). So, I'll give you some suggestions for the more common problem areas: attention, memory, and responding.

What topic do you struggle to really listen to? Don't let boredom get the best of you!

© Luc Sesselle/Shutterstock.com

Beep . . . Beep . . . Beep . . . Improving Your Attention Scanner

After you receive a stimulus in the listening process, it's up to you to decide to attend to something. Sometimes that's easier said than done. Motorcycle engines may be one of my least favorite topics. Once, at a faculty cocktail party, I was talking with two men, one of whom was droning on about motorcycle engines. OMG! I can't imagine anything more dreadful. I had no interest or desire to listen. It took substantial effort from me to stay attuned to the conversation. One way to help *you* focus on things that you struggle to attend to is to simply acknowledge it as it happens. Identifying—in the moment—that you're struggling *because* it's a topic boring to you can actually help you focus more. Making ourselves aware of which topics require more energy and effort helps us be better not only at interpersonal listening but will help in class as well. Simple awareness of what takes energy on our part actually helps exert that energy!

Another skill we can add to our superpower repertoire is to assess the demands of a listening situation and match our effort and interest to those demands. It might seem strange to try to increase your interest in something, but it's possible. One way is to ask questions. If you're ever bored in class, one way to reduce this boredom is to ask questions. It's verbal, so we're forcing ourselves to be active, which will wake us up a bit. It's also informative—you'll learn something (you never know when that useless fact will come in handy in trivia games!). Further, it will improve both the relationship (the person will appreciate being asked) *and* your identity (they'll think better of you as someone interested in their topic).

Swish . . . Tink . . . Slash . . . Honing Your Memory Blade

Consider a classroom example: Your professor just explained a concept. You know you heard what she said, and at the time, you knew what she meant. Why isn't that enough to answer the exam question? Because you didn't make enough effort to commit the info to memory. People want to improve their memories so much that entire bookstore sections are devoted to this skill. Really, what they all break down to is generally a *retrieval failure*, when you can't access the "box" where your brain stored it. Luckily, knowing this, researchers have uncovered techniques that work best for each memory type (Schacter, 2001). So, once you identify which memory type you struggle with, you can go right to the appropriate strategy.

Short-term memory strategies

There are three particularly effective (and simple) techniques to improve short-term memory: repetition, chunking, and logical patterns.

First, *repetition* helps by keeping the stimulus in our short-term memory. It's like constantly putting it back into your immediate memory on purpose. I use repetition when I go to the grocery store without a list: I repeat "cat food, paper towels, grapes" over and over again. That way I get everything I went in for (it doesn't mean I don't also pick up a snack, though). The same simple technique can help you remember someone's name. As you're introduced, repeat their name back (e.g., "It's nice to meet you, Regina.").

Next, we can use *chunking* to group items for easy "brain box" access in our short-term memory. We recall phone numbers using chunking: the area code, exchange/prefix, and the line numbers exclusive to one person's phone.

Finally, we can *form logical patterns* by using stuff we already have in our heads (e.g., the alphabet) to similarly "shape" the info we've listened to for short-term use. Let's say you need to remember five mobile media terms for a test. Luckily, each term starts with a sequential alphabet letter

There's no reason phone numbers are separated into sections other than it helps us chunk them for memory.

(assumingly learned in grade-school): A, B, C, D, and E. That pattern helps us recall terms: **a**irplane mode, **b**luetooth, **c**arrier, **d**ashboard, and **e**lectrophoretic. Depending on the info and your need for it, logical patterns can also be used as a long-term strategy. But, if you think about it, you've probably forgotten most of what you've tried to remember via patterns in the past—illustrating why they're great for short-term use.

Long-term memory strategies

To improve long-term recall, it's important to store memories carefully. Though some of these may happen implicitly/passively (without us trying to do them), there are five general ways to explicitly store long-term memories: association, mediation, categorization, mnemonic devices, and imagery.

First, paying attention to *associations* when storing can help (Tomes & Katz, 1997). I listen to lots of audio books. To this day, there's a bridge in Hartford where I recall listening to *Madame Bovary* while driving under it, so every time I drive under this bridge, I recall that book. That's

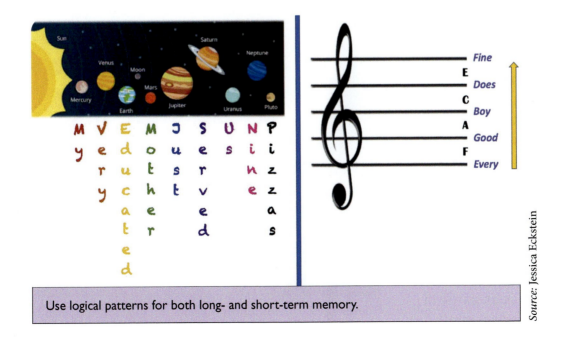

Use logical patterns for both long- and short-term memory.

Source: Jessica Eckstein

an extra association with that book that helps me recall it. This memory often comes unbidden (passively), but I can capitalize on my mind's tendency to work that way to remember a slew of related ideas. It's helpful, for example, to remember names by adding an association when you first hear it: "Hi, Helen, nice to meet you. My sister's name is also Helen."

Next, *mediation* relies on making new connections to/with previously memorized info. I had a student many years ago whose name was Sanchia Petrovitch. The middle part of her name sounded like "chee-ah," so she went by Sancy. To remember her name, I had to first think of a Chia Pet (perhaps what she was trying to avoid in the first place), then think SanCHIA PETrovitch, and then I could remember "Sancy" was what she wanted to be called.

Third, *categorization* helps recall similar items. It's sort of like a long-term version of chunking where you rely on logical patterns simultaneously. Let's say one Saturday you have a bunch of homework assigned in CHE 102, MAT 100, COM 163, and HIS 350. You can categorize the assignments by discipline to make sure you don't forget any.

Fourth, *mnemonic devices* create associations of otherwise unrelated ideas so they're easier to recall. Many of us were taught to remember the colors of the rainbow remembering ROY G. BIV. But, mnemonic devices also might incorporate a fifth strategy, *imagery*, using visual cues to help remember something (like tying a string to your finger, which is also symbolic mediation). A classic example of a mnemonic device incorporating imagery is "S" (a man with extraordinary memory, described by Russian scientist Luria, 1997). "S" remembered very long lists of items by visualizing a familiar childhood street and "walking down" the street in his mind, then "placing" objects in familiar, easily recallable "places." The next time he reviewed the street in his mind he remembered them. This technique connects the familiar with the new and is highly visual. Ancient orators like Cicero (1942) taught students to build visual "memory villas" in their heads to remember entire books, lectures, and speeches!

Flap . . . Flap . . . Vroom . . . Responding Quickly and Accurately to the Bat-Signal

Remember (see what I did there?), the final step in the listening process is responding, and because it's pretty automated, we can't often control the first, initial reaction we have. However, we can control what we choose to DO with our initial responses. In other words, although his immediate reaction to seeing the Joker may be to jump back or startle in fear (that dude is pretty

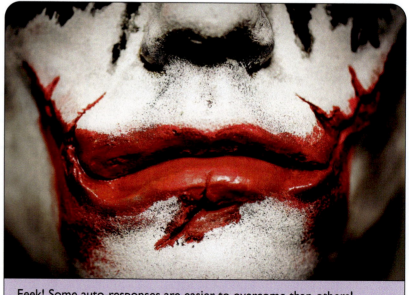

Eeek! Some auto-responses are easier to overcome than others!

© Bottle Top Photography/Shutterstock.com

creepy-looking nowadays!), Batman can control that bodily signal to instead stand firm and speak calmly. You can do this, too! Overall, you can get better at your responding through questioning and gauging accurate feedback.

A primary way of responding is to ask questions. Rather than assuming our first interpretation and evaluation are correct, we can self-question our emotional responses by verbally asking someone for clarification. *Closed questions* invite a yes or no answer or a simple perfunctory response. They're often necessary and are good for some simple tasks and interactions: "Do you have time to talk now?" *Open-ended questions* invite a broader array of responses from your communication partner. They're more often "how" or "why" questions. Because they're designed to explore and understand—not argue—they can be effective in strengthening relationships and increasing understanding. Let's say you're walking out of class feeling overwhelmed and you see a classmate with a frown on their face. Rather than assuming your interpretation is correct and feeling "OMG, the whole class is freaking out like me!" you can simply verify if that's true (before you unnecessarily panic). Look at the difference between asking a friend after class: "That class sucked, didn't it?" (a response to your emotions) versus "What did you think of class today?" (questioning if your own response is also theirs). Questions can clarify and inform, but we must be careful to avoid judgmental wording.

Another type of response is *feedback*, or info (good or bad) provided about how a process unfolded. It's almost an automatic part of interaction because we tend to hear responses as feedback on how interesting or important others think we are (see altercasting, Chapter 6). But, the more we plan our feedback, the better equipped we'll be. The "rules" for giving constructive criticism (see Activism Hero box on next page) apply to all feedback you give.

Give a Damn, Batman!

I'm sure this doesn't include you, but some people think listening is nothing more than polite turn-taking: We wait for the other to finish so we can turn the topic to ourselves (like stage hogs). We can, however, choose to develop extreme superpowers (perhaps like Superman), instead of "just" relying on our utility belt of tricks like Batman. As an actual superpower, listening is essential for building better friendships, being liked, and advancing at work. There are three ways we can do this, and I recommend they be done together: active listening for others, evaluative listening for ourselves, and self-listening—which is actually for us *and* others.

Activate Empathic Concern!

Active/effective listening relies on basic interpersonal skills (see Chapter 10 for how these overlap) to SHOW someone you care and are trying to understand, AS you provide active listening feedback (largely nonverbal but some verbal) *while* the sender is communicating, and simultaneously verify for yourself that you've correctly understood the sender. This process involves several techniques we more or less do in a particular order. You can certainly jump back to earlier techniques, but you'll want to make sure you hit each one repeatedly throughout the conversation: encouraging, restating, reflecting, and summarizing.

Activism Hero: Constructive Criticism to Create Change

Change requires feedback, and while it may be necessary, it needn't be *negative*. Too often, criticism puts up barriers to effective listening, so if you need to change someone's behavior, *constructive criticism* helps them listen and you get results. Research suggests we should *always* do five things to offer feedback:

1. **Start positive.** Don't start with the problem! Soften them up; always show you care about the relationship (even if you don't) by giving them approval/compliment first. Otherwise, their defenses go up, and they won't listen to anything you say. Anger auto-reduces compliance likelihood because it makes us feel uncertain (Zhang, 2014); compassion, on the other hand, has reverse effects. The compliment should relate to your goal, so try: "I appreciate how you interact with customers . . ." or "I'm so happy to have a man who washes dishes—you rock!"

2. *Specific behavior, not person.* State exactly, precisely what you want addressed—*not* ANYTHING about them personally. Instead of "You're so irresponsible!" [which you may feel], be specific to the behavior: "If you say you'll be here at 6, I need you here at 6, not 6:30." Replace "You never do your share around here!" with "We agreed you'd clean the bathroom, and I'd do the kitchen." Avoid all global and personal attacks.

3. **Explain why, show benefits.** Why should they bother doing it? Tell them! It could be how happy/relieved it'd make or help you—that should be enough for someone who cares about you. For example, "It bothers me when you borrow clothes without asking; sometimes the shirt I plan to wear is in the laundry." With others, make the benefit about them: "I like doubling our wardrobes by sharing; I'd just like to be asked so I can plan around it." This also addresses any misperceptions causing the behavior; it clears up any questions about WHY you're asking (e.g., motives, credibility), so they're less likely to assume it's *only* because you're angry, spiteful, or mean.

4. **Offer help.** You *can* (but don't have to) offer help. If it's something they must do alone, just say you're available for any questions. If it's something to bring you closer consider lending a (*minor*, not doing it for them) hand: "If you need some better supplies, I'll grab some tonight so we can get this place cleaned up."

5. **Limit amount.** Don't list *every* issue in a single encounter. Just mention the most important or easiest (so they accomplish something minor before working the way up). We can't cognitively process too many change-requests at once—especially hurtful/overwhelming ones. Some suggest covering 2-3 at a time. If you've never dealt with them before (or you *know* they won't take it well), just stick to one at a time!

As you implement feedback, increase its success by making sure to do it promptly (immediately, *unless* in public or you're angry—then wait), use helpful nonverbals (scowling ≠ constructive), and make dialogue (rather than lecture). The next time you need to give feedback, remember these basics to ensure listening.

Contributed by J. Eckstein

© barbaliss/Shutterstock.com

Encouraging is where you show you're listening. It's like the responding stage of the general listening process. The point of this step is to get the speaker to keep talking—not to do so yourself. You may nod your head, lean forward, maintain eye contact, or verbalize ("mmmhmm" or "oh really?"). The hardest part for people in this step is not to agree or disagree. If you're *actually* practicing active listening, it's not your job to tell them what you think. Use only noncommittal words in a positive tone: "I see . . .," "uh-huh . . .," "That's interesting," "What did you say then?," or "What did he say when you said that?" Make sure you do these sincerely; just imagine them with a monotone voice—it's much different.

At appropriate moments while listening, an effective listener will also "check in" with the speaker to verify the factual accuracy by **restating** what *they're* understanding. The goal here, after you've incorporated consistent encouragement (and keep that going throughout! See, I told you, it's hard work!), is to get your own clarification of *their* message. It's just like the "clarification" final stage of perception-checking (see Chapter 5). Some ways to do this involve statements like . . . "If I understand you, you're saying. . ." or "In other words, your decision is . . ." But, do not interpret or judge in this stage. This step is only to ensure understanding of the message (i.e., content level).

Then, after that, you can **reflect**, where you figure out your interpretive accuracy. This is where you go beyond checking in to understand the message and instead show you're listening to their feelings; it's where you check in to make sure you're getting their meta-message. By using **empathic statements** ("You feel that . . ."), you restate the other person's basic feelings to perception-check with them. This shows you've gone beyond processing at the surface level to really engage them as a human being, not just as a reporting machine.

Finally, **summarizing** is doing little recap responses to establish interpersonal progress at key times. You pull all the important ideas/facts together to establish a basis for further discussion. Essentially, it's like a mini-recap in the conversation (think of our "internal previews/reviews" in a speech, see Ch. 2) where you review progress to make sure communication is *effectively* occurring. Even though it's called the summarizing stage, you're not just relisting things. Here's where you restate, reflect, and sum up all the *major* ideas and feelings you've encountered. Really obvious ways to voice active listening in this stage could be: "These seem to be key ideas you've expressed . . ." or "If I understand what you're saying, you feel this way about . . ."

This stuff is hard work! It takes a lot out of us when we do it (so, don't do it every single day—you'll be exhausted!), which is one reason effective teachers, counselors, or social workers get burned-out if they don't take vacations from it. Active listening on a constant basis takes an emotional *and* physiological toll on whoever does it.

That having been said, if and when we do want to be good at active listening, it's important to practice—just like with high-impact, technical sports. Start by practicing one step at a time on people with whom you're comfortable (i.e., safe space!) until you're good at that one step. Then, move to incorporating that *plus* the next one, and so on, adding a step in practice until you're competent at all of them. Like many skills, if you don't keep up the practice, you lose it . . .

Critically Evaluate!

A lot of interactions are devoted to persuasion, so to get better at listening in ways that actually help us, it's important to excel at critical or evaluative listening. I once had a student buy a "Flex Belt Stimulator" from a late-night infomercial. Needless to say, a belt that pings your abs while you lie around watching TV probably won't give you six-pack abs. Could she have listened in a way to save herself three easy payments of $39.99? Yep!

To critically listen, we need to ask ourselves if our understanding or assigned meaning is accurate—if it's fact, opinion, or inference. Currently, I have

Critical listening skills usually don't develop until we're older (and sometimes not even then!).

© Lorelyn Medina/Shutterstock.com

some electricians working in my house while I'm not there. If I come home and nothing's been moved, I infer they haven't been there (although they might have). And, separate from this is my opinion about what they're telling me, if it's true, and if they're good electricians. Speaker credibility (McCroskey & Young, 1981) has its roots in listening to public speakers, but we can apply the standards to all interactions. If we perceive someone positively, we're more likely to attend and retain info we get from them. So, if I perceive my electricians as positive, I'm more likely to listen to and believe them. This is why you must be aware of how your view of a speaker may unduly influence you. Checking our perceptions when listening actually makes all types of listening (therapeutic, appreciative, evaluative) richer experiences. But, what's an even higher-powered skill you can work toward? Something called self-listening.

Look Inward, Bruce Wayne

Self-listen to your REAL self to more effectively listen to others.

According to Brownell (2016), *self-listening* "influences all other relationships [because] the process of listening to oneself is integrally linked to the process of listening to others" (p. 16). It involves paying attention to our perceptions (how/why we have the ones we do; perception-checking, see Chapter 5). "Deliberate self-reflection" makes us get in our heads to use a "wise mind" rather than an "emotional mind" to inform our responses. It's important to use self-listening to also look outward (it's not all about you, Karen!), so we don't pay too much attention to our internal monologues, allowing them to actually become "noise" in our listening process. This can be particularly difficult (yet even more important!) to do when emotional or sensitive topics come up.

Self-reflect if you're offended by something. It probably wouldn't get under your skin if it didn't have some truth ...

Obviously, people have varying responses to "sensitive" topics like violence, racism, ableism, sexism, or other forms of privilege. In fact, *most* of us struggle with them in some form. And, that's OK! DiAngelo (2018) talked about "White fragility," a strongly emotional response and resistance to learning about, recognizing, and ending White supremacy. Although I like to think of myself as a White person committed to anti-racism, White fragility is a term I wasn't initially comfortable with. It irritated me every time I saw a Facebook post from a "woke" White friend about it. I kept quiet because I thought my emotional response was overly strong. Then, I decided to read DiAngelo's book. Even though I still have reservations about the term, I now have a greater understanding of her argument. We can do something similar in listening to difficult topics. We can turn everyday listening skills into a superpower—get curious, ask questions, and make sure we correctly assign meaning on difficult topics.

There's a big difference between "bad" discomfort and discomfort we should feel to embrace change.

Just like with speeches, considering your audience and your goal helps you craft effective messages to others. It can also be useful to just *listen* to those we may not agree with so that we can take in the important parts of their message. Manji (2019) said we need to explore our tendency to be offended by others with two goals in mind. First, learn not to offend others unnecessarily. Offending others disconnects people, especially those who seem different from us. As a result, we don't get a chance to learn from each other. That's why a second goal should be to embrace offense. She argued that becoming offended isn't a barrier to diversity. Rather, it's the *path to* diversity, if we can overcome that initial feeling of offense. In other words, Manji believes we must self-listen to reflect enough to be able to rise above our immediate emotions—to not let being offended linger and hinder our ability to *truly* listen.

Conclusion

A U.S. citizen, Fran Peavey (2003), once set up listening booths in other countries with a sign posted: "American Willing to Listen", and she sat waiting until a wide variety of people came to speak to her for all sorts of reasons. If you think about it, it's a pretty brave thing to do, and she felt it helped improve non-Americans' views of the USA. We don't need to travel overseas to make a difference with our listening; there are many ways you can listen to improve your community or make some sort of difference for those around you. Who are some people in your life you usually avoid listening to? Could you set aside some time in an upcoming day to actually listen to them with an open mind? Make yourself accountable to attend to and remember at least two new things that you never knew before listening to them. As you do it, *seriously consider* your feelings and how your reactions reflect what you just learned in this chapter. There! You just leveled-up to a new superpower! Hold yourself responsible; exercise effective listening more often in your daily life to see how *your own* worldview changes along with the world around you!

Listening is the first step to breaking through barriers!

© Michele Paccione/Shutterstock.com

References

Ashby, H. (Director), & Higgins, C. (Writer). (1971). *Harold & Maude* [Film]. USA: Paramount.

Baddeley, A. D. (2001). Is working memory still working? *American Psychologist, 11*, 851–864. doi:10.1037/0003-066x.56.11.851

Bohlken, B. (1999). Substantiating the fact that listening is proportionately the most used language skill. *The Listening Post, 70*, 5.

Broadbent, D. (1958). *Perception and communication*. London, England: Pergamon Press.

Brownell, J. (2016). *Listening: Attitudes, principles, and skills* (5th ed.). Boston, MA: Pearson.

Cicero. (1942). *De oratore* (E. W. Sutton & H. Rackham, Trans.). London, England: Heinemann.

DiAngelo, R. J. (2018). *White fragility: Why it's so hard for White people to talk about racism*. Boston, MA: Beacon Press.

International Listening Association. (2019). *ILA homepage*. Retrieved from listen.org

Janusik, L. A., & Wolvin, A. D. (2009). 24 hours in a day: A listening update to the time studies. *The International Journal of Listening, 23*, 104–120. doi:10.1080/10904010903014442

Kahneman, D. (1973). *Attention and effort*. New York, NY: Prentice-Hall.

Luria, A. (1997). *The mind of a mnemonist: A little book about a vast memory*. Boston, MA: Harvard University Press.

Manji, I. (2019). *Don't label me: An incredible conversation for divided times*. New York, NY: Macmillan.

Marzano, R. J., & Pickering, D. J. (2010). *The highly engaged classroom: Generating high levels of student attention and engagement*. Bloomington, IN: Marzano Research Laboratory.

McCroskey, J., & Young, T. (1981). Ethos & credibility: The construct & its measurement after three decades. *Central States Speech Journal, 31*, 24–34. doi:10.1080/10510978109368075

Peavey, F. (2003). American willing to listen. In M. Brady (Ed.), *The wisdom of listening* (pp. 60–80). Somerville, MA: Wisdom Books.

Purdy, M., Roca, M., Halley, R., Holmes, B., & Christy, C. (2017). Five personal worlds of listening: An auto-ethnographic approach. *International Journal of Listening, 31*, 1–18. doi:10.1080/10904018.2016.1151606

Rajadurai, J. (2007). Intelligibility studies: A consideration of empirical and ideological issues. *World Englishes, 26*, 87–98. doi:10.1111/j.1467-971X.2007.00490.x

Schacter, D. (2001). *The seven sins of memory: How the mind forgets & remembers*. New York, NY: Houghton Mifflin.

Smith, L. E. (1992). Spread of English and issues of intelligibility. In B. B. Kachru (Ed.), *The other tongue: English across cultures* (2nd ed., pp. 75–90). Urbana, IL: University of Illinois Press.

Tomes, J., & Katz, A. N. (1997). Habitual susceptibility to misinformation and individual differences in eyewitness memory. *Applied Cognitive Psychology, 11*, 233–251. doi:10.3758/BF03193059

Weil, S. (1970). *First and last notebooks*. New York, NY: Oxford University Press.

Wolvin, A. D., & Coakley, C. G. (1996). *Listening* (5th ed.). Dubuque, IA: William C. Brown.

Zhang, Q. (2014). Emotion matters in serial arguments: The effects of anger and compassion on perceived resolvability and relationship confidence in dating relationships. *Communication Research Reports, 31*, 102–109. doi:10.1080/08824096.2013.846256

Chapter 10:
Interpersonal
Communication

Contributed by
Dr. Nancy Brule

"Hi! My name is Dr. Nancy J. Brule. I'm your professor for this communication class. You can call me Nancy. If you're uncomfortable with that, call me Dr. Brule, Professor Brule, or Dr. B. I know that by the end of this class, we'll all know each other so well you'll call me Nancy!"

This is how I always start my classes, and by the end of the term, the only people still identifying me as "Dr. Brule" are those students who either didn't come to class or who *really* pissed me off during the semester. I believe interpersonal communication is the most important class you can take—whether you're a communication major or not. Currently, you're in an interpersonal relationship, interested in entering a relationship, or want to know how to improve your relationships (with family, friends, colleagues, or the love of your life). Understanding interpersonal communication is one of those skills you'll use in *every* life aspect, and frankly, a superpower you'll soon wish everyone had. In fact, you'll arguably do more interpersonal communication throughout your lifetime *than any other type* of communicating.

Many years ago, I taught at a university where engineering students were required to take an interpersonal communication class. As I walked into that room, I was greeted by 30 guys (engineering field, dominated by men) who didn't feel they needed this class—that it was a waste of their time. These students valued the hard sciences; "soft skills" such as knowing how to communicate with people and maintain relationships were not something they respected. Hostility radiated from their every pore toward this cheery, short, female professor (that's me!) who thought interpersonal communication was the greatest thing on earth! As I warily eyed this class, I decided to try cutting through their hostility using **emotional intelligence**, an interpersonal "superpower" used to "read" a person by observing their nonverbal communication cues and knowing how to appropriately respond. I asked this class of men, "How many of you are in romantic relationships?" No one raised their hand. So, I said: "When you're done with this class, you'll be able to get a date!" The students laughed, sat up, and our semester began with a renewed interest in the benefits of interpersonal communication.

As our plastic hero, GI Joe, says, "Knowing is half the battle."

© Norberto Mario Lauria/Shutterstock.com

They ended up being some of the most eager students I've ever taught; we laughed our way through the semester as we role-played skills to help them develop active listening techniques, verbal and nonverbal communication skills, empathy and emotional intelligence, interviewing tips and tricks, and of course . . . the strongly desired relational development and maintenance skills—or as I like to call them "how to get a girl/boyfriend and keep them" (you'll read more detail on this last one in the next chapter on romantic relationships). It's not just "close" relationships, though. Corporations say *the* most important skills they want in employees fall into four categories: verbal (see Chapter 7 and all the speech-making chapters), listening (Chapter 9), written (Chapters 2 and 3), and nonverbal (Chapter 8) communication skills (e.g., Carnevale & Smith, 2013; Robles, 2012). You've already touched on these in other chapters, so I'll focus here on how they merge to make you a communication superhero. I'll put all the pieces together (while also showing you some new ideas) to see how to be the absolute best you can be.

Obviously, this chapter can only give you a taste and get you excited (much like a good attention getter!)—you can take entire courses or get a degree in interpersonal communication, so I'll present some key interpersonal concepts to help you understand why (or not) you're successful when communicating. After a brief history of how/why we study interpersonal the way we do today, I'll cover some concepts currently used in the field, and then tell you what it takes to be an interpersonal superhero!

Where "We" Came From: An Interpersonal Origin Story

In the past, interpersonal communication often was viewed as an interdisciplinary field, sharing studies with language, social cognition, and social psychology. It wasn't until the 1960s that "interpersonal communication" became the official term used to identify it. By then, it was accepted that relationships and well-being could be improved through effective communication (Heath & Bryant, 2000). It's pretty sad it took us until the 1960s to realize communication was important to our relationships . . . what were all those people doing before then? By the 1970s, interpersonal communication research began to focus on social interaction, relational development, and relational control, among many other areas.

I remember taking one of the first interpersonal communication classes offered in 1980 (long before you or even some of your authors were a twinkle in parents' eyes). It consisted of sitting around in a circle, talking about our feelings, talking about our thoughts, talk, talk, talk. Think of being *forced* to take part in a social support group with strangers, being asked to share feelings about *everything*! That's how my first interpersonal class was taught. As the communication discipline began to expand, interpersonal's focus flowed into using cognitive approaches, followed by behavioral, and then communicative adaptations.

Be glad your communication classes aren't like this anymore!

© Photographee.eu/Shutterstock.com

Currently, interpersonal communication is a full-blown social science and is one of the largest areas of the communication discipline, with many branches having expanded from it: personality, identity, and cultural influence; knowledge structures and social interaction; language and nonverbal signals; emotion experience and expressive, supportive communication; social networks and personal relationships; influence; conflict; computer-mediated communication; sports communication; workplace communication; escalation and de-escalation of romantic or platonic relationships; healthcare interactions; family relationships; and communication across the life span.

In fact, interpersonal is often thought of as a sister discipline to psychology, sociology, social work, and marriage/family therapy. Many of my students who focus on interpersonal communication end up going to graduate school or careers in the fields of business, human resources, counseling, marriage and family therapy, social work, ministry, student life . . . the list goes on. I often ask people across many areas of work what's made them successful; 9 times out of 10, they report it's their interpersonal communication skills and knowing how to interact and work with people. So, if you don't know what you want to do specifically—just that you want to work with people, then studying interpersonal communication is perfect because you use it in so many ways (#drinktheKool-Aid)! And, like those engineering students, even if you know what you're going to do, having great interpersonal skills can help your career *and* your personal life.

Definitional Concepts: Why Interpersonal Comm Is Unique

Most interpersonal scholars agree certain characteristics make interpersonal communication unique among all other communication types. Many of these derive from the definition itself. At its simplest, interpersonal communication is just an exchange of information between two people (Berger, 2008). A bit more in-depth view, taken from numerous definitions,

Some of my nontraditional interpersonal relationships.

considers ***interpersonal communication*** a common, dyadic communication process on an evolving continuum that continually re/defines the nature of a relationship (Burleson, 2010; Cappella, 1987). Let's break this down by focusing on four key aspects.

Dyadic and Frequent

First, interpersonal communication is ***dyadic***, meaning it takes place between two or more people. And, we have *many* interpersonal relationships! For example, I have a different interpersonal relationship each with my husband, my daughter (another author in this book; can you guess which one?), my son, and (I strongly argue) with each of my two dogs, six cats, four horses, and each of my 16 female and two male goats! We can't be certain animals (or humans) feel the same way, but we can perceive on *our end* unique interpersonal relationships. From my perspective, I have a unique relationship with each of these mammals (humans are just other mammals, after all), and if you ask me which is my favorite, on some days I'd be hard-pressed to choose between my children or my head herd-goat Lolli (but, don't tell my son or daughter that!). The point is, we have many interpersonal relationships, which take place between any two, unique parties.

Interpersonal communication differs slightly in its definition from the earlier "communication" definition (in Chapter 1) because it goes deeper into the personal realm and very specifically involves another person's intrapersonal thoughts, metacommunication, and their identities in specific interactions. Interpersonal relationships are like snowflakes—each is different and means something different to each of us—because they combine the six selves of interpersonal communication: who I think I am, who I think you are, and who I think you think I am × 2. These selves meet to create something that can't be re-created. I'm an identical twin, and although we laugh alike, talk alike, and look alike, we're unique in our relationships with people we both know. For example, even though we both know and appreciate my ex-husband Terry, we each have a totally different relationship with him; our "social" history changes the meaning of our communication even though we may say the exact same thing to him. When she says "Terry, you're an angel," this means something very different than when I say those same words to him. To her, it has a positive meaning (appreciation for his freely offered, helpful advice), whereas for me it may be negative (resentment that everyone thinks he's perfect while I've lived with his stubbornness). The fact that every second of the day—no matter the context—is a potential opportunity for interpersonal communication means it's one of the most frequent forms of communicating we do. So, added to all its unique complexities, it NEVER, EVER STOPS!

Processual

Interpersonal communication is an ongoing process, which means it's uniquely inescapable and continuous, as well as unrepeatable. Many scholars have tried breaking it down into discrete, ordered parts, but in reality, because there're so many variables at play (history, setting, emotions, moods, contexts), it's never a simple process. Nevertheless, it *is* a *unique* process.

Uniquely Inescapable and Continuous

Back when I worked at a very conservative church, I had a car bumper sticker that said: *God made man. Then, He had a better idea and created woman.* Imagine my surprise when, at the next church board meeting, an agenda item read: "Pastor Nancy's bumper sticker." What ensued was a "spirited discussion" regarding what this was/wasn't communicating. I thought it was funny; the all-male board members? Not so much! I spent the next hour trying to scrape my bumper sticker off without scratching my car.

Communication in general has the potential for multiple interpretations. But, interpersonal communication is *never* just about the message sent. All the nonverbals of every person

LAUGHTER IS THE BEST MEDICINE, UNLESS YOU HAVE DIARRHEA

Too bad all churches don't have this sense of humor.

© Thomas Alan Schneider/Shutterstock.com

involved, their perceptions and previous relationships, the power dynamics among different members—all came into play to make this "discussion" a very *interpersonal* process (one that didn't end when the meeting was over!). It was continuous; I was communicating even when I wasn't speaking. It's also inescapable; I intentionally put the bumper sticker on my car to make people smile, but I unintentionally communicated supposedly controversial beliefs. Remember: It doesn't matter whether you mean to or not; communication is inescapable and continuous—so it impacts all potential relationships!

Because it's all around us and always changing, just like communication in general, interpersonal communication can't ever be repeated in the exact same way twice. However, with interpersonal communication, many hundreds (if not thousands) of layers of repeat-impossibility are factored into that process; it involves a process that is uniquely unrepeatable.

Uniquely Unrepeatable

I smile remembering an unrepeatable instance that fills me with love each time I think of it: My three tiny children were each strapped into their car seats in the back of our little compact car. They were poking at each other, starting a ruckus, when I glanced into the rearview mirror and sternly said, "Stop poking each other and keep your hands to yourselves!" I continued to watch their reactions to my rebuke in the mirror as my youngest son's mouth dropped open, his eyes growing wide. He asked in his little 3-year-old voice, "How'd you know we're doing that?" I responded, "Moms have eyes in the back of their heads." A short while later, I felt tiny little fingers softly digging through my hair. I said, "Jake, what are you doing?" He replied, "I'm looking for your eyes . . ." He'd squirmed out of his car seat to create an interaction that can never be repeated. I've told this story many times, and even though it occurred only once, it remains a symbol of how one-time interpersonal processes/events define our relationships.

You already know (from Chapter 1) that in a process, everything is continually changing and therefore, an interpersonal interaction can never be the exact same again. We can't recapture an identical meaning because the time (if only 1 second), our frame of mind (maybe I'm bored or stressed), and physiology (maybe I'm tired or hungry now, and I'm already older!!) are all different. Each interpersonal episode changes from one point to another—largely because it's influenced by the ongoing relationship being built/growing between the parties. I'll never be able to repeat or replace the "looking for eyes" interaction in the car. As we communicate interpersonally, we're experiencing a process we'll never experience again.

Interdependent

One of the reasons we can't re-create experiences is due to interpersonal ***interdependence***, meaning both individuals are mutually reliant, and the behaviors of one inherently influence the other and vice versa. For example, my husband loves to chat, and after a day of teaching, counseling, and doing nothing BUT talking, I just like to sit and "not talk." He's constantly talking to me, telling me about every little detail of his day (right down to how his hamburger was cooked), sharing with me how *much* he loves me, how *much* he loves our life together . . . you get the idea—he's MUCH too talkative. And yet, I relax knowing I don't have to converse back. If I insisted on talking the entire time, he would be forced to talk less, keeping him from meeting his needs. Our behaviors intrinsically influence each other and if/how our needs are met.

Beyond met-needs, interdependence can also occur through feelings of attachment. So, if we're watching TV, my husband's sitting across the couch, and I hear a sniffle and see tears in eyes, of course I *have* to ask, "What's wrong?" He'll reply, "I just love you soooooooo much! I am verklemmt!" (a German word used often by my African American husband to illustrate just *how so moved* with love he is. Ha!). My reply to this outburst of affection? "Okaaayyy . . ." As you can see, we definitely don't have equality and balance in our communication amount/types with each other, but we're balanced and equal in meeting each other's needs *and* in the felt-emotions we have for one another. He couldn't be verklemmt if our needs weren't intertwined, and truthfully, my needs wouldn't be met if he weren't verklemmt! The first step in achieving interdependence is interpersonal communication (Stafford & Canary, 2006).

Evolving Continuum of Continual Redefinition

Finally, interpersonal communication occurs on a continuum, ranging from impersonal to highly interpersonal. Before I go on, it's important to distinguish between interpersonal *communication* and interpersonal *relationships*. Remember, interpersonal communication is the process; the interpersonal relationship is what is (potentially) built from that. I can communicate interpersonally with someone I don't know yet (in an attempt to build a relationship). I can also communicate *impersonally* with someone I have a relationship with (see Buber, 1958). The point is that when we study interpersonal communication, we're interested in focusing on how relationships evolve and change based on the interpersonal communication we use.

On one end of the spectrum, you have ***impersonal communication***, which is informal, superficial, and covers topics that are necessary to accomplish a specific goal. It occurs in interactions based purely on the social roles of interactants (like salespersons with potential customers). In Minnesota (where I'm from), when you go to a store and someone helps you, the talk is almost always about the weather—an impersonal "interpersonal" interaction. You can think of interpersonal communication ranging on a scale between 1 (impersonal) to 10 (highly interpersonal). My communication with my husband tends to be a 10 (even when I call to tell him I just chased the horses all over the country for 5 hours because he

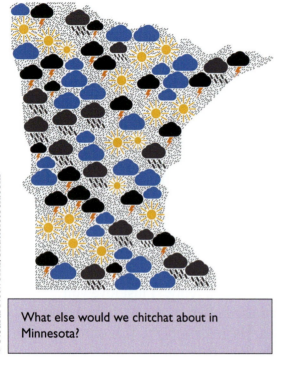

What else would we chitchat about in Minnesota?

forgot to close the gate and I use "@#!!%$#!" to communicate my feelings), and may be an 8 with my colleagues, 7 with Lolli, and 1 with the store clerk helping me at the checkout.

But, we don't always interpersonally communicate with those we have interpersonal relationships with (e.g., I can just "chitchat" superficially with my husband). The level at which we communicate interpersonally can even vary based on context or environment. When I was in doctoral school, two of my kids were undergrads at the same university. Because they were communication students, they ended up taking some classes I taught. When my son took one of my courses, he was adamant that no one know I was his mom—so he wouldn't be treated differently by classmates. He'd call me "Professor" or "Nancy," and I'd treat him like any other student (actually, I graded him harder because I knew his abilities or when he'd just half-assed it; moral: Don't take classes from your parent if you want an easy "A"!). One day, we were in the food court (like most students he was broke, so always happy for me to buy lunch), and he did what all great children do to say goodbye to their mothers: gave me a big hug and a kiss on the cheek and told me he loved me. As I turned to go, I saw a few students from our class standing there, mouths agape. I knew our ruse had to be over; I told Jake we had to let the class know our relationship or I'd risk big trouble with a "harassment" suit.

The next class period, I walked into the room and could tell "word" had gotten around: Jacob loved his teacher and not only that, he'd kissed her! Students were very uncomfortable, and Jacob, sensing everyone's obvious discomfort, stood up dramatically (a good actor, he always knew how to play the "scene"). He walked to the front, gave me a huge, smacking kiss on the cheek and said, "I love you . . . Mom!!" You could hear the class sigh in relief! A highly interpersonal relationship isn't something that happens overnight. Relationships are built over time. Luckily, even our "bad" moments contribute to our interpersonal histories.

Interpersonal communication is *indexical*, meaning that *how* we communicate shows the emotional temperature (called *relational climate*) of our relationship at any given time. A *confirming* relational climate is one where you feel supported and valued; a *disconfirming* relational climate makes you feel devalued, criticized, and demeaned. Three things affect the tone of a relational climate. First, the *relational trust* level is how much we can depend or rely on another. Interpersonal relationships high in trust (where interpersonal communication has been confirming) allow people to depend on each other, expect faithfulness and fidelity, enact support, and avoid intentional harm (Eckstein, 2005). Next, *relational power* is the degree to which we can influence the direction and flow of the relationship or interactions within it, such as decision-making, resources, and power. Like any superpower, relational power can be used for both good and evil in any relationship; it just depends on how we interpersonally communicate. Finally, *relational intimacy* is based on the connection, acceptance, and disclosure we communicate on emotional, physical, intellectual, spiritual, and experiential levels (Schaefer & Olson, 1981). The more intense our intimacy across these different realms, the more highly interpersonal relationships are considered

Some things require more trust and intimacy than others . . .

to be. Beyond contributing to the relational climate, intimacy also affects what we "label" our relationship. All of these factors are in flux—causing us to continually reassess how interpersonal our communication may or may not be, redefine our relationships, and figure out which relationships we do/not need.

It Takes Twoooo, Baby . . . Me and You!

Both people have to be "in" for a relationship to be successful.

Even though we *could* choose to interpersonally communicate with everyone (though it'd be so exhausting we'd probably become hermits), we can't have an interpersonal relationship with everyone—nor should we want to! True interpersonal relationships take a lot of time, development, and nurturing. Who/how many you choose will largely depend on your individual needs and preferences. Abraham Maslow and William Schutz each offered models to explain why we need to interpersonally communicate and how our needs may vary. And, Relational Dialectics Theory explains how we attempt to manage these needs.

Maslow's Hierarchy of Needs

Maslow's (1943) hierarchy is the simplest representation of individual needs. Looking at the pyramid on the next page, we can see that all people need Levels 1 and 2 (at the bottom of the pyramid) to survive. *Physical needs* provide us with sustenance for our bodies (e.g., food, water, needed medicine) and *safety needs* make sure we don't die (e.g., shelter, security, protection from Minnesota weather). Interpersonal communication may be necessary if we rely on family members to provide us with physical and safety needs. For example, you don't want to get kicked out of the house in a blizzard because you pissed off your dad during Christmas dinner. Of course, once those needs are met, we begin to

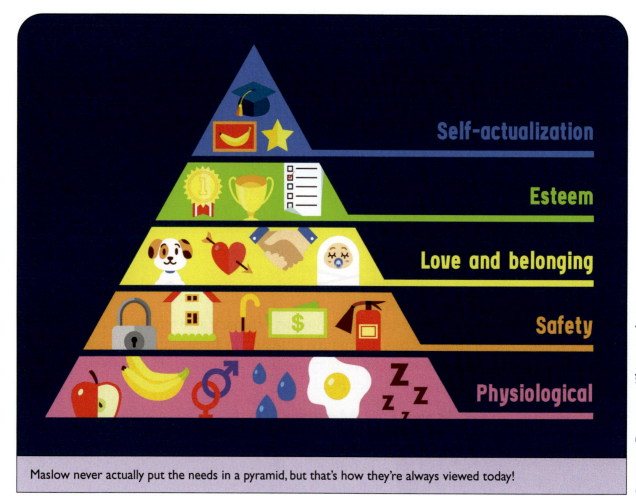

Maslow never actually put the needs in a pyramid, but that's how they're always viewed today!

crave/seek companionship for Level 3's ***love and belongingness needs***, which are desires to feel like we're part of a larger unit and that someone cares for us. This is where interpersonal communication plays a much larger role in meeting our needs. Next, we'd develop to Level 4, our ***self-esteem needs***, to grow and develop our identity and understanding of who we are (see Chapter 6). Then, we start to reach for ***self-actualization*** (Level 5), or a desire to perceive control or empowerment in our lives—to be all we can be. Very few of us attain *full* self-actualization, but that's the whole point. Merely striving for it gives meaning to our lives (Maslow, 1970).

Based on personal observations, Maslow (1943) originally argued the top levels were important for living happy/successful social lives, BUT he said Levels 1 and 2 (the "basics") were the only ones absolutely necessary to stay alive. However, research from the 1900s all the way up through the 1990s questioned this assertion by showing other levels (Level 3) were *just as important* to our physical survival. One notable (and horrible!) study involved taking away baby monkeys from their mothers (replaced with wire re-creations to feed the babies) or even placing the babies in an isolation chamber intentionally called the "pit of despair" (Harlow, 1959). Compared to babies who got touched, loved, and "babied" as much as possible (meeting *all* their needs), those who had *only* the physiological (Level 1) and safety (Level 2) needs met were much more likely to die. Studies as recent as the

1990s of adoptees from Romanian orphanages (where the children received little affection and attention) showed severe physical and psychological deficits in these children long after their adoption into loving homes (Nelson, Fox, & Zeanah, 2014). Maslow's hierarchy is controversial because it's hard to "prove" with research. However, it does model the importance of love/belongingness and esteem needs; they're just as crucial to our long-term survival as food, water, and safety! Looking at this "needs" perspective of interpersonal communication, we see how some needs get met/used, and ultimately, preferred more than others by different people.

Public Speaking Power: Using Maslow to Persuade

Maslow (1970) determined some core needs, so use them to persuade your audience. To get them more invested in your argument, show how your topic meets each need:

- *Physiological*—explain how a topic helps them be healthier (e.g., why buy a particular vitamin brand? drink more water?)
- *Safety*—show how a topic protects them (e.g., why they need preparedness kit, alarm system, self-defense skill?)
- *Belongingness*—describe how they'll have more/better relationships (e.g., join a dating website? frat/sorority?)
- *Self-Esteem*—illustrate how a topic helps them feel better about selves (e.g., buy a flattering clothing brand? take better selfies?)
- *Self-Actualization*—explore how a topic helps them work toward being their best selves (e.g., volunteer/contribute to charity? earn good education/better grades?)

Contributed by B. Ribarsky

Schutz's Theory of Interpersonal Needs

When they were in high school, I'd ask my sons about their friends and chuckle as they'd say, "We don't have friends, Mom; we have associates." When they were even younger, I'd encourage them to make more friends. "Mom, why do I need friends?" That's a very good question. Now, I know they didn't have the same need for friends as others; therefore, they chose their friends very carefully, having only a few, deep friendships they continued as adults.

My youngest son lived all over the U.S. and overseas, so I often wondered if, constantly moving, he had strong interpersonal relationships. When he died unexpectedly at age 35, I was overwhelmed when people all over the world who considered him a close friend sent me pictures and videos, sharing stories of how much he'd meant to them, their adventures together, interests and fun shared, and more interestingly, how long they'd known each other. Hearing from his friends showed how even as a preferred-loner, his relationships met many different needs. You, too, must consider what your own needs are and what/why you need from others.

Schutz (1958) created the Fundamental Interpersonal Relations Orientation (FIRO) to explain how our needs vary. He argued our needs differ across three main categories: affection,

FIRO
Fundamental Interpersonal Relations Orientation

<u>NEED</u>	Want FROM Others	Express TO Others
Inclusion	Acceptance	Interest
Control	Guidance	Leadership
Affection	Closeness	Liking

Schutz's (1958) model of our interpersonal needs

Source: Jessica Eckstein

inclusion, and control. For each need, we have separate preferences for how much we want it from others and how much we desire to express it to others. Our differences explain why we each seek out various types and levels of interpersonal relationships.

First, **affection** is our desire to be liked/loved and appreciated—a need basic to all humans but with differing expectations. *Closeness* measures how much affection we want from others, whereas *liking/affiliation* is how we give it to others. **Underpersonals** are people who want to limit their social interactions and don't need constant approval from others, whereas **overpersonals** strongly desire to be liked and constantly seek attention. My son's friends were all **personals** (a healthy balance between the two).

Next, **inclusion** is a need to belong. We typically want it from others via *acceptance* and give it to others by showing *interest* in them. **Undersocials** seek fewer interactions and prefer smaller groups (to large gatherings), whereas **oversocials** crave the spotlight and seek group belonging. A **social** person strikes a healthy balance between the two.

Finally, Schutz (1958) recognized humans' need for **control**, to influence people and events. From others, we get *guidance*; to others, we *lead*. Many of my son's friends are **autocrats** (high desire to control others) who often met up in Washington, DC to attend rallies or post online to challenge/influence their role in the world. Some of his friends, who may have been **abdicrats** (shifting control burden from self to others), didn't share as close a relationship with my son as others because Jacob had very little tolerance for people lacking energy/desires to be active about social problems. It's very clear my son's friends were not **democrats** (balanced need between individual and group); they operated on extremes. Most interpersonally successful people learn to adapt to extremes by finding a balance between needs that works for everyone.

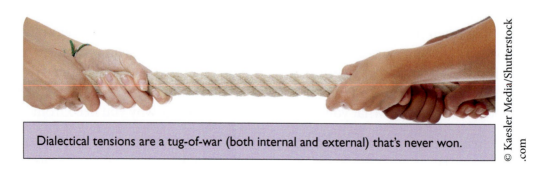

Dialectical tensions are a tug-of-war (both internal and external) that's never won.

© Kaesler Media/Shutterstock.com

Managing Needs

Once you've figured out your needs, the next step is to manage them by examining how your needs interact with those of others. **Relational Dialectics Theory** says we constantly feel tension (which isn't necessarily a bad thing!) to meet our own needs/desires in relationships *while* we still want to satisfy the other person's needs as well (Baxter, 1990). These tensions/forces are extremely strong, so if not handled correctly, can affect other people.

Baxter and Montgomery (1996) argued we can't predict relationships in formal, rule-like ways because people are so different, emotions and past experiences impact our responses, relationships are constantly in process, and because we're always dealing with different forces (or needs) in a relationship. According to Baxter (1990), three main **dialectics**, opposite forces, pull us both as internal tensions (within the dyad) and as external tensions (between the dyad and everyone outside it). First, we manage a dialectic of how integrated or separated we want to be. People manage this internal **connection–autonomy** tension between doing/sharing everything together versus living totally independent, separate lives. That same pair externally manages an **inclusion–seclusion** tension, deciding how much they want to include "outside others" (e.g., inviting extended family to join in) or maintain separate time "just as a couple" in their lives. Second, we manage a dialect of how expressive or private we are with information. Within the dyad, internal **openness–closedness** tensions vary from telling each other every single thing about your day (ah, I love my chatty husband) to expressing little by keeping things completely private. Externally, the pair manages **reveal–conceal** tensions, figuring out how much to tell others about the relationship or how much to protect info so it's known only by the couple. Finally, we manage a stability/change dialectic. An internal **predictability–novelty** tension coordinates how much we need set patterns versus how much to "mix it up" every day. A dyad's external **conventional–unique** tension manages how they'll appear to the outside world—ranging from wanting to present as traditional/"normal" friendship/couple/family to being a norm-violating pair. All of these tensions vary from person to person (I may be less open than my husband), relationship to relationship (I'm more open *with* my husband than with my stylist), and day to day (sometimes I just need a little alone time).

Even though it sounds like it, tensions are NOT something bad or to be avoided. Rather, they just exist. Because both our own and others' tensions are always in flux, it's impossible to permanently balance them. Instead, we learn to constantly manage them. Tensions aren't either/or—we don't just choose one need over the other. Tensions are both/and—we want both, often at the same time. They're simultaneous and both always present, but one or the other might be more salient, or obvious or important, to us at different times. The only way to deal with

Even great momma bears need some alone time.

tensions in relationships with others (who might have different needs than us) is to engage in **metacommunication**, which is talking *about* the relationship's communication.

You shouldn't think of any of these categorizations (Maslow's hierarchy, FIRO, or Dialectics) as "personality types" or set in stone. We can choose to develop each aspect in ourselves at higher and lower levels—which is important because these needs are used to accomplish the key purposes of interpersonal communication, such as sharing meaning, meeting social goals, managing personal identities, and conducting relationships. To excel in these important life-aspects, it's imperative we become competent interpersonal communicators.

Interpersonal Superpowers: Achieving Competence!

For all those times Betsy becomes YOUR new Bestie.

© Yaoinlove/Shutterstock.com

Many of us have experienced some version of the following situation: You're sitting on an airplane or at a coffee shop, and just when you begin reading, the stranger next to you ("Betsy My New Bestie") decides it's time to begin talking. Because I've been raised not to be rude, I often give in and have a *very* long flight talking to someone I didn't want to entertain for the whole trip. Reflecting on this, I often think, "I'm an incompetent interpersonal communicator" because I allow myself to be drawn into a conversation I don't want to have. "Betsy" is also not a competent interpersonal communicator because either she doesn't accurately read my nonverbal cues silently screaming "I don't want to talk" OR she knows I don't want to talk and engages me anyway. Either way, we've both failed each other in this interaction.

Interpersonal competence refers to using context (what's the situation?), goals (what do you want?), and knowledge (who's the other person?) to inform your use of effective and appropriate communication patterns; being effective and appropriate depends on your ability to adapt (Spitzberg & Cupach, 1984). Research concurs on 10 basic skills anyone can develop/improve to become interpersonally competent (Rubin & Martin, 1994). These powers are important not just for personal relationships; they're all skills desired by employers.

1 and 2: Empathy and Altercentrism

First, *empathy* means that you communicate with someone while putting yourself "in their shoes," so to speak. For example, if your friend informs you that his dog Rin Tin Tin just died, you likely wouldn't try to make them laugh by saying, "What do you get when you cross an attack dog with Lassie? A dog that bites off your arm and then runs for help" or "I went to the zoo hoping to see lots of animals, but they only had one small dog. It was a shih-tzu" while you laugh

This is my Ridley. Pups really do make the best empathizers!

Source: Dr. Nancy Brule

hysterically. Pretty funny, but you'd obviously be lacking in empathy, unaware such statements make your friend feel worse about his own sad situation. Empathy is a skill we can hone or work to develop further (Péloquin & Lafontaine, 2010). We can develop our empathy skills by asking ourselves what someone might be thinking or experiencing. Empathy doesn't mean you agree with them, just that you consider what the other might be going through.

A second, similar skill is **altercentrism** where you focus consciously and rationally on the other person (Helgeson, 1994). You show interest in, concern for, and attention to them while conversing. We usually notice this skill most when it *doesn't* happen; we have no problem remembering times people *lacked* altercentrism. Ever conversed with someone who continually scans the room while you talk? It's as though they're looking for someone more interesting to talk to. Their lack of attentiveness to what you're saying makes you feel as if you weren't important to them (Wheeless, Frymier, & Thompson, 1992). Practice nodding affirmatively, asking questions to encourage talk, and other skills of effective listening (see Chapter 9).

From 1954 to 1973, Lassie was the most altercentric friend—rescuing Timmy, who apparently wasn't very bright, as he was always falling into wells or getting lost, bullied, mugged, or hunted by animals.

© Ingrid Pakats/Shutterstock.com

3: Social Relaxation

If you have a ton of anxiety or worry in everyday social interactions, you clearly need to work on your **social relaxation**, or feeling of comfort communicating with others regardless of their negative reactions or criticism. It should be pretty obvious that when we're more comfortable, or not experiencing stress in social interactions, it's easier to communicate and be involved interpersonally. Our social relaxation varies by situation. Even though I hate chitchatting, I have no fear of doing it. Do I like it? No!! Can I do it? Yes!! I'm a competent interpersonal communicator when it comes to chitchatting with my farmer neighbors, my colleagues, students, "Betsy My New Bestie" from the plane, train, or automobile . . . you get the picture. However, if I'm conversing with people I strongly dislike, don't respect, or distrust, then my chitchatting skills go downhill, and I become silent and sullen. A helpful first step to achieve social relaxation is to understand no one's perfect; we all make mistakes in communication interactions. No one can be competent in every situation, regardless of their skills or training.

4: Self-Disclosure

Another skill to practice with others is **self-disclosure**, intentionally revealing personal info not readily known to others, such as your motives, desires, dreams, goals, failures, feelings, fears, thoughts, and experiences (Fisher, 1984). Disclosing these thoughts/topics requires courage and trust. Even with people who mean a great deal to us, we may hesitate to share

Ogres (and self-disclosure) are like onions, according to Social Penetration Theory—the dirtiest sounding theory in communication.

© Anton_Ivanov/Shutterstock.com

deep feelings for fear of what they'll think. Self-disclosure isn't something we can just expect from people; it's both a gift and a compliment. If I feel safe enough to share something that could damage our relationship and it's something that very few (if any) people know, then obviously, I trust you to care and respond appropriately and reciprocally (a self-disclosure "rule").

Why would we want to do this? ***Social Penetration Theory*** explains self-disclosure is how we move relationships from impersonal to interpersonal (Altman & Taylor, 1973). An overused illustration is that we're all like onions with layers (or ogres, like Shrek); each disclosure peels back another self-layer for the person who receives it. This "peeling" occurs on two levels varying in *breadth* (all the types of things you could possibly share about yourself) and *depth* (how deep you go in sharing details of a particular topic). I could self-disclose there were seven children in my family, name them all and their careers (breadth) and then tell you secrets about how I feel toward each of them (depth). The more one self-discloses, the more intimate the relationship often becomes. But, it's not a guarantee. Remember "Betsy My New Bestie"? She self-disclosed deeply to me, but it didn't make our relationship more intimate.

5 and 6: Interaction Management and Environmental Control

Next, we can work on ***interaction management***, our ability to handle specific conversations (Rubin & Martin, 1994). This skill includes negotiating which topics to discuss, taking turns, knowing when to start/end talking, and introducing conversation topics. Yes, this skill involves *many* separate components (which we don't have time to cover here; again, take an interpersonal class!), so to balance them all, you must be highly perceptive or interpersonally sensitive *and* then communicate accordingly (i.e., appropriately; Bernieri, 2001). Being good at interaction management means because it's expected of us, we actively engage when we don't necessarily want to. To avoid offense, you can hold unsolicited conversations with someone.

Similar to managing specific interactions with others is the sixth skill of "managing the room" or ***environmental control***. This skill allows you to accomplish your goals by modifying your communication according to the environment or context (e.g., high self-monitor from Chapter 6; Snyder, 1987). When he was in my speech class, my son *knew* he was a very strong public speaker and that his speeches would've been As for anyone else; but, he never properly cited his sources, so I kept assigning him Cs. Giving his final speech, he was doing great (as usual) when he suddenly remembered he must use sources (or I'd drop his grade again, at this point a running joke between us). So, he said, "That information was from . . . the original source . . . God!" Reading the room, he realized this was a bit of a stretch, so (using his years of prior scripture memorization for competitive Bible Quizzes) he began incorporating specific, applicable Bible verses throughout the rest of his speech. Well, he got me . . . he implemented environmental control because he accomplished his goal (source-citation) *while at the same time* he cited only the verse numbers (instead of quoting the scripture) to adapt to the class (who was perhaps not as Biblically interested). In this instance, he was a very competent interpersonal communicator: effective because he knew I'd find it humorous and he'd meet his goal of sourcing, AND appropriate because he adapted to the context of an audience with diverse needs and interests. And, yes, his environmental control finally got him an A.

7 and 8: Expressiveness and Immediacy

Another skill relying on nonverbal communication is *expressiveness*, using appropriate cues such as smiling, gestures, paralanguage, and body language (see Chapter 8) to convey your thoughts and feelings with clarity (Pittam & Scherer, 1993). How expressive you are helps people distinguish between the message (content) and meta-message (relational) you're trying to convey (Toner & Gates, 1985); it also makes you more attractive to people (Golle, Mast, & Lobmaier, 2014)—something that'll help you achieve your goals.

People who excel at expressiveness are often good at an eighth skill, *immediacy*, or using verbal and nonverbal behaviors to communicate positive feelings toward others (Mehrabian, 1981). Immediacy is what we project when we want to show we're approachable and open to communication from/with others. In the U.S., some ways we communicate immediacy include verbal compliments and nonverbal smiling, eye contact, and focus using active listening cues (Myers & Avtgis, 1997). Immediacy is highly related to success at work (Kay & Christophel, 1995) *and* in relationships (Niven, Holman, & Totterdell, 2012).

9: Supportiveness

With the ninth skill, *supportiveness*, we confirm others' thoughts and actions to encourage them to be the best person they can be. Support is often expected from us spontaneously (Rubin & Martin, 1994) in the form of problem-solving, empathy, and showing equality. The general ways we offer social support include informational (e.g., telling how to fix a computer), emotional (e.g., letting someone cry on your shoulder), esteem (e.g., complimenting someone on their abilities), social network (e.g., inviting them to a gathering), and tangible (e.g., buying someone groceries; Cutrona & Suhr, 1992).

10: Assertiveness

Finally, standing up for your own rights and beliefs while still recognizing that others also have rights and beliefs is the skill of *assertiveness*. When you use assertive communication, you speak conversationally, maintain a friendly tone, have relaxed posture and open expressions, speak to the point and openly share your thoughts, and reach your goal without alienating others. The trick to being assertive is to not become *aggressive*. Being

Public Speaking Power: Can You Relate?

Immediacy, self-disclosure, expressiveness—these aren't just interpersonal skills. Research confirms these skills make BOTH interpersonal partners *and* speech audiences like, relate with, and listen to people. Make them *want* to hear your message! To bring your audience *along with you*, here are practical tips to increase immediacy and perceptions of caring and affinity:

- **Self-disclose!** Drop a personal tidbit about yourself so they sense familiarity and companionship (Kay & Christophel, 1995) and feel more sympathetic to what you have to say.
  - ○ Don't make "creepy" or inappropriate disclosures that ruin it (Schrodt, 2013); they must also be topic-relevant (Frymier & Shulman, 1995).
- **Verbally & vocally express!** To draw people in, catch their attention and keep it (Schwarz, Bless, & Bohner, 1991). Be animated; if this is outside your comfort zone, realize audiences don't see it that way—they just see an exciting speaker and pay attention (Lang, Bradley, & Cuthbert, 1990).
  - ○ Verbally, use "we/us/our" rather than "I" or "you" whenever possible - a simple change that stresses your similarity (remember, we like people who are like us) and creates perceptions of "concern" and "understanding" (Martin, Chesebro, & Mottet, 1997).
  - ○ Monotone is the opposite of immediacy (Wheeless et al., 1992)! Speed up your pace (to show energy/enthusiasm), then slow down (to show seriousness). Raise (to show passion) and lower your volume (to show gentleness).
- **Physically express!** Bodily nonverbals create immediacy and audience-connection.
  - ○ Increase your eye gaze and gestures, move your body purposefully (walk the room at key points, avoid those nervous fidgets), and relax your posture (Burgoon, 1991). Lean forward slightly, like you have a big, juicy secret to tell. Move close enough (if you can; Argyle & Dean, 1965) so they see your facial expressions.
  - ○ Make those facials LOOK caring. Frown, scowl, grimace when describing something "bad"; look meek and concerned (like you're begging for a favor) when the topic is sensitive or sad; and force a happy face, smiling with big eyes when talking about a potential good future (Golle et al., 2014).

Contributed by J. Eckstein

able to talk assertively is so important that I often have my students practice this skill by identifying the various parts to an assertive message (see Kolb & Stevens-Griffith, 2009); it's a surprisingly easy formula to apply by filling in the blanks: Use (a) an "empathy statement" showing your effort to see things from the other's perspective, followed by (b) the "I feel" statement to name your emotions, then (c) a "when/because" statement to identify what specifically bothers you about their behavior and why it bothers you, and finally (d) the "I wish/need/would like" statement where you request what you'd like from them.

For example, let's imagine my eldest son isn't a cat lover and as a result, doesn't appreciate my new rescue kitten, Oreo, who tries to run outside every time the door opens. When my son helps on the farm, he takes no special effort to close the door, putting Oreo's life in danger. Rather than aggressively yell, I'd use my assertiveness skills to say:

> "Aaron, I appreciate you taking time to help me on the farm, and I understand you're not a cat lover *(empathy)*, but I feel responsible for my animals' lives *(I feel)*. When you don't keep Oreo from running outside, I worry he'll die because you don't tell me he got out *(when/because)*. I need you to take extra care to keep Oreo inside, and if he gets out, I'd like you to bring him inside right away to make sure he's safe *(need/would like)*."

Assertiveness makes us interpersonally competent; it also helps save one of little Oreo's nine lives.

As much as he disagrees, Oreo just isn't ready to go out into the world on his own yet!

To be interpersonally competent, you must not only know how to use but also continually work on *practicing* these skills. Start by knowing how good you actually are at each one so you have a baseline to gauge improvements. Just because we know something is appropriate and effective for the situation doesn't mean we necessarily choose to be appropriate and effective in our communication. Remember, these are skills you *choose* to practice—or not.

Conclusion

We often see people make deliberate choices to communicate inappropriately because they just don't care. In fact, recently I was in a very small parking garage, trying to maneuver my husband into the car from his wheelchair when I heard a huge commotion. A woman at the checkout (let's call her Mary Misfortunate) didn't know it was a pre-paid ticket machine and had five other vehicles waiting behind her when three cars back, a woman in a huge SUV (let's say Tina the Terrorizor) started yelling and swearing *at* Mary Misfortunate: "Back up, you stupid dumbass! Back up, @*#*%!!" Now, it's clear Tina Terrorizor wasn't very bright because poor Mary Misfortunate was trapped by five cars and couldn't simply back up (or do anything else). As we were in a concrete parking garage, the noise was *very* amplified and as a result . . . chaos ensued. As a result of *that*, I TOTALLY stressed, my blood pressure skyrocketed, making me yell at my husband who couldn't get his legs in the car—wait—did I say "make me yell"? (Memorize the following phrase: *I'm not responsible for others' actions; I'm only responsible for my reactions.*). My very sensitive husband started crying, which made me cry, which made the dog in the next car howl/cry, which made the baby next to him cry, which made the mother cry . . . and as you can see, our communication choices affect the world.

Communication doesn't just happen *to* us—WE decide how to interpersonally communicate. Think about it: Who you want to be or be perceived as, whether you'll succeed in love and life, whether you'll be able to leap tall interpersonal interactions in a single bound—it all depends on the effort you put into building skills as a competent interpersonal communicator.

Activism Hero: Conflicting to Overcome

Fixing inequalities or injustice inevitably leads to conflict, but that's not a bad thing! When handled appropriately, conflict can be constructive and is *essential* for social change! Simple *awareness* of your options (and others' tactics) lets you address it more easily. If one style doesn't work, simply try another. Wilmot and Hocker (2018) explained five conflict approaches:

Competition *(win/lose)*—directly (or indirectly, hello guilt trips!) get power over others
BUT ... *it "burns bridges" and can hurts relationships*
Collaboration *(win/win)*—develop a creative solution benefiting everyone
BUT ... *it takes massive time/effort and only works if all parties invest*
Compromise *(lose/lose)*—everyone gets, but also loses, something
BUT ... *no one fully wins, so it can create resentment among everyone*
Avoidance *(lose/lose)*—pretend everything's fine and problem doesn't exist
BUT ... *nothing gets solved, and you look like you don't care*
Accommodation *(lose/win)*—sacrifice or give in to whatever they want
BUT ... *you may do it now so you can get something you want later*

This figure shows conflict styles based on: (a) how important your relationship is, (b) your goal's value, (c) time limits, and (d) anticipated future interactions. You have a *choice* in the style you use!

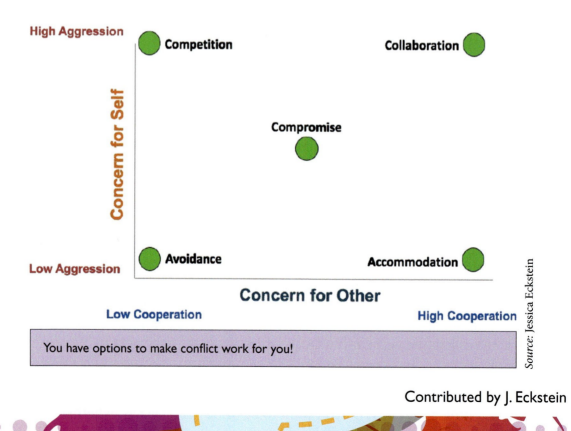

Source: Jessica Eckstein

You have options to make conflict work for you!

Contributed by J. Eckstein

References

Altman, I., & Taylor, D. (1973). *Social penetration: The development of interpersonal relationships*. New York, NY: Holt.

Argyle, M., & Dean, J. (1965). Eye contact, distance, and affiliation. *Sociometry, 28*, 289–304. doi:10.2307/2786027

Baxter, L. (1990). Dialectical contradictions in relationship development. *Journal of Social and Personal Relationships, 7*, 69–88. doi:10.1177/0265407590071004

Baxter, L., & Montgomery, B. (1996) *Relating: Dialogues and dialectics*. New York, NY: Guilford.

Berger, C. (2008). Interpersonal communication. In W. Donsbach (Ed.), *The international encyclopedia of communication* (pp. 3671–3682). New York, NY: Wiley-Blackwell.

Bernieri, F. (2001). Toward taxonomy of interpersonal sensitivity. In J. Hall & F. Bernieri (Eds.), *Interpersonal sensitivity: Theory & measurement* (pp. 3–20). Mahwah, NJ: Erlbaum.

Buber, M. (1958). *I and thou* (2nd ed., R. G. Smith, Trans.). New York, NY: Scribner.

Burgoon, J. (1991). Relational message interpretations of touch, conversational distance, and posture. *Journal of Nonverbal Behavior, 15*, 233–259. doi:10.1007/BF00986924

Burleson, B. (2010). The nature of interpersonal communication: A message-centered approach. In C. Berger, M. Roloff, & D. Roskos-Ewoldsen (Eds.), *Handbook of communication science* (2nd ed., pp. 145–164). Thousand Oaks, CA: Sage.

Cappella, J. (1987). Interpersonal communication: Definition & fundamental questions. In C. Berger & S. Chaffee (Eds.), *Handbook of communication science* (pp. 184–238). Newbury Park, CA: Sage.

Carnevale, A., & Smith, N. (2013). Workplace basics: The skills employees need & employers want. *Human Resource Development International, 16*, 491–501. doi:10.1080/13678868.2013.821267

Cutrona, C., & Suhr, J. (1992). Controllability of stressful events & satisfaction with spouse support behaviors. *Communication Research, 19*, 154–174. doi:10.1177/009365092019002002

Eckstein, J. (2005, November). *Intimacy & trust: Variable links suggested (yet never tested) by Social Penetration Theory*. Presented at National Communication Association, Boston, MA.

Fisher, D. (1984). A conceptual analysis of self-disclosure. *Journal for the Theory of Social Behaviour, 14*, 277–296. doi:10.1111/j.1468-5914.1984.tb00498.x

Frymier, A., & Shulman, G. (1995). "What's in it for me?": Increasing content relevance to enhance students' motivation. *Communication Education, 44*, 40–50. doi:10.1080/036345295-09378996

Golle, J., Mast, F., & Lobmaier, J. (2014). Something to smile about: The interrelationship between attractiveness and emotional expression. *Cognition & Emotion, 28*, 298–310. doi:10.1080/02699931.2013.817383

Harlow, H. (1959). Love in infant monkeys. *Scientific American, 200*(6), 68–74. doi:10.1038/scientificamerican00659-68.

Heath, R., & Bryant, J. (2000). *Human communication theory & research*. Hillsdale, NJ: Erlbaum.

Helgeson, V. (1994). Relation of agency and communion to well-being: Evidence and potential explanations. *Psychological Bulletin, 116*, 412–428. doi:10.1037/0033-2909.116.3.412

Kay, B., & Christophel, D. (1995). The relationships among manager communication openness, nonverbal immediacy, and subordinate motivation. *Communication Research Reports, 12*, 200–205. doi:10.1080/08824099509362057

Kolb, S., & Stevens-Griffith, A. (2009). "I'll repeat myself, *Again?!*": Empowering students through assertive communication strategies. *Teaching Exceptional Children, 41*(3), 32–36. doi:10.1177/004005990904100304

Lang, P. J., Bradley, M. M., & Cuthbert, B. N. (1990). Emotion, attention, and the startle reflex. *Psychological Review, 97*, 377–395. doi:10.1037/0033-295X.97.3.377

Martin, M., Chesebro, J., & Mottet, T. (1997). Students' perceptions of instructors' socio-communicative style and the influence on instructor credibility and situational motivation. *Communication Research Reports, 14*, 431–440. doi:10.1080/08824099709388686

Maslow, A. (1943). A theory of human motivation. *Psychological Review, 50*, 370–396. doi:10.1037/h0054346

Maslow, A. (1970). *Motivation and personality*. New York, NY: Harper & Row.

Mehrabian, A. (1981). *Silent messages: Implicit communication of emotions & attitudes* (2nd ed.). Belmont, CA: Wadsworth.

Myers, S., & Avtgis, T. (1997). The association of socio-communicative style and relational type on perceptions of nonverbal immediacy. *Communication Research Reports, 14*, 339–349. doi:10.1080/08824099709388686

Nelson, C., Fox, N., & Zeanah, C. (2014). *Romania's abandoned children: Deprivation, brain development and struggle for recovery*. Cambridge, MA: Harvard University Press.

Niven, K., Holman, D., & Totterdell, P. (2012). How to win friendship and trust by influencing people's feelings: An investigation of interpersonal affect regulation and the quality of relationships. *Human Relations, 65*, 777–805. doi:10.1177/0018726712439909

Péloquin, K., & Lafontaine, M. (2010). Measuring empathy in couples: Validity and reliability of the Interpersonal Reactivity Index for Couples. *Journal of Personality Assessment, 92*, 146–157. doi:10.1080/0223890903510399

Pittam, J., & Scherer, K. (1993). Vocal expression and communication of emotion. In M. Lewis & J. M. Haviland (Eds.), *Handbook of emotions* (pp. 185–197). New York, NY: Guilford.

Robles, M. (2012). Executive perceptions of the top 10 soft skills needed in today's workplace. *Business Communication Quarterly, 75*, 453–465. doi:10.1177/1080569912460400

Rubin, R., & Martin, M. (1994). Development of a measure of interpersonal communication competence. *Communication Research Reports, 11*, 33–44. doi:10.1080/08824099409359938

Schaefer, M., & Olson, D. (1981). Assessing intimacy: The PAIR inventory. *Journal of Marital and Family Therapy, 7*, 47–60. doi:10.1111/j.1752-0606.1981.tb01351.x

Schrodt, P. (2013). Content relevance and students' comfort with disclosure as moderators of instructor disclosures and credibility in the college classroom. *Communication Education, 62*, 352–375. doi:10.1080/03634523.2013.807348

Schutz, W. (1958). *FIRO: Three dimensional theory of interpersonal behavior*. New York, NY: Holt.

Schwarz, N., Bless, H., & Bohner, G. (1991). Mood and persuasion: Affective states influence the processing of persuasive communications. *Advances in Experimental Social Psychology, 24*, 161–199. doi:10.1016/S0065-2601(08)60329-9

Snyder, M. (1987). *Public appearances, private realities*. New York, NY: Freeman.

Spitzberg, B., & Cupach, W. (1984). *Interpersonal communication competence*. Thousand Oaks, CA: Sage.

Stafford, L., & Canary, D. (2006). Equity and interdependence as predictors of relational maintenance strategies. *Journal of Family Communication, 6*(4), 227–254. doi:10.1207/s15327698jfc0604_1

Toner, H., & Gates, G. (1985). Emotional traits and recognition of facial expression of emotion. *Journal of Nonverbal Behavior, 9*, 48–66. doi:10.1007/BF00987558

Wheeless, L., Frymier, A., & Thompson, C. (1992). A comparison of verbal output & receptivity in relation to attraction & communication satisfaction in interpersonal relationships. *Communication Quarterly, 40*(2), 102–115. doi:10.1080/01463379209369826

Wilmot, W., & Hocker, J. (2018). *Interpersonal conflict* (10th ed.). New York, NY: McGraw-Hill.

Chapter 11:
Romantic Relationships

Contributed by
Dr. Beth Ribarsky

Honesty is the best policy, so let's start with that. I've looked through many intro to communication textbooks and have yet to see one that includes an entire chapter devoted to romantic relationships. So, why did we decide to include one? First, chances are you're currently in, have been in, or desire to be in a romantic relationship at some point, so you're apt to have a bit of interest in the topic. There's no better place to learn about romantic relationships than in a course introducing relationships' very essence—communication. I like to think this chapter arms you with x-ray-vision into romantic relationships. Second, communication in romantic relationships is my main area of research; I even teach a "Dating and Relating" class. I could write a whole book just about relationships, so cutting it down to just one chapter was a challenge, but I get to share my passion and knowledge with you. And finally, because we wanted to.

But, there's an important caveat to this chapter: I *can* get you laid, but I won't. I'll teach you about long-term, happy, and stable relationships. To put you on the road to relational success, I'll talk about attraction, finding partners, first dates, falling in love, sex talk, relational progression, relationship maintenance challenges, and breaking up.

"When you decide not to be afraid, you can find friends in super unexpected places"

—Ms. Marvel

Main Attraction(s): Why We Seek Out the People We Do

Before we even get into romance and actual relationships, it's important to understand why and how we're attracted to others. What's attractive will vary based on your priorities at certain times of life, but I'll focus here on attractors that are overwhelmingly research-based.

© wavebreakmedia/Shutterstock.com

Humans are such vain creatures!

First, when I ask students what attracts them to potential romantic partners, they list things like humor, honesty, or hard work ethic. Oddly, I have to urge them to say the thing that plays the primary role in our attraction—physical attributes. No one wants to seem shallow for admitting it, but it *is* the first reason people catch our attention. Although "beauty is in the eye of the beholder" is true to some extent, there are some common things that physically attract us to others. For example, you already know from other chapters that we tend to be attracted to taller people (Pierce, 1996) and gauge beauty by proportions/layout of faces (see Chapter 8) and bodies (e.g., women's hips 30% wider than waist; Singh, 1993). We also tend to be attracted to people who seem more physically familiar to us, and therefore, may be more likely to date/marry people who look like our siblings. Creepy, yes, but more narcissistic because YOU look most familiar to you. Familiarity increases attraction; the more we run into/ see someone, the more attractive they are to us (Zajonc, 1968), which also connects to a second attraction factor—proximity.

Proximity helps foster familiarity by allowing us to interact with, smell, touch, and even taste each other. Further, proximity often means we share similar characteristics or familiar experiences. I grew up and did my undergrad and master's degrees (Fire Up Chips!) in Michigan. It's a big part of who I am. Now that I live in Illinois, anytime I meet someone from Michigan, we instantly connect. We talk about where we're from, things we eat/drink (mmm . . . Koegel hot dogs, Blue Moon ice cream, and Vernors), and our mutual hate for *THE* Ohio State University (don't worry Buckeyes, I know you hate us too). Because of these shared (even though separate) experiences, we have a connection/attraction.

Blue Moon ice cream—the way to Dr. Beth's heart. To learn more about how your beliefs/values/ characteristics impact your attraction, see the *Love Compatibility Book* (Hoffman & Weiner, 2003).

This sense of connection leads to a third reason for attraction— similar beliefs and values. You've probably heard "opposites attract," and they do but only if complementary (Nowicki & Menheim, 1991). For example, I'm Type-A and tend to be attracted to laid-back people who equalize me. BUT, "birds of a feather flock together" is more accurate. How awful would it be if all you did was argue about your values? We like people who validate our opinions and beliefs (Aronson, 1998). Plus, it's nice to have a "partner in crime"—someone to share similar interests. I'm a foodie, so if I learn a potential partner eats ONLY chicken nuggets and ketchup and has no desire to try new restaurants, we probably won't work out in the long run.

Fourth, we don't just spend time with partners because they agree with us (unless you're an egomaniac); we also hope they have moderate competency, or *at least* half a brain. Physical attraction is all fine (*verry fiiine*) and dandy, but if we can't hold a conversation, a one-night stand is more likely than an actual relationship. This doesn't mean you have to be brilliant— just able to converse on something a partner also finds interesting.

Finally, we're attracted to people who provide rewards. Thibaut and Kelly's (1959) **Social Exchange Theory** takes an economic view of relationships to show how, like any good business, we like more rewards than costs. Romantic relationships have copious rewards (e.g., companionship, safety, money, sex) and costs (e.g., time, independence, money, sex). Of course, as unique individuals, we might see some things as rewards that others view as costs, *and* these views of costs/rewards vary from relationship to relationship (you might not consider sex as a reward for friendships) *and* change throughout our lives. I doubt that when you were in high school you prioritized partners who'd be excellent moms/dads. However, if you're ever ready to raise kids, parenting skills might become an attractor. It's great to understand why we attract; it's even better to know where and how to find your dates.

Finding Partners

You're attracted to people! Woohoo! But, now you need to know where to find those people and how to draw them in to recognize just how awesome you are. Today, you have so many ways to find a partner, so we'll see how to adapt to any (new/old) context.

E-Mail My Heart—Finding Dates Online

Love might just be a click away . . .

There are plenty of in-person options to find a date (e.g., bars, worship centers, gyms), but today, you don't even have to leave your house (or put on pants) to meet a potential partner! Swipe left. Swipe right. One of the biggest changes to/ influences on dating stems from technology (Ştefăniţă, 2019). As recently as 5 years ago, whenever I discussed online dating, my students would look at me in disgust, saying "only 'losers' go online to find dates" (insert a disheartened me who was online dating). But, in a 2017 study of over 5,000 people, 39% of mixed-sex couples and 65% of same-sex couples met online (Rosenfeld, Thomas, & Hausen, 2019), suggesting online dating stigma has significantly decreased, and places to meet people online have significantly increased. Plenty of Fish, Grindr, Match, eharmony—endless online dating options have many foci: hookup, long-term, religious, farmer, pet lover, and so on.

As much as I sometimes hate online dating, I remain one of its biggest proponents. First, it helps users cast a wider net. Whether small-town or giant city-living, you can connect with people you wouldn't typically meet. Second, it makes sorting easier. I can filter to eliminate men old enough to be my dad who smoke and hate dogs; I don't have to waste time meeting people before I eliminate them as an option. Third, it's phenomenal for shy people. It takes a LOT of courage to ask someone out in-person (although I give tips for this shortly), but with an app, you can just swipe the screen. Getting told "No" online isn't nearly as face-threatening as being rejected in person. Finally, you get to shape your profile and messages to show your best self; of course, this won't help you once you meet in person, but it's a great foot in the door.

But, Dr. Beth, what if they're lying? A recent study of dating app users' messages found only 7% of messages were deceptive, with lies primarily to boost attractiveness to others ("OMG, I love that show too!") or skew availability ("I'm sorry, I already have plans this weekend"; Markowitz & Hancock, 2018). As much as I love the show *Catfish*, the prevalence of big deceptions like cheating or being a different sex is largely exaggerated.

However, this doesn't mean you shouldn't be careful when meeting someone online (or frankly, from anywhere). It should be obvious, but you'd be amazed at how many people don't ALWAYS do these basics: Meet

This is most likely not your date.

(and stay) in a public place, have your own form of transportation, tell a family member/ friend where you're going, and check in with them (or have them call you halfway through— also, giving yourself an "out" if you need it). And, to make meeting them slightly less awkward, have clear descriptions (e.g., "I'll be the girl with the short-hair, wearing a polka dot shirt, sitting at the corner of the bar"). I have a friend who chatted with a guy for 20 minutes before *he* realized she wasn't the date he was there to meet.

Yes, online dating and apps can be exhausting, but just think of them as *additional* tools to help you meet others. YOU are the one who makes tools work. However you meet potential partners, there are things you can do to stand out from the crowd—online and in-person.

What Makes You Beautiful—Online and In-Person

First and foremost, play up your physical attractiveness. Many of the things we do to attract people are the same in any context. Look clean, presentable, and put-together (see Chapters 5, 8, 14). When luring (and NOT being a creep) online, pick an attractive, CURRENT pic of yourself with: (a) No sunglasses so we see your eyes (sorry, Cyclops!); (b) You *alone* so we know which one you are; (c) Clean (e.g., No dirty dishes!) and nice background (for the love of all things holy, if I see one more urinal in profile pic . . .); (d) Non-mirror selfies so we know you have friends (who could've taken the pic); (e) A smile (I really have to say it again in this book? It makes you more attractive!); and (f) A shirt so you (guy or gal) don't look like just a body with no personality (what kind of person are you trying to attract, exactly? Remember my earlier caveat?!?). And, within your profile (yes, you should have actual descriptions), it sounds cliché, but you have to be HONEST to get the person you want/need. Share your intent (long-term versus hookup) and true passions to find someone who loves trashy reality-TV as much as you do.

And although I think online dating is great, you never know when an in-person opportunity will arise, so you have to be ready and approachable anywhere. For example, a *ridiculous* amount of flirting is done at the grocery store! Get your mind out of the gutter; it's not all about melons and meat (see my interview with the *Washington Post*, Wiggins, 2011). But, it *is* true that "you attract what you put out" (see Chapters 4 and 10). Ever been to a restaurant where someone's hunched over a drink, immersed in a book or on a computer (I'm totally not currently typing this at my local brewery) with a scowl on their face? Most people won't chat you up looking like this. Simple welcoming/friendly nonverbals make all the difference in attracting the attention you desire.

Finally, you don't want to just *look* at your potential romantic partner, so let's talk to them. How about some pick-up lines? I know what you're thinking, "But, Dr. Beth . . . pick-up lines are so cheesy." Yes, they can be. But, pick-up lines come in three major forms: flippant, compliments, and indirect interactions. *Flippant lines* are the "cheesy" ones: "Are you from Tennessee? Because you're the only ten I see!", "Are those pants made of mirrors? I can see myself in them!" Kleinke, Meeker, and Staneski (1981) found most men underestimate how much women are put off by these flippant pick-up lines. These tend to work only if they're *actually*, purposefully jokey. Humor can be a good initial attractor.

Are you a parking ticket? Because you've got "fine" written all over you!

© VdZ/Shutterstock.com

Beyond those crazy, cheesy pick-up lines, there are better and more simplistic ones. How about a simple compliment that genuinely flatters (not skeeves out) another person? Who doesn't want to hear they have a great smile? A compliment sets a positive tone for an interaction, especially if it's something non-bodily (think, personality).

Finally, and perhaps the best, is the ***indirect approach***, where you begin a conversation with them like you're already friends. I recently overheard two guys discussing Michigan beers (three things I'm obviously into . . . Michigan, beer, and attractive fellows). So, I jumped in like we were already friends, "Michigan? Really? What's your favorite Michigan brewery?" This same concept works great (once again) at those grocery stores: "If you were buying a steak, which one would you go with?" Not only do you jump into the conversation like you know them, but you ask their opinion, which makes them feel valued. No matter which approach you use, remember that "pick-ups" are advertisements of who you are and what you bring to the table.

Public Speaking Power: Wooing Your Audience

It's not that weird; you need to woo your audience like a date. Winning them over involves attracting their attention *and* keeping them interested. So, let's learn to flirt with our audience:

- **Smile!** No one wants to date *or* listen to a disgruntled fuddy-duddy. Even a slight smile during demo speeches makes you more interesting and attractive. But, be appropriate—not the asshat smiling during sad, disturbing info.
- **Nod Your Head!** While flirting, a subtle head-nod may subconsciously suggest "yes" to your date, making them more likely to say "Yes" when you ask them out. Try this during your persuasive speech solution to increase audience compliance.
- **Use 3-Yes (Foot-in-the-Door) Power.** As you build to asking out a date, get them in the habit of agreement: "This weather's been great, right?" (Yes). "This bar is packed! It must have great reviews" (Yep). "We should grab a drink sometime" (OK). Do this with an audience; get them agreeing with your evidence (yea Chapter 3!) to eventually comply with your solution.

Contributed by B. Ribarsky

© Artem Kovalenco/Shutterstock.com

Getting to Know You . . . Through Dating

After you get a potential mate's attention, it's time to date—figure out who they are and if they're a good match. Two concepts can guide you: dating scripts and uncertainty reduction.

Dating Scripts

Most research today *still* looks at ***dating scripts***, sets of prescribed behaviors for first-date interactions, in very stereotypical 1950s-style ways. In this very heteronormative context, a man actively dominates (e.g., asks girl out, drives, pays, makes first "move"), and a woman passively reacts (e.g., waits to be "courted," does guy's planned activities, "resists" his advances; Rose & Frieze, 1993). Thinking about this script as "dating" raises the question, do we still date?

Students today typically say they're more likely to just "hang out." Dating has become less formal, influenced by a greater acceptance of fluid gender roles, less pressure to marry, and overall acceptance of casual sex and "dating around." However, there's a major problem: People *report* engaging in more casual dating practices but continue to desire traditional first date scripts (Sanchez, Fetterolf, & Rudman, 2012). This creates ***cognitive dissonance***, where we feel anxious because our beliefs and actions don't match up, and sets up any dating interactions not following those scripts for dissatisfaction.

I've already alluded to another problem with traditional dating scripts—they focus on relationships involving mixed-sex partners, which is pretty heterosexist. The good news is researchers are slowly changing their relational focus. Although limited same-sex dating-script research exists, we do know same-sex and mixed-sex couples are *MUCH* more alike than different, something found consistently over the past 40 years (Cardell, Finn, & Marecek, 1981; Kurdek, 2004; Pollitt, Robinson, & Umberson, 2017)! In an era of changing norms/expectations, it's crucial to see dating processes as continually morphing—much like Mystique—and needing our continued attention.

Uncertainty Reduction Theory

One of the key functions of dating, or even hanging out, is getting to know the other person to decide if they're worth our time, emotions, or even financial investment. *Many* theories posit how we get to know others. ***Uncertainty Reduction Theory*** (URT) is one of the most enduring theories explaining how uncertainty (not knowing what someone will say or do) makes us uncomfortable, so we try to reduce it (Berger & Calabrese, 1975). URT describes any initial interactions with anyone, but it's particularly useful for looking at potential dating partners. The main way we attempt to reduce uncertainty is by gaining more info—passively, actively, and interactively.

Passive information gathering is all about observation. Although it sounds very stalker-ish, we learn a remarkable amount just watching others—perceiving and listening to their verbals *and* especially nonverbals. What do their clothes (or lack thereof) say about them? Are they loud, gesturing wildly or standing meekly in a corner? If you know the people they're with, you may assume they're similar (see Chapters 5 and 14). You probably even

Who do you imagine picking up this drink? Whiskey and beer are considered traditionally masculine (Nurin, 2017). We assign personality attributes even based on perceived taste buds!

© Karavanska Alina/Shutterstock.com

make assumptions based upon what they're drinking! The great thing about passive info gathering is that it's very safe; you don't have to approach the other person or risk embarrassment (see Chapter 6). However, you *are* relying upon assumptions—and when you assume, you make an ass out of "u" and "me."

Active information gathering learns through third parties. If I get set up on a blind date, I would ask my friend a lot of questions about who they set me up with. A more modern, and increasingly common, way we actively gather info is via Google. Active gathering may give us more info, but it's not necessarily accurate; third parties and search engines are inherently biased. It's still safe and easy, though, because we don't have to interact with the one we're reducing uncertainty about.

Finally, ***interactive information gathering*** actually engages the person you're trying to discover more about, typically in two ways. First, we use questions. If I want to know where you're from, I simply ask you. Second, we use the ***rule of reciprocity*** to get disclosures back at similar levels (Miller & Kenny, 1986). To know where you're from, I'd say, "I'm originally from Michigan but now live in Springfield" so you'd respond with similar info. Interactive info is usually (assuming it's not a lie) the most accurate. But, it requires actual interaction with the target, which makes you susceptible to face loss if you're inappropriate or make a fool of yourself.

URT isn't perfect, though. For one thing, it assumes all uncertainty is bad, which it isn't. Remember Dr. Brule's husband in the last chapter? Sometimes a little mystery is nice; you don't need to know every single detail about someone. Further, just because you get more info doesn't mean it'll reduce uncertainty. If your date tells you she's an axe murderer (or is *reeeeally* into superheroes), you may learn about their occupation/interests, but your overall uncertainty would likely *increase* dramatically. That's why other theories are necessary (#TakeMoreCommClasses).

You know more about them, but do you feel LESS uncertain now?

© DarkBird/Shutterstock.com

What's Love Got to Do With It?

You've had an amazing first date—let's work on falling in love. Up to 60% of people swear they've fallen in love at first sight (Naumann, 2004). BUT, before you get all mushy, stop right there! Love at first sight does NOT exist. Plenty of people report falling in love the moment they see someone, but that's a **reflective statement**, falsely transferring current feelings onto a past memory. What they likely experienced was *lust* at first sight (Zsok, Haucke, DeWit, & Barelds, 2017)—and that's perfectly okay (you're human after all), but it's not *love*! When we see and interact with someone we're attracted to, our brains let off an exhilarating chemical explosion of endorphins and serotonin (that happy chemical mentioned in antidepressant ads) causing our hearts to beat a little faster, hands to sweat a bit, and even creating those tummy butterflies (Fisher, 2004). These feelings are exciting and feel good, but those initial feelings are lust.

So, what IS love? (Baby don't hurt me . . . don't hurt me, no more). Despite thousands of songs about it, love is still considered a relatively complex construct, but plenty of scholars have broken it down. **Love** is communicatively constructed intimacy. But, I like a former student's description best: Love is an intimate connection where you experience safety and comfort while simultaneously feeling incredibly vulnerable. As such an ever-present factor in our lives, music, movies, and pizza orders, it's not surprising there are so many approaches to explaining love. To really understand love, it's important to look at both sides of it—the way it's *felt* (cognitively, emotionally) and the way it is *expressed* (communicated).

In My Feelings—Felt Love

Lots of different people (largely, social psychologists) have hypothesized how we experience love. One of the most prominent is Sternberg's (1986) **Triangle of Love**—a nice, concise conceptualization saying three components make up love. Each side pairs with another to form different types of relationships. For example, if I have only **intimacy** (close, personal bond) and **passion** (physiological attraction/reaction), then I'm probably in a passionate romance. Pairing intimacy and **commitment** (ongoing decision to maintain involvement) describes families, friends, or long-term couples no longer having sex. Finally, if I have commitment and passion, then it's superficial, perhaps all about the sex.

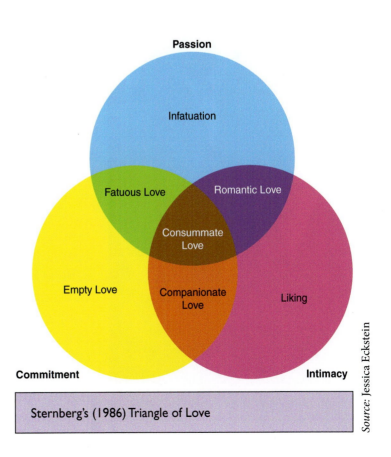

Sternberg's (1986) Triangle of Love

Source: Jessica Eckstein

Sternberg (1986) said "ideal" romantic relationships have all three aspects, experienced at/ in different times/ways.

Another love theory is also a student favorite: Lee's (1973) **love styles** recognize that we all experience/feel love differently. Sorry, it's not nearly as dirty as it sounds. None are good/bad (they're situational), and they're not innate; we may use any of them in different relationships, with different people (even non-romantic contexts!). Three primary love types exist. First, **Eros** is romantic, passionate love (Hendrick & Hendrick, 1986). It's very intense, fast-paced, and usually involves passion but doesn't *have to* be sexual. When we fall in love with Eros, we fall hard and fast—so it's pretty emotional, with super highs and deep lows. Marvin Gaye's "Let's Get It On" epitomizes Eros love. Next, **Ludus** loves love. Also called "game playing" love, it's where people like the attention and excitement falling in love brings, so they want more of it. Inherently playful, Ludus can become manipulative if/when lovers get bored quickly; they may have multiple relationships at a time, using each one to fulfill different wants/needs. Finally, **Storge** (pronounced "store-gay") is practical and platonic, characterized by friendship. Perhaps long-time friends eventually fall in love or romantic partners eventually grow to be besties. Either way, Storge lovers want companionate partnerships.

If you pair each primary love style, their combos produce three more secondary love styles. First, **Pragma**, a combo of Storge (practical) and Ludus (game-playing), is a logical

love. It's very goal-oriented and so sometimes called "shopping list" love. Just like with Social Exchange Theory (where we weigh relational pros/cons), this kind of lover desires people who meet a checklist of ideal qualities. Next, **Mania** combines Eros (passion) and Ludus (game-playing) for a possessive (sometimes obsessive), dependent love. This can get a bit extreme (sometimes, even dangerous), as with crazy stalkers or obsessive lovers! Mania lovers get completely enmeshed—sometimes even losing a bit of their own identity to the relationship. Their intense focus on the romance may mean they neglect other things (e.g., family, friends, job). Finally, **Agape** combines Eros (passion) and Storge (practical) for all-giving, selfless love. It can be platonic (family/friends), but it doesn't have to be; it could be a long-term couple, too. Agape puts others' needs/desires first (e.g., give up dream job to move elsewhere with a romantic partner; forego buying something they wanted to get partner's desired item instead). Again, none are better than another—just different ways we *feel* love.

Arm candy, funny, *and* a millionaire? Check!

How Will I Know That S/He Really Loves Me?—Expressed Love

These approaches to felt love are interesting but merely descriptive. A more practical approach is how we express love. *Love languages* are how we express our relational love intent to others (Chapman, 2010). These apply across many contexts, which is why people find it to be one of the most helpful tools in their own lives—with parents, friends, lovers, and so on.

There are five basic love languages (again, no one being better than another). *Words of affirmation* are verbal appreciation, compliments, or encouragement communicated with kindness (i.e., nonverbally consistent with loving message) and humility (i.e., "requesting" as opposed to "demanding"; Chapman, 2010). *Quality time* is distraction-free attention given to another. It may include shared activities and common experiences, or quality conversation involving "effective listening" techniques (see Chapter 9). Third, *gifts* are objects provided for the sole purpose of conveying affection. Gifts may be bought, found, or created by the giver, and thus, are not limited to those with funds. Fourth, *acts of service* involve doing tasks your partner would like; this involves conscious, advance consideration and time/effort (e.g., unexpectedly getting your car cleaned). Finally, *touch* uses body or objects and can be platonic or sexual, but couples must agree on appropriate time/place it occurs.

Knowing your own love languages allows you to TELL others what they can do for you to make you feel loved. And, knowing another's preference means you can adjust how you communicate to whatever makes *them* feel most loved/appreciated. Chapman (2010) argued major relational breakdowns come when languages aren't being "appreciated" or recognized by the other party. Partners have different love languages, so metacommunication is essential. It's so easy to just ASK (and then do) what makes them feel most loved. There's no excuse for ignorance in this context.

"I'd just as soon kiss a Wookie"
—Princess Leia

Let's Talk About Sex, Baby

Now that you've fallen in love, it's time for some sex. No, I'm not a total fuddy duddy; I know people don't need to fall in love before they have sex. Maybe you're reading this, realizing you've never really been in love, but you've had sex. Nonetheless, having a solid foundation and open communication with your partner sets you up for positive sexual experiences.

Despite living in what sometimes feels like a sex-driven society, when I bring up the topic in my classes, students still manage to turn red and act all awkward. This reaction doesn't surprise me, though. We know that talking about (and *having*!) sex in romantic relationships is important, but we've created a culture that makes talking about it difficult, so we still shy away from it for several reasons. First, the United States is a rather conservative culture (Foucault, 1990). Seeing sex and talking about sex in a public setting is still largely seen as taboo (Montemurro, Bartasavich, & Wintermute, 2015). By sustaining its taboo nature, we're less likely to broach the subject or feel comfortable discussing sex.

© iQoncept/Shutterstock.com

Second, we've created gendered sexual stereotypes and expectations for males and females. Despite supposed sexual progress, it's *still* true that males are expected to be sexual conquerors (man + many sex partners = stud), and females are expected to be pure (woman + many sex partners = slut), which creates a very outdated view of sex (Hamilton & Armstrong, 2009). Because of this, men may be more likely to view sex as a *way* to escalate relationships, and women are more likely to see sex as a *sign* of relationship escalation (Bogle, 2008). Thus, men and women stuck in these norms may have difficulty discussing sex from the same perspective.

Third, we learn most of our communication skills from our parents. Therefore, we often talk about sex the way our parents talk to us about sex, which often means not at all (Flores & Barroso, 2017). Some parents mistakenly believe talking to their kids about sex gives them a green light to do it (have sex, that is), but research finds the opposite—kids whose parents discussed sex (e.g., setting rules/standards, delaying sexual activity) were safer and delayed first sexual encounters for longer (Aspy et al., 2007).

Fourth, we lack good language to talk about sex. We have words that are medical ("I like when you do that with your penis"), derogatory ("I've been thinking about your snatch all day") or childish ("Your wee wee makes me hot and bothered"). They all sound ridiculous, don't they? How can we expect people to talk about sex when we don't have a comfortable language for it?

Because of these factors, people are more likely to communicate about sex nonverbally (Babin, 2013). A moan might be a way to indicate "keep doing that" or moving someone's hand could mean "don't put that there." But, that's the problem . . . it *could* mean that. As you've already read, nonverbal communication can be incredibly ambiguous. If someone moves your hand away, does that mean "not now" or "never again"? That's why verbal sex communication is essential.

Verbally communicating about sex has several benefits. First, couples who talk about sex are more likely to be sexually satisfied because they actually know what their partner likes/wants (Blunt-Vinti,

You only need to be embarrassed to **NOT** talk about sex!

© Pernataya/Shutterstock.com

Jozkowski, & Hunt, 2019). They have clearer expectations about what, when, and how (including safety) to have sex. Second, couples able to talk about sex often find it easier to discuss all areas of their relationship. Finally, being sexually content and engaging in open communication makes these couples much more satisfied in their relationships overall (Montesi, Fauber, Gordon, & Heimberg, 2010). Still feel embarrassed talking about sex? Too bad. If you can't discuss sex, you shouldn't be having it.

> *"I'm looking for someone to share in an adventure"*
>
> —Gandalf

Stairway to . . . Relational Progression

As much as we'd like to be able to predict what people do in romantic relationships, it's incredibly difficult because people and their relationships are so unique. Knapp (1978) created a "staircase" model of relational escalation and de-escalation. Some have attempted to apply it to other voluntary relationships, but this model really focuses on romantic relationships. Further, as a model (not a theory), it *describes* tendencies at each stage; it doesn't predict what or when things happen. Knapp's model has five "coming together" steps and five "coming apart" steps.

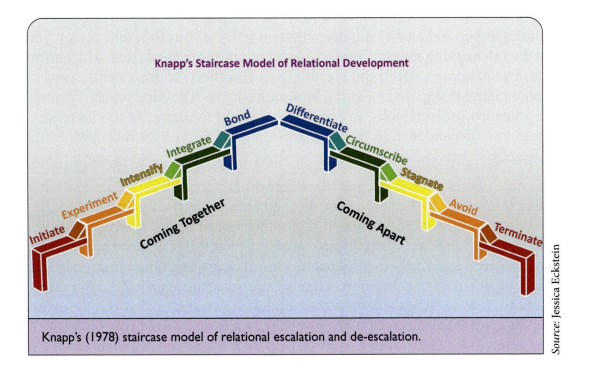

Knapp's (1978) staircase model of relational escalation and de-escalation.

Source: Jessica Eckstein

Stages of Escalation

The first stage of coming together is ***initiating***, where we recognize one another's existence. It's obvious, but it reminds us relationships don't exist unless you BOTH know you're alive. Sorry, but your "relationship" with Arianna Grande or Michael B. Jordan isn't really a thing (unless they actually know you, too). Most info exchanged at this point is nonverbal (think back to passive info-seeking). All relationships, romantic or otherwise, must enter this stage.

Lil' dude—we find people exhausting too!

© Aleksey Boyko/Shutterstock.com

Second, *experimenting* is the small-talk stage where you test to see if you're a good match and if the person's worthy of further investment. Because you don't know them very well, you likely only disclose surface info (remember Social Penetration Theory, Chapter 10?); you don't want to scare them off with your secrets, and you don't know if you can trust them with *your* info. Most relationships never make it past this stage because anything beyond experimenting requires investment (Knapp & Vangelisti, 2009), and it'd be *exhausting* to escalate ALL of our relationships. We see most people in this step as acquaintances.

Next, if (during experimentation) you deem them worthy of your time and energy, you move into the *intensifying* stage to develop greater commitment and trust, which means your disclosures have more depth and breadth. This also affects address terms, which become more informal (e.g., schnookums, love muffin). You'll develop private symbols like inside jokes or wordless "looks" to express what you're thinking. As you increase commitment, your dependence on the other goes up too. We consider most people in this stage our friends.

The fourth stage of escalation is *integrating*, where other people begin to see and value you as a couple. If you're invited to a party, it's assumed your partner is invited too. An easy way to detect people in this stage is to notice their use of inclusive terms; "she or he" and "I" become "we" and "us." There's deep commitment at this point, and unsurprisingly, self-disclosure keeps growing in depth/breadth. Social circles begin merging; your friends become each other's. And, you begin to exchange or create shared artifacts. For example, you might begin leaving things at their place (yes, leaving your toothbrush is the equivalent of a dog peeing on a tree—this is MINE!), give them a key, or share a lease. Physical touching also increases a LOT at this point (Knapp actually said intensifying was "holding hands," and integrating was "holding genitals"). Obviously, this stage characterizes romantic partners (finally!).

The final stage of escalation, *bonding*, is public acknowledgment of your commitment to each other. This may come in the form of an engagement, commitment ceremony, or wedding. But, of course, this public acknowledgement ritual varies culturally.

Stages of De-Escalation

The first stage of coming apart is
differentiation, when people begin stressing
their contrasting characteristics. If I know
you hate sushi, guess what I'll bring home
for dinner? Couples bounce in and out of
this stage all the time when they annoy each
other. It's easy to push buttons, but it's also
simple to recover from this stage, returning
to the previous escalation step (wherever on
the staircase you happened to be).

Differentiating is often characterized by subtle aggressions, like picking something your partner hates to eat.

© Aaron Amat/Shutterstock.com

Next, if things continue to go poorly, the
couple moves to ***circumscribing*** (say that
very carefully), where tension increases, and
communication between partners decreases.
In this stage, if I ask how your day was, you'd
probably just say "Fine." Because the couple may still recover, they often don't want others
to have a bad impression of the relationship, so usually, those outside the couple don't know
anything's wrong at this stage (Knapp & Vangelisti, 2009).

Third, ***stagnating*** is much like it sounds—not moving. The couple isn't getting better or
worse. For example, couples who stay together "for the sake of the kids" are often in the
stagnating stage. Also known as the eggshell stage, the relationship is still relatively solid at
this point but could break with one wrong move.

Fourth, if things continue going south, the couple moves to ***avoiding***, where they no longer
just elude communication but now also physically separate from each other as much as
possible. They avoid phone calls/texts and perhaps stay out late or move out altogether.
There isn't much chance of recovery at this point.

The final stage is ***termination*** or the end of the relationship. Termination doesn't have to come
after the other steps; it can happen abruptly at any point. If you suddenly discover someone's
disgusting hobby during the experimenting stage, you can drop them right there. In more
invested relationships, this is where you separate your stuff, set the terms of the break-up (e.g.,
I'll only see you in class), and say your goodbyes during what Duck (1982) called grave-dressing.

Progression Considerations

Knapp's (1978) staircase works well as an analogy for romantic relationships. First, if you're
anything like me, when you try to take more than one step at a time, you may trip and fall (often,
back to the beginning). Knapp said we generally don't skip stages, and if we do, we go back to
the beginning and still go through those stages eventually. For example, a couple who meets and
marries in Vegas (jumping to bonding) will still need to intensify, integrate, etc. once they start
living together or getting to know each other. Second, just because I start going up/down the

stairs doesn't mean I have to go all the way up or all the way down. It's not unusual for a couple to move in and out of multiple stages, and many relationships don't completely escalate (pretty sure it'd be illegal to marry everyone we ever met . . . not to mention exhausting) or completely dissolve. Plus, I can just hang out on one stair as long as I want. Just because you're standing on a step doesn't mean you're not moving within/on that step; maybe you're enjoying the view from that particular stair-position. You can easily move *within* a stage without moving up or down. And, it's an "open" staircase with no walls/rails; I can jump off from any stair. If we haven't gone very far up the staircase, it's much easier for us to jump all the way to the bottom. In other words, if we don't have much invested, we can try to jump to termination. Finally, sometimes we run up the stairs like we're on a mission; sometimes we methodically take each step slowly and carefully. There is no one, perfect rate of escalation or de-escalation.

Overall, Knapp's (1978) model is a nice, simple explanation for traditional romantic relationships—particularly for how they come together and pull apart. But, the model doesn't describe what we *should* do to stay on the "moving up" stairs. So, let's talk about how we maintain our relationships.

> *"Love is . . . a (decision you'll) have to make again and again"*
>
> —Black Panther

Stuck in the Middle With You—Relational Maintenance

Maintaining relationships isn't easy. That's because even long-term, healthy couples will encounter challenges, boredom, or "growing pains" now and then. In this section, I integrate tips *all* couples should consider to keep their relationships going (i.e., maintenance), but I'll also focus on an increasingly common, yet not often talked about/ planned for dynamic: long-distance relationships.

About 40% of college students report being in a long-distance romantic relationship (LDRR; Merolla, 2010), but with increasing use of technology to meet and maintain relationships, this number will likely continue to grow for all individuals. There are many reasons for physical separation: job or educational positions, military service, jail, deportation, or cross-country family care (Kelmer, Rhoades, Stanley, & Markman, 2013). The nature of the relationship and its daily management determine if it's an **LDRR**, typically any distance it's inconvenient to see your partner daily (if you wanted to;

Technology has made forming and maintaining long-distance romantic relationships (LDRRs) easier!

© alexmillos/Shutterstock.com

Guldner & Swensen, 1995). Living 20 miles apart may be a mere 15 minute drive in Central Illinois but would be an LDRR (over an hour commute) in New York City. People in LDRRs have high levels of individual and relational stress (DuBois et al., 2016), often due to uncertainty caused by the distance (Maguire & Kinney, 2010). In other words, individuals in LDRRs face similar stresses to those in geographically-close relationships with the possibility of additional stressors due to the distance.

Relationship Maintenance Challenges

Whether geographically close or far, trust is foundational to any romantic relationship. When you're not with your partner, it's impossible to know who they're with and what they're doing. It's perfectly easy to cheat in the same town as your partner (most cheating *does* happen in proximally-close relationships; Labrecque & Whisman, 2017). But, for many people, adding distance exacerbates the uneasiness they feel, making it easier for them to jump to conclusions and experience relational uncertainty when they're farther apart (Dainton & Aylor, 2001).

Second, mundane actions make up most of our lives (Canary & Stafford, 1992). In an LDRR, you miss out on some of the little things that become relational glue, such as running errands, making dinner, watching TV. Plus, all those in-person episodes are *physical*—we touch, smell, even taste our partners when they're around us in the same room—all things that increase our sense of intimacy with them (Yoo, Bartle-Haring, Day, & Gangamma, 2014). Missing out on those little things also fosters a potential to grow apart. You have different, separate life experiences. You develop different friend groups, and when you do have LDRR problems, you're apt to talk to these friends about your relational woes, giving them a negative image of your partner and your relationship—in turn, creating an unsupportive network (Le, Dove, Agnew, Korn, & Mutso, 2010).

Unsurprisingly, there's a long-held belief that LDRRs are more likely to break up than geographically-close relationships (Sahlstein, 2004). But, most current research says there's no significant difference in stability based on a partner's distance (Kelmer et al., 2013). So, to improve the likelihood of ANY relationship succeeding in the long run (no matter how far or near your partner may be), there are a number of strategies we know work for couples.

Maintenance Success Strategies

Tactics that increase LDRRs' success are the same as those for ANY romantic relationship . . . just sometimes with a bit of adaption. First, have clear (and positive) relational expectations; it's a strong predictor of relational success (Lemay, 2016). It's fine to have an open, "let's see how things go" timeline—if you both agree to that. But, if you have different expectations, you'll only encounter problems (and perhaps, have wasted your time) if you wait to discuss it. Specifically for LDRRs, it's key to verbally discuss a planned end-point to the distance so you both know when to expect the ongoing uncertainty to end; this helps reduce your day-to-day feelings of uncertainty as well. For example, deployed couples know after a military tour is done, they'll be reunited (for at least some time), whereas commuter couples with across-state jobs may never know if/when they'll become geographically-close. Either one can work—as long as both parties have agreed and discussed it explicitly.

Don't you wish you knew what his partner sent him?

© AJR_photo/Shutterstock.com

Second, employ some common relational maintenance techniques. Stafford and Canary (1991) highlighted five relational maintenance strategies for any romantic relationship: positivity, openness, assurance, social networks, and shared tasks. *Positivity* focuses on affirming communication and avoiding criticism (e.g., "We're doing great!"). If you do end up criticizing or using negative communication, use relationship guru John Gottman's (1999) golden ratio—for every one negative thing you say, have five positive comments. *Openness* highlights discussion of plans, actions, and relational future (e.g., "I'm gonna hang out with my boys tonight, but I can't wait to see you this weekend"). Use technology to communicate more openly and frequently (even in geographically-close relationships) or see each other face-to-face (e.g., Skype) to reduce your uncertainty! *Assurances* reaffirm commitment to the partner and relationship (e.g., "Distance is tough, but I love you, and we can make it through anything."). *Social networks* involve your circle of family and friends to support the couple (e.g., introducing and talking positively about your partner to family/friends). Finally, *shared tasks* contribute to the relationship "together" through everyday actions (e.g., do laundry or wash dishes together when one visits; take turns being the one to travel to the other).

Third, romantic rituals are important in LDRRs *and* in geographically-close relationships. Establish communication habits (e.g., "Good morning/night!" text). Knowing how and when you'll hear from them reduces some relational uncertainty. Whether near or far, check in and connect with your partner routinely. You don't have to go "out" to go on a date; watch a movie together on the same couch, or while you chat (with each other) on the phone/online. LDRRs can be difficult, but that doesn't mean they can't be successful—you just need to be the type of relational superhero to leap long-distance barriers in a single bound (or, at least with some open communication). However, despite many ways to improve relationships, not all of them are meant to be.

We Are Never Ever Getting Back Together—Breaking Up Is (Not) Hard to Do

Breaking up with people is an inevitable part of finding a match. Perhaps you grow apart, there's infidelity, or you just don't make a good pair. No matter the reason, breakups are difficult for everyone. Whether you're ghosted or part agreeably, there are a few things you can do to handle breakups more effectively.

Activism Hero: Dear Dr. Beth . . .

Many of our book's Activism ideas focus on making larger societal impacts, but the little changes we make for the people around us (or even ourselves) are equally (or more!) important. A first step toward positive change is to recognize relationships aren't perfect or easy—they ALL have flaws. You can't change the world without awareness, right? Superheroes *embrace* the struggle by diagnosing the issue and formulating a solution—before diving in to solve it. Further, the ones who succeed don't do it alone; they know when to recruit help or seek new knowledge. Should you choose to answer the call, you also can change how people manage relationships.

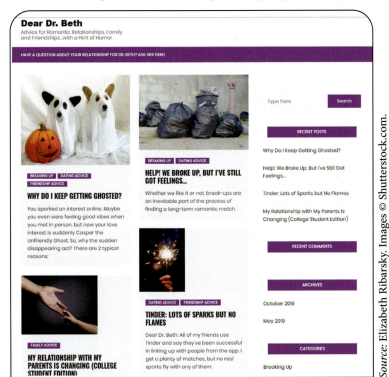

Source: Elizabeth Ribarsky. Images © Shutterstock.com.

After over a decade of students, friends, and even strangers (after they find out what I do) coming to me for advice about how to address problems in their relationships (romantic and otherwise), I created www.deardrbeth.com. Based on solid grounding in the field of romantic relationships (i.e., established research, *not* pop culture stereotyping, myths, or personal opinions), I provide simple, practical, *do-able* advice on what works (and doesn't). Consider me your go-to knowledge source for your specific relational (romantic, family, whatever) issues. Equip yourself with the superpowers (don't worry, I'm not that cheesy on the site) to make positive changes in your relationships. If you're ready to make a change in your life, tackle some relational problems, or just learn to decipher the unknown when you see it in the world around you, don't be afraid to reach out and get help—actively asking or passively reading. When you realize you're not only helping yourself (and those you care about) but actually setting an example for healthy relational communication for observers as well, you'll see how this can really be the truest form of micro-activism!

Contributed by B. Ribarsky

Revenge body! Happier and healthier!

First, take time. Too often, people try to jump into a new relationship, creating the infamous **rebound**, attempting to start new relationships to "replace" (e.g., at same level) the old. Not only are you not giving yourself time to reflect on the breakup, but you're likely skipping a bunch of the steps Knapp (1978) outlined.

Second, take care of YOU. You might be tempted to drown yourself in ice cream or booze, but carbs create temporary highs and alcohol is a depressant—only exacerbating your sorrow. Instead, start forcing yourself to exercise; it's a natural mood booster (Rocheleau, Webster, Bryan, & Frazier, 2004). Plus, there's great satisfaction in looking hot, showing your ex what they're missing. Finally, take control and get help if you need it. The period immediately after a breakup can seem like torture, and you're NOT being overdramatic if it hits you like a ton of bricks! Divorce, for example, is a major life-span reducing stressor (Sbarra, Nojopranoto, & Hasselmo, 2014) and breaking up with a close partner isn't that far off! You'd see a specialist for an injury, so why not see one for a breakup?

Instead of continuously grieving what you've lost, take a *little* bit of time to do that (maybe a night out with pals), then wake up the next day ready to heal (you won't feel better right away, but you'll *start* healing)! How you frame challenges actually affects you mentally and physically. Start dreaming about all the opportunities you'll now have to find someone or some*thing* (e.g., job, friends, activities) better/different! Take time to reflect on what you really NEED from a relationship. What you think you want and what you need might be very different things. If you find yourself dating the same types—or literally the same person—repeatedly with similar results (insanity's definition), you clearly haven't figured out what you really need.

Finally, as you move forward, instead of thinking about the time/effort you invested in the relationship, think about it all as *practice* for the next, better one! When handled in these healthy ways, breakups can be a tremendous source of personal growth

Love is LIKE A FART. If you have to force it, it's probably SHIT

(Tashiro & Frazier, 2003). There's no such thing as The One; that's yet another pop-culture myth (Galloway, Engstrom, & Emmers-Sommer, 2015). There are better and worse fits, and dating is the *process* of finding the best fit for YOU.

Conclusion

It's not you; it's me. Time to call it quits . . . on this chapter. Hopefully, you now have some clarity on how/why relationships work and how you can be better at them. That doesn't mean it's easy. Romantic relationships require vulnerability, some bad dates, and work. Anyone who says "If it's meant to be, it should be easy" is full of crap (and in denial). Relationships take constant maintenance. You must continue communicating *effectively* and *appropriately* (which means sometimes you shut up), and you never stop dating—even if you've been together for 20 years.

References

Aronson, E. (1998). *The social animal* (7th ed.). San Francisco, CA: Freeman.

Aspy, C., Vesely, S., Oman, R., Rodine, S., Marshall, L., & McLeroy, K. (2007). Parental communication and youth sexual behavior. *Journal of Adolescence, 30*, 449–466. doi:10.1016/j.adolescence.2006.04.007

Babin, E. A. (2013). An examination of predictors of nonverbal and verbal communication of pleasure during sex and sexual satisfaction. *Journal of Social & Personal Relationships, 30*, 270–292. doi:10.1177/0265407512454523

Berger, C. R., & Calabrese, R. (1975). Some explorations in initial interactions and beyond: Toward a developmental theory of interpersonal communication. *Human Communication Research, 1*, 99–112. doi:10.1111/j.1468-2958.1975.tb00258.x

Blunt-Vinti, H., Jozkowski, K. H., & Hunt, M. (2019). Show or tell? Does verbal and/or nonverbal sexual communication matter for sexual satisfaction? *Journal of Sex & Marital Therapy, 45*, 206–217. doi:10.1080/0092623X.2018.1501446

Bogle, K. (2008). *Hooking up: Sex, dating, & relationships on campus.* New York, NY: New York University Press.

Canary, D. J., & Stafford, L. (1992). Relational maintenance strategies and equity in marriage. *Communication Monographs, 59*, 243–267. doi:10.1080/03637759209376268

Cardell, M., Finn, S., & Marecek, J. (1981). Sex-role identity, sex-role behavior, and satisfaction in heterosexual, lesbian, and gay male couples. *Psychology of Women Quarterly, 5*, 488–494. doi:10.1111/j.1471-6402.1981.tb00588.x

Chapman, G. (2010). *5 love languages: Secret to love that lasts* (4th ed.). Chicago, IL: Moody.

Dainton, M., & Aylor, B. (2001). A relational uncertainty analysis of jealousy, trust, and maintenance in long-distance versus geographically close relationships. *Communication Quarterly, 49*, 172–188. doi:10.1080/01463370109385624

DuBois, S., Sher, T., Grotkowski, K., Aizenman, T., Slesinger, N., & Cohen, M. (2016). Going the distance: Health in long-distance versus proximal relationships. *The Family Journal, 24*, 5–14. doi:10.1177/1066480715616580

Duck, S. (Ed.). (1982). *Personal relations 4: Dissolving personal relationships.* New York, NY: Academic Press.

Fisher, H. (2004). *Why we love: Nature & chemistry of romantic love.* New York, NY: Owl Books.

Flores, D., & Barroso, J. (2017). 21st century parent-child sex communication in the U.S.: A process review. *Journal of Sex Research, 54*, 532–548. doi:10.1080/00224499.2016.1267693

Foucault, M. (1990). *The history of sexuality* (R. Hurley, Trans.). New York, NY: Vintage Books.

Galloway, L., Engstrom, E., & Emmers-Sommer, T. M. (2015). Does movie viewing cultivate young people's unrealistic expectations about love and marriage? *Marriage & Family Review, 51*, 687–712. doi:10.1080/01494929.2015.1061629

Gottman, J. (1999). *The marriage clinic: A scientifically based marital therapy.* New York, NY: W.W. Norton & Co.

Guldner, G., & Swensen, C. (1995). Time spent together and relationship quality: Long-distance relationships as a test case. *Journal of Social & Personal Relationships, 12,* 313–320. doi:10.1177/0265407595122010

Hamilton, L., & Armstrong, E. A. (2009). Gendered sexuality in young adulthood: Double binds and flawed options. *Gender and Society, 23,* 589–616. doi:10.1177/0891243209345829

Hendrick, C., & Hendrick, S. (1986). A theory and method of love. *Journal of Personality & Social Psychology, 50,* 392–402. doi:10.1037/0022-3514.50.2.392

Hoffman, E., & Weiner, M. (2003). *The love compatibility book: 12 personality characteristics that can lead you to your soulmate.* Novato, CA: New World Library.

Kelmer, G., Rhoades, G., Stanley, S., & Markman, H. (2013). Relationship quality, commitment and stability in long-distance relationships. *Family Processes, 52,* 257–270. doi:10.1111/j.1545-5300.2012.01418.x

Kleinke, C., Meeker, F., & Staneski, R. (1981). Preference for opening lines: Comparing ratings by men and women. *Sex Roles, 15,* 585–600. doi:10.1007/BF00288216

Knapp, M. (1978). *Social intercourse: From greeting to goodbye.* Boston, MA: Allyn & Bacon.

Knapp, M. L., & Vangelisti, A. L. (2009). *Interpersonal communication and human relationships.* Boston, MA: Pearson.

Kurdek, L. (2004). Are gay & lesbian cohabiting couples *really* different from heterosexual married couples? *Journal of Marriage & Family, 66,* 880–900. doi:10.1111/j.0022-2445.2004.00060.x

Labrecque, L. T., & Whisman, M. A. (2017). Attitudes toward and prevalence of extramarital sex and descriptions of extramarital partners in the 21st century. *Journal of Family Psychology, 31,* 952–957. doi:10.1037/fam0000280

Le, B., Dove, N. L., Agnew, C. R., Korn, M. S., & Mutso, A. A. (2010). Predicting nonmarital romantic relationship dissolution: A meta-analytic synthesis. *Personal Relationships, 17,* 377–390. doi:10.1111/j.1475-6811.2010.01285.x

Lee, J. A. (1973). *Colors of love.* Toronto, Ontario, Canada: New Press.

Lemay, E. P., Jr. (2016). The forecast model of relationship commitment. *Journal of Personality and Social Psychology, 111,* 34–52. doi:10.1037/pspi0000052

Maguire, K., & Kinney, T. (2010). When distance is problematic: Communication, coping, and relational satisfaction in female college students' long-distance dating relationships. *Journal of Applied Communication Research, 38,* 27–26. doi:10.1080/0090988090348357

Markowitz, D. M., & Hancock, J. T. (2018). Deception in mobile dating conversations. *Journal of Communication, 68,* 547–569. doi:10.1093/joc/jqy019

Merolla, A. J. (2010). Relational maintenance and noncopresence reconsidered: Conceptualizing geographic separation in close relationships. *Communication Theory, 20,* 169–193. doi:10.1111/j.1468-2885.2010.01359.x

Miller, L., & Kenny, D. (1986). Reciprocity of self-disclosure at the individual and dyadic levels: A social relations analysis. *Journal of Personality & Social Psychology, 50,* 713–719. doi:10.1037/0022-3514.50.4.713

Montemurro, B., Bartasavich, J., & Wintermute, L. (2015). Let's (not) talk about sex: Gender of sexual discourse. *Sexuality & Culture, 19,* 139–156. doi:10.1007/s12119-014-9250-5

Montesi, J., Fauber, R., Gordon, E., & Heimberg, R. (2010). The specific importance of communicating about sex to couples' sexual and overall relationship satisfaction. *Journal of Social & Personal Relationships, 28,* 591–609. doi:10.1177/0265407510386833

Naumann, E. (2004). *Love at first sight: The stories and science behind instant attraction.* Naperville, IL: Sourcebooks.

Nowicki, S., Jr., & Menheim, S. (1991). Interpersonal complementarity and time of interaction in females relationships. *Journal of Research in Personality, 25,* 322–333. doi:10.1016/0092-6566(91)90023-J

Nurin, T. (2017, May 12). Why we don't talk more about whiskey-loving women. *Forbes.* Retrieved from www.forbes.com/sites/taranurin/2017/05/12/why-we-dont-talk-more-about-whiskey-loving-women/#4c164b19519e

Pierce, C. A. (1996). Body height and romantic attraction: A meta-analytic test of the male-taller norm. *Social Behavior & Personality, 24*, 143–149. doi:10.2224/sbp.1996.24.2.143

Pollitt, A., Robinson, B., & Umberson, D. (2017). Gender conformity, perceptions of shared power, and marital quality in same- and different-sex marriages. *Gender & Society, 32*, 109–131. doi:10.1177/0891243217742110

Rocheleau, C., Webster, G., Bryan, A., & Frazier, J. (2004). Moderators of the relationship between exercise & mood changes: Gender, exertion level, & workout duration. *Psychology & Health, 19*, 491–506. doi:10.1080/08870440310001613509

Rose, S., & Frieze, I. (1993). Young singles' contemporary dating scripts. *Sex Roles, 28*(9), 499–509. doi:10.1007/BF00289677

Rosenfeld, M., Thomas, R., & Hausen, S. (2019). Disintermediating your friends: How online dating in the United States displaces other ways of meeting. *Proceedings of the National Academy of Sciences, 116*(36), 17753–17758. doi:10.1073/pnas.1908630116

Sahlstein, E. M. (2004). Relating at a distance: Negotiating being together and being apart in long-distance relationships. *Journal of Social & Personal Relationships, 21*, 689–710. doi:10.1177/0265407504046115

Sanchez, D. T., Fetterolf, J. C., & Rudman, L. A. (2012). Eroticizing inequality in the United States: The consequences and determinants of traditional gender role adherence in intimate relationships. *Journal of Sex Research, 49*, 168–183. doi:10.1080/00224499.2011.653699

Sbarra, D., Nojopranoto, W., & Hasselmo, K. (2014). Divorce & health outcomes: From social epidemiology to social psychophysiology. In C. Agnew & S. South (Eds.), *Interpersonal relationships & health* (pp. 89–105). New York, NY: Oxford University Press.

Singh, D. (1993). Adaptive significance of female physical attractiveness: Role of waist to hip ratio. *Journal of Personality & Social Psychology, 65*, 293–307. doi:10.1037//0022-3514.65.2.293

Stafford, L., & Canary, D. (1991). Maintenance strategies & romantic relationship type, gender, & relational characteristics. *Journal of Social & Personal Relationships, 8*, 217–242. doi:10.1177/0265407591082004

Ştefăniţă, O. (2019). Facebook and romantic relationships—A troubled couple. *Romanian Journal of Cognitive-Behavioral Therapy & Hypnosis, 6*(1/2), 1–12.

Sternberg, R. J. (1986). A triangular theory of love. *Psychological Review, 93*, 119–135. doi:10.1037/0033-295X.93.2.119

Tashiro, T., & Frazier, P. (2003). "I'll never be in a relationship like that again": Personal growth following romantic relationship breakups. *Personal Relationships, 10*, 113–128. doi:10.1111/1475-6811.00039

Thibaut, J. W., & Kelly, H. H. (1959). *The social psychology of groups*. New York, NY: Wiley.

Wiggins, O. (2011, February 17). New Prince George's Wegmens becoming a social hot spot. *The Washington Post*. Retrieved from www.washingtonpost.com/national/picking-up-dinner-and-maybe-a-date/2011/02/16/ABr5VVH_story.html

Yoo, H., Bartle-Haring, S., Day, R. D., & Gangamma, R. (2014). Couple communication, emotional and sexual intimacy, and relationship satisfaction. *Journal of Sex & Marital Therapy, 40*, 275–293. doi:10.1080/0092623X.2012.751072

Zajonc, R. (1968). Attitudinal effects of mere exposure. *Journal of Personality & Social Psychology, 2*, 1–27. doi:10.1037/h0025848

Zsok, F., Haucke, M., DeWit, C., & Barelds, D. (2017). What kind of love is love at first sight?: An empirical investigation. *Personal Relationships, 24*, 869–885. doi:10.1111/pere.12218

Chapter 12:
Small Group
Communication

Contributed by
Dr. Joshua Hammonds
Dr. Beth Ribarsky
Dr. Jessica Eckstein

"If you want to go fast, go alone. If you want to go far, go together."

After Dr. Hammonds graduated from college, he took a few months "to find himself" and gain some direction. He thought spending a summer in Tanzania, Africa, teaching and building in Masai villages with a group of eight people would help him do just that. Nothing teaches you more about yourself, others, and the importance of communication than living for 6 months in mud huts with eight people of vastly different cultural upbringings, values, and norms, all assembled to carry out common goals. From negotiating shared living quarters to navigating conflicts that naturally emerge from spending 18+ hours/day together for 6 months, this particular trip was one of the most challenging, and yet, life-enhancing experiences he'd ever had. He may never quite recover from the time all eight of them were forced to sleep in a broken down ATV in the middle of the Serengeti, but this experience was a 6-month survival course showing how vital communication is in how we reflect who we are, treat others, and accomplish major goals as a small group.

© jo Crebbin/Shutterstock.com

Mud huts like the ones Dr. Hammonds lived/worked in

"Class, this semester you'll be working in groups." You hear it every semester. To many, this is a chance to meet new people, collaborate, share workloads, and develop creative projects that can't be accomplished solo. For others, it brings up negative emotions from past experiences that didn't go according to plan – working with others who don't share your excellence standards or sense of responsibility (Bachrach, Bendoly, & Podsakoff, 2001). Regardless, the concept of "working in groups" isn't going anywhere. Classrooms, co-curricular events, and especially corporations increasingly involve team-based formats to develop ideas/products and to generate solutions (Volini et al., 2019). In this chapter, we look at important small group characteristics. Then, we discuss how communication influences group members' power, decision-making, team-transformations, and leadership. Finally, we suggest ways to be effective in your small groups.

Characteristics of Small Groups

Small groups come in many forms, across many contexts. Your sports team, course-project group, clique of friends, company work-team, online gaming guild, or hobby-based (music, TV, shopping) forum, even the cool new cult you just joined (uhh . . .)—all are types of small groups with similar characteristics. So, let's dig in to raise your awareness of small group dynamics (their definition, pros/cons, roles) so you can be an effective group member. Then, whether you use this superpower for good or evil will be up to you.

Before we dive into the many facets of small groups, it's important to define the parameters of what small group communication is. In short, we define ***small group communication*** as communication among a group of people coming together for a common purpose, who experience a sense of belonging and interdependence with one another. Let's break those down.

Group Size

It's a bit of a debate in the communication research world: What's the appropriate number of people for a "small" group? To stay with a running joke in this textbook (did you notice?), size matters. You've already read the chapter on interpersonal communication (Chapter 10), so you know there has to be *more* than two people to be a group. However, with more than 20 people, the group turns into a public forum, taking on the characteristics of a public speaking event. Through deduction, we know the number

should be somewhere between 3 and 20 people. But, team dynamics researchers note that in larger groups (e.g., 13–20), individuals lose their mutual influence over each other, resulting in alliances and subgroups within the group (Mueller, 2012). This leaves an ideal size between 3 and 12 to maintain the other defining aspects of effective small group communication. However, most researchers agree 5 (actually, 4.6, but we'll round up to a whole person) to 7 people is ideal; it's enough members to garner small group benefits without allowing people to slack off (Hackman & Vidmar, 1970). Also, ideal groups should be odd-numbered to facilitate quick majority-rule votes (Menon & Phillips, 2008).

Common Purpose

Another defining element of small group communication is that those involved must share a common purpose or collective goal. Often, this is what distinguishes a mere group of people and a small group. Just because groups of people gather (like waiting for a bus) doesn't mean they have a collective goal. Yes, they each have a goal to ride the bus, but they don't share a destination or concern about how others get there. However, if we placed this group in an Escape Room and told them they couldn't ride the bus until

Isn't riding the bus painful enough? Now, you must do an "escape room" to get to your destination?!

they completed the tasks to escape, you might find they quickly transition into a true small group with a common purpose.

Sense of Belonging

Another thing that defines a small group is whether or not members feel a sense of belonging. Has your teacher ever put you in groups to work on some in-class activity for 20 minutes? Yes, you're a group of people, and you have a common purpose (at that moment), but do you really feel a sense of commitment/belonging to the group? Small group members, in some capacity, must feel this sense of belonging to the group, especially if the group wants to achieve shared goals (Walton, Cohen, Cwir, & Spencer, 2012). Group names or other unity-builders (e.g., team shirts, norms) can increase belongingness (Tindale & Kameda, 2000).

But, keep in mind your identity is linked to the group as much as theirs is linked to you. For example, if you're a frat/sorority member and you do well in your speech class (because you read/implemented this textbook's suggestions), the next time your instructor has someone from your frat/sorority in their class, they'll be excited! So, although a sense of belonging and group identity is important, keep in mind that this group identity also reflects on you.

Interdependence

Lastly, a small group must have members who exert influence on one another. Think about a recent class group project. In what ways did the communication and actions of each member affect other group members? Perhaps you felt motivated by the contagious energy in the group? Maybe you felt less overwhelmed knowing you had others to rely on? Or, maybe that interdependence wasn't positive. Was a member's absence noticed? Did anyone's procrastination affect others' workload or even the project's timeline? Although it's great to have group members to supplement your work, this level of interdependence comes with risks.

Balancing Small Group Disadvantages and Advantages

Think back to the last time you heard, "All right, for this next project, I'll be putting you into groups." Did you groan or feel relieved? Working and communicating with others is messy. Balancing egos, sifting through misconceptions, juggling schedules, leveling out the workload—group work has its fair share of challenges. Conversely, you may recall a memorable small group experience with plenty of healthy, positive interactions, individual growth, and a final project result everyone was proud of. In this section, we'll highlight some challenges you may encounter working in groups. But first, let's address the individual, relational, and task-based benefits that emerge when groups work through such challenges.

Public Speaking Power: Presenting Group Speeches

We often think public speaking is a solo mission, but group presentations are common. The good news? You've got a built-in support group and back-up if you're nervous. And, there are a few things that make group presentations smoother:

- **Stress structure.** You each have your own intros/conclusions (*right?*), but be sure to have a *group* intro/conclusion, too. A group attention getter/clincher draws us in, sets the tone, and leaves a strong last-impression for all the presenters. But, more importantly, group intros/conclusions provide structure for the *entire* presentation, not just your own—something even MORE important for the audience when paying attention to longer presentations. Your preview and review must specifically highlight who will/did talk about what.
- **Link it together.** Just as you transition between main points, you also want to bridge speakers to provide smooth, clear links: "I discussed X, now Gary will present Y."
- **Take a seat.** Don't stand awkwardly in front of the audience while one person speaks (it's weird for both the group members and the audience); set chairs to the side and sit! Your speaker transitions will give you time to change places.
- **Simplify!** Use time wisely. Change speakers only when necessary; it's distracting and wastes speech time if you're constantly transitioning. Also, don't repeat info other members already covered.
- **Share responsibilities.** One person dominating negates others' roles. Each person should have similar speaking times. And no, clicking/holding a visual aid does NOT count as a presentational role.
- **Practice as a group.** Students often assume they can just practice individually, and it'll all magically come together later. It doesn't; we can tell when you didn't practice as a group. Not only do group rehearsals ensure you're meeting time requirements (group speeches take longer), they also give you a chance for additional feedback. Be each other's practice audience to hone your skills individually and as a group.

Contributed by B. Ribarsky

Benefits of Working in Groups

As we've mentioned, group work isn't going anywhere, and your professors aren't simply assigning it to make your life more difficult. Organizations have been adopting team-based projects at growing rates—to the point that organizations today have been referred to as a "network of teams" (Volini et al., 2019). Few of you will find careers with completely autonomous tasks. Long gone are the days of hiring one person with one specialized skill to do one task, alone. Organizations are interested in small groups because they yield several advantages.

Productivity

More people can get more done. Have you ever watched a construction crew? They're a group for a reason. Not only can they physically accomplish more ("Here, hold this while I nail it"), they each bring

different skills (an electrician doesn't do the same work as a roofer) and more information to the group. Competent small group members from rich, diverse backgrounds can provide valuable info for developing creative solutions to complex problems. So, if 2 heads are better than 1, then 6 to 12 heads should be great! There's a reason superheroes tend to team up—they get more done!

Creativity

Not only do groups tend to get more done, their outcomes are generally more creative than ideas generated individually. Even as your authors and editors worked on this book (and chapter), we found bouncing ideas off one another led to better ideas than if we'd tried to do it alone (Hello, do you think we came up with our cheesy superhero theme on our own?!). It's important to note that creativity doesn't simply happen. It's a process involving the generation, application, combination, and extension of new ideas (Johnson & Hackman, 1995). Certain people may be able to generate new ideas from nothing, but the most creative ideas are built from discussions with OTHERS, applying existing ideas to new contexts or combining two ideas in new ways others fail to see (see Chapter 2 for brainstorming tips). Diverse people with varied experiences are needed to foster this kind of creativity in groups.

Accuracy

Your group might generate numerous amazing ideas, but some of them will be less than stellar. Having other people critique our work helps ensure we generate the best solution possible. Ever tried to proofread your own work just to find it still has errors, even after you've gone through it several times? Our brains are quick to fill in and correct errors, making them nearly impossible for us to see ourselves (Kalfaoğlu & Stafford, 2014). Those additional sets of brains/eyes help ensure accuracy. Providing plentiful input lets small group members see all sides of an issue, critique it rigorously, and arrive at a compelling solution that satisfies the project's goals (Laughlin, Hatch, Silver, & Boh, 2006). We're sure that even in this book, we could've benefited from even more additional team members looking over our work!

Enthusiasm

Finally, small groups can generate enthusiasm and simply be fun. It's one thing to celebrate your own victory, but there's something great about celebrating as a group. Plus, your group can also help light a fire under you. Energy is contagious! In putting together this book, Dr. Beth and Dr. Eckstein, along with their publisher's prompting, got into a nice back-and-forth (almost competitive) pattern to get tasks done to "keep up" with each other's work. If you're a procrastinator, it's easy to put off your work until the last minute (not that *you* ever do that). But, if you know other people are waiting/depending on you, you're more likely to start earlier and work harder.

Challenges to Working in Groups

Unfortunately, we're pretty certain you've had a not-so-great group experience at some point in your life. Have you ever: Been afraid to rock the boat? Dealt with nightmare personalities? Ended up doing all the work? Found it impossible to find mutual meeting times? There are many reasons to groan when told you'll be working in a group.

Groupthink

Have you ever disliked a group decision but thought you were the only one against it and so you didn't speak up? Perhaps you later found out you weren't the only one feeling this way. If so, you were a victim of ***groupthink***, the conformity of group members afraid of disrupting harmony; it limits creativity and creates a sense of invulnerability and the illusion of consensus (Janis, 1971). Groupthink occurs for several reasons (#TakeSmallGroupComm) but most commonly to avoid conflict. People would rather go with the flow than deal with conflict's disruptive stress.

Further, because they're attempting to maintain harmony, those subject to groupthink don't solicit others' opinions (Viega, 1991). A group might even have ***mindguards*** who avert dissenting opinions (perhaps "forgetting" to invite opposing members to meetings or dismissing them as "crazy"; Janis, 1971). Or, a group might be apathetic about a topic; if they don't care, they're not invested in generating discussions or ensuring good decisions . . . again, fostering that illusion of consensus.

Some of the biggest disasters in history were due to groupthink and a highly persuasive, credible, and/or powerful individual whom others were afraid to oppose. For example, although many members of his cabinet were concerned about a Bay of Pigs invasion (This isn't a history book—Google it), people found President JFK highly persuasive (and obviously high-ranking) and were afraid to speak against him—resulting in a botched invasion. Even if decisions aren't life-changing, we're still susceptible to groupthink if we fear challenging others or feel invulnerable.

Activism Hero: Don't Be a Bystander!

Admit it! We're all guilty of being a bystander at some point. We don't want to rock the boat, ruffle feathers, or any other clichés. But, complacency leads to bad decisions—which prevents social change. Janis (1989) proposed group members can do the following to avoid groupthink:

- **Diversify!** We tend to group with people we like, but friendships aren't ideal groups (similar opinions = fewer critical, creative ideas). Start off right; get as many diverse members as possible. You might not like everyone, but your group will make better decisions!
- **Encourage debate!** Ask questions, actually *listen* to responses, and do *not* get defensive! Good debates/arguments encourage clear rationales for ideas/decisions. If members are too nervous to speak up (of course, *you* won't be with your new superpowers), find ways to incite/spark debate (e.g., confidential, written comments and questions).
- **Shut up, Step away!** Leaders have sway, especially over more timid group members. If you're leading, avoid starting discussions with YOUR idea; let the group come up with their own ideas before you insert yours. If your mere presence as a leader influences/skews conversations, don't be afraid to step away for a bit.
- **Appoint a devil's advocate!** A *devil's advocate* annoyingly questions ALL ideas by thinking like an enemy, and that's what you want! It ensures critically thinking through decisions. Further, by appointing a devil's advocate, that person isn't subject to retribution for it—they're simply playing their appointed role.
- **Reach out!** Sometimes we get too close or invested in our ideas and no longer see the flaws. Seek outside council (those not affected/involved) to get clear eyes on the project.

Contributed by B. Ribarsky

© barbaliss/Shutterstock.com

Opposing Communication Styles

Although diverse members help avoid groupthink (Janis, 1989; see Activism Hero box, above), working with others who have different communication styles can be frustrating. Have you ever "talked" with someone who won't let you get a word in? Maybe you've dealt with the other extreme where you can't get someone to speak up? Or, someone who's always defensive, seeing even your nicest comments as attacks? Whatever their communication style, there's no guarantee you'll mesh well. That's why metacommunication, or communication about communication, plays a vital role; it allows the group to talk about what's working (or not) with their communication. Before Dr. Beth invited Dr. Eckstein to co-edit this book, they knew each other socially and professionally but had never worked together on an actual project. So, to avoid future conflicts over communication styles, Dr. Eckstein was explicit: "Ok, here's how I work, my style . . . what parts of that are you ok (or not) with?" It's such an easy thing to say/ask!

Unfair Workloads

When we assign group work, one of the most common complaints we hear from students is about unfair workloads. Frequently, this comes from *social loafing*, with individuals not pulling their weight. Because of small groups' high interdependence, when one person doesn't do their work, it forces others to step in and step up or risk failure. This is the

"Well, I like having on our team someone who obsessively chats about Christmas."

© Cartoon Resource/Shutterstock.com

Don't be a social loafer!

© mishanik_210/Shutterstock.com

more common complaint, but the opposite sometimes happens—someone takes over the entire project and doesn't let others participate. This can be nice for small tasks if you don't care, but we generally don't want our opinions/contributions ignored. Plus, having one person do all the work means it's not group work, meaning the previously mentioned benefits don't occur. It's important everyone actually discuss group norm- and work-expectations (we provide tips for this later).

Time Commitments

Recall the proverb at the beginning of this chapter: If you want to go fast, go alone; if you want to go far, go together. It's true; group work is rarely quick. Dissecting problems, brainstorming options, and implementing solutions among several people are time-consuming feats. And, don't forget about logistics! For instance, you alone have many time commitments—work, other classes, familial engagements, friendships to maintain, and yeah, you should probably sleep every now and then. Sometimes it can be hard enough to find time for one thing in your busy schedule, but now you're trying to make this magical time slot work for five or six individuals?!? It can be darn right impossible. It can help to keep a set meeting day/time rather than trying to figure out something new each time. Further, just talking about schedules can be confusing. We find doodle.com is great (easy, free) to line up people's times/days for scheduling.

Additionally, not every decision needs a whole group to solve a problem. If an efficient, quick solution (e.g., emergency decision-making) is prioritized over a high-quality, creative solution, it may be best to delegate this quick decision to one person—or people with particular roles—and reserve group discussions for more appropriate contexts where they're needed.

Small Group Roles

Our communication constitutes our relationships. That means our roles are determined by how we interact in an ongoing process of negotiation. In small groups, however, the relational roles that emerge are even more varied and complex. Have you noticed how some groups really bring out the leader in you, but in other groups, you play more of a passive, observing role? Group members' particular knowledge of the group's tasks combine with members' relational histories to affect how roles emerge. Although some may be assigned formally (e.g., chair, note taker), roles more often come about informally through interactions over time (Bray & Brawley, 2002). Pioneer small group researchers Benne and Sheats (1948) discovered both task and relational roles are necessary for a group's success.

Task roles are positions group members take to advance the group's agenda to achieve group goals. *Maintenance roles* support group social functioning, meeting relational needs by building a positive social climate. Sometimes it's possible that one dominates over another, but they aren't really mutually exclusive—they're both needed for success. When the Avengers work together to conquer a foe, they don't exactly worry about "hanging out" (task roles dominate); they each do the tasks they're there to do (few, if any, maintenance roles are actively present). When it's all work, the goals get accomplished, but there's not always a great sense of unity or belonging outside those contexts; Captain America, Tony Stark, and The Hulk all leave until another "task" presents itself again. Conversely, when Thor sinks into a depression, scarfing pizza and beer and playing Fortnite with his small group (friends Korg and Miek), *all* they focus on are those maintenance roles. They might be enjoying their time together (and it *does* serve a purpose in uniting them as "bros"), but they don't accomplish any larger task group goals. A great group recognizes the importance of both role types.

Humor is a great tension-reliever, but a jokester keeps the group from staying on track!

© Jenn_C/Shutterstock.com

However, not all small group roles are beneficial. *Individual roles* are self-serving and bring focus to a member's behavior/agenda (hidden or explicit). For example, even though The Torch's bombastic humor may relieve group tensions, the *joker/clown* role can prevent the group from staying on task, as can a *self-confessor* who uses group's time as a therapy session. You'd learn more about role types in a small group communication class (#shamelessplug), but for now, just recognize the importance of having an honest conversation about group roles.

Communication in Small Groups

Small groups both affect and are influenced by communication. Because of their nature, small groups have some dynamics that make the communication within them unique. Let's discuss some ways this plays out in terms of power dynamics, decision-making, team-transformations, and leadership.

Power in Small Groups

Power is present in every single group. Whether there are clear group role differences or social status inequalities, members can access power and control in many ways during group interactions. *Power* is an ability to control or influence another person (Franz, 1998). After talking about some different forms of power that might emerge in your group and its sources, we'll discuss how these can play out in actual small group interactions.

Power Sources

Using French and Raven's (1959) framework, six types of power are typically discussed: legitimate, referent, expert, reward, coercive, and informational. We add a seventh type: connection.

Legitimate power is the influence someone has granted to them because they're appointed, elected, or assigned an "official" role by either the group or an outside entity. It's sometimes referred to as "position power" and relies on a given culture's social structure (Weber, 1947). Colonel Nick Fury's job (S.H.I.E.L.D.'s Executive Director) is an example of this. Decisions and group directions may rest with this individual because they've been legitimately given this authority. However, it's not unusual for people to also have legitimate power due to seniority, like Dr. Xavier over *X-Men* or Captain America over the *Avengers*.

"I have the POWER!!!"
© Elizabeth Winterbourne/Shutterstock.com

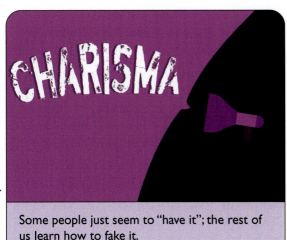
Some people just seem to "have it"; the rest of us learn how to fake it.
© Artur Szczybylo/Shutterstock.com

Referent power is someone's control or influence due to their charisma. Whether socially (fun to be around), task-wise (you like that they get things done), or physically (they're hot)—if you're attracted to someone, they have a certain power over you. This is one of the few power bases that can get used without the user fully realizing it. It may also explain why close friends can ask (and receive) big favors; admiration grants referent power (Simpson, Farrell, Oriña, & Rothman, 2015). We give others referent power because we want to (or already do) identify with them

(Newcomb, 1958). A perfect example is the friend/group member who can talk you into anything simply because they're so darn likable. And, even though some of us are a bit more likeable than others, *all* of us can increase our likeability through simple immediacy cues (see Chapter 10): Appear friendlier, smile a bit more, and REALLY listen to others.

Compliments make the world a nicer place—even in small groups!

© astudio/Shutterstock.com

Expert power is the authority someone has because of how much they know about a subject or how skilled they are at something specific. When we feel someone is more knowledgeable than us, we tend to give them a *lot* of flexibility in determining our thoughts and actions for us (Festinger, 1953)! If you're working on a project on the efficacy of food delivery apps and someone in your group has already created multiple successful apps, you'll most likely accept their advice and direction. Because they're an "expert" on the subject, they suddenly have more power. However, this type of power shifts quickly, according to the subject at hand. Captain America may know the political climate of World War II, but Spiderman is the expert when it comes to knowing pop culture.

"Please! If you do this for me, I'll be your best friend forever." The ability to reward someone if they succumb to your demands is known as *reward power*. Rewards can be tangible (money, candy, hugs) or intangible (friendship, love, compliments), but a person must actually think the reward has worth for it to have power. Companies use overtime weekend pay, and small groups assign good/fun tasks (versus bad) or give verbal praise. Simply being approved of by someone we like is a powerful form of reward power (Raven & Kruglanski, 1970)!

Perhaps the darkest of power types, *coercive power* is the ability to punish someone for noncompliance. Financial, material, physical, and psychological punishments can be used to control another person. For example, corporations use threats of demotion, firing, and docking pay to control employees. Small groups may resort to bullying or social stigmas to have group members conform (Goffman, 1963). But, that doesn't mean coercive power shouldn't be used when necessary; it still gets things done. Parental discipline and the legal system (with threats of fines/jail) are also examples of this. Overall, it can create a negative climate, but it works!

Sometimes your power doesn't come from your expertise but simply info you have (like the little kid sing-songing, "I know something you don't know"); that's *information power*. Let's say you're on an awards committee and you have inside knowledge that a particular student being considered for the collegiality award had recently sent a mean, harassing email to a classmate. You might not be an expert on which awards to give, but you have access to pertinent info to help the committee make a better decision—thus, giving you power. To apply this in your own life, some research suggests it's more effective to present your info indirectly ("I heard this student harassed people, so we might want to consider that as we proceed") rather than directly ("This student is mean and not collegial enough for the award"; Falbo & Peplau, 1980).

Finally, sometimes it's less about *what* you know and more about *who* you know, or **connection power** (also known as third party invocation; Lewin, 1952). Dr. Beth recently needed to rent a local organization's hall for a fundraiser. However, only members or those "sponsored" by members were allowed to rent the hall. Because one of the fundraising group's members was good friends with, and so got sponsored by, one of the organization's members, the group could rent the hall. Although this group member typically played more of a follower role, simply knowing the right person increased her power in the group.

Understanding Power Dynamics

As you can see, power in its many forms is used continually throughout small group interactions. It's important to note that power is neither innately destructive nor negative. Nonetheless, we should always be conscious of how it's used to influence—especially by people who possess several of the power bases at once (e.g., a teacher or coach). These are considered "power relationships," and both parties should be aware of the benefits and potential risks associated (Raven, 1993). For example, all three of your authors certainly take advantage of their legitimate (professor title), expert (relevant Ph.D. knowledge), referent (cute, interpersonally likeable), reward (verbal praise, extra credit points), and coercive (point deductions, lower grades) powers with students to get them to behave or participate in class. But, the more power someone has, the more opportunities are present to manipulate or coerce others against their will; this is especially the case for people insecure in their positions (Kipnis, 1976).

It's also important to realize that power is *given*, which means these bases only have power if we "let" them. We can choose to ignore someone's supposed expertise by believing we know more than them or showing it's irrelevant to the situation. Or, consider that attraction (referent power) or authority/credibility (expert or legitimate power) are in the eye of the beholder; what persuades you about someone may be a turn-off to another. Although it's *much* easier said than done, we have the choice to not allow some power bases to influence us. Ultimately, all these power types influence how groups communicate and make decisions.

Making Decisions

No matter what project your group is working on, decisions need to be made. However, that doesn't mean the *best* decision will be chosen. A lot depends on HOW groups come to these decisions, and there are numerous ways (each with benefits and drawbacks) this can occur, including consensus, authority, majority, expert, and random.

"What was the decision making process that led to hiring a cat?"

First, *consensus decision*, where everyone agrees, is great because it means you're all on the same page. However, coming to a consensus can take a while (sometimes, seemingly forever!), which is one reason group work takes so long. And, an *illusion* of consensus, where we assume everyone else agrees so we do too (peer pressure), is a symptom of harmful groupthink.

Second, *authority decision* is just that—the leader makes the decision. Of course, these decisions are easy for the group (they don't have to do anything!) and quick because there's no need for discussion. But, it also means that valuable feedback isn't necessarily taken into account, which also puts the group's climate at risk.

Third, *majority decision*, or voting, can be an efficient method. However, because the solution rests on the majority, it inherently means at least some people will be pissed off. Actually, if you go with a "simple majority," it could mean almost half your group (49.9%) might be angry. Further, in even-numbered groups, you might not solve anything if it's a tie between split-decisions. It's unrealistic to think people will change their minds based on group discussion.

Fourth, *expert opinion decision* relies on those considered best-informed to make choices. Of course, if someone really is an expert, they might be ideal to decide, and it'll often happen quickly! However, there's no guarantee someone truly is the expert they claim to be *and* even their expertise doesn't mean they'll make the best decision for the group or situation.

Finally, *random decision* leaves the choice to fate: flip a coin, pull from the hat, the nose goes, throw a dart, pick a straw, and so on. Clearly, this can be efficient if clear, good solutions are already developed; it CAN work when equally good options exist. But, people often just take this easy way out so they don't have to think/talk through choices. Dr. Hammonds and Dr. Beth have gone to many a bar (when we were younger and not wiser) where we've seen people suckered into choices via dartboards/spinning wheels of shots. It never ends well.

Should you use a Magic 8-Ball to make your decisions? Signs point to "No."

Group Phases

Figuring out roles, learning who has power and who doesn't, and testing decision-making methods—all impact how a group comes together and how well they perform. Tuckman (1965) famously explained the ups and downs of a group's existence through four stages of group formation: forming, storming, norming, and performing. First, in the *forming* stage, people try to figure out each other, what's expected of them, and how they fit (or don't) together. Because of the awkward uncertainty of this stage, group members tend to stick to safe topics. Second, *storming* is where conflicts arise. Being a bit more comfortable together, people begin to express ideas/feelings more openly and challenge others when they disagree. The third stage is *norming* . . . and thank goodness because it's a relief after the storming stage! Now, roles/responsibilities are clearer/accepted, norms (hence the name) are established, and members are usually more committed to the group/goals. This is necessary for *performing*, the action phase where members work on the task at hand (rather than figuring out group dynamics).

Although it appears linear in theory, in real life, groups slip in/out of stages as groups evolve. Someone may leave or join the group or your group may accomplish a task but then get new tasks with different needs, which might cause groups to revisit the storming and norming stages. Once a group learns to effectively work together, they can begin working to become a team.

Making a Group a Team

Although we've discussed them interchangeably in this chapter, they're not necessarily the same thing: It's one thing to be a group; it's another to be a *team*, which is essentially a high-functioning group. In other words, all teams are groups, but not all groups are teams. Athletes are obviously on teams, but co-curricular programs, organizations, corporations, and even class projects can function as teams. So, what makes the difference? Ultimately, group communication has to occur in ways that enhance team performances and facilitate effective leaders. Larson and LaFasto (1989) described eight defining characteristics that transform groups into teams: clear and elevating goal, results-driven structure, competent members, unified commitment, collaborative climate, standards of excellence, external support/recognition, and principled leadership.

Clear and Elevating Goal

All groups need to strive for clear goals. But, a team can't exist without them. Team members must thoroughly understand the goal before them—to the point that each of them can articulate (automatically, if asked) exactly what that goal is; everyone's on the same page. Think back: In how many of your group experiences could everyone have independently, clearly stated the goal? It's much more common in team experiences than across most "groups" we've been in.

Team goals must not only be clear but also elevate. As with our clichéd (but true) superhero, you can't reach an elevating goal with your feet flat on the ground; you have to strive for team goals. Groups may do this, but only teams require hard work, determination, cognitive strain, and perseverance. Although they first appear insurmountable in how much they focus on elevating the team, a team's goals must be realistic and obtainable. Of course, there's a fine line between elevating and unobtainable.

For example, if you're trying to lose weight and set a goal of 50 lbs./month, you're setting self-defeating (and unhealthy/dangerous!) goals . . . so much so that you might not bother trying. On the other hand, if you decide to lose 3 lbs. by month's end, you might not be motivated enough to start, and by the time the month comes to an end, you might find it too late to accomplish even this small goal. The same goes for a team's goals. Groups might initially be unsure of their direction, so the earlier they set goals, the sooner they can focus on tasks and be on their way to becoming a true team. Take advantage of this feature: For your next group project, articulate with absolute clarity a goal that tests your limits, creates urgency, and is obtainable.

Results-Driven Structure

Groups may have situations where it's unclear what's expected. Sometimes, you may even duplicate efforts, finding someone else doing work you thought YOU'RE supposed to be doing. Teams eliminate this confusion with clear structures, identified roles and responsibilities, established rules and expectations, and clear lines of communication. On baseball teams, the pitcher doesn't go out to play at first base (because they know that's not their position/responsibility), and the team knows the manager calls the shots (so, the entire team knows who they should be listening to). To help your group become a team, establish expectations and roles up-front, not later as tasks come up.

Competent Team Members

Can you imagine if that baseball team had *only* pitchers? (Hello, designated hitter rule). Or, a Fantastic Four team of only Things? It just doesn't work. Team members are not only committed to team goals (see below), they also each bring unique skills/knowledge to the team. As much as you want your friend to join, if she or he doesn't have role-specific skills, they won't add to a team. In fact, randomly selected groups may be more diverse *and* perform more effectively than self-selected ones (Chapman, Meuter, Toy, & Wright, 2005)!

So, though you may not enjoy it, if an instructor randomly assigns you to a group, thank them for giving you "real world" experience and setting you up for a better chance at success (Blowers, 2003).

Unified Commitment

We've all worked in groups where not everyone's committed: They arrive late, are distracted, and don't prioritize group goals. These behaviors (and the attitudes behind them) block goals and contagiously affect others' attitudes (Janis, 1971): "*He* showed up late, so why should *I* bother coming on time?" On teams, knowing you're ALL "all in" increases trust and interdependence. In teams with unified commitment and collaborative climates, members value team goals over their own.

Collaborative Climate

It's important, especially early in developing, that members foster a collaborative spirit, sharing positively as they work toward goals. Supportive climates produce open communication, leading to more ideas and solutions. In "teams" where one person wants to be the star, they're so focused on achieving individual goals that they'll often keep info to themselves or try to undermine others. A focus on working together deters ego-driven behaviors to achieve greater results.

Standards of Excellence

How good is "good enough" for your group? That should be clearly established. Standards of excellence vary among members, so successful teams will agree on what constitutes excellence. Is the bar set at a championship victory or an undefeated season? An A+ on the presentation or a perfectly acceptable B–? Mentioned before, teams have elevating, stretched-to-the-limit-goals. It's necessary to have a team-discussion to determine what that level of excellence is for everyone.

External Support and Recognition

Home field advantage: Whether it's psychological or physical familiarity, teams win more at home than away (Smith, 2003). Corporate/organizational teams are no different. There may not be thousands of people chanting for your team as you splice together PowerPoint slides in the 11th hour before your presentation, but research overwhelmingly shows that teams who receive recognition (and often, praise) from management tend to perform better. It's not just the recognition and accolades; teams need appropriate resources to get the job done.

Trophies are nice, but even praise from a boss or instructor helps a group feel more like a team.

© Kseniia Kolesnikova/Shutterstock.com

Principled Leadership

Phil Jackson. Vince Lombardi. Pat Summitt. Professor X. What do they all have in common? They're considered great leaders. You may have the most skilled team members, but even great teams need leadership. Effective leaders moderate conversations, create vision, motivate, and focus. But, what works for one team/situation doesn't work for all. Leadership (both good and bad) comes in all shapes and sizes.

Leadership in Small Groups

Dr. Hammonds's 4-year-old daughter started preschool last year, eagerly growing to like her classmates and excited about her new activities. After 2 months, at the first Parent–Teacher Conference, her teacher mentioned their daughter was deemed "The Class President." Delightfully surprised, Dr. Hammonds asked when they'd held Preschool Elections and why so early? Her teacher responded, "Oh no, we don't have elections. That's just what everyone calls her." After climbing down from his Proud Papa chair, he began to wonder: How much of his daughter's early leadership was innate (born from DNA-linked personality characteristics), and how much was due to her "in-the-moment" communication with classmates (how she refers to people, frames ideas, and communicates generally)? There are numerous ways leadership has been studied. We'll discuss three: traits, style, and emergence.

Trait Perspective

Some people are just born leaders, right? *Right*? This common belief has been researched for decades. Early leadership studies focused on good leaders' specific traits: intelligence, self-confidence, enthusiasm, dominance, and social participation (Hare, 1976). These *can* be great traits, but as a society, we don't always select leaders so prudently. Most Americans pick leaders based on charisma and attraction, things we assume reflect their character (Finkelstein, 1991).

A famous example is the first televised U.S. Presidential debate (1960 Kennedy/Nixon). Kennedy was undoubtedly more attractive than Nixon, but JFK also wore makeup

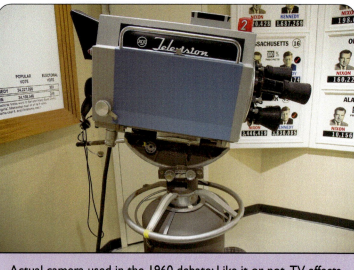

Actual camera used in the 1960 debate: Like it or not, TV affects our perceptions of leaders!

© Joseph Sohm/Shutterstock.com

(whereas Nixon refused and proceeded to sweat profusely) during the debate (pro tip: A little blush prevents looking like a corpse on black/white TV!). Many people *watching* the debate thought JFK won—he looked cool, calm, collected, and frankly, just attractive. However, many *listening* on radios thought Nixon won (Lehrer, 2011). People were unsurprisingly influenced by the candidates' appearances. (FYI: Nixon later wore makeup and won the next two debates but not the election.)

Do attractiveness, charisma, or intelligence guarantee good leaders? No! Believing traits are innate allows some people to be valued over others and also relies on race/sex bias, with masculine traits tied most to "good" leadership perceptions (Jackson, Sullivan, & Hymes, 1987). Trait-based perspectives also don't consider contexts or situations. Although we still choose many leaders this way (Hochschild & Borch, 2011), research acknowledges there are better ways to choose leaders.

Style Approach

Rather than believing we're just born that way (sorry, Lady GaGa), communication scholars argue we become leaders. Barnlund and Haiman (1960) argued effective leaders are those who act/communicate in leader-like ways (i.e., specific behaviors to guide, influence, and direct others toward group goals). There are three major communication leadership styles (each with its appropriate time and place): autocratic, democratic, and laissez-faire.

First, *autocratic leaders* are much like dictators who lead with a "My way or the highway" approach. Group morale is often low with autocratic leaders because they often allow members little say in group decisions. However, there's still a time/place for this style. If groups lack knowledge or experience, autocratic leaders can guide them in what/how they do tasks. Also, in a time crunch, you can accomplish things quickly by letting such leaders make the decision (again, little input from the group).

Authoritarian leaders aren't for every group, but they can work in particular situations.

Second, *democratic leaders* are moderators, encouraging others to share opinions/ideas and focus on coming to decisions *together* as a whole. A democratic leader encourages creativity and communication, so group members feel their input matters, which in turn, increases group morale. It sounds like a great leadership style, but it's not always ideal. As much fun as it is to boost morale with active communication, if we're in a car crash, we don't want a long group discussion. Save our lives! We'll worry about morale later.

Finally, *laissez-faire leaders* take a hands-off approach, letting groups lead themselves. It can be difficult for outsiders to even tell *who is* the leader in laissez-faire groups. Of course, this method can be disastrous if groups lack direction or experience, but it's ideal for highly skilled and motivated groups. Freedom in this hands-off approach promotes creativity. High-functioning groups with laissez-faire leaders are often called *self-directed work teams*, who might meet together before branching off to do individual work, then reconvene to share results.

Because each style has benefits and drawbacks, leaders can switch from one style to another when deemed appropriate/necessary. You may find your current group leader favors one style, so different people with other leadership styles might take on leadership roles depending on the situation.

Leadership Emergence

Each semester, Dr. Hammonds puts his class into five-person groups, assigns them a project, doesn't designate a leader, and gives intentionally ambiguous operating instructions. At the term's end, groups present their final projects and are asked one final question: Who was your leader? Over 90% of students (confidentially *and* unanimously) select the exact same leader in each group. Looking at peer-chosen leaders like this, Bormann (1975) focused on "leaderless groups" and observed a ***method of residues***, where all members are initially potential group leaders but are each eliminated from contention until one leader remains.

Using the method of residues, you might end up with a great leader … or great cup of coffee.

© NonLoeiterd/Shutterstock.com

Leadership emergence using the method of residues looks at how people are eliminated from leadership for various reasons. The first to go are the quiet ones. Observant, listening members are valued, but Bormann (1975) found being *too* quiet during early group formation prevents them from being seen as leaders. Next, overly talkative or dogmatic people are removed, with nearly half of potential leaders taken out of contention in the first two meetings. After this, groups tease out future leaders based on behaviors such as contributions, help-seeking, and reticence. After several interactions, groups may still have one or two potential leaders, so they assess who has the best relational/task balance. In the end, one is left standing (or two—one task, one relational), and the other may become a lieutenant supporting the leader. Emergent leaders can be great for groups' situational needs, but as new tasks are presented and challenges evolve, new leaders may emerge.

Evolving Technology and the Small Group

The most obvious, pervasive, recent societal change involves ever-evolving technologies. It's not surprising that, having inundated our lives, technology also impacts small group communication. Technology allows small groups to meet, form, and conduct business around the globe through synchronous apps (e.g., GoToMeeting, Google Hangouts, ReadyTalk, Skype, Zoom). Virtual teams may never meet, but they have many small group benefits—plus a few more. First, more organizations are opting for virtual teams because they lower costs, allowing work from home (Volini et al., 2019). Remote work also reduces overall commuting time; why fly around the world when you can meet online? Second, research shows virtual teams

Virtual teams allow you to work from anywhere … wearing anything. Some of your authors "may" have written this textbook in their pajamas.

© Andrey_Popov/Shutterstock.com

can reduce power differentials and encourage members to be vocal (Panteli & Tucker, 2009). We tend to speak more openly online (it's easier to say how you really feel when people aren't literally across the table), so it may lessen groupthink potential and heighten creativity.

Despite these benefits, depending solely on technology to meet with your group creates some problems in addition to those already present for small groups. First, technology can be isolating. Even though you *are* a virtual team member, it doesn't mean you *feel* like a member of that team. Second, if/because you don't feel team-unity, the group's overall cohesiveness, commitment, and productivity might be lower. So, how can we address both technological and face-to-face group challenges?

Grab Your Capes! Tips for Small Group Superheroics

Hopefully, you now recognize you can't avoid small groups—they're an essential part of our lives, whether we like it or not. Let's discuss how groups can work to be more effective. First, mesh team goals with members' individual goals if possible. When our own goals are recognized and (at least somewhat) met, we have higher team commitment (Larson & LaFasto, 1989). This also helps build cohesion—the social glue connecting and committing you to your team. Emphasize each other's commonalities and recognize even little group victories. Make it through your first meeting? Yay. Develop a timeline? Yay! Complete a project? YAY! Little celebrations drive momentum. You should also minimize in-group and maximize out-group competitions. Inner rivalries lead to distrust and lack of cooperation, BUT, external competition bonds people together (Puurtinen & Mappes, 2008). Sports teams do it all the time: Together, we'll crush them! Even with class projects, you're probably inspired to outdo other groups.

Next, establish positive group norms early. The most common complaints we hear from student groups involve latecomers and loafers—behaviors that spread, exacerbated when they're not addressed early on. LuLu wasn't on time because no one seemed to care when Bogart was late before; but then, because LuLu wasn't called out for *her* tardiness, Bogart thinks he can be even later next time. It's a vicious cycle! In your first meeting, stress the expectations and consequences for not meeting them. For example, set a rule that someone more than 10 minutes late (without notice or valid excuse) must bring snacks to the next meeting. Whatever your norms/rules/punishments are, be sure they're developed early so your group spends more time on tasks than trying to figure out what's expected of them. And, don't just *set* desirable norms; follow them. In other words, don't be a bad group member. Be on time. Do what's asked of you, and do it well. Don't be afraid to use your newfound superpowers to get ideas rolling, but also, know when to shut up! Don't be a jackass dominating discussion; be the member you wish everyone was.

In the end, groups are complicated. You're dealing with different goals, communication styles, and schedules. Simple awareness of challenges prepares you to lead and, more importantly, to be a better group member. Think of groups as opportunities, not burdens. No matter how you derive cohesion or what your goals/norms, good communication remains the key to your group's success.

A small group used their communication superpowers to write a small-group chapter!

© Malchev/Shutterstock.com

References

Bachrach, D. G., Bendoly, E., & Podsakoff, P. M. (2001). Attributions of the "causes" of group performance as an alternative explanation of the relationship between organizational citizenship behavior and organizational performance. *Journal of Applied Psychology, 86,* 1285–1293. doi:10.1037/0021-9010.86.6.1285

Barnlund, D., & Haiman, F. (1960). *Dynamics of discussion.* Boston, MA: Houghton Mifflin.

Benne, K. D., & Sheats, P. (1948). Functional roles of group members. *Journal of Social Issues, 4*(2), 41–49. doi:10.1111/j.1540-4560.1948.tb01783.x

Blowers, P. (2003). Using student skill self-assessment to get balanced groups for group projects. *College Teaching, 50*(3), 106–110. doi:10.1080/87567550309596422

Bormann, E. (1975). *Discussion and group methods* (2nd ed.). New York, NY: Harper & Row.

Bray, S. R., & Brawley, L. R. (2002). Role efficacy, role clarity, and role performance effectiveness. *Small Group Research, 33,* 233–253. doi:10.1177/1046496402033002

Chapman, K., Meuter, M., Toy, D., & Wright, L. (2005). Can't we pick our own groups?: The influence of group selection method on group dynamics and outcomes. *Journal of Management Education, 30,* 557–569. doi:10.1177/1052562905284872

Falbo, T., & Peplau, L. A. (1980). Power strategies in intimate relationships. *Journal of Personality and Social Psychology, 38,* 618–628. doi:10.1037/0022-3514.38.4.618

Festinger, L. (1953). An analysis of compliant behavior. In M. Sherif & M. O. Wilson (Eds.), *Group relations at the crossroads* (pp. 232–256). New York, NY: Harper.

Finkelstein, J. (1991). *The fashioned self.* Philadelphia, PA: Temple University Press.

Franz, R. S. (1998). Task interdependence and personal power in teams. *Small Group Research, 29,* 226–253. doi:10.1177/1046496498292005

French, J., & Raven, B. (1959). The bases of social power. In D. Cartwright (Ed.), *Studies of social power* (pp. 151–164). Ann Arbor, MI: University of Michigan Press.

Goffman, E. (1963). *Stigma: Notes on management of spoiled identity.* New York, NY: Simon & Schuster.

Hackman, R. J., & Vidmar, N. (1970). Effects of size and task type on group performance and member reactions. *Sociometry, 33,* 37–54.

Hare, A. P. (1976). *Handbook of small group research* (2nd ed.). New York, NY: Free Press.

Hochschild, T. R., & Borch, C. (2011). About face: The association between facial appearance and status attainment among military personnel. *Sociological Spectrum, 31,* 369–395. doi:10.1080/02732173.2011.5 57132

Jackson, L. A., Sullivan, L. A., & Hymes, J. S. (1987). Gender, gender role, and physical appearance. *The Journal of Psychology, 121,* 51–56. doi:10.1080/00223980.1987.9712642

Janis, I. (1971). Groupthink. *Psychology Today, 5*(6), 43–46, 74–76.

Janis, I. (1989). *Crucial decisions: Leadership in policymaking & crisis management.* New York, NY: Free Press.

Johnson, C. E., & Hackman, M. Z. (1995). *Creative communication: Principles and applications.* Prospect Heights, IL: Waveland Press.

Kalfaoğlu, C., & Stafford, T. (2014). Performance breakdown effects dissociate from error detection effects in typing. *Quarterly Journal of Experimental Psychology, 67*(3), 508–524. doi:10.1080/17470218.2013.820762

Kipnis, D. (1976). *The powerholders.* Chicago, IL: University of Chicago Press.

Larson, C. E., & LaFasto, F. M. J. (1989). *Teamwork: What must go right/what can go wrong.* Thousand Oaks, CA: Sage.

Laughlin, P. R., Hatch, E. C., Silver, J. S., & Boh, L. (2006). Groups perform better than the best individuals on letters-to-numbers problems: Effects of group size. *Journal of Personality and Social Psychology, 90*(4), 644–651. doi:10.1037/0022-3514.90.4.644

Lehrer, J. (2011). *Tension city: Inside the Presidential debates.* New York, NY: Random House.

Lewin, K. (1952). Group decision and social change. In G. Swanson, T. Newcomb, & E. Hartley (Eds.), *Readings in social psychology* (2nd ed., pp. 459–473). New York, NY: Holt.

Menon, T., & Phillips, K. W. (2008, November). *Getting even vs. being the odd one out: Conflict and cohesion in even and odd sized groups.* Paper presented at meeting of International Association for Conflict Management, Chicago, IL. doi:10.2139/ssrn.1298497

Mueller, J. S. (2012). Why individuals in larger teams perform worse. *Organizational Behavior and Human Decision Processes, 117,* 111–124. doi:10.1016/j.obhdp.2011.08.004

Newcomb, T. (1958). Attitude development as a function of reference groups. In E. Maccoby, T. Newcomb, & E. Hartley (Eds.), *Readings in social psychology* (3rd ed., pp. 265–275). New York, NY: Holt.

Panteli, N., & Tucker, R. (2009). Power and trust in global virtual teams. *Communications of the ACM, 52*(12), 113–115. doi:10.1145/1610252.1610282

Puurtinen, M., & Mappes, T. (2008). Between-group competition and human cooperation. *Proceedings of the Royal Society, 276*(1655). doi:10.1098/rspb.2008.1060

Raven, B. H. (1993). The bases of power: Origins and recent developments. *Journal of Social Issues, 49*(4), 227–251. doi:10.1111/j.1540-4560.1993.tb01191.x

Raven, B., & Kruglanski, A. W. (1970). Conflict and power. In P. G. Swingle (Ed.), *The structure of conflict* (pp. 69–109). New York, NY: Academic Press.

Simpson, J., Farrell, A., Oriña, M., & Rothman, A. (2015). Power and social influence in relationships. In J. A. Simpson & J. F. Dovidio (Eds.), *APA handbook of personality and social psychology: Interpersonal relations* (pp. 393–420). Washington, DC: APA.

Smith, D. (2003). The home advantage revisited: Winning & crowd support in an era of national publics. *Journal of Sport & Social Issues, 27,* 346–371. doi:10.1177/0193732503258637

Tindale, R. S., & Kameda, T. (2000). "Social sharedness" as a unifying theme for information processing in groups. *Group Processes & Intergroup Relations, 3*(2), 123–140. doi:10.1177/1368430200003002002

Tuckman, B. W. (1965). Developmental sequence in small groups. *Psychological Bulletin, 63*(6), 384–399. doi:10.1037/h0022100

Viega, J. F. (1991). The frequency of self-limiting behavior in groups: A measure and an explanation. *Human Relations, 44*, 877–895. doi:10.1177/001872679104400807

Volini, E., Schwarts, J., Roy, I., Hauptmann, M., van Durme, Y., Denny, B., & Bersin, J. (2019). Global human capital trends survey. *Deloitte Insights*. Retrieved from www2.deloitte.com/ content/dam/insights/us/collections/HC-Trends2019/DI_HC-Trends-2019.pdf

Walton, G., Cohen, G., Cwir, D., & Spencer, S. (2012). Mere belonging: The power of social connections. *Journal of Personality & Social Psychology, 102*, 513–532. doi:10.1037/a0025731

Weber, M. (1947). *The theory of social and economic organization*. Oxford, London: Oxford University Press.

Chapter 13:
Organizational
Communication

Contributed by
Dr. Wendy Papa
Dr. Michael Papa

Communication is at the core of what allows organizations to function. Organizational communication allows people to work together productively and harmoniously, but it also may create an oppressive environment or interfere with work getting done effectively. We, your authors, have a *lot* of organizational communication experience around the world and have found that, unsurprisingly, no organization is perfect. Between the two of us, we've previously worked at Allstate Insurance Company (Wendy was a corporate trainer), Uppsala University (Sweden), Michigan State University, Hong Kong Baptist University, Bangkok University, Ohio University, and University of North Carolina-Greensboro. We've conducted research on organizations' social change initiatives and economic developments in the U.S., Bangladesh, India, and Thailand; conflict in the U.S., Sudan, and Uganda; and technology diffusion, management selection and development, and decision-making processes.

In this chapter, we use all of this experience to show you some key aspects of org comm. There are MANY topics and issues that org comm scholars study, so we'll focus on just those topics we feel will give you an introductory understanding of this subset of the communication discipline. We'll use real-world organizational examples to describe and explain the importance of org comm, how it works, and what should be considered in the future.

What Is Organizational Communication?

At its core, organizational communication focuses on two verbs: organizing and communicating. Karl Weick (1979), one of the most prominent organizational theorists of the 20th century, defined **organizing** as a set of rules people negotiate to reduce their uncertainty about how to interact, behave, and coordinate to accomplish their work. Organizing occurs in many places. Simple forms might be a group of kids choosing sides and negotiating rules to play baseball at a local park or a family figuring out how to prepare, cook, and serve a holiday meal (Papa, Singhal, & Papa, 2006). More complex forms of organizing occur when corporations design systems for people working together to make, sell, and distribute products to millions of people; on such a large scale, these processes involve thousands of workers organized into dozens of departments. Organizing is also central to people figuring out how to work cooperatively within and between departments to accomplish more abstract organizational goals.

The communicating part of this subfield focuses on people's processes for creating shared meanings through interactions. You already know these shared meanings allow us to create and sustain relationships and coordinate our efforts; without shared meaning, people can't accomplish their goals. It's not always easy, however; people within organizations often struggle over meanings (Papa, Daniels, & Spiker, 2008) because org comm essentially combines interpersonal, small group, and even mediated communication into one giant, complicated system. Interpersonally, people write and receive messages to/from others, seek information, converse about tasks, provide feedback, and sustain positive (it's always nice when you actually like the people you work with and don't have to *only* talk about work) and productive (even if you really like your coworkers, you should probably get *something* done) relationships. In small groups, members engage in problem-solving, decision-making, and conflict management.

Communicating is also needed between organizations and various publics (consumers, neighboring communities, government officials, and regulators). Obviously, 21st century org comm is no longer just face-to-face—it comes in every mediated form imaginable. Simply put, organizational communication isn't simple.

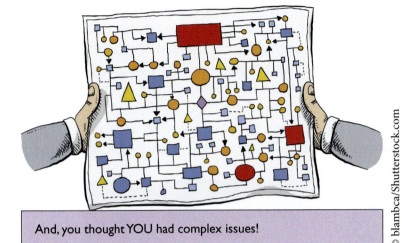

And, you thought YOU had complex issues!

© blambca/Shutterstock.com

We know most of you aren't communication majors (although we hope you're realizing how amazingly interesting and applicable communication is and will be sucked into the superpowers of our discipline). But, even if you're not a comm major/minor, there are two primary reasons to study org comm. First, you'll better understand your current and future organizational experiences. Second, you'll develop some org comm superpowers to soar above the crowd.

Understanding Organizations

First, you're likely already a member of several organizations right now. From a frat/sorority, athletic program, workplace, or nonprofit to recognizing you're an essential (yep, they can't run without you!) part of your college/university, our lives are inextricably tied to organizations. And, because people can't describe their life experiences within organizations without communication, we need to understand the human processes that take place there. Conflict, cooperation, decision-making, uses of power and authority, compliance-gaining, resistance, innovation and change, and the creation and maintenance of organizational culture are all based in communication. And, the ways we engage in these various communication forms are constantly evolving. For example, websites and social media have become integral not only to how organizations communicate internally but also how they communicate with the public. We hope to guide you through looking at how your various organizations communicate and consider what they could do to be more effective. As we said, no organization is perfect. Perhaps, like Tony Stark, you can be the one striving to make your organizations better.

Awareness of Skills

By looking critically at how organizations communicate internally and externally, you'll come to appreciate the very skills that make you a top choice to employers. There's broad, general agreement that well-developed communication skills are essential to personal effectiveness in organizations for all workers and particularly, for managerial, professional, and leadership positions (Papa et al., 2008). Surveyed organizations place "communication" prominently among skills most desired from new hires (National Association of Colleges and Employers [NACE], 2019), and other highly ranked skills are actually all communication skills as well (just called different things): presentation skills (Chapter 4), verbal (Chapter 7) and nonverbal (Chapter 8) abilities, writing and reading skills, critical thinking/problem-solving (Chapters 2 and 3), teamwork/collaboration (Chapter 12), negotiation (Chapters 9 and 10), intercultural fluency (Chapter 14), and data analysis using digital technology (NACE, 2019). Communication skills, flexibility, adaptability, and curiosity help get you hired and advance in your career, in any field. Clearly, there are many reasons to increase your understanding of org comm. Even if you never take another communication class again, it'll help you in jobs you currently work as well as any job you later pursue.

Your communication superpowers can keep you from resorting to this tactic!

© CREATISTA/Shutterstock.com

How Organizational Communication Works

To understand the practical skills that help you in organizations, it's important to see them in terms of some major org comm concepts, including understanding organizations in terms of systems, communication patterns, and organizational culture.

Organizations as Systems

Because organizations consist of so many people, relationships, and moving parts, they're often thought of as a system. A useful theory to understand this concept is *Systems Theory*, which views groups or organizations as living organisms experiencing birth, development, and death (von Bertalanffy, 1968). This means organizations are dynamic and act in purposeful ways to survive, accomplish goals, and thrive. Systems Theory explains how organizations do this using several key concepts: wholeness, openness, feedback, and hierarchy.

Wholeness

An organizational system consists of parts (groups, departments, members) that link together interdependently, which means each part affects another (it's the highly interdependent nature of small groups . . . × 100!). If the relationships are *highly* interdependent, a change in one part of the system can lead to changes throughout the entire system—much like a super-ripple effect (Hello, Dr. Who!). Interdependence among parts results in an integrated whole.

Wholeness means the effect of parts working together differs from the effect of their isolated, individual actions taken collectively; in other words, wholeness refers to *synergy*, where the whole is *greater* than the sum of its parts. Think of your favorite band performing a song. You could listen to each member's solo parts and perhaps enjoy them just fine, but their combining gives a more dynamic performance. It's not just about the individuals performing as one . . . their *interactions* got them to this point. Band members brainstorm playing songs in different keys, tempos, or members' solos. Intermingling, they build on and modify their ideas until they arrive at something that sounds good *and* reflects both their individuality and who they are as a group. What'd happen if we asked each musician to generate ideas by working in isolation from one another? We might see ideas similar to what came from group-brainstorming, but the individually compiled list wouldn't include ideas emerging from creative, spirited group discussions. The band's musicians

Like a great (or even average, garage) band, it's how they work together—as a whole—that makes the magic happen!

working as an integrated group (a *system*) produce something greater than they would've in a simple collection of isolated, individual efforts.

It's no different than if we tried to understand your family just by meeting you. Even if we met all your family members individually, we still wouldn't come close to a complete picture until we saw and understood how you interacted together as a system. We can't simply *add up* individual actions in order to understand how they function as a system. And, *that* is wholeness.

Openness

If we tried to understand organizations just by looking at how their parts interact, we'd be missing something crucial: Systems don't operate inside bubbles (only Aquaman can do that). Instead, they interact with other organizations and the environment. In your body's system, all your organs interact to make you unique and functioning, but everything around/outside you influences how effectively your parts work. Unlike your body, however, organizations can usually choose (to some extent) how much "outside" environment they want to let in, usually along a continuum of options. ***Open systems*** allow or encourage active exchange with others in the outside environment. They allow lots of ***input***, or energy and materials (e.g., ideas, skills, plastics), which they transform in some way via a process called ***throughput*** (e.g., analyzing data, physically making/manipulating materials), and then return products and by-products of throughput (e.g., solutions, physical products) to the environment, which is ***output***. Because these things are both entering and exiting, an organization can't exist without some connection with the outside environment. In stable outside environments, it's tempting to ignore the fact that organizations are open systems because this is when they operate smoothly, in a steady, machine-like state: Performance is regular and routine because nothing in the environment demands anything else. But, ignoring the environment's role can be hazardous if/when surroundings change in some dramatic way.

For example, you've probably heard of Kodak, but there's a good reason you've probably never used their products. Kodak dominated the photography market for much of the 20th century. Although they developed the first digital camera in 1975, they ignored this major technological advance, fearing that introducing this new technology *they* developed would ruin their film market. Unsurprisingly, someone else—Logitech-Fotoman (the maker of a wireless mouse you may be using now)—eventually released the Dycam digital camera in 1991. By refusing to acknowledge the continually changing environment and inevitable role technology would play in our lives, Kodak set itself up for failure, filing for bankruptcy in 2012. Environmental adaptation is key to any organization's success, and systems adapt through feedback.

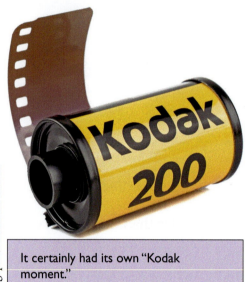

It certainly had its own "Kodak moment."

Feedback

Feedback involves negative or positive responses to system actions; these responses provide info that organizations can use to adjust to environmental changes. Feedback functions in two ways: *maintenance processes*, regulatory methods to keep system conditions within acceptable ranges ("maintaining the status quo") and *adaptive processes*, bringing about change and growth ("shaking things up").

Negative feedback indicates deviations or changes from normal conditions. Negative doesn't mean bad, though; think of it more like the negative charge in a battery or ion. Systems prefer *homeostasis*, staying the same; so any change (whether "good" or "bad") will result in negative feedback. Organizational systems adjust to this change by correcting the deviation and taking some action. Maintenance processes depend on negative feedback to maintain this status quo. Let's say a restaurant wants to reduce waste while also being prepared for sudden increases (busy season) and decreases (slow season) in patrons. If the food inventory rises above a certain level as busy season slows down, a chef sends negative feedback (Conditions are changing; the beans are piling up!) to the owner so that they reduces food purchases (no more beans!) until business picks up again. Similarly, if food inventory drops below a level needed to feed a sudden busload of off-season bean-lovers, the owner receives negative feedback to order more beans until the shortage is corrected. Negative feedback keeps things within a normal range, to maintain a system's homeostasis.

Rather than signaling for a correction, *positive feedback* reinforces deviations, creating new system conditions rather than maintaining old ones—a key factor in adaptive processes. The Magical Bean restaurant may use positive feedback by "dealing with" their influx of beans (e.g., creating more bean-based dishes or ads/special promotions). The deviation in the status quo is having too many beans, but rather than stopping more beans from coming in, they continue with the deviation and engage in more adaptive processes, *using* the positive feedback.

Did you know beans are a common part of a traditional "English Breakfast"? Yet another way to deal with the influx of beans!

Of course, feedback in living, open systems isn't simply a mechanical process of auto-responses to deviation-correcting or -reinforcing messages. Imagine if you depended on autocorrect to make all the changes it assumes to be right. It'd be incredibly frustrating for both you and the recipient and even more disastrous for an organization. Feedback isn't always a simple process.

Hierarchy

Finally, relationships among a system's parts are governed by rules. One of the more important rules, particularly for organizations, is the principle of **hierarchy**, which is how different parts are organized into subsystems, often showing who has more or less power. Subsystems all relate to one another to form the overall organizational system. Again, think about your immediate family. You and your siblings are a separate subsystem from your parents' subsystem, and chances are, your parents had/have the most power. Further, all organizations operate within a larger hierarchy. Even your immediate family doesn't exist alone—it's part of a larger system of all your other relatives. An organization has individual workers, who make up work groups, departments, or divisions, who all combine (like the Thundercats) to create an organization. Even organizations that depart from traditional ideas about labor divisions are still characterized by a basic systems hierarchy going upward from elements (workers) to subsystems (departments) to systems (organization). This hierarchy influences if, and how, parts communicate.

"Those of you who like big families will be happy to hear we now have a parent company."

Taken collectively, the basic concepts of Systems Theory—wholeness, openness, feedback, and hierarchy—thoroughly explain organizations in action. The theory is influential in org comm because it puts the *organizing* role of communication in a new light (Littlejohn, Foss, & Oetzel, 2016). Communication doesn't just occur in organizations nor is it solely a tool for managerial control. *All* the human processes that define an organization arise from communication.

Organizational Communication Patterns

Relationships among individual organizational members are defined by communication. When we study org comm, we don't just look at person-to-person communication; we also examine how small groups communicate internally and with other groups in the organization. Communication within and between these individuals and groups can be formal or informal.

Formal Communication

Happening in officially designated channels between org members, *formal communication* tends to occur in four directions: downward, upward, horizontal, and diagonal.

Downward communication. Sending messages from upper to lower levels of the organization's hierarchy (i.e., from manager to employee) is *downward communication.* Some organizations view communication primarily as a tool for managers to control and coordinate; this focuses downward communication on orders and regulations from superiors to subordinates. Five message types are typical of downward communication: job instructions (what, how work should be done), job rationales (why tasks should occur, its place in relation to the big picture), procedures/practices (policies, rules, benefits), feedback (subordinates' performance appraisals), and indoctrination (foster commitment to an organization's values, goals; Katz & Kahn, 1978).

Although it's studied a lot by scholars, research usually focuses on the *ineffective* kind (info inadequacy, inappropriate diffusion) of downward communication. Downward messages present a puzzling paradox. On the one hand, downward messages frequently create overload. Advances in technology, and ironically, the importance attached to the idea of effective organizational communication, have led to floods of emails and social media messages. On the other hand, some organizational members report they don't receive enough info on topics important to them. It's possible that members receive too much of the *wrong* information—not that the info itself is flawed; it just may not relate to their job and/or organizational concerns. Think about all the school email you get that doesn't pertain to or interest you.

© Trukhachev Kirill/Shutterstock.com

Downward communication doesn't have to be like this.

Although downward communication is incredibly important in having clear direction from those in charge, it can ultimately be overwhelming. And, if an organization *only* relies on downward communication, employee/member morale often suffers because it feels like they're always being talked down to. Think about the last time you had a class when the instructor didn't care about your questions or input (of course, your instructor for this class would never do that). It's nice to have direction, but it's also important to feel like you matter.

Upward communication. Because sending messages only from the top down provides an incomplete picture, organizations also implement *upward communication*, messages sent from lower to higher levels (namely, communication initiated by workers and sent to managers). Primarily concerning task-related matters, upward communication can be used to promote morale, like encouraging employee involvement in decision-making (e.g., employee meetings), problem-solving (e.g., suggestion systems), and development of policies and procedures (e.g., systematic grievance reporting, attitude surveys).

Upward communication provides superiors with information on job performance, job-related problems, fellow employees and their issues, and subordinates' perceptions of organizational policies and practices (Katz & Kahn, 1978). If upper management is too far removed from what's happening, how will they know there's a problem to fix? Even as a student, you know of issues that administrators are unaware of because *you're* the one experiencing it. Send it up the chain!

Managers may value upward communication, but its actual use is limited when management doesn't establish effective ways to make it happen. Then, it seems like only a token gesture ("Here's a suggestion box we'll never check"). Or, employees might be too nervous to provide feedback, fearing retribution for denigrating something management implemented. This is understandable given superiors may not be receptive to upward communication attempts (Papa et al., 2008). Once people get the impression their boss only wants to hear good news or support for their own ideas, those workers will filter what they communicate upward, telling only what they think their boss wants to hear or only what *they* want their superiors to know (i.e., to make themselves look better for raises or promotions). No one wants to be the bearer of bad news; those are the first henchmen killed off by the evil villain in any movie! And, in extreme cases, death has resulted from upward communication failures in real life.

Make yourself heard!

© Irina Qiwi/Shutterstock.com

One of the most tragic instances of a failure in upward communication was at NASA prior to the launch of the Challenger space shuttle. In previous flights, NASA workers had noticed abnormal O-ring erosion (allowing high-pressure rocket fuel to escape), but instead of reporting it up the chain of command (by requesting an investigation), NASA Management ignored the problem (told to them by the workers) and chose instead to increase the (systemic) tolerance for erosion (i.e., Systems Theory's positive feedback). The night before the launch, NASA had a conference call with Morton Thiokol, manufacturer of the Saturn Rocket Booster. A group of Morton Thiokol engineers *again* expressed their deep concern about a possible O-ring failure in cold weather and recommended postponing the launch. But, with pressure from NASA, Thiokol Management gave launch-approval, showing tragic groupthink. An upward communication failure, combined with management allowing NASA to bypass safety requirements, killed seven Challenger crew members (Raval, 2014)!

Groupthink-type situations like this could be helped with more open and debate-encouraging communication (see Chapter 12), but that's sometimes easier said than done. Another way some organizations have encouraged upward communication is by using appointed representatives. For example, rather than an entire student group showing up at a dean's office, that group might create a list of grievances and send 1-2 people to deliver them. The ideas still get heard, but it takes the focus off any particular person, reducing stress for everyone involved.

Horizontal communication. Messages sent across same-level functional areas (e.g., production, marketing, HR, PR) of an organization are lateral or ***horizontal communication***. This gives flexibility to the organizational structure by facilitating problem-solving or info-sharing across work groups and task coordination between departments or project teams. Horizontal communication is basically what each individual member of the Avengers does—they're all their own parts of the system and coordinate with every other part directly, without going through upward/downward channels. Because there's a certain freedom to it, horizontal communication can enhance morale, help resolve conflicts, and allow for participative decision-making. Although it may not be as efficient as downward communication, it can be more effective. In many Japanese organizations, decision-making and problem-solving occur through horizontal communication at lower levels: There's continued discussion until consensus is reached (i.e., everyone on board with decision), at which point that info is transmitted upward to management for review and approval (Kopp, 2019). This often creates long, drawn-out processes for making decisions, but employees are happier with the decisions eventually made.

Although horizontal communication can be effective, it's not immune to problems such as territoriality, rivalry, specialization, and separation (Papa et al., 2008). One inhibiting value is *territoriality*, where task-controllers regard others' involvement in their defined/fixed jurisdictional area as invasive/encroachment; departments (and people) value their turf and strive to protect it. For example, some schools run into territory problems when one department begins offering classes that might align too closely with another department. Because communication often pulls from numerous disciplines (e.g., sociology, women's and gender studies, psychology), these other departments might view communication as an encroachment on their "territory" and not be as open to sharing and working together for the good of the students and school. Instead, they may go straight to the top to complain about encroachment on "their" area.

Public Speaking Power: Audiences as Organizations

Being involved in any organization means you'll inevitably be responsible for sharing info with others. However, because of increased organizational specialization, it sometimes feels like we're speaking completely different languages. But, you can practice speaking to different groups now—just think of your class as an entire organizational system. Seeing it as an org, rather than just a bunch of other students, will help you shape your message like you would in a company or larger organizational setting. Here are some things to consider for both contexts:

- Recognize not everyone has your expertise. *You're* the specialist; avoid jargon.
- Recognize the systemic hierarchy to deal with downward (prof's instruction), upward (feedback to teacher, turning in assignments), horizontal (feedback to/from classmates), and perhaps diagonal (TA questions, contacting college IT or librarians) communication.
- A good organizational message—just like all other communication forms—is both effective and appropriate. USE messages you receive horizontally (Classmates offended or confused by something? Fix it! It's your job to adjust to *them*, not the other way around.) AND vertically (Teacher tells you how to improve? Don't assume it's arbitrary preference; it's to make you better!).

Contributed by B. Ribarsky & J. Eckstein

© Artem Kovalenco/Shutterstock.com

Next, this problem may be made worse if intra- and interdepartmental *rivalries* arise from win/lose competition for rewards/resources. Again, if workers (even within the same department) are competing against one another, they may be reluctant to be as open with communication or sharing resources for the good of the organization. Years ago, a large company's sales force (aka, Sales Studs) believed the marketing department (aka, Market Men) took too much credit for the Studs' hard work (e.g., sales via maintaining personal and professional networks, traveling cross-country to meet potential buyers). Conversely, the Market Men felt the Studs didn't recognize how *their* efforts had opened the door to new markets (i.e., pre-inclined potential customers to buy company products from the Studs). This rivalry reduced communication between the departments, which inhibited their cooperative work and sometimes sabotaged success for entire departments. Senior management intervened by (a) *making* (yes, like they were children) the Studs and Men meet weekly to share product-promotion ideas and (b) increasing sales-based bonuses to *both* departments—both practices shown to significantly increase corporate sales precisely because they address rivalries (Carucci, 2018).

Comedy genius Richard Ayoade perfectly portrays specialization in *The IT Crowd.* Check it out!

Third, **specialization**, or specific focus on a particular skill, also may hamper horizontal communication. For example, because their specialty is so technical, horizontal communication is often difficult between Information Technology (IT) specialists and other employees. Technology can be simple to IT people, so when software problems or changes occur, their abbreviated explanations and **technical jargon**—terms not understood by those outside the profession—make it difficult for others to implement IT's suggestions. Employees may get angry or frustrated with IT because they can't do their work until the technology is fixed. IT gets annoyed that others don't understand their explanations *or* can't solve simple problems on their own ("Did you try turning it off and back on again?").

Finally, horizontal communication often fails because of **separation**—the org simply isn't set up to make lateral messages easy. Departments may be on different floors, in different buildings, or across the country. People may be unwilling to make additional effort to connect with others who aren't sitting close by or have a different work schedule (hours, time zone, etc.). And, even in shared spaces, you may be separated (sometimes intentionally, by the company's design!) by other physical barriers like cubicles in an awkward maze of semi-private barriers. If horizontal communication isn't *encouraged* by how the company is set up (both literally and figuratively), you may not get to know people, which makes it even more challenging when you do need to reach out to them.

Diagonal communication. When messages cross both levels *and* functions/departments within an organization, it's called **diagonal communication**. It may be officially recorded and occur through organizational channels like company newsletters or interdepartmental memos, but the frequency and expectations for it aren't usually defined (like they are with upward or downward communication). Let's say you work for a theme park. Your job is to manage the cafeteria. One day, you need to get some extra help cleaning up all the debris because there has been an influx of customers. You can't go through typically prescribed channels to "order" assistance from your higher-ups and wait for them to contact the other departmental managers because the trash is piling up NOW! So, you avoid the rigmarole by calling the manager of the custodial services directly ("We need help stat! Trash cans are overflowing!").

In its most simple form, diagonal communication creates an up/down and over direction. As technology evolves, this form of communication increases in organizations, so it's a newly recognized org comm flow. As a result, compared to the other formal types, comparatively less research has been done on it. But so far, diagonal communication has been touted for its openness; it allows people at all org levels to communicate with one another as-needed, according to the organization's *or* department's needs—creating cross-functional relationships.

Formal communication is important and is one of the key things that distinguishes org comm from other subfields. But, the communication studied in other subfields (e.g., interpersonal, nonverbal) is just as crucial in the context of organizations. This is most illustrated in org comm contexts when we discuss informal communication.

Informal Communication

Any messages occurring outside officially designated channels are considered *informal communication*, which is often just as (or more) important and much more frequent than formal channels. Informal communication can be particularly useful for unforeseen day-to-day problems. It can be a substitute for inadequate formal messages, such as insufficient or ambiguous ones. For example, if you weren't quite sure what to take from the latest university email on the grievance policy, you might ask one of your classmates or a professor in one of your classes (even if they're from another department) for their take. There's not a formal link between the two of you, so, informal communication fills in the gaps.

Because it often occurs in clusters of people talking together, informal org comm has been called the *grapevine* (Hellweg, 1987). Grapevine communication can be incomplete because there are no "fact-checkers," and those using it aren't responsible for making sure messages are correct. But, overall, it tends to be more accurate (e.g., there isn't any ambiguous language used by management to make things "sound good for the company") than inaccurate and usually spreads fast. Grapevines typically deal with people-oriented, social information—although other info can be diffused here. The grapevine also serves as a rumor mill.

Grapevine communication is also called "water-cooler talk" because that's where people meet to chat—or at least, they used to ...

Three types of rumors spread through the grapevine: anxiety rumors, wish-fulfillment rumors, and wedge-driving rumors. *Anxiety rumors* focus on something negative that's going to happen to people in the organization (e.g., layoffs). *Wish-fulfillment rumors* reflect something positive that workers want to happen (e.g., pay raises). And, *wedge-driving rumors* pit groups of workers against each other to fight so only one group succeeds (Papa et al., 2008). Although gossip and rumors have an inherently negative connotation, research has shown gossip can play a positive role, helping people get information they won't otherwise hear, release their frustrations productively, and learn unwritten rules of an organization's culture (Hafen, 2004).

Organizational Culture

You've already been part of many organizations in your life, so you know each one is unique in how it functions. There are clear differences in what each organization values, how things are "done" there, and how members interact. This is why organizations can be seen as having their own culture, with org comm being a performance of this culture (Pacanowsky & O'Donnell-Trujillo, 1984). You'll learn more in Chapter 14, but for now, it's helpful to know that a culture exists when people come to share a common frame of reference (e.g., language, values) for interpreting and interacting in their world. Like all other types, *organizational cultures* consist of shared values observable in community features such as rites, rituals, celebrations, legends, myths, and heroic sagas (Bormann, Howell, Nichols, & Shapiro, 1982). This culture arises from a dynamic tension and interplay within/between members of the system and surrounding environment. Communication is what constructs and maintains this culture. An organization's culture can be seen in its opportunities for growth, sociability, job autonomy, degree of structure, achievement awards, tolerance for change, and emotional support.

First, imagine going to the same job, doing the same task, knowing nothing will change/happen Every. Single. Day. Sounds miserable, right? For some organizations (or rather, their employees), this is the reality. Others have found integrating growth opportunities to be a great way to motivate employees and increase morale. *Opportunities for growth* can come in the form of promotions (moving up the ladder/rank) or from additional (organization-provided/paid for) training, licensing, or schooling. This added training means that even if employees eventually leave the organization, they're able to take the results of these growth opportunities with them—which also makes them more appreciative employees *while* they work for the organization providing these benefits. Growth opportunities help the person *and* the company (Bassi & Van Buren, 1998)!

Second, **sociability** is how friendly an organization's environment is. It sounds counterintuitive, but actually allowing/encouraging workers to socialize helps the

workplace be more productive. We're talking effects in the *trillions* of dollars (Gallup, 2017)! Found time and time again for the past 80 years, employees who enjoy not only where they work, but perhaps more importantly with *whom* they work, tend to be more productive at work *and* more committed to their workplace, resulting in less worker turnover, and ultimately, saving an organization money and time (Zelenski, Murphy, & Jenkins, 2008). Sociability can come in lots of forms: celebrating birthdays, happy hours after work, even workplace sports teams.

Boring workplaces also lead to less sociability.

© CREATISTA/Shutterstock.com

Third, **job autonomy** specifically looks at how much independence employees have to do their own work how they want. Do they have freedom to be creative or try new things? Or, even in non-creative jobs, is someone always looking over their shoulder, double-checking their work? Even at entry-levels, having some autonomy develops greater trust between employees and management (Bond & Galinski, 2011). There may be more or less autonomy, depending on the job, the organization, or the person (a boss shouldn't let bad workers run wild, after all).

Fourth, degree of structure is often linked to **power distance** (see Chapter 14), how equally power and influence are distributed across groups or people. Organizations with **lattice designs** are non-hierarchical structures with no bosses. New members (who aren't assigned departments) find a team they'd like to join and voluntarily commit to achieve outcomes as part of that team. Direct communication is encouraged, so there aren't intermediaries or approval-seeking. Rather than fixed or assigned authority, "natural leaders" emerge through fellowship among team members (see Chapter 12). Lattice organizations recognize sponsors (individuals who guide and mentor) rather than bosses (Magloff, 2016). One example of a company using this design is Gore & Associates (which makes products like GORE-TEX®), a large, international corporation who needed to grow without violating their founder's views (he believed workgroups > 200 people lose cohesion) regarding organizational size. Their solution was to spawn "clusters" where each building houses only 150 to 200 employees. All clusters are located near each other, however, "so expensive resources can be shared and functional groups of people can come together easily to share

Achievement rewards can be tangible (like a gold star) or intangible (like praise).

© JellyRollDesigns/Shutterstock.com

knowledge, expertise, and experience" (Natural Leadership, 2004, p. 2), encouraging people at all levels to interact, sharing power and resources.

Fifth, *achievement rewards* recognize people's contributions. Much like opportunities for growth, achievement awards are designed to motivate, but instead of promotions, they're based on recognition for tasks done within one's position (e.g., finishing a job, leading sales). Achievement awards come in many forms, including simple recognition (employee of the month), preferential treatment (closer parking spot), bonuses (money), or celebrations (lunch for your work group). They can be small ("I brought in doughnuts because you've all been working so hard") and still go a long way to increase morale or motivate. However, if overused, we may expect rewards just for showing up, resulting in rewards' lost value and reduction of people's intrinsic motivation (Davis, Winsler, & Middleton, 2006).

Sixth, *change tolerance* is how innovative/flexible an organization typically is (again, see Chapter 14 for more). Some are willing to try (and built to allow) new methods, whereas others tout the "We've always done it this way, so we'll always do it this way" mentality. Like all other organizational culture features, this exists on a continuum. For example, you may want Apple to develop new and innovative products, but you probably want your McDonald's fries to continue tasting the same. Some change is good—Kodak's refusal to adapt resulted in its demise. However, too much change makes employees uncertain/uncomfortable.

Finally, *emotional support* is how much concern is given to an employee's mental well-being—both at work and outside the system. For example, does the organization provide bereavement leave? Do managers and other employees express condolences for an employee's loss? This may seem like an emotional extreme, but increasingly, companies' leave policies include "personal days" that aren't just about being sick or going on vacation—they recognize the importance of employee mental health and well-being. Life is stressful (duh!) and whether that stress comes from personal issues or *emotional labor* (the psychologically taxing part of jobs: putting on a happy face for customers or being worried about patients or students), providing emotional support simply creates better employees (Vincent, 2011).

Doctors and nurses, like teachers, often have difficulty "checking out"—they worry about their patients/students even when "off the clock."

© vectorfusionart/Shutterstock.com

Each organizational culture is different and may exhibit cultural factors in many ways. Each employee, organizational goal, etc. has different needs, and every culture reflects that. Whether it's good or bad depends on your perspective. Cultures aren't right or wrong—they're just different, which is good! And, just because a particular org culture exists today doesn't mean it can't/won't change. In fact, larger global issues often necessitate organizational change.

Global Issues in the Org Comm World

Remember, organizations are living, dynamic entities that evolve and change. In this final section, we consider changes to org comm emerging recently. Over time, these changes will continue to affect both organizational leaders and the people who interact with them. Many changes are happening in today's organizations (take an org comm class!), but we'll just look at technology in light of the work/life separation and globalization.

Technology and Work/Life Separation

It's obvious that significant change emerges as digital technologies (e.g., cell phones, iPads) evolve. Using these tools, people are linked to organizations from anywhere—a convenience giving workers flexibility to work remotely. But, it also reduces work/life separation, particularly for salaried employees. For those who can't "clock out" and go home, when does work stop and private life begin? If a task demands immediate attention or there's an emergency, is a worker able to choose to ignore it—without repercussions? The separation of work/life has become increasingly muddied.

Nearly 30% of American workers feel they need to stay connected to work 24/7, *even* during weekends, breaks, or holidays (InterCall, in Collins, 2015). Can you imagine your professor calling *you* on nights/weekends regarding a class project!? And yet, have you ever sent a night/weekend email to your professor, hoping for a quick response? Teachers, in particular, have difficulty with the work/life distinction because technology creates an expectation of 24/7 availability. Even when they're not in the classroom or in their office, they're often grading, making lesson plans, doing committee work, researching, writing, or responding to email. Such expectations can cause fatigue, emotional stress, and even larger health issues. For example, teachers who experience occupational stress even report more gastrointestinal problems (Howard, Giblin, & Medina, 2018)! These pressures to perform 24/7 and their resulting outcomes may be exacerbated even further with increasing pressures to perform globally.

Alas! Your profs can only dream . . .

© Willow Dempsey/Shutterstock.com

Marketplace and Global Competitive Pressures

Globalization, increasingly expanded interaction among people around the world, has significantly impacted organizations, their workers, and understandings of org comm. On the positive side, globalization has enormous potential for people around the world (Stiglitz, 2007). Some benefits include the following:

> Income increased globally for both rich and poor, decreasing poverty. Increased wages for the well educated. Increased wages for technologically skilled. Improved economic conditions in countries and regions that successfully compete in the global economy. Increased access to more goods. Reduced prices due to competition with local monopolies. Increased food supply in some countries. (Osland, 2003, p. 141)

Overall, expanding the diversity of our experiences is never bad IF we handle it with communicative expertise. Unfortunately, not all humans do this—leading to some negative outcomes of globalization. Although sometimes seemingly macro-level, these problematic issues no doubt affect us and those we care about on a personal level—both at work and outside it.

First, globalization has created human rights violations with respect to labor. For example, Osland (2003) warned about a "race to the bottom" where competition determines work (and thus, environmental) conditions in a perpetual downfall to the "lowest common denominator" (p. 141). This means that multi-national corporations look for the cheapest ways and easiest/cheapest places to do business, even if people aren't protected in those places (International Relations, 2019).

A tragic example of how global competitive pressures drive down the costs of business operations in ways that cause human rights violations was the 2013 Savar building collapse in Bangladesh. At about 9:00 a.m. on April 24, the Rana Plaza building collapsed. The massive weight of this eight-story building crushed workers inside, resulting in 1,134 deaths and 2,500 severe injuries. People nearby described the collapse as a thundering earthquake (Marriott, 2013). The reason for the collapse? The owners' ignored building regulations that would've driven up costs and reduced profitability. Global competitive pressures meant these owners put profits ahead of human lives. Sadly, similar choices are made all over the world. Another example is Nike, one of the most recognized brands in the world, which deals with increasing scrutiny for its unsafe/unfair labor practices, including using child labor—something possible *because* of an open global market that allows (and encourages) companies to outsource.

However, there is hope . . . is it a bird? A plane? Nope, (you guessed it) it's super communication! Pervasive communication technologies assist anonymous whistleblowing and allow documentation of negative practices. Further, the media (see Chapter 15) plays a crucial role in heightened public awareness (often sharing images of unsafe conditions), creating a public relations nightmare for companies like Nike. Remember Systems Theory? Organizations can't operate in a bubble; eventually, they have to deal with the outside environment.

Activism Hero: Organize for Power

Organizational communication is at the heart of social movements and change! For example, consider the Black Lives Matter Global Movement. Committed people developed this "chapter-based, member-led organization whose mission is to build local power and to intervene in violence inflicted on Black communities by the state and vigilantes" (Black Lives Matter, 2019, para. 1). Organizing such a social movement requires building camaraderie and coordinating people's efforts to bring in as many supporters as possible. An organization such as Black Lives Matter energizes the organizational process so that a disempowered group can assert its human rights and gain control of its future. You, individually, might create change, but learning to communicate and coordinate with many groups can make it a global phenomenon.

Contributed by W. Papa & M. Papa

© barbaliss/Shutterstock.com

Second, globalization inherently increases our need for cultural sensitivity and awareness. This is where you can emerge as a superhero! You'll learn more about this in the next chapter, but for now, know that change and acceptance can start with YOU! Recognize your biases, read up on the cultures of those you work with, and here's a crazy idea . . . ask questions. Too often, we get so caught up in "not offending" that we forget how vital open communication is. People are just as curious about you as you are about them—open the door and start the conversation.

Conclusion

This chapter focused on organizational communication. As we've observed, communication is at the core of how organizations function and how people experience the organization and accomplish their work. We've defined and explained the importance of org comm, talked about how it works, and illustrated some changes within org comm. As society continues to change, so must organizations if they wish to survive and thrive. Communication, in all its varied forms, will always be central to how organizations evolve and respond to the changes around them.

References

Bassi, L. J., & Van Buren, M. E. (1998). The 1998 ASTD state of the industry report. *Training & Development, 52,* 21–43. doi:10.1108/jeit.1999.00323gab.001

Black Lives Matter. (2019). *About*. Retrieved from blacklivesmatter.com/about/

Bond, J. T., & Galinsky, E. (2011). Workplace flexibility and low-wage employees. *National Study of the Changing Workforce*. New York, NY: Families & Work Institute. Retrieved from familiesandwork.org/site/research/reports/WorkFlexAndLowWageEmployees.pdf

Bormann, E., Howell, W., Nichols, R., & Shapiro, G. (1982). *Interpersonal communication in the modern organization* (2nd ed.). Englewood Cliffs, NJ: Prentice-Hall.

Carucci, R. (2018, September 25). How to permanently resolve cross-department rivalries. *Harvard Business Review.* Retrieved from hbr.org/2018/09/how-to-permanently-resolve-cross-department-rivalries

Collins, D. (2015). *Survey reveals conference call on-hold habits.* Retrieved from www.westuc.com/en-us/blog/conferencing-collaboration/survey-reveals-conference-call-hold-habits

Davis, K., Winsler, A., & Middleton, M. (2006). Students' perceptions of rewards for academic performance by parents & teachers: Relations with achievement & motivation in college. *Journal of Genetic Psychology, 167,* 211–220. doi:10.3200/GNTP.167.2.211-220

Gallup. (2017). *State of the global workplace* [Report]. Retrieved from www.gallup.com/workplace/238085/state-american-workplace-report-2017.aspx

Hafen, S. (2004). Organizational gossip: A revolving door of regulation and resistance. *Southern Communication Journal, 69,* 223–240. doi:10.1080/10417940409373294

Hellweg, S. (1987). Organizational grapevines: State of the art review. In B. Dervin & M. Voight (Eds.), *Progress in communication sciences* (Vol. 8, pp. 213–230). Norwood, NJ: Ablex.

Howard, K., Giblin, M., & Medina, R. (2018). The relationship between occupational stress and gastrointestinal illness: A comprehensive study of public schoolteachers. *Journal of Workplace Behavioral Health, 33,* 260–275. doi:10.1080/15555240.2018.1542310

International Relations. (2019). *Pros and cons of globalization.* Retrieved from internationalrelations.org/pros-and-cons-of-globalization/

Katz, D., & Kahn, R. L. (1978). *The social psychology of organizations.* New York, NY: Wiley.

Kopp, R. (2019). Thinking of working in Japan? It's good to know what you're in for. *The Japan Times.* Retrieved from www.japantimes.co.jp/community/2019/01/30/how-tos/thinking-working-japan-good-know-youre/

Littlejohn, S. W., Foss, K. A., & Oetzel, J. G. (2016). *Theories of human communication* (11th ed.). Long Grove, IL: Waveland Press.

Magloff, L. (2016). How does a lattice organization work? *Houston Chronicle.* Retrieved from smallbusiness.chron.com/lattice-organization-work-3486.html

Marriott, R. (2013). The house of cards: The Savar building collapse. *Libcom.* Retrieved from libcom.org/news/house-cards-savar-building-collapse-26042013

National Association of Colleges and Employers. (2019). *Career readiness defined.* Retrieved from www.naceweb.org/career-readiness/competencies/career-readiness-defined/

Natural Leadership. (2004). WL Gore & Associates. *Hewitt Quarterly Asia Pacific, 3*(2), 1–5.

Osland, J. S. (2003). Broadening the debate: The pros and cons of globalization. *Journal of Management Inquiry, 12,* 137–154. doi:10.1177/1056492603012002005

Pacanowsky, M., & O'Donnell-Trujillo, N. (1984). Organizational communication as cultural performance. *Communication Monographs, 50,* 126–147. doi:10.1080/03637758309390158

Papa, M. J., Daniels, T. D., & Spiker, B. K. (2008). *Organizational communication: Perspectives and trends.* Thousand Oaks, CA: Sage.

Papa, M. J., Singhal, A., & Papa, W. H. (2006). *Organizing for social change: A dialectic journey of theory and praxis.* New Delhi, India: Sage.

Raval, S. (2014). Challenger: A management failure. *Space Safety Magazine.* Retrieved from www.spacesafetymagazine. com/space-disasters/challenger-disaster/challenger-management-failure/

Stiglitz, J. E. (2007). *Making globalization work.* New York, NY: W.W. Norton & Company.

Vincent, S. (2011). The emotional labour process: An essay on the economy of feelings. *Human Relations, 64,* 1369–1392. doi:10.1177/0018726711415131

von Bertalanffy, L. (1968). *Organismic psychology & system theory.* Worcester, MA: Clark University Press.

Weick, K. E. (1979). *The social psychology of organizing.* Reading, MA: Addison-Wesley.

Zelenski, J. M., Murphy, S. A., & Jenkins, D. A. (2008). The happy-productive worker thesis revisited. *Journal of Happiness Studies, 9,* 521–537. doi:10.1007/s10902-008-9087-4

Chapter 14: Cultural Communication

Contributed by
Dr. Jessica Eckstein

Too often, culture is treated as a "modifier" or addition to our communication. But, how we communicate and exist in the world is inherently impacted by our culture. It's impossible to separate culture from communication, and therefore, your authors often address culture in their own chapters. However, the enormous role culture plays in our communication and relationships is worthy of its own chapter. Usually covered near the end of intro textbooks (hey, waddya know?), ***intercultural communication*** is the creation and exchange of meaning among, between, and across cultural groups. Although similar, ***cross-cultural communication*** focuses more on comparing different cultures (Omori, 2017). I cover both here.

There *are* certainly differences across cultures, but how (and how much) we stress them matters. Difference is emphasized everywhere, in every field, by all humans, in all situations for a number of reasons. Most prominently, it's natural. Perception involves selecting and organizing (Chapter 5). When something "sticks out" or is different, we're more likely to pay attention to it. Further, when trying to figure out where something we've perceived fits, we depend on our brain categories. But, with more life experiences, we quickly learn nothing is truly identical and develop more brain boxes to sort things. These differentiations help us perceive both similarities and differences (Geertz, 1988). BUT, this gets influenced by another reason we dwell on differences—they're sexier than similarities. It's interesting to explore the novel and unique. Lastly, cultural differences are easy excuses (Hofstede, 1984). They provide rationales for lazy, bad behaviors like prejudice and discrimination.

Originally a serious song about racial integration, "Black and White" (Arkin & Robinson, 1954) is most remembered from Three Dog Night's hippy-dippy version of it: www.youtube.com/watch?v=4f65mO146Zo

© MM_photos/Shutterstock.com

However, *celebrating* difference is another story! And, THAT's what I'll do here by looking at differences among us (they *are* fun to learn about) in ways that illustrate how (a) ALL cultures exist as more alike than different (and not in cheesy, kumbaya ways); (b) our differences make communication more interesting and worth pursuing (same = boring!); and (c) we can revolutionize our world on superhuman levels (assuming you *want* to put in effort from time to time). Check out the YouTube link on the previous page to listen to "Black and White" while you read this to set the mooood . . .

What Makes a Culture? It's Similar for Everyone!

Even though cultural *enactments* differ, the cultural *concepts* are the same everywhere. A *culture* is *any* grouping of characteristics and/or behaviors that influence people's shared meanings and the lenses by which they perceive and communicate. Back in the day, before transportation was easy, most people spent their whole lives near home. So, to them, culture often took on an "us" versus "everyone else" perspective. For example, where/when my parents grew up, two big distinctions were town-people vs. farmers and Lutherans vs. Catholics. Like Batman and Catwoman, my parents thwarted divisions—stressing their similarities to eventually produce the very awesomeness writing this chapter. Nowadays, this seems overly dramatic; we can interact with anyone, anywhere, any way or time, and so, we must view culture in new ways.

Traditionally, cultures were grouped (by anthropologists and sociologists) by major, often visible differences like country, race, ethnicity, religion, or socioeconomic status (SES) and any divisions *within* cultures were called sub-cultures. But, those are rather "old-school" approaches; a "sub"-culture label implies that some identity aspects influence us less and that the only ones worth study are big, visible ones. You can probably already guess how this can be problematic.

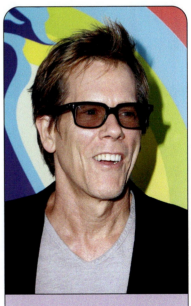

"Six degrees of Kevin Bacon" (star of original *Footloose* film) is a game connecting seemingly random film actors.

© Kathy Hutchins/Shutterstock.com

In response to these problems, an alternative term was proposed (Orbe, 1996): A *co-culture* is any social (e.g., race, sex, religion) OR personal (e.g., gamer, athlete, dog-lover) group whose members share norms/rules, meanings, and worldviews. This term is more useful for us because who's to say what culture affects our communication most? I'm certainly more consciously influenced as a dog-mom than by my Whiteness . . . which doesn't mean my race or nation don't influence me. It just means I don't *usually* consider my race when communicating (though that's *because* I'm White, which I'll discuss) as much as I constantly adapt to my fur-babies! Further, *each* co-culture I belong to separately influences me (and thus, those I interact with). And, because endless co-cultures exist, we're each a "Kevin Bacon" (the link disparate people share) to two other people. Multiply that by the world population, and that's a LOT of *Footloose*! Any one thing people can bond over or share can group/designate a co-culture.

All the co-cultures I belong to make up what's unique about me (Chapter 6), while I simultaneously share each trait with millions of others—my fellow co-culture members. **Intersectionality**, or "simultaneity" (Combahee River Collective, 1983), examines how multiple self-aspects congeal, modifying our interactions as we attempt to manage more than one identity (particularly, culturally subordinated ones). Originally used to label how oppression is multiplied (e.g., being Black *and* female; Crenshaw, 1989), lately the term refers to people's numerous identities.

My co-cultures and inherent intersectionality are based on sex (female), race (White), ethnicity (Nordic/German), sexuality (hetero), eye/hair/skin color and type (pale blue/near-sighted, dark brown/thick-straight, pale/clear), age/generation (late-30s/Millennial), education (Ph.D.), raised religion (Pentecostal), current religion ("spiritual" Christian), birthplace/hometown (rural Minnesota), raised SES/parents' jobs (upper-middle class, white-collar), parents' and my relationships (divorced, married), achieved SES (DINKs), mental health (clinically depressed, in treatment), physical health (superb immune system, able-bodied), hobbies (hiking, reading), interests (fashion, sociology, animals), and priorities (spatial freedom, independence, mental stimulation)—each just a sprinkling of differences I exhibit.

© MoreVector/Shutterstock.com

You can tell if something's a co-culture by checking Google or Facebook; if there's a "group" devoted to it, then, it's an obvious co-culture.

To understand how our culture and co-cultures influence our identities and communication, let's break down cultural components further: Every culture must have (a) membership norms and rules and (b) meanings shared, understood, and informed by (c) a defining worldview lens. Each co-culture we belong to has its own version of these three things, all intersecting in one person! But, many co-cultures overlap, so it's not like we (usually) live contradictory lives—luckily for our communication!

Norms and Rules

First, all cultures have an understanding of what is/isn't appropriate communication—or "ways of being" for each member (Goffman, 1959). *Norms* are what people (are expected to) do, whereas *rules*, which also tell us how to live, focus more on what NOT to do. For example, a norm is that people often drive slightly over the speed limit. The rule is the speed limit. So, although we have rules, we may be more likely to follow the norm. But, both rule and norm violations can result in explicit or implicit punishments. Norm/rule-breakers may be punished by cultural *sanction* or restricted access to group benefits, *ostracization/ stigma* singling out violators for shame, or even *penalization* requiring "paying" for violations (Goffman, 1963). Knowing we otherwise risk punishment, we usually end up following norms/rules to stay in good cultural-standing.

We're not only influenced by our cultural rules/norms; we influence them with our communication, too. You already know that communication is ambiguous and arbitrary, so it may have multiple interpretations but doesn't have ANY meaning until a group decides/ teaches it to us. In other words, the groups give meaning to rules/norms, and in turn, help identify AND limit themselves through customs, folkways, mores, and laws.

First, *customs* are what we assume as "normal" rituals or "just the way it's always done." Customs support cultures' survival and growth (Sumner, 1906) by sustaining a group's identity and— through repeated practices—reinforcing cultural values. Beginning school at a certain age, having a church wedding or exchanging rings, and holding an "open-house" graduation party are all examples of American customs. *Not* practicing these things may be considered odd by some, but nothing really bad happens for not doing them; they're just traditions. Your grandma may shake her head if you decide to get married while skydiving, or you may be snubbed or gossiped about, but nothing's set in stone to punish people who skip customs. Until the 1840s, most U.S. and European brides just wore a dress or nice suit to get married. White "wedding" dresses weren't customary until people sought to emulate English Queen Victoria (Rubinstein, 1995). That's because customs emerge over time, usually after repeatedly practiced as folkways.

We even get marketed to differently based on our particular co-cultural folkway intersections. This is a company marketing specifically to pale, female Christian Millennials!

© Enola99d/Shutterstock.com

Changing fashions are one example of folkways. Whereas customs tend toward ritual or "special" events, folkways deal more with everyday encounters. Usually taken for granted when we grow up with them, *folkways* are informal norms based on *current* practices (Sumner, 1906). Some behaviors include how we greet people, ride the bus (looking at our phones), or catcall attractive women. No one (I hope!) is instructed, "Make sure to yell obscene comments when an attractive lady walks by," but it's done anyway. If you think that's offensive, it shows how folkways progress across history or social moments. They also differ by co-culture. You may believe holding the door open for someone is an obvious, expected courtesy OR you may only do it when someone's struggling, very old/young, female (and attractive), and/or it's raining/cold. Living in Missoula, Montana, I saw people held doors for *everyone*, even while people crossed parking lots! Now in Connecticut, I've discovered holding doors is rare within this co-culture, except when old or attractive people are approaching, and if *you* hold doors, you rarely get thanked. When someone doesn't follow cultural folkways, it's not the end of society—it's just rude. It also shows you're challenging norms or just identifies you as an outsider.

Third, **mores** (pronounced "more-rays") use co-cultural values to indicate right/wrong via unspoken societal rules. As a result, there's severe (albeit informal) punishments for violating them. In some co-cultures, like vegans for example, people believe it's wrong to eat animals. If you eat a burger in front of them, they might chastise you and think you're a bad person, but it's not like you're going to jail for it . . . until the culture in charge decides to make it a law. Smoking (or however you imbibe) weed is a great case because it used to be considered counter-cultural or deviant by the "mainstream" U.S., but popular opinions changed significantly. Most no longer see it as morally wrong, so the mores surrounding marijuana are now influencing laws.

Finally, mores that get officially sanctioned are **laws**. For example, most people today frown on slavery, child-sex, and animal abuse. But, these used to be just mores; some people felt them perfectly acceptable to do, whereas others within the same culture disagreed. Nowadays, they're illegal in most places and so result in severe punishments. If cultural standards change, laws can always revert back to mores. For example, prohibition in the U.S. was reversed, so now only certain co-cultures view drinking alcohol is wrong. But, laws can be enforced across co-cultures. Your animal-lover co-culture might mean you want to bring your dog into a restaurant, but you can get into trouble in U.S. restaurants (assuming they want to keep their federal health-code status). Until 1964, only White people could use particular bathrooms and water fountains and marry other White people (Zinn, 1997). Simply doing something while *belonging* to particular co-cultures was against the law! That's because laws were created to officially enforce the shared moral-meanings of mores (say that 10× fast!).

We're proud of what unites our particular groups . . . right up until we don't like it anymore. Then, we realize we helped enforce it for others all along! We thrive on how we're "cultured" (verb) because it bonds us while we subject ourselves to restrictions created because they made us "similar" in the first place!

Shared Meanings

A second feature of (co)cultures is they all have their own shared meanings. We expect to understand things similarly to others within our co-culture. Although there are many ways we share meanings, I'm going to talk about some of the more interesting (to me!) ones here (see how MY cultural bias is informing YOUR learning?): appearance and language.

Appearance

Because it's so obvious, what we look like was/is often used to identify group co-members. We clearly rely on skin color (even when we don't want to admit it), but there're many additional ways appearances get grouped—so much so that at certain times historically, appearance was dictated by law. For example, to separate males/females, women could get the death penalty in Medieval Europe

Legally, they could have burned Joan of Arc just for wearing men's clothing; they didn't need to invent the witchcraft charge as well!

© matrioshka/Shutterstock.com

for wearing men's clothing (Bullough & Bullough, 1993). Today, we still shop in "men's" or "women's" departments for clothing and shoes. What has changed (in some places) are the repercussions for norm violations. I assume plenty of females reading this book are wearing traditionally male clothing (e.g., pants, suitcoats); I know I am! Personal appearance still communicates specific social meanings, which in turn reflect what particular co-cultures value or prioritize. Appearances shape meanings via endowment, modification, and adornment.

Believed to occur "naturally," **body endowments** are appearance aspects that indicate (seemingly permanent) co-cultural memberships. Their supposed innateness

© Basheera Designs/Shutterstock.com

Hair can be highly political within co-cultures. See Chris Rock's documentary *Good Hair*.

communicates intrinsic codes (supposedly unintentional meanings) to others. Thus, endowments (e.g., skin, hair, eye colors) get used a lot to group people culturally. Of course, they *can* be changed (e.g., tanning, contacts), but people generally presume we're born with these features (Etcoff, 2000), so they become cultural identifiers. For example, black hair accompanying almond-shaped eyes was typically seen as "Asian" and blond/red hair with round eyes as "European" ethnicities. Today, most of us aren't nearly as comfortable admitting we assign ethnic cultures *solely* by appearance (though we still do it), but we often have no problem identifying co-cultures (e.g., senior citizens, potheads, jocks) based on looks.

When someone doesn't naturally have traits their culture values, they're typically expected to do something about it—to adapt to the norm. This is usually accomplished via *body modification*, an attempt to change how our "natural" endowments appear to others (Etcoff, 2000). Bodies are modified temporarily (e.g., diet, dyeing, contacts) or more permanently (e.g., surgery, tattoos, piercings, scarification). For example, large breasts for women are valued so much, it's the #1 cosmetic plastic surgery procedure in the U.S., *still* increasing in frequency each year (American Society of Plastic Surgeons, 2018). Some cultures value women's long hair so much that women do painful modifications to adapt (e.g., chemical or iron straightening, wigs, weaves, or extensions to replicate particular co-cultural understandings of "ideal" hair).

Seventeenth century eyebrows that didn't meet European norms were often masked by tiny pieces of mouse-skin (Howell, 2013).

© Kseniia Vladimirovna/Shutterstock.com

A final appearance code is *body adornment*, the temporary, changeable ways we physically communicate culture (Boucher, 1987). Adornments are a primary way we communicate "ourselves" (personality, style, aspirations, status—and combining all of these, *culture*). The most obvious adornments are clothing, accessories, and makeup. Around the world, laws dictate/d what different people wear. Furs; hats; dressings for carriages and horses; length of cloak, dress, or gloves; height of shoes, hair up-dos; and many other appearance features were limited to particular social classes, each also assuming co-cultural memberships by race, ethnicity, education, wealth, and lineage (Boucher, 1987).

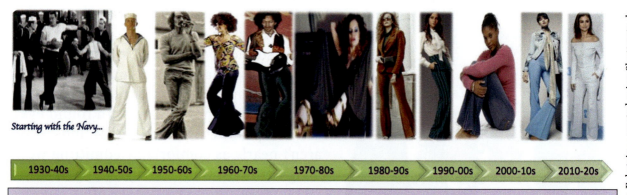

Starting with the Navy...

| 1930-40s | 1940-50s | 1950-60s | 1960-70s | 1970-80s | 1980-90s | 1990-00s | 2000-10s | 2010-20s |

Folkways shift. One appearance code, many different co-cultural meanings: Bell-bottoms worn in World War II by U.S. Navy as backup flotation devices were adopted by 1960s hippies, then 1970s discos, then 1980s yuppies, and as "boot cut" pants today.

Source: Jessica Eckstein—created using Shutterstock images

We don't always have a choice in how/if we alter our appearance . . . which brings us back full circle to skin color as the great separator. It isn't just about Black/White dynamics. Every culture has used skin shades to delineate identity; even non-"White" cultures valued *lighter* skin more highly (Etcoff, 2000). White powder was so highly valued (among White people!) because it reduced looking sun-exposed (attributed to labor/farm/serf co-cultures), so both sexes used toxic metals to look like ghosts (Howell, 2013). Whenever we use makeup or dye our hair or change our clothes, we're saying one look is preferred over another, reinforcing meanings within *and* outside our co-cultures. So, I might wear a long skirt to a conservative church/school but change to a mini for clubbing. It's not just situational; it communicates desires to "fit in" or identify with a co-culture.

Language/Voice

You already know language includes both verbal and nonverbal components. Co-cultures use both aspects to distinguish themselves. One vocalic indication of culture is a ***regional accent*** (locational vocalics). Although arbitrary, we nonetheless use it to identify people (and assign meanings to those attributions, see Chapters 5, 6, and 8). For example, U.S. Southerners are thought "slow/dull" because of their drawl and slow speaking rate (Öhman, 1975). As a result, many people intentionally change vocalics to identify with different co-cultures (most people don't knOw I'm from Minnesota unless I *Oh*verly emphasize my *O*s when speaking). Our speech ties to who we are/where we're from, but we can train ourselves to use different phrases or speech forms. Sometimes, we just adapt *naturally* to whomever we're with.

Communication Accommodation Theory says we either emphasize social differences (***diverge***) or minimize differences/emphasize similarities (***converge***) with others. In terms of vocalics, we converge most on "pronunciation, pause and utterance lengths, vocal intensities, [&] nonverbal behaviors" (Giles & Smith, 1979, p. 46), but not necessarily all at once. Phwew! When we diverge, we intentionally focus on difference (not necessarily negatively) when it's key to an interaction (e.g., to value diversity or maintain cultural identity). If you had a Southern accent, you might intentionally avoid drawling when not around other Southerners because you don't want to be seen as "dull." In contrast, convergence reveals our desire to fit in, so the more I need/want someone to like me, the more I'll converge with them. When I go "home" to Minnesota, I instantly (naturally, without thinking) adjust my words/sounds to "assimilate" to the co-culture. Bilingual people do this ***code-switching*** (adjusting word use/tone/accent based on who you're with), too, which is why first generation immigrants often pass as "natives" of more than one language. They know not only the words but also the nonverbals (tone, pitch, etc.) to speak those words (Chapter 8), AND they know shared meanings of things like slang (Chapter 7).

In addition to our vocalics, the way we address or refer to people reflects and creates meanings cultures share. Address can be verbal or nonverbal and is used culturally in pronouns, gendered grammar, and direct-address terms. First, pronouns in some languages indicate status or respect to order relations within cultures. In Spanish (and German and

Italian), I'd refer to someone formally or respectfully as "you" using *Usted* (or *Sie* or *Lei*) rather than *tú* (or *du* or *tu*), which I'd use informally with friends. Someone who only learned words for literal translation misses rules governing when it's appropriate to use each form (Norris, 2015). Japanese keigo differentiates between honorific, plain/casual, and humble ways of addressing people, with the voice-tone modifying things even further to indicate polite forms of any of these. Pronouns are used more than names or titles, so they're pervasive and also reflect a lot about the culture.

Another formal, respect demonstration is in how we identify/address people, particularly interpersonally. For example, in China and Japan, a "family" name is always used first (rather than as a "last name"), showing the importance of the family or community unit above that of the individual. In the U.S., there's variation in if/how we change our surnames on marrying: Many adopt their spouse's surname, others keep their "maiden" name or hyphenate both surnames, and some even create an entirely new name both partners share. In many Spanish-speaking co-cultures, multiple surnames are the norm to maintain family-of-origin identities. Or, in some very small nations like Iceland, where people were originally all from the same few families, last names end in "der"/"son/sen"—literally, "son/daughter of." These variations also expand to address titles. In academic co-cultures, female professors with doctorates tend to be called "Ms." or "Mrs." more than males (even without Ph.D.'s!) get called "Mr.". Thus, address forms reveal a lot about how respect gets assigned within co-cultures.

Winnie the Pooh's author: If English was better, there'd "be a word which meant both 'he' and 'she,' and I could write 'If John or Mary comes, heesh will want to play tennis' which would save a lot of trouble" (Milne, 1931, p. vi).

© tulpahn/Shutterstock.com

Further, "gendering" language is particularly obvious in cultures that rely on **articles**, words used to modify a noun, showing grammar (specific vs. general, singular vs. plural). English articles are neuter (no gender), Spanish and French indicate nouns as feminine/masculine (Graves & Hodge, 1943/2018), and Japanese doesn't have gender even in pronouns! This reveals shared meanings within those cultures. For one thing, it shows who's part of the culture (saying "el montaña" or "la museo" reveals improper usage *and* a lack of belonging). Further, some people argue this **grammatical gendering** reveals cultural priorities (Norris, 2015). If some words are innately masculine and others innately feminine, those power associations (e.g., postman, male nurse, fireman) reflect a culture's valued roles (Kramarae & Treichler, 1992). Word choice (language) or delivery (voice) determine and express cultural belonging.

Worldviews and Values

A final cultural characteristic involves *worldviews*, or the lenses that shape how we interpret life and communicate accordingly (Chapter 5). We've already seen that culture isn't just country/ethnicity/race; it's actually multi-leveled because it operates both on the personal, learned life experiences we share with others AND on commonly communicated values, norms, and traditions we get from our co-cultures. Although *no one* is identical to another (even twins), *no one* is 100% different from any other person, either; it's impossible if they're both human. Like a merry-go-round, our communication is influenced by our culturally shared meanings, but those meanings are created by (and in turn, create) the worldviews of our cultures (which then influence our communication again). Worldviews typically vary by meaning complexity, uncertainty tolerance, power distance, gender framework, communality, and contact.

Do you know what these florals each say? Members of a high-context Ikebana co-culture do!

© Lily Studio/Shutterstock.com

Meaning Complexity

Meaning complexity has to do with HOW a culture shares meaning. Hall (1976) discussed *context level* as how much meaning is drawn from direct language versus more subtle, nonverbal and situational cues. *High context* (HC) groups infer meaning from surroundings, or highly complex *contextual* cues. People in these cultures both communicate and notice nonverbal cues (e.g., specific meanings of floral arrangements, averted gaze, belted knot, parted lips) others may not even see. Historically, entire nations (Native American tribes, Japan, China, Korea) were put in this category. American HC co-cultures could be communities who don't prioritize spoken words (e.g., Buddhist or Catholic monks). Often, HCs are focused on face-saving, so their messages (especially negative ones) are communicated in indirect manners. Have you ever had someone communicate something to you with "the look"? In HCs, this happens continually across situations/relationships.

On the flip side, *low context* (LC) cultures value what's said verbally and directly. LCs tend to get their messages across bluntly. Yes, nonverbals still play an important role in their communication. But, there's less focus on face-saving and more on getting to the point—even if feelings/relationships are threatened. Often, you can tell a culture's complexity by how much they talk. LCs aren't comfortable with silence; they gab! Obviously, the U.S. joins other Chatty Cathy nations (Germany, Canada, France).

Public Speaking Power: Am I Speaking Your Language?

This is just a metaphor, but it works for speeches: Think about going to a place you don't speak the language. Imagine how difficult trying to communicate would be. Even if you speak a *little* of the language, so many concepts/experiences don't have word-equivalents. As public speakers, we try to do the best we can to learn about our audience's experiences and cultures so that we can *speak their language* and reduce culture shock—thus, increasing understanding and impact. To do this, avoid both EGOcentrism and ETHNOcentrism.

First, avoid **egocentrism**, or selfish thinking. From the examples you use to explain concepts to the words you choose (words an audience might not know), they all come from who you are, so it makes sense to you. But in public speaking, we need to make sure that we are *making sense to our audience*. It'll help if, in addition to your adapted language, you increase your communicative clarity by using a lot of expressive gestures and animated facial expressions. Avoid egocentrism; don't assume everyone thinks and sees the world like you do.

Next, avoid **ethnocentrism**, or culturally self-centered thinking. For example, high-context cultures value relational communication. For people from low-context cultures, communicating with high-context cultures can feel like torture; everything takes longer, and more time is spent on socializing (not just task-info). This matters if speaking to a high-context audience because if you use any language criticizing them for "wasting time," they're going to be confused (it isn't a waste to them), *and* they won't listen to someone who doesn't care about them as people. Avoid ethnocentrism; your culture and worldview aren't superior to others'.

Contributed by K. Scholten

Uncertainty Tolerance

Although we all differ individually in our degree of uncertainty tolerance, cultures can be distinguished by how their norms/rules function during change or instability (Hofstede, 1984). *Uncertainty avoidance* is the desire to stay traditional in our habits/routines. A culture's overall policies or laws (and how easily changeable those are) tell you how they manage uncertainty. *High uncertainty avoidant* groups are (duh!) very change-resistant in both their culture (macro) *and* their interpersonal patterns (micro). They act negatively toward anyone who disrupts the status quo (Hofstede, 1984). Recent historic examples include Greece (Reactions to new government-employee policies bankrupted the nation!), Spain, France, or Portugal (clinging to colonial European mores), and Japan (with ancient codes/holidays/laws *still* built directly into the national system). U.S. co-cultural examples are any fundamentalist group adhering to tradition by punishing deviants, like churches who "kick out" violating members (e.g., women who cut their hair short).

In contrast, **low uncertainty avoidant** cultures are typically unthreatened by change. That doesn't mean they *want* all the changes, just that they probably won't get aggressive and emotional if/when changes do come. As a result, they're willing to try out new things, even at the risk of failing. Some examples of countries that operate like this include Singapore (the lowest!), Jamaica, and Nordic countries (the most "liberal" social policies *and* personal norms in the world!). An example low uncertainty avoidant co-culture is a company stressing innovation, like Google; they're always trying new methods to motivate employees: nap rooms, bringing pets to work, laundry service, and slides/fire poles to get to lower floors.

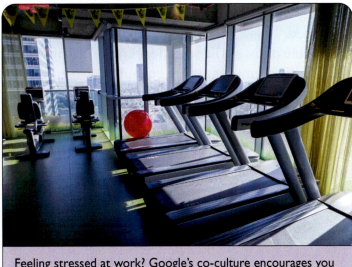

Feeling stressed at work? Google's co-culture encourages you to take a run with gyms around the corner from your desk.

© ColorMaker/Shutterstock.com

Power Distance

Power distance examines power disparities and people's tolerance of them, which affect interpersonal relations (Hofstede, 1984). **High power distance** (HPD) cultures exhibit greater inequalities, and people tolerate this by communicating a lot of respect for high status persons. Power distance comes in many forms, including sex (men > women), age (old > young), or income (rich > poor). HPDs include Malaysia (the highest!), Mexico, India, Brazil, and co-cultures like militaries or frats/sororities.

Groups who are **low power distance** (LPD) believe in equal power/role distribution and often go out of their way to practice it. Striving to minimize class differences, LPDs accept interpersonal challenges to power roles. Example countries are Austria (the lowest!), Israel, Canada, and Denmark—all places that value what citizens *do* and *say* and *live* and *earn* over born-characteristics (age/sex/class). Start-ups, feminist collectives, Antifa, and the hacker collective Anonymous are LPD co-cultures.

Soo . . . where does the United States as a whole land when it comes to power distance? It's tricky. On the one hand, things are unfair in both practice AND legal codes. Yes, women still continually earn less than men for doing the same work, and the rich continue to benefit from tax breaks. On the other hand, the Constitution is founded on the principles of liberty/justice/"for all"/equality and all that jazz . . . The way to see this is in *overall* interpersonal encounters: Do people act/react differently based on perceived power? Does the region you live in affect this?

Gender Framework

Remember (from Chapter 6) that when we talk about *gender*, we're not talking about sex but a style of communicating/acting. ***Masculine*** cultures (Mexico, Italy, Japan) value competitiveness, strength, material success, and division of labor according to sex roles (Hofstede, 1984). Some masculine U.S. co-cultures include East Coast Catholics (in terms of sex-role divisions) and college frats/sororities. ***Feminine*** cultures (Thailand, Costa Rica, and Nordic countries) value equality between the sexes (in theory), nurturing government, quality of life for all, supportiveness, and affection. One could argue a feminine co-culture is the Democratic Party (in its current form, at least), whereas the Republican Party is currently more masculine in its valued communication priorities. Undoubtedly, the way we understand gender frameworks implicitly ties to power distance and uncertainty avoidance.

Check out countries' ratings on Hofstede's (1984) categories: http://clearlycultural.com/geert-hofstede-cultural-dimensions/

Communality

Cultures are also distinguished by their worldview in terms of how much they prioritize community versus autonomy (Hofstede, 1984). ***Individualistic*** cultures value people's independence more than anything else (which gives the U.S. chant "We're #1!" a whole new meaning), whereas ***collectivist*** cultures (Guatemala, Ecuador, Japan) value the group. The group can include country, community, organization, or even family. For example, in Japan, the collectivist focus can be seen in something as mundane as presenting a business card—you must ensure you don't cover the company's logo when handing it out because the company is ultimately more important than the individual. And, although the U.S. is typically known as an individualistic culture, co-cultures that value collectivism could include a sports team or a frat/sorority. Individualism/collectivism overlaps with other concepts (power distance, uncertainty, gender) because no culture is JUST all one group/aspect—everything's nuanced, intersectional. If we only look at one type of distinction, we miss the whole picture.

Contact Level

Finally, contact is highly related to communality (Hall, 1976), which makes sense; the more I value/rely on people around me, the more I'm likely to be physically close to them. *Contact* cultures include many Middle-Eastern and Latin American countries and Southern European locales, where people not only tend to be physically closer to one another but also engage in more touching . . . think Italians kissing one another on the cheek to greet. *Non-contact* countries are in North America, Northern Europe, and East Asia. Like the cultural characteristics, these can also be seen within co-cultures. U.S. Southerners tend to touch others much more often than East-Coasters.

Contact isn't always tied to space—it just has a role in it. Touch also matters. For example, India and Pakistan are considered non-contact countries, but the level of "acceptable" personal space in these countries is closer to that of many contact cultures. Indians standing in lines usually have *very little* (compared to Western norms) space between each other; super close, but no touching. In Western-Euro spaces like the U.S., lots of room is given (but still no touching!). Whether the dominant culture is contact or non-contact, much of this is still dependent upon sex roles—*who* is it okay to touch and *how* can you touch them? For example, in the U.S., it's seen as "normal" for women to hug/touch each other. Men can hug too, but how often do you see them hug with an arm between their bodies (limiting full physical contact) and simultaneously beating each other on the back (Dibiase & Gunnoe, 2004)? How we use space says a lot about us and our relation to others.

Our worldviews are mostly unconscious, implemented without thinking (Hall, 1959). As you consider each distinction, realize one isn't necessarily better than another—just different. Being aware of these differences allows us to see others' perspectives. If we only look at our own groups, we "can't see the forest for the trees" and see only personal nuance, not our overwhelming tendencies as they appear to others. Remember, any *actual* differences are "in degree"—no culture *totally* embodies any worldview. ALL incorporate elements of many co-cultures, too.

Culturally Communicating to Change the World!

You've seen how cultures differ in their norms/rules, their shared meanings, and their worldview. I've shown how no one person differs entirely from anyone else; we all share some co-cultures, whether we want to or not. That similarity means we need to begin embracing these similarities WHILE celebrating any differences! Difference is too often an excuse for people to get away with things. It's not surprising (or, at least, it shouldn't be nowadays) that inequality exists in the world. But, how did it get that way and why isn't it changing faster if people acknowledge it's not great (#understatement)? You have the power to change that! In this final section, we'll look at some cultural inequalities as a target for your attack. Simple awareness urges doing something about it (even if it's "only" changing our own communication patterns).

Reinforcing Inequality

There are two ways to look at cultural inequality, examining how (a) justice is practiced (how cultures' driving forces, morals, and ideals operate) and (b) beliefs are reinforced (how communication maintains values).

Macro-Level Perpetuation: Justice or Lack Thereof

Justice (or fairness) creates, sustains, and thwarts change due to inequality in the world. You already know we naturally stereotype (Chapter 5); we may then act prejudicially or biased (positively or negatively); we may even discriminate against others; and it could end there . . . but it doesn't. They're *perpetuated* when a group (via folkways/customs/mores/laws) ALLOWS this to happen in three main forms: distributive, substantive, and retributive justice.

Distributive justice looks at whether things are given out fairly (on the surface, at least). Cultures don't just punish to maintain norms; they also use rewards (power, money, status) to show some people are more valued. More "equal" cultures don't think wealthy people deserve their wealth more than those without it, BUT in cultures with huge income disparities (e.g., United States), people assume those with more money probably deserve it more (Heiserman & Simpson, 2017)—the ol' "If I just work hard enough, I'll get it too" philosophy or individualist worldview.

Instead of focusing on outcomes, **substantive justice** is the morality driving a culture's distributions. It includes what a co-culture considers "crime," punishment, and members' rights/responsibilities. You can see how this could be problematic if even one person becomes selfish or discriminatory. For example, people are supposed to be pulled over for driving violations, *not* for being Black. **Procedural justice** (a subset of substantive justice) is concerned with the process itself—how the ideals/norms are actually practiced to maintain fairness. These often are the legal procedures governing police officers', lawyers', and other enforcers' allowed operations. For example, how a store chooses Employee of the Month tells you if the requirements are "fair" (procedural/substantive) and actually allow everyone a chance (distributive) to get the honor. Let's say it's only given to adult workers—what's the incentive for teenage employees who fill the same hours/positions to work hard?

Finally, **retributive justice** punishes people for violating mores or laws. Across cultures, humans want to be treated fairly; what differs is what this looks like in practice. Formally, we have fines or prison sentences; people want to know they're equally applied to the same crime (no matter *who* someone is or how well they "play" the system). This also concerns a "victim's" payback—if it's fair (based on their suffering) and if everyone gets it equally. Plato (1994) discussed some ways cultures "restore balance" after cultural violations. First, cultures that practice *retributivism* seek to restore norms by making punishments fit the crime. Like the Biblical "eye for an eye," if someone does something bad, the equivalent should be done to them (theft = return and yours taken; murder = "the chair"). *Deterrence* makes you not want to do it again (get caught with cigarette so dad forces you to smoke the entire pack) or at least not get caught any time soon! When the punishment is so bad, people follow norms! Finally, *rehabilitation* shows benefits of following norms after a violation (church shows "mercy" to bring ex-members "back into the fold") to re-sustain cultural balance. These are all ways cultures (re)enforce norms in top-down ways. Both macro and micro practices keep cultures' worldviews intact for members, but individual ways are used much more often to keep people in line.

Micro-Level Perpetration: How We Do It in Our Lives

Interpersonal and implicit public strategies are the most common, taken for granted, and thus, most effective methods reinforcing cultural values/inequalities. To understand how communication shapes/is shaped by these practices, let's look at why and how this works.

Why. Group norms and rules have always kept people in line, supposedly for the good of the group. As written, the Judeo-Christian Golden Rule (a theory foundational in *most* cultures, see Activism Hero box on next page) applied only to those in the group—not to

Cross-Cultural Equality Principle

Judaism	*What's hateful to you, do not to your fellow men. This is the entire law: all the rest is commentary.*
Islam	*No one of you is a believer until he desires for his brother that which he desires for himself.*
Buddhism	*Hurt not others in ways that you yourself would find hurtful.*
Hinduism	*The sum of duty: Do naught unto others which would cause you pain if done to you.*
Confucianism	*Surely it's a maxim of loving kindness: Do not unto others that you wouldn't have them do unto you.*
Taoism	*Regard your neighbor's gain as your own gain & your neighbor's loss as your own loss.*
Zoroastrianism	*That nature alone is good which refrains from doing unto another whatsoever isn't good for itself.*

Source: Jessica Eckstein

What we know as the Golden Rule is actually found cross-culturally.

those who weren't "our own" people. To accomplish conformity, outsiders were considered "other" by simply *looking* different or having different beliefs, practices, and habits (Geertz, 1988). That's how we get to good ol' racism; we wrongly correlate internal with external differences.

Common in many cultures, the "bad is black" perception means that, regardless of someone's *actual* race, people assume more immoral acts are committed by those with darker skin tones (Alter, Stern, Granot, & Balcetis, 2016). Consider age: We perceive people ARE their "generation," which we determine based on their *looks* (Etcoff, 2000). The adage "Women age, but men mature" shows how we perceive male versus female balding/wrinkles. We're influenced A LOT by these thoughts, whether we want to be or not—at least until we get to know people past surface levels.

External features like race or nationality may be what we *say* are our reasons for labeling and determining who's different from us, but it's our internal processes—ones we actually all share in common—that really make problems for us. For example, even though all cultures shared it, syphilis has historically been blamed on whatever group of people a country wanted to view as dirty and "other" (even in cultures with basically the same ethnicities as the ones they blamed!). It was called the Polish- (in Russia), German- (in Poland, Russia), Chinese- or Korean- (in Japan), and French-Disease (in England), depending on which country was being blamed for it (Brown, 2006). Such attributions create issues because they rarely stay internal and can emerge in many forms—like Mystique.

Activism Hero: Use the Platinum Rule

The so-called Golden Rule is a standard taught in almost every culture. A transcultural perspective of this rule, which applies a general standard across humanity, recognizes we're all humans to be treated equally and responsible for holding people accountable for certain actions no matter what. The problem is that most often, the nation/people with the most power (e.g., Western, modern societies) get to dictate the "right" way to act in a global society. Another perspective, multiculturalism (or **cultural relativism**, the idea that morality depends on where you're from) has merit for allowing each culture to set its own standards. But, in reality, we don't all value the same things. One way to incorporate both perspectives has been called the Platinum Rule: *Treat others as we'd want to be treated IF we were in THEIR position.* This helps us avoid ego/ethnocentrism, forcing us to see things from others' perspectives—the basis of all truly positive social change.

Contributed by J. Eckstein

How. How we "other" outsiders takes many forms, which are subtle, ongoing, and pervasive, and all work to silence anything not fitting norms. And, unless we intentionally act *against* these processes, we're supporting them: silence = compliance. According to *Muted Groups Theory*, those in power shape our realities through domination, which is communicated in four ways (Ardener, 1975). First, cultural *ridicule* occurs when speech of "outside" groups is trivialized, such as when conversations about "women's topics" (childcare, fashion) are framed as less "serious" or important to talk about than are men's areas (sports, business). Second, *rituals* reinforce particular group values (over others) in ceremonies or traditions, like fraternity "rush" periods for pledging membership worthiness. Rituals continually reinforce group "specialness" (e.g., annual ceremonies, celebrations). Third, *control* allows access to the creation of knowledge standards for members by *excluding* others from these things. Think about it: Who wrote your cultural rules (e.g., legal system), decided a word's "correct" meaning (e.g., wrote dictionaries), chooses what media to air/broadcast/produce, or has the power to easily change these things? *That's* control. Finally, *harassment* is the most obvious tactic: Physical and verbal assaults are *major* deterrents to members AND to outsiders trying to join a culture or simply survive outside a dominant one. To show they didn't belong, women in the workplace were (and still are, though it's now illegal) harassed via lewd comments, "jokes," or sexual assault. According to Muted Groups Theory, these tactics all support the *process of silencing*, whereby less powerful groups feel pressure to either assimilate or risk repercussions (Ardener, 1975). Luckily, the theory shows how subordinate co-cultures can address their silencing/muting done by the dominant groups.

Ways to Fix It!

They may vary in effectiveness, depending on the cultural context, but five overarching communication tactics can be practiced *publicly* (and this is key, so other co-cultures see it happening) to address the silencing process: naming, reclaiming, elevating, celebrating, and creating. One act may accomplish multiple goals simultaneously, but I'll cover each individually.

First, *naming* calls attention to the issue by simply identifying, or bringing to light, the fact that silencing/muting is occurring. If you observe a bully and then "call them out" on their behavior, you're practicing naming. At a broader cultural level, this could involve classroom discussions, written articles, films or music about it, or even suing someone for an unjust behavior. You can't begin to fix something until it's problematized. Even Ardener's (1975) creation of Muted Groups Theory was naming because it identified something as a problem.

© Vlada Young/Shutterstock.com

Next are three often-intertwined (yet distinct) strategies. ***Reclaiming*** is "taking back" a term or practice that another culture used/viewed negatively and "making it your own" as a source of pride. Obvious examples of this reappropriation include the American "Black is Beautiful" campaign in 1960s–70s or when GLB (as known then, but now, LGBTQ+) culture embraced "queer" as an identifying term. You can embrace prejudicial terms used against you, too! Are you someone who embraces the term "geek" and are proud of it? Or a female who embraces "bitch" because it basically means you haven't communicated "femininely" enough. These examples also illustrate ***elevating***, or raising something formerly denigrated to something newly important. If a hotel owner begins paying (typically female) maids equally to (typically male) desk-clerks, they've elevated a formerly "lesser" co-culture to a new priority level within the company. In money-driven cultures, we elevate certain things through what we buy; dollars = support. So, support local businesses; don't shop at places whose values you object to. You can elevate in your own life by what you purchase! This may overlap with another similar strategy: ***celebrating***, which not only elevates roles, making them equally worthy but also pushes to make previously ignored (because seen as lesser) practices publicly prevalent. Gay pride parades are an obvious, public example. Another is how feminist hipsters took up sewing, weaving, or farming as important art (previously limited to "mere" homemakers or traditionalist women)—a practice celebrating these skills by giving them "street-cred" outside and above their devalued status.

Finally, ***creating*** is forming something NEW that's unique to members' norms *and* also challenges, replaces, and/or substitutes a dominant group's version of it. Basically, the new thing created reflects the co-culture's priorities—*their own* experiences, values, and worldviews. A notable case, *A Feminist Dictionary* emphasizes English words from a female cultural perspective (i.e., terms understood differently by women than as originally defined by men; Kramarae & Treichler, 1992). For example, Webster's dictionary defines "cuckold" as "the husband of an unfaithful wife" but has no term for a wife with an unfaithful husband. She's simply called a wife. Creating a new source from which to understand language illustrates co-cultures' options for prioritizing their own values, without denigrating others' worldviews.

© Kopytin Georgy/Shutterstock.com

Doll (noun): A toy playmate given to, or made by, children. Some adult males continue their childhood by labeling adult female companions "dolls" (Kramarae & Treichler, 1992)

Conclusion

Once again, we're all more alike than different because we ALL have myriad identities, each one based on varying interactions with others who are similar to and diverse from us. So yes, it's important to be aware of potential differences (particularly when they perpetuate injustice or inequality to maintain their own norms), but if focusing on difference is all we ever do, we're screwed. As you've seen, we share co-cultures with people on the other side of the planet—maybe even more than with people next door or in our family! And, it's not in a touchy-feely, "let's hold hands," one-world-unite sort of way. Nowadays, cultural communication unites us quite literally because we do it across multiple co-cultures, day-to-day in interpersonal interactions in-person and online. By learning *how* those differences affect or can be affected by our own communication based on them, we can begin to *celebrate* difference!

References

Alter, A. L., Stern, C., Granot, Y., & Balcetis, E. (2016). The "bad is black" effect: Why people believe evildoers have darker skin than do-gooders. *Personality and Social Psychology Bulletin, 42*, 1653–1665. doi:10.1177/0146167216669123

American Society of Plastic Surgeons. (2018). *New statistics reveal the shape of plastic surgery*. Retrieved from www.plasticsurgery.org/news/press-releases/new-statistics-reveal-the-shape-of-plastic-surgery

Ardener, S. (1975). *Perceiving women*. London, England: Malaby.

Arkin, D. I., & Robinson, E. (1954). Black and white [Recorded by E. Robinson]. On *A walk in the sun and other songs and ballads* [Record]. New York, NY: Folkways. (Recorded 1957)

Boucher, F. (1987). *20,000 years of fashion: The history of costume and adornment*. New York, NY: Harry Abrams.

Brown, K. (2006). *The pox: The life and near death of a very social disease*. Stroud, England: The History Press.

Bullough, V., & Bullough, B. (1993). *Cross dressing, sex, & gender*. Philadelphia, PA: Penn Press.

Combahee River Collective. (1983). A black feminist statement. In L. Nicholson (Ed.), *The second wave: A reader in feminist theory* (pp. 63–70). New York, NY: Routledge.

Crenshaw, K. (1989). Demarginalizing the intersection of race and sex: A Black feminist critique of antidiscrimination doctrine, feminist theory and antiracist politics. *University of Chicago Legal Forum* (pp. 139–168). Retrieved from chicagounbound.uchicago.edu/cgi/viewcontent.cgi?article=1052&context=uclf

Dibiase, R., & Gunnoe, J. (2004). Gender and culture differences in touching behavior. *Journal of Social Psychology, 144*, 49–62. doi:10.3200/SOCP.144.1.49-62

Etcoff, N. L. (2000). *Survival of the prettiest: The science of beauty*. New York, NY: Anchor Books.

Geertz, C. (1988). *Works and lives: The anthropologist as author*. Stanford, CA: Stanford UP.

Giles, H., & Smith, P. (1979). Accommodation theory: Optimal levels of convergence. In H. Giles & R. N. St. Clair (Eds.), *Language and social psychology* (pp. 45–65). Baltimore, MD: University Park Press.

Goffman, E. (1959). *Presentation of self in everyday life*. Englewood Cliffs, NJ: Prentice Hall.

Goffman, E. (1963). *Stigma: Notes on management of spoiled identity*. New York, NY: Simon & Schuster.

Graves, R., & Hodge, A. (1943/2018). *The reader over your shoulder: A handbook for writers of English prose* (Reprint ed.). New York, NY: Seven Stories.

Hall, E. T. (1959). *The silent language*. New York, NY: Doubleday.

Hall, E. T. (1976). *Beyond culture*. Garden City, NY: Doubleday.

Heiserman, N., & Simpson, B. (2017). Higher inequality increases gap in perceived merit of the rich & poor. *Social Psychology Quarterly, 80*, 243–253. doi:10.1177/0190272517711919

Hofstede, G. (1984). *Culture's consequences.* Beverly Hills, CA: Sage.

Howell, H. M. (2013, March 27). A history of humanity's disgusting hygiene. *Owlcation.* Retrieved from owlcation.com/humanities/A-History-of-Dirty-Habits

Kramarae, C., & Treichler, P. A. (with Russo, A.). (1992). *Amazons, bluestockings, and crones: A feminist dictionary* (2nd ed.). Ontario, Canada: Pandora.

Milne, A. A. (1931). *The Christopher Robin birthday book.* New York, NY: Dutton.

Norris, M. (2015). *Between you & me: Confessions of a comma queen.* New York, NY: Norton.

Öhman, S. (1975). What is it that we perceive when we perceive speech? In A. Cohen & S. Nooteboom (Eds.), *Structure & process in speech perception* (pp. 36–47). Berlin, Germany: Springer.

Omori, K. (2017). Cross-cultural communication. In M. Allen (Ed.), *The SAGE encyclopedia of communication research methods* (pp. 309–312). Thousand Oaks, CA: Sage.

Orbe, M. (1996). Laying the foundation for co-cultural communication theory: An inductive approach to studying "non-dominant" communication strategies & factors that influence them. *Communication Studies, 47*(3), 157–176. doi:10.1080/10510979609368473

Plato. (1994). *Republic* (R. Waterfield, Trans.). Oxford, UK: Oxford UP. (Original work published c. 380 BC).

Rock, C. (Creator), & Stilson, J. (Director). (2009). *Good hair* [Motion picture]. USA: HBO.

Rubinstein, R. (1995). *Dress codes: Meaning & messages in American culture.* Boulder, CO: Westview.

Sumner, W. G. (1906). *Folkways: A study of the sociological importance of usages, manners, customs, mores, and morals.* Boston, MA: Ginn & Company.

Zinn, H. (1997). *A people's history of the United States.* New York, NY: New Press.

Chapter 15: Mediated Communication

Contributed by
Dr. Scott Sochay

A VERY Short History of Media

For the majority of human existence, oral communication was the dominant way to share, store, and pass on information to future generations. As a result, languages, story-telling, and other methods developed to refine the communication process. People learned how to master oral communication and understand the nuances of speaking. Literacy then, was based on not only who could speak well but also on who learned to decode and process speech efficiently.

Did you know Gutenberg didn't actually invent the printing press? He "stole" the patent from his business partner!

© Everett Historical/Shutterstock.com

As time passed, we created different *media*, a term encompassing any tool used to communicate with others. Before the printing press came along in the 1450s, words had to be written and copied by hand—an expensive and time-intensive process. However, books, newspapers, and magazines became more affordable in the 1800s as our printing technology advanced. For the first time in human history, print slowly started to take the place of oral communication as the dominant way to share, store, and pass on information to future generations (Ong, 1988).

Fast-forward to the 20th century. New mediums such as film and radio were invented to communicate on a societal scale. Print still retained its dominance but only for a while. When television was invented and started to become popular, this new medium began to rival print. The ability to create visually stimulating information became more and more valued. Audiences started spending more time watching rather than reading. We had now entered the age of television.

But, TV's reign as a dominant medium wouldn't last long. With the invention of the Internet, and then Tim Berners-Lee's creation of the World Wide Web, humanity entered the digital age. As the medium you probably use most today, the internet turned mediated communication technologies from passive to interactive mediums (Rideout & Robb, 2018).

The length of time any one particular mass medium is dominant is decreasing, with oral communication (tens of thousands of years

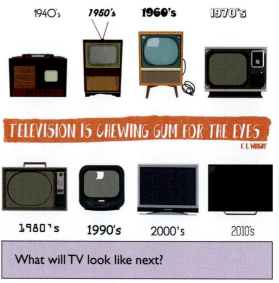

1940's   1950's   1960's   1970's

TELEVISION IS CHEWING GUM FOR THE EYES
F. L. WRIGHT

1980's   1990's   2000's   2010's

What will TV look like next?

© gigi rosa/Shutterstock.com

ago, at the latest estimates), print (about 500 years), and TV (roughly 60 years if we don't count streaming internet) giving way to internet as our current dominant medium. One thing is for sure: Even internet likely will be replaced by something else sooner rather than later.

"By the end of next week, these fads such as social media, automobiles and making fire will all be over."

© Cartoon Resource/Shutterstock.com

This increasing pace of media development has concerned many people for generations. When print first developed, some thought it to be a societal step backward. In fact, Socrates, as quoted by Plato in *The Phaedrus*, warned writing would create forgetfulness because people wouldn't

Is the news meant to entertain or inform?

© architect9/Shutterstock.com

use their memories. Then, when TV came along, it, too, was met with concern and skepticism. Neil Postman (1986) believed television would turn content (including news and information) into entertainment. Internet has also come under critique for, among other things, making us dumb (Carr, 2008). Because of these concerns, it's important for us to consider how much media affects us and if we actually understand what we're reading/viewing.

Media Literacy: Being an Educated, Skilled Audience Member

Because orality and print have been with us for so long, societies have developed ways to teach and measure *literacy*, a general ability to evaluate and otherwise engage with a text via set standards (Potter, 2001). For example, this textbook is written at a certain reading level (hopefully, at a level you can understand!). If you were writing for an average American audience, you probably wouldn't want to write it at more than a 6th- to 8th-grade reading level. Think about one of the most common books out there—the Christian Bible. The King James Version of the Bible has long been considered the gold standard for Biblical translations. Did you know the KJV is approximately at a 12th grade reading level? That means the average American would have a difficult time understanding what they were reading. This isn't good if you want to understand (or want others to understand) the Bible! In contrast, one of the most popular, modern translations of the Bible is the New International Version (which has been recently revised yet again). The NIV is about a 7th-grade reading level, much more in the wheelhouse of the average American reader.

Now translate that example to TV or internet. We don't have a similar grade-level to attach to what we might watch or view. Intuitively, we know that some programming will contain content that's more difficult to process. For example, most cartoons are far easier to process than news programs with scrolling text, graphics, and other on-screen information. But, schools don't assess watching skills in the way they assess reading skills. So, how can we teach media literacy in our quickly changing digital, technological age? Understanding how and why the media affect us the way they do can actually go a long way toward making us more conscientious consumers. Let's start with how media can affect us and then move to how our own choices affect media (which then, in turn, tries to affect us again); it's a continual loop!

Two main approaches used in the communication(s) (the *s* is there because media actually involves the study of technologies and channels; it's slightly different than communication, as introduced in Chapter 1) field clarify how/why we engage with media the way we do today: media ecology and the media literacy movement.

How We Engage With Media: Media Ecology

A broad approach to understanding media is taken by the field of ***media ecology***, which is based on the idea that the characteristics of a medium influence how we interact with and process texts' content (Postman, 1986). These characteristics influence our processing regardless of the content, so media ecologists explore how our engagement with printed texts, for example, might differ from how we engage with a TV program. To understand the basics of media ecology, think about a book or graphic novel you read where you've also watched the movie based on the book. The Harry Potter series? Marvel's *Avengers*? DC's *Superman* or *Batman*? What's different in your experiences with each of these texts? If you're like me, one thing you'll notice is that it takes longer to read the book than watch the movie. This is a key characteristic of print: It needs more time to process. Or, when one of my favorite books is turned into a movie, I find that a character or a place doesn't look like I imagined them. This is another characteristic of print: It engages the imagination.

In my classes, I often show half the class a cartoon called *Gertie on Tour*—a 2-minute black and white silent cartoon from 1921 about Gertie the Dinosaur—which I can safely assume none of my students have seen (McKay, 1921). The other half of the class instead reads a print version (with no pictures) of *Gertie on Tour*. I then provide crayons (but don't require their use) and ask each of them to draw a picture of Gertie the Dinosaur. After more than 20 years doing this exercise, the results are always the same. Students in the watching group each draw pictures that, to the best of their ability, try to copy what Gertie looked like in the cartoon, while students in the reading group draw very diverse pictures of what they think Gertie looks like. In other words, they can't copy Gertie from what they saw; they have to use their imagination. Other things also differ between the groups. The reading group takes longer to draw their picture, they use the crayons more often to incorporate color, and they're far more likely to add background elements from the story into their drawing. Finally, when asked about their drawings, the reading group is far more likely to tell a story, taking longer to talk about their images.

What does all this prove? Not all mediums are the same, and we engage with different mediums in different ways. That's basically what the study of media ecology contributed to our world. Now, take this one step further to see some media ecology-based implications. Does the Gertie the Dinosaur exercise prove that students who read have better imaginations? Of course not! But, imagine if this trend were to continue for months or even years. Eventually, the groups might begin to display very different ways of processing information that could transfer over to how they process information in other contexts.

Media affects how we process information.

© solar22/Shutterstock.com

We might also tie this to **Media Richness Theory** (Daft & Lengel, 1986), which says the communicated content depends on a medium's *richness*, or the level at which detail can be conveyed. Face-to-face communication is very rich, with lots of verbal and nonverbal cues possible. However, miscommunication via text messages is quite common because it lacks richness by eliminating many nonverbal cues. Media richness affects how fast we can understand, reduce uncertainty regarding, and resolve ambiguities related to media. In consequence, the richness of the medium should be tailored to the level/type of information presented in order to aid understanding (or prevent misunderstanding). You wouldn't want to convey something really complex via handouts or flyers, for example, because they lack the richness to get a complicated notion across without confusing people. Or, as much as you might love texting, sometimes you can accomplish a lot more in a shorter period of time if you just make a 5-minute phone call.

To see some specific ways the study of media ecology has affected what we know about how we process information, let's consider print and TV—which are where the field made its initial contributions. I'm about to show you how, just by looking at some characteristics unique to each type of media, you're actually *developing/increasing* your media literacy—developing another superpower that can put you above others without your even realizing it!

How We Read: Print Mediums

Print media has several characteristics that distinguish it from other types: It's (a) linear and logical, (b) in an active environment that (c) encourages reflection, and (d) delayable gratification (Ellul, 1985). You already know from this book's Chapter 1 (remember Dr. Ribarsky's friend, "A-Hole the Cat"?) that, presented with symbols that make up the word "cat," our brain takes logical steps to process and then assign meanings to this word. For me, that meaning would be "evil" (I usually get groans when I say this!).

As we read, this process continues in a logical, linear fashion. In American culture, we read in a "Z" pattern (from left to right, top to bottom). But, did you know we read online print differently, often in an "F" pattern (reading text at the top of the page and then reading less and less as we scroll down—if we scroll all the way through it at all)? We combine

© Mallmo/Shutterstock.com

Text content is linear, processed actively and reflectively, and delays gratification.

letters into words, words into sentences, sentences into paragraphs, paragraphs into chapters. It's very logical *and* very linear. Because we're so used to it, it'd seem silly to try to read any other way.

Print also presents an active environment. For example, sometimes when I'm reading, I blank out and realize a minute or two has passed, and I'm still on the same sentence (I'm sure none of you reading this text have ever done this!). In other words, I have to be engaged with the text in order to process what I'm reading. It's an active environment.

When I'm reading, I can pause to think about what I just read because reading encourages reflection. Few of us usually read a book in its entirety in one sitting. I use a bookmark and then set the book down to resume later, reading from where I left off. With print, it's not only easy to automatically access certain points in the text (let's say a really juicy scene I want to revisit), but we can also delay processing (and gratification) for extended periods.

How We Watch: Visual Mediums

Many "texts" today are in the form of filmed programs. But, do you remember being taught in school how to watch a TV show? I certainly don't. Yet, somehow we seem to manage. Visual mediums have their own set of unique characteristics, including being (a) personal and emotion-driven, (b) encouraging largely passive, and (c) continuous processing that (d) allows for instantaneous gratification (Ellul, 1985).

When we look at an image (moving or still), there isn't any logical starting point. We can look anywhere in the image we want or even choose to ignore part of the image. When you watch a play from an American football game, before the beginning snap, what do you focus on? Most people say they look wherever the ball goes. And, that certainly makes sense. But, you don't have to watch the ball. In high school, I played offensive guard and defensive end, so *I* love to watch the blocking schemes of

Filmed content is personal, processed passively and continuously, and instantaneously gratifies.

© gpointstudio/Shutterstock.com

the offensive line and the stunts and blitzes of the defensive line. None of this involves watching the ball. It's no more "correct" to watch the ball than it is to watch the two lines clash. Images don't demand we look at things in a linear, logical fashion, so we engage with them in personal, emotion-driven ways that *we* enjoy looking at most (Ellul, 1985).

Although it includes factors similar to reading, watching is executed in different ways. Remember how I said earlier that I can zone out when I read but advance no further down the page when I'm not focused? With watching, the images move on, and I advance as I'm taken through the program (and in most cases am none the worse off for what I've missed). In other words, watching is more passive than reading. It happens with or without me fully engaging. It's why you can do other tasks while you watch a show.

Finally, how often do you actually pause what you're watching to sit and think about what you just saw before pressing play again? Not so much? Or, how often do you stop a movie, go and do other things, and come back to the movie later? Probably not, if it's good. That's because watching encourages continuity instead of discontinuity, and as a result, also favors immediate gratification over delayed gratification.

How Medium-Type Matters

I'm not going to argue that reading is better than watching (or that watching is better than reading, though some media ecology scholars such as Neil Postman would say reading IS better than watching). What I am saying is that reading and watching, based on their characteristics *alone*, influence how we process and decode information. Notice my emphasis on "alone." Media ecologists argue these differences occur regardless of the content we're engaged with. They're properties of each medium.

McLuhan (1994) summed up this idea rather neatly with his title-phrase "The medium is the message." In other words, setting aside content, the fact *that* we read or *that* we watch is what's significant. At this point, you might be thinking, that's interesting, but how is that really relevant to anyone? That's a good question to ask because talking about the implications of the dominant medium in a society—and how that applies to us helps us become better audiences, which actually helps us improve our communication in all other aspects of our lives as well!

Media ecologists argue the dominant medium in a society influences how we process information. Consider TV. If we're cognitively trained (without even realizing it!) to process information in a certain way, then this way of processing is potentially how we auto-process most other information too! Postman (1986, 1999) postulated a TV-dominated society would actually develop hostility toward science because the linear, logical reasoning required by science takes too much time (and effort). Although his conclusion seems a bit far-fetched, the idea that we try to make our gratification more and more immediate has relevance for us as individuals and as a society. Postman even extended this argument about instant gratification to say being dominated by TV would lead to increased divorce rates! Again, this seems a little sketchy. But, he argued if we're used to a TV-style of information-processing and romantic love gives us immediate gratification (so we get married in the happy rush of feelings), when those endorphins run out (sometimes I dearly feel love for my wife, but I'll admit, other times I don't), it seems easier to end the relationship because the instant gratification has run out. Although this argument seems a bit ridiculous when applied to our lives, the reasoning behind it is certainly present in some of our interactions. How long do you wait for particular websites to load or channels to come up on cable TV? If it takes "too long," we get frustrated and often turn to another option. Think about that the next time you're ready to call it quits! You've let your medium-determined, steadily decreasing tolerance for delayed gratification regulate your life choices for you.

Why We Engage Media: Media Literacy

In addition to media ecology, other approaches focus not only on what media we consume but how much. We live in a media-saturated society. In fact, recent surveys show that the average American spends up to 11 hours a day exposed to media (Nielsen, 2018). The number isn't actually quite that high, as some of that exposure is due to multi-tasking (e.g., listening to music while on social media). But, it's estimated we're exposed to anywhere from 4,000 to 10,000 ads per day! Spending so much time with media affects us. Don't believe me? Go on a media fast. I challenge you to spend at least 24 hours with no access to any form of media. You might groan at the thought of being disconnected from your smart phone for so long or even think it's impossible. But, after completing the fast, most students tell me how much they learned about all the ways media influences their lives (often, vowing to limit their future media-dependency).

Beginning in the 1990s, scholars began taking a serious look at media literacy with the goal of helping people become aware of media and how it might affect us. Basically, this

Honestly, how addicted are you to your cell phone?

approach helps people gain control over their media exposure by understanding it better. Potter (2001) defined *media literacy* as "a set of perspectives that we actively use to expose ourselves to the media to interpret the meaning of the messages we encounter" (p. 19). This approach argues we tend to engage media because of two main factors: increasing access and pervasiveness *and* levels and types of media exposure.

Access and Pervasiveness

In the 1960s and 1970s, when I was growing up in the Upper Peninsula of Michigan, I had access to one TV channel. One. Imagine that! Later, when I moved to the Lower Peninsula (and became a troll; they live under—AKA south of—the bridge), I had access to ABC, NBC, CBS, PBS, and if weather conditions were right, the CBC out of Canada. Now, I have access to hundreds of channels (and yet, I often complain there isn't anything to watch). While growing up, if I missed a movie in the theater, my next best hope for seeing it was *if* it showed up on TV years later (or in some cases, was re-released in theaters). Whereas it used to be risky to miss a theater release, now through multiple platforms and on-demand, I have access to most movies ever made. This level of *access* feeds into the amount of time I'm exposed to content in any one platform. If I miss the theater, no worries, in a few months it'll be streaming, and shortly after, available for home-use (e.g., DVD, download).

Basically, this is all to say that media are ubiquitous, or all around us and available everywhere. Well, almost. There's a digital divide in the United States (and globally) in terms of who has access to digital technologies. The *digital divide* is the idea that there are inequalities not only in terms of access but also in terms of the knowledge and skills needed to use these resources. Do you ever find yourself frustrated with your parents or grandparents (or maybe even instructor) because they can't seem to get their technology to "work"? This divide, or gap, can also be along lines of ethnicity, region, income, and/or educational levels. This means that not everyone has similar

338   Chapter 15: Mediated Communication

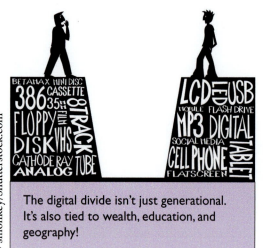

The digital divide isn't just generational. It's also tied to wealth, education, and geography!

© smonkey/Shutterstock.com

access to information—something that maintains and even *increases* existing gaps in economic, social, and educational opportunities (Rainie, 2017)! Imagine you need to submit an online job application, but you can't afford a phone or computer. Your only access to internet is at your local library, which is only open during the same hours you work your current job. Your financially driven lack of access only perpetuates your lack of access by preventing you from being able to apply for the better paying job.

But, it's not just your access that's important—media's *pervasiveness* also influences our beliefs. *Cultivation Theory* (Gerbner, Gross, Morgan, & Signorielli, 1986) considers how a culture's dominant medium (previously TV, now internet) becomes a "storyteller" that shapes thoughts, attitudes, and behaviors that would otherwise be formed by alternative sources (e.g., family, church). This influence isn't just the result of being exposed to one particular message. Rather, the theory says repeated, cumulative exposure results in a *cultivation effect*. Originally created to explain TV's impact, Cultivation Theory looked at how shows (and the news in particular) were far more violent than the real world, *and* viewers were exposed to thousands of murders, brutal attacks, explosions, and other violent activities across many hours of programming. As a result of something called *mean world syndrome*, TV causes unrealistic understandings of violence. Most of us don't see nearly as much violence in reality, so heavy viewers are cultivated into seeing the real world as far more violent than it actually is. For example, individuals who watch all the *Law & Order* series are apt to think if they visit New York City, they'll be raped and/or murdered. The same unrealistic cultivation can occur on anything the media portrays. For example, frequent viewers of shows like *The Bachelor* tend to have inflated, unrealistic expectations for romantic relationships (Ribarsky, 2009). So, if you're still looking for a magical, fairytale romance, think a bit more about what you've been reading/watching. Cultivation effects can also be examined across different types of mediums, such as music and social media, which raises the question: Does it matter *what* type or *how much* of a particular media form we engage with?

Exposure Types and Levels

Does your own media exposure tend to be *selective*, where you consciously choose to engage with a particular product, or is it more *habitual*, where you simply get online and/ or turn on the TV just to see what's on? The more habitual our exposure, the more likely the media is to influence us. Media literacy, then, would have us become more *selective* in our media engagement.

Public Speaking Power: Push YOUR Agenda

Becoming a more conscientious consumer of media can help you pick great topics and develop better speeches. First, if you're still struggling to come up with a topic, let Agenda-Setting Theory (covered later in this chapter) do its thing and tell you what to think about. Flip on the news or scroll an online news site. Not only are you apt to find a lot of material but also a lot of CURRENT material. But, remember to make sure you're still applying those good source criteria! Buzzfeed is fun (who doesn't want to take a quiz and find out what type of cupcake they are?), but it may not be the most credible or unbiased of sources.

Second, if you pick something that's currently a media "hot" topic, but from doing your audience analysis (from Chapter 2) know they might not be entirely invested in it (talking to college students about social security), there may be a trick to persuading your audience more effectively: QUANTITY of arguments. That means you should bring in a ton of supporting examples, statistics, stories, trends, etc. from various media sources: conservative and liberal media; online and print sources of world news, local news—and of a highly interactive media variety (Braverman, 2008). When an audience doesn't really care much about your topic, they'll be more likely to listen to and be persuaded by you with a high variety and quantity of evidence.

Contributed by J. Eckstein and B. Ribarsky

Relatedly, why do we engage with the media in the first place? Why do we listen to music, or watch TV, or surf online? And, why do we, as individuals, choose different types of mediums and exposures? Some people rarely read a newspaper, love to listen to music, and spend a fair amount of time with social media. Others love to read, could care less about social media, and watch TV occasionally. These different choices suggest we have some control over our media exposure. To explain these choices, consider ***Uses and Gratifications Theory***, which posits that we engage with the media because it meets our perceived needs (Katz, Haas, & Gurevitch, 1973).

Imagine you just got a breakup-text from your romantic partner. You probably have several needs at the moment, and media is good at meeting most of them! Some of the needs media researchers identify are *surveillance* (what's happening in the world), *correlation* (how things relate to or affect us), *cultural heritage* (how things fit socially), and *entertainment* (the "need" to be stimulated). Katz et al. (1973) noted several more fundamental needs too. In the case of a breakup-text, you might have a *cognitive* need (wanting more information about why it's happening), so you "stalk" their social media. Or, maybe you need to blow off some steam and throw on a comedy (*tension-release* need) or need comfort so you seek support on your social media feed (*affective* or *social integration* needs). As this array of needs comes to the surface, you're faced with choices—which need is most important to meet, and how might we use the media to meet it?

Why Media Engages Us

To understand more about how media can satisfy your needs, you'll need to raise your awareness by considering some basic reasons media chooses to engage with us: who we are and who "they" are.

Who We Are: Audience

As an audience, we all process media in different ways. Think about how there's always someone who finds subtly placed hints/messages (for tons of "Easter eggs" see www.eeggs.com) that you missed in movies. Or, maybe you know someone who always asks you to explain what just happened in a novel. Try making it through Milton's *Paradise Lost* or Dante's *Inferno* without annotations. I dare you! Clearly, we don't all have the same skill levels when it comes to processing media content. Some of us are more proficient with decoding visual information, some audio, and some print. The ability to process and decode media content relies on different *media filters*, or the abilities or perceptual lenses we use to help us better understand what we're exposed to. Three basic filter types impact our ability to decode media messages: informational/linguistic, psychological, and cultural.

© Anton Watman/Shutterstock.com

Does your informational filter let you know what this references?

Informational/linguistic filters, which rely on intelligence and cognitive skills, include our ability to understand words and languages. When I read a media effects book, I'm likely to understand most (OK, probably all) of what I'm reading without having to search for a definition or more information. But, for a quantum mechanics book, I'll probably have to stop every sentence or two to look something up. This filter doesn't just cover intellect; it also includes our ability to understand social references. In my family, knowing the movie *Monty Python and the Holy Grail* inside-out is practically a requirement for family membership. Thus, terms such as "killer rabbit" and "holy hand grenade"; characters such as Tim the Enchanter and brave Sir Robin; and scenes such as the French taunting of King Arthur and the "Bridge of Death questions" are things most of my family immediately understand when brought up in conversation. If, however, I use a *Grail* reference with someone who hasn't seen the movie (perhaps you, if you're entirely confused by the examples I just mentioned), they have no idea what I'm saying (and think I'm a bit strange).

Psychological filters are the ways emotions, attitudes, and experiences affect how we perceive media. These can affect our ability to process and decode what we're engaged with. When I'm sad, it's harder for me to concentrate on media content, and I tend to miss things. I'll focus for a while, then sadness will distract me, and pretty soon I've missed part of the content. Thus, I can't decode as well when I'm in that emotional state. Next, our attitudes also affect how well we can decode. I like watching televised political debates. My wife decidedly does not. So while I'm dissecting every word and looking for logical fallacies, she's barely paying attention and asking me to change the channel. Thus, my positive attitude toward the debate tends to increase my attention as well as my decoding

What do you LOVE to watch that others hate? What's your guilty pleasure show?

© Rommel Canlas/Shutterstock.com

ability. Finally, if we have positive experiences with it, we're far more likely to be better processors of media information than if we've had negative experiences (Hiebert, Ungurait, & Bohn, 1991).

Cultural filters are ways that our values, political or religious beliefs, or biases affect our media processing. All media content has values explicitly or implicitly embedded; it's made by humans, after all. Watching a show such as *Friends*, one quickly learns that sex outside of marriage is normal. The show may not come out and say that directly, but it's implied in just about every episode. This may or may not be a value you hold. Whether or not you agree with a portrayed value affects how you process information in that program. For example, someone's religious beliefs can affect filtering processes. Even if media isn't explicit in stating a religious or non-religious viewpoint, it's often

© Christian Bertrand/Shutterstock.com

Which shows/movies have values that strongly contradict yours?

there in the background. A show, for example, may poke fun at Jesus and/or Christianity, and most American audiences will roll with it. It may not come to mind immediately as a show that has religious content, but in *The Big Bang Theory*, the Sheldon character often mocks anything related to religion (including his mother's devout Evangelical faith, which is depicted as nutty). For someone of deep faith, that mockery can be deeply offensive, which will affect the way the show is viewed by them.

Biases are important cultural filters. Right now, our country is deeply divided along liberal-conservative lines. What liberals see as true or right is seen by conservatives as false or wrong, and vice versa. This affects not only how we process media we engage with, but also affects our media *choices* from the get-go. Conservatives often watch/listen to/read material only from conservative outlets; liberals do the same from only liberal outlets. We call this **selective exposure** (as you might remember from Chapter 5), the deliberate choice to refuse to process certain kinds of media content. Because of this, we live in a **dual climate of opinion**, in which what we perceive as reality is a highly different reality for those who watch different outlets (Noelle-Neumann, 1974). When we can't avoid content we disagree with, we typically have two options—we can try to tune it out or we can argue with it. For example, recently people have begun to label whatever they don't agree with as "fake news" in an attempt to dismiss anything not fitting their worldview. Actual **fake news** is news that serves an ideological or political agenda rather than an objective presentation of facts.

Activism Hero: Don't be THAT Person!

Do you ever get frustrated with someone who spouts "news" and "facts" that are clearly biased? It's easy to get sucked into what the media tells us, so don't be that ill-informed person ... or, at the very least, be more aware of how your media choices might inform what you know/believe. Here's one way to explore framing and bias in the news media. Watch MSNBC (liberal) and FOX News (conservative) on the same day. Look for several things. First, what news stories do they cover? Second, what parts of stories do they emphasize? And, finally, when they cover the same story, how do they frame it (think about the language they use and even the pictures they show). By developing better awareness of how and where you get the information that influences your beliefs, you can challenge yourself to become better informed about the issues you're most passionate about.

Contributed by S. Sochay

© barbaliss/Shutterstock.com

Who "They" Are: Industry and Content

Although how we use/view media is important, it's vital to understand who "they" *were* and who "they" *are*. In the early 1970s, media industries were relatively separated. Phone companies provided phones and call services. Film studios produced and distributed films. TV networks produced and provided programming. Music labels produced and distributed music. Publishers produced and distributed books, magazines, and/or newspapers. There were certainly cases of media companies owning and producing across various media, but economically each industry was relatively distinct.

Fast-forward to today and media companies are far more likely to be conglomerates whose products span multiple industries. In fact, it's difficult to talk about something like the phone industry, for example, when phones now include internet, TV, video streaming, music, and also actual phone call services. There are several reasons for this move to conglomeration. First, technological innovation made devices into multi-purpose tools, like I just mentioned with smartphones. Second, companies began acquiring both hardware (distribution networks, devices) and software (programming, content) due to these multi-purpose technologies, resulting in **vertical integration**: one company is involved in more than one stage, several different mediums, or combined synergies of an industry. For example, Disney produces not just a movie but also the soundtrack, book, apps, and other media associated with that film. Third, this caused companies to get bigger and more diversified to compete on the global scale. In doing so, they began to **horizontally integrate**, or acquire smaller companies within their industry, such as when Disney acquired Pixar.

In the United States, most media companies are for-profit entities driven to produce media content that generates revenue. This capitalistic marketplace encourages production of content audiences *want* at the expense of content audiences *need*. Media in socialist or government-controlled countries say that, freed from the burdens of creating content for a profit, they're better situated to produce content audiences need (e.g., educational) rather than want (e.g., reality TV). This isn't necessarily better. It simply raises a different question: Who determines what audiences need?

How are both vertical and horizontal integration shown in this Disney store in China?

© J. Lekavicius/Shutterstock.com

One major influence in determining what audiences need is advertising. In general, advertisers want to reach younger demographics, typically aged 18–34 years old. Why? Younger audiences are believed to be more persuadable and willing to try new things (CrowdTwist, 2019). As we age, we develop brand loyalty and become more set in our purchasing habits. Interestingly, this same demographic group has grown up with tools to skip commercials—something advertisers don't want! How are advertisers responding? One way is via ***product placement***, where products are placed seamlessly into storylines so that even if ads are skipped, products are still brought to consumers' attention. Therefore, media increasingly are creating content aimed at these audiences in order for advertisers to reach *their* audience.

It isn't just about American audiences anymore (even if they are a primary audience). As more international markets open, producers must now consider how their content will play at home *and* in diverse world-markets. This has implications for content. Not all genres perform equally well across cultures. Humor is often culturally bound; it's not universal. On the other hand, action and explosions (i.e., little-to-no reliance on words) transfer more easily across cultural borders. It's not too difficult to see why action content (such as a superhero movie) is on an upswing, and comedy is on a downswing in both film and TV industries.

Even if media reaches a huge audience, it may be considered a failure if it doesn't reach the "right" audience. In earlier decades, media producers tended to produce content that was called ***lowest common denominator programming***, content designed to reach large audiences with relatable, non-objectionable material (*Leave It to Beaver*, anyone?). Why? In an era with few media outlets, reach mattered. Today, that philosophy has shifted. With thousands of choices (so many channels, subscriptions, etc.), consumers are more fragmented than ever. Aside from special events such as the Super Bowl, it's incredibly difficult to garner a large audience. With so much competition, media producers have to create content that stands out from the crowd. Content is aimed at specific audiences and designed to cater to smaller population segments, or ***niche programming***. An educated media consumer—like I hope you're trying to be—will be conscious of media's goals and make themselves aware of the three Rs: reality, representation, and risk offending.

Reality. Ask yourself: When you engage with programming primarily designed to be entertaining, is what you see actually related to reality? In most cases, NO. Not even "reality" shows are real. They're scripted and edited to foster storylines and keep the "plot" moving forward in a way that keeps audiences tuning in for more. What we see is content exaggerating real life. If what we saw was real, it'd have to show people sleeping for about 1/3 of every episode! And, wouldn't it be wonderful if every problem in life were completely solved in 30 to 60 minutes with no future repercussions?

Children (typically those 5 and under) often don't have an ability to understand what's real or not on media (it's one reason commercials showing multiple toys being played with are required to say, "Items sold separately"). Increasingly, however, it's becoming more difficult for even mature adults (yes, that includes *you*) to discern what's real. Digital editing is so effective that Hollywood's digitally de-aging of characters is hard to notice without close attention. Other trends along these lines include "deep fakes" where prominent people, such as former-President Obama, are "filmed" giving a speech in their "own" voice that they never actually gave. Most deep faking isn't sophisticated enough to fool many, but the day is coming when it'll be virtually impossible to tell the real from the fake.

Representation. In addition to exaggerating reality, media also engages stereotypes to keep storylines simple and to save time. Imagine a "computer hacker" character for TV. Do you picture a socially awkward 20- to 30-year-old White male living in his parent's basement, scrawny from no exercise or overweight from eating junk food? If we all have a common understanding of this stereotype (remember from Chapter 5 how stereotypes affect our perceptions?), using this character means there's no need to take time developing his backstory or explaining much about who he is; the audience will get it. If, however, the producers cast an 80-year-old African American female who lives in a mansion and teaches sculpting classes on the side, audiences would need to know more about this character to understand how/why she's a computer hacker. It bogs down the story and takes time producers often don't have.

Which of these brings to mind a typical computer hacker?

© Rocketclips, Inc./Shutterstock.com

© Arina P Habich/Shutterstock.com

I'm Native American, a member of the Little Traverse Bay Band of Odawa Indians. In my "Native Americans and the Media" course, we explore how appearances by Natives in mainstream media are "stuck in history" and/or they're only cast in historical pieces. Rarely are Native Americans shown in contemporary settings holding contemporary jobs. In fact, a recent poll done by the Reclaiming Native Truth project found 40% of respondents didn't think Native Americans still existed (First Nations Development Institute, 2018)! This means that to many, Native Americans are invisible in modern American society. Now, connect this to what I said in the previous paragraph. For a content producer to cast a Native American in a contemporary story line, it would require a backstory, which there often isn't time for. Thus, Native Americans are in a catch-22. If Natives were cast more often in contemporary roles, people would begin to see Natives in a more contemporary light, and thus, less backstory would be required. But, in present societal conditions, casting Natives in contemporary roles requires backstory, and thus, we aren't cast in those roles.

Risking offense. In an era of significant cases of microaggressions and trigger words, content producers have to be careful not to offend or they risk a backlash against their creations. This issue can be more complex when you're exposed to content created by past generations with different social norms. Nowadays, even one slip can doom a production. And, coming full circle to who "they" are in the industry, we can see how not wanting to lose money would make people want to "play it safe" with their content and casting. But, this doesn't just concern the reasons (the *why*) that drive media; it also influences the process (the *how*) used to reach us as audience members.

How Media Engages Us

When asked if media affects them, most people say "No!", but when asked if it affects other people, most say "Definitely yes!". What this tells us is that we aren't very good at evaluating how the media affects us. It's easier to see in others. When I ask my students to think about kids watching a Disney movie, they come up with lots of examples of how kids role-play Disney characters, ask their parents for Disney merchandise, and sing Disney songs (If I hear "Let It Go" one more time, I might consider sticking a pen in my eardrum). It's not hard to see these effects exist. But, what *are* typical media effects? They can be intentional or unintentional. Horror movies want us to be scared; that's intentional. But, the 1938 "War of the Worlds" radio broadcast of a fictional Martian invasion didn't intend to fool people. Some people, predisposed to accept the story based on geographic, social, or religious factors, thought the invasion was real and panicked (Lowery & DeFleur, 1983)! Media effects break down into categories that go from easiest to hardest for media to produce: cognitive, affective, parasocial, behavioral, and macro or societal-level effects.

Considered the easiest one for media to accomplish, ***cognitive effects*** deal with how we process information or how the media influences how/what we think. In fact, a cognitive effect is happening at this very moment. As you read this sentence, your brain is processing it into learning. This is a direct, individual-level cognitive effect. A more significant, macro-level effect is examined by ***Agenda-Setting Theory***, which looks at whether or not media determine (i.e., "set our agenda" for) what we think and talk about (McCombs & Shaw, 1972). Did you talk

Who do you see? How the media presents stories can influence what we see/believe.

with others about the ending of *Game of Thrones* or *Avengers: Endgame*? If so, you're part of an agenda-setting effect. In the early days of mass media when radio and TV were drawing large national audiences, some people were concerned that the media could control or brainwash us into thinking what "they" wanted us to think. Even though study after study has dispelled this notion (Katz & Lazarsfeld, 1955), this doesn't mean that media don't affect our agendas.

© Fishman64/Shutterstock.com

In general, we've learned media is very good at telling us WHAT to think about but not what to think ABOUT what we think about (McCombs, 2004). You might want to read that last sentence one more time! Basically, media influence what's on our minds and what we pay attention to but have much less influence on our values and opinions related to those topics. But, it's not totally powerless. News media *can* affect how we understand things through *framing*, or influencing how we see an issue by presenting it a certain way. In immigration stories, do those trying to cross the border into America get called "refugees" or "illegal aliens"? How these people are labeled creates a *framework* for how we think about this issue (Scheufele, 1999).

Offensive? Or just another affective effect?

© VolkovART/Shutterstock.com

Next, *affective effects* address things such as our emotions and attitudes. They account for how quickly, how long, and with what intensity the media can cause change. Consider comedy; media often wants to make us laugh:

> I went to see my psychiatrist.
>
> I said, "Doc, you gotta help me, I keep hearing voices."
>
> My psychiatrist replied, "You don't have a psychiatrist."

Ba-dum-dump-bing! I'll give you a minute to get off the floor and stop laughing . . . Even if your sense of humor is clearly not as amazing as mine, this joke still produces an affective effect (perhaps exasperation or disgust?). Researchers looking at affective effects also study things like how quickly a joke spreads and if its effect persists over time. Think about cases with more viral potential than my joke, such as a YouTube video by GrumpyCat, a Presidential Tweet, or a Kim/Kanye Instagram post.

Third, as media consumers, we're often engaged with media at levels deeper than simple exposure. We cheer for certain characters and root against others. When we watch sports, we can be heavily invested in our favorite teams and whether they win or lose. These are *parasocial effects*, where we're immersed with our teams, our characters, or our programs—sometimes to the point we feel they're real or that we could influence what happens to them. I'm thoroughly convinced that if I sit a certain way when I watch my beloved Minnesota Vikings, we'll win every time. If I fail to adhere to proper posture, the Vikes will lose, and I'm partially to blame.

A fourth type, *behavioral effects* are considered one of the hardest for media to achieve. Certainly, advertisers believe media content convinces audiences to buy products. And, if media couldn't produce *any* behavioral effects, there would be no advertising! Behavioral effects can also (like all the other effect types) be positive or negative. Media researchers typically focus on studying potentially negative media effects (e.g., whether violent content is mimicked by children after exposure). Positive behavioral effects of media could include campaigns to encourage kids not to smoke, for example.

Finally, *macro/societal effects*, which can potentially encompass all four of the previous effects, concern media potentially influencing entire cultures. It may be as innocent as spreading a new catch-phrase, influencing fashion, or starting a new craze (Please tell me you didn't eat a Tide Pod.). More significantly, it could influence our thinking, attitudes, and behaviors toward politics, economics, or religion. In a media-saturated world, the potential for media to influence us at macro/societal levels is greater than it's ever been. With these effects possible, some people believe we should enact macro-level/societal protections against media.

Considering the Future: Media Protections?

Potentially the most powerful gatekeeper/censor of all media is the government. *Censorship* (or in a broader context, *gatekeeping*) is when content is suppressed, prohibited, or limited. The

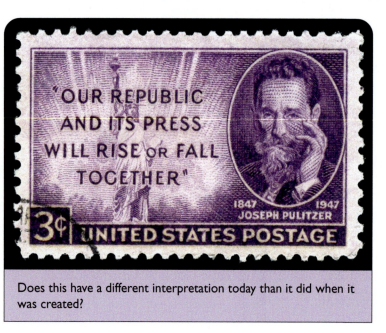

First Amendment to the U.S. Constitution outlines how far our government can go in terms of censorship (other regulations affect government's ability to censor but are beyond this chapter's scope): "Congress shall make no law . . . abridging the freedom of speech or of the press." At first glance, this seems to indicate the government has no power to censor. Doesn't "no law" mean "no law"? Well, actually it doesn't. In practice, it means there are circumstances under which government can act as censor. What are some of those circumstances?

Does this have a different interpretation today than it did when it was created?

The Founders never considered all speech to be equal. When America was founded, many came here for religious and political liberty. As a result, political and religious speech tends to be highly protected. On the other hand, commercial speech (such as advertising) doesn't receive that same level of protection. Government has a greater ability to censor advertising. This is why when you see an ad for a prescription drug, the first half of the ad talks about how wonderful the drug is, and the second half talks about all the possible horrible side effects. Drug companies certainly don't want to highlight these effects so prominently, but government mandates these disclosures.

Over the course of history, the U.S. Supreme Court outlined several types of speech that fall outside of First Amendment protection. These include speech related to:

National security (e.g., we don't have rights to know nuclear launch codes or info that may put our military in harm's way),

Public safety (e.g., we don't have rights to jokingly yell "fire" in crowded theaters),

Defamation (e.g., we don't have rights to say knowingly false things about someone to damage their reputation), and

Obscenity (e.g., no one has rights to create, possess, or distribute child pornography).

Further, when our Founders wrote and ratified the First Amendment, the term "the press" didn't mean journalists; it meant the literal printing press (Pember, 2018). From those origins, courts have determined not all mediums should have the same level of First Amendment protection. Print mediums generally receive the highest protections; it's difficult for the government to censor books or magazines, for example. TV receives much less protection. The explanation is complicated, but in short, because TV uses airwaves, which belong to the public, government mandates that broadcasters must broadcast in the "public interest," opening the door for government to act as censor in ways it can't with print (e.g., government banned cigarette commercials from TV, but you can still see them in magazines).

What speech should or should not be protected online?

© TheVisualsYouNeed/Shutterstock.com

An interesting question moving toward the future will be, where does internet fit? After all, it has characteristics of print and of broadcasting. In *Reno v. ACLU* (1997), the U.S. Supreme Court decided the Internet was more like print mediums and thus deserved the highest levels of First Amendment protection. But, when used for its social media capabilities, should those standards still apply? For example, should cases of cyberbullying also be protected this way? What about when someone posts private information that then affects your right to privacy?

Protecting privacy is becoming essential to our interaction with media. How many times have you heard stories about someone's social media post coming back to haunt them? Or, people having their information or identities stolen online? Unfortunately, these issues aren't going away (see Eckstein, 2020). Privacy issues are changing so rapidly that anything I say, or offer in the way of advice, will be outdated by the time you read this—a fact that should illustrate more than anything how fast media change all the time.

At this point, we've covered a lot of ground in terms of understanding media literacy, but this is just a glimpse (#TakeaMediaLiteracyCourse!). As you go back to your media-saturated world outside this text, recall one of the main purposes of this chapter: To help you become aware of media and its possible effects. Become more conscientious consumers! Simply *noticing* some of the things I've mentioned will make you already a more-informed media consumer than many other people out there . . . giving you a superpower you perhaps didn't even know you needed.

© Rawpixel.com/Shutterstock.com

References

Braverman, J. (2008). Testimonials versus informational persuasive messages: The moderating effect of delivery mode and personal involvement. *Communication Research, 35*, 666–694. doi:10.1177/0093650208321785

Carr, N. (2008, July/August). Is Google making us stupid? *The Atlantic*. Retrieved from www.theatlantic.com/magazine/archive/2008/07/is-google-making-us-stupid/306868/

CrowdTwist. (2019). *Gen Z vs. Millennials: The changing landscape of loyalty.* Retrieved from https://resource-center.crowdtwist.com/reports/genzvsmillennials

Daft, R. L., & Lengel, R. H. (1986). Organizational information requirements, media richness and structural design. *Management Science, 32,* 554–571. doi:10.1287/mnsc.32.5.554

Eckstein, J. J. (2020). What is violence now: A grounded theory approach to conceptualizing technology-mediated abuse (TMA) as spatial and participatory. *The Electronic Journal of Communication, 30,* www.cios.org/www/ejc/

Ellul, J. (1985). *The humiliation of the word.* Grand Rapids, MI: William B. Eerdmans Publishing Company.

First Nations Development Institute. (2018). *Reclaiming Native truth research findings: Compilation of all research.* Retrieved from https://rnt.firstnations.org/research

Gerbner, G., Gross, L., Morgan, M., & Signorielli, N. (1986). Living with television: The dynamics of the cultivation process. In J. Bryant & D. Zillman (Eds.), *Perspectives on media effects* (pp. 17–40). Hillsdale, NJ: Lawrence Erlbaum.

Hiebert, R. E., Ungurait, D. F., & Bohn, T. W. (1991). *Mass media VI.* New York, NY: Longman.

Katz, E., Haas, H., & Gurevitch, M. (1973). On the use of the mass media for important things. *American Sociological Review, 38,* 164–181. doi:10.2307/2094393

Katz, E., & Lazarsfeld, P. F. (1955). *Personal influence: The part played by people in the flow of mass communications.* Glencoe, IL: Free Press.

Lowery, S., & DeFleur, M. (1983). *Milestones in mass communication research.* White Plains, NY: Longman.

McCombs, M. (2004). *Setting the agenda: The mass media and public opinion.* Malden, MA: Blackwell Publishing.

McCombs, M., & Shaw, D. (1972). The agenda-setting function of mass media. *Public Opinion Quarterly, 69,* 813–824.

McKay, W. (1921). *Gertie on tour* [Motion picture]. Rialto, CA: Rialto Productions.

McLuhan, M. (1994). *Understanding media* (Critical ed.). Corte Madera, CA: Gingko Press.

Nielsen. (2018). Time flies: U.S. adults now spend nearly half a day interacting with media. *Nielsen Total Audience Report.* Retrieved from www.nielsen.com/us/en/insights/article/2018/time-flies-us-adults-now-spend-nearly-half-a-day-interacting-with-media/

Noelle-Neumann, E. (1974). The spiral of silence: A theory of public opinion. *Journal of Communication, 24*(2), 43–51. doi:10.1111/j.1460-2466.1974.tb00367.x

Ong, W. J. (1988). *Orality and literacy: The technologizing of the word.* London, England: Routledge.

Pember, D. (2018). *Mass media law* (20th ed.). New York, NY: McGraw-Hill.

Postman, N. (1986). *Amusing ourselves to death.* New York, NY: Elisabeth Sifton Books.

Postman, N. (1999). *Building a bridge to the 18th century.* New York, NY: Vintage Books.

Potter, W. J. (2001). *Media literacy* (4th ed.). Thousand Oaks, CA: Sage.

Rainie, L. (2017). Digital divides. *Pew Research Center.* Retrieved from www.pewinternet.org/2017/02/09/digital-divides-feeding-america/

Reno v. American Civil Liberties Union, 521 U.S. 844 (1997).

Ribarsky, E. N. (2009). *"I don't kiss on the first date": Symbolic convergence through women's ritualistic watching of reality-dating television.* Doctoral dissertation. Retrieved from Digitalcommons @University of Nebraska-Lincoln (AAI3344727).

Rideout, V., & Robb, M. B. (2018). *Social media, social life: Teens reveal their experiences.* San Francisco, CA: Common Sense Media. Retrieved from www.commonsensemedia.org/sites/default/files/uploads/research/2018_cs_socialmediasociallife_fullreport-final-release_2_lowres.pdf

Scheufele, D. A. (1999). Framing as a theory of media effects. *Journal of Communication, 49*(4), 103–122. doi:10.1111/j.1460-2466.1999.tb02784.x

Nancy Brule, Ph.D.

Academy Training: University of Nebraska-Lincoln; Mankato State University
Origin: Red Lake Falls, Minnesota, United States
Fortress/Lair: Communication at Bethel University in St. Paul, MN
Mission Status: Professor
Battle/Focus: Interpersonal relations; Adolescent-parent comm; Abusive relations
Superpowers: Engaging students; Running a farm; Managing conflict in all species
Energy Sources: Watching football; Singing; Good wine
Foes: Animal mistreatment; Incompetence coupled with arrogance

Jessica Cherry, M.A.

Academy Training: Western Kentucky University
Origin: Newtown, Connecticut, United States
Fortress/Lair: Communication at Post University in Waterbury, CT
Mission Status: Instructor
Battle/Focus: Many areas within interpersonal communication
Superpowers: Ensuring students' "lightbulb" moments
Energy Sources: Her dogs; Cooking and eating all types of FOOD!
Foes: People who are late; Taking too long to get to the point of a story

Jessica Eckstein, Ph.D.

Academy Training: University of Illinois Urbana-Champaign; University of Montana
Origin: Kasson-Mantorville, Minnesota, United States
Fortress/Lair: Communication at Western Connecticut State University in Danbury, CT
Mission Status: Professor
Battle/Focus: Destigmatizing taboo topics, identities, and relationships
Superpowers: Reading people; Performing for an audience
Energy Sources: Solitude in the forest; Diet Coke; All pups
Foes: Smoke; Cars; Bull-shitters

Joshua Hammonds, Ph.D.

Academy Training: University of Nebraska-Lincoln; Ball State University
Origin: Evansville, Indiana, United States
Fortress/Lair: Communication at Rollins College in Winter Park, FL
Mission Status: Assistant Professor
Battle/Focus: Examining comm management of relationships
Superpowers: Using data to predict behavior; Persuasive speaking; Teaching team-adaptation
Energy Sources: Playing guitar, singing; Undiscovered pretentious foodie spots
Foes: Tight social-schedules; Meetings to plan meetings; Mean people

Russell Luce, M.A.

Academy Training: Miami University
Origin: Cadillac, Michigan, United States
Fortress/Lair: Communication at Horry-Georgetown Technical College in Conway, SC
Mission Status: Professor
Battle/Focus: Political comm; Communicating across generations
Superpowers: Teaching people how to persuade their local government
Energy Sources: Dogs; Chocolate-covered bacon; His three boys
Foes: 90% of people driving in parking lots

Stevie Munz, Ph.D.

Academy Training: Ohio University; Illinois State University
Origin: Sycamore, Illinois, United States
Fortress/Lair: Communication at Utah Valley University in Orem, UT
Mission Status: Assistant Professor
Battle/Focus: Humans' cultural identity, power, politics, and gender
Superpowers: Supporting students in their critical exploration
Energy Sources: Hiking, biking, running in the mountains or desert
Foes: Peanut butter

Richard Murphy, Ph.D.

Academy Training: University of Nebraska-Lincoln; Illinois State University
Origin: Meredosia, Illinois, United States
Fortress/Lair: Communication & PR at McKendree University in Lebanon, IL
Mission Status: Associate Professor
Battle/Focus: How social media highlight/modify individual & group identities
Superpowers: Seeing multiple perspectives in every utterance; Best Dad (minus trophy)
Energy Sources: Lesson-planning; Bingeing group shows (e.g., *Parks & Recreation, Lost, Arrow*)
Foes: Know-it-alls; One-uppers; Braggarts lacking humility/vulnerability

Michael Papa, Ph.D.
Academy Training: Temple University; Central Michigan University
Origin: Bronx, New York, United States
Fortress/Lair: Communication at Central Michigan University in Mt. Pleasant, MI
Mission Status: Professor
Battle/Focus: Organizational comm applications; Technology diffusion
Superpowers: Empowering organizational-level social change internationally
Energy Sources: Music; Skiing; Writing
Foes: Techno-pop; Clogged drains; Wet shoes

Wendy Papa, Ph.D.
Academy Training: Ohio University; Central Michigan University
Origin: Indianapolis, Indiana, United States
Fortress/Lair: Communication at Central Michigan University in Mt. Pleasant, MI
Mission Status: Professor
Battle/Focus: Pedagogy; Social justice; Diffusion of innovations
Superpowers: Training future instructors; Conflict management
Energy Sources: Teaching; Skiing; Crispy bacon
Foes: Horror films; Mean people; Coconut

Beth Ribarsky, Ph.D.
Academy Training: University of Nebraska-Lincoln; Central Michigan University
Origin: Frankenmuth, Michigan, United States
Fortress/Lair: Communication at University of Illinois Springfield
Mission Status: Associate Professor
Battle/Focus: Examining individual and relational identities
Superpowers: Teaching others how to date; Public speaking; Dad jokes
Energy Sources: Cute animals; Potato chips; Craft beer
Foes: Loud chewers; Littering; Rudeness

Kristi Scholten, Ph.D.
Academy Training: University of Nebraska-Lincoln; Central Michigan University
Origin: Cadillac, Michigan, United States
Fortress/Lair: Communication at Ferris State University in Big Rapids, MI
Mission Status: Associate Professor
Battle/Focus: Political debates; Games in education; Identities in gaming
Superpowers: Teaching others how to win arguments; Public speaking
Energy Sources: Surviving and thriving with crazy 6-year-old twins
Foes: Time management; People who "reply all" in group emails

Scott Sochay, Ph.D.

Academy Training: Michigan State University
Origin: Upper Peninsula, Michigan, United States (a Yooper!)
Fortress/Lair: Communication at Bethel University in St. Paul, MN
Mission Status: Associate Professor
Battle/Focus: Media law; Native Americans and the media
Superpowers: Convincing students my generation's music/TV/film is better than theirs
Energy Sources: Pasties (traditional UP food from Cornwall, UK); Baseball
Foes: Anything related to that other unnamed Big 10 school in Michigan

Katy Wiss, Ph.D.

Academy Training: University of Massachusetts, Amherst
Origin: Riverside, Illinois, United States
Fortress/Lair: Communication at Western Connecticut State University in Danbury, CT
Mission Status: Professor
Battle/Focus: Perception and listening; Teaching awareness meditation
Superpowers: Accepting people as they are; Great Germanic sound shift and ablaut
Energy Sources: Meditation; Audio books; Good beer
Foes: When lunatics are valorized over hard workers

Lesley Withers, Ph.D.

Academy Training: University of Connecticut; University of Maine
Origin: Chelsea, Maine, United States
Fortress/Lair: Communication at Central Michigan University in Mt. Pleasant, MI
Mission Status: Professor
Battle/Focus: Exploring emotional connections & connection-threatening behaviors
Superpowers: Helping others understand comm's "dark side"
Energy Sources: Family (Nate, E. Aubrey, Elise); Playing D&D with SoR Radio crew
Foes: Malignant narcissists; Emotional immaturity; Social stigma